The New Politics of Race and Gender

Education Policy Perspectives

General Editor: Professor Ivor Goodson, Faculty of Education, University of Western Ontario, London, Canada N6G 1G7

Education policy analysis has long been a neglected area in the UK and, to an extent, in the USA and Australia. The result has been a profound gap between the study of education and the formulation of education policy. For practitioners, such a lack of analysis of new policy initiatives has worrying implications, particularly at a time of such policy flux and change. Education policy has, in recent years, been a matter for intense political debate – the political and public interest in the working of the system has come at the same time as the breaking of the consensus on education policy by the New Right. As never before, political parties and pressure groups differ in their articulated policies and prescriptions for the education sector. Critical thinking about these developments is clearly imperative.

All those working within the system also need information on policy-making, policy implementation and effective day-to-day operation. Pressure on schools from government, education authorities and parents has generated an enormous need for knowledge among those on the receiving end of educational policies.

This Falmer Press series aims to fill the academic gap, to reflect the politicalization of education, and to provide the practitioners with the analysis for informed implementation of policies that they will need. It offers studies in broad areas of policy studies, with a particular focus on the following areas: school organization and improvement; critical social analysis; policy studies and evaluation; and education and training.

The New Politics of Race and Gender

The 1992 Yearbook of the Politics of Education Association

Edited by

Catherine Marshall

University of North Carolina

The Falmer Press
(A member of the Taylor & Francis Group)
Washington, DC • London

USA	Falmer Press (North America) 1900 Frost Road, 101, Bristol, PA 19007
UK	Falmer Press Ltd, 4 John Street, London WC1N 2ET

First published 1993

Library of Congress Cataloging-in-Publication data are available on request

A catalogue record for this book is available from the British Library

ISBN 0 75070 176 5 cased

Set in 11/12 Bembo, by Graphicraft Typesetters Ltd., Hong Kong

Cover Design by Caroline Archer

Printed in Great Britain by Burgess Science Press, Basingstoke on paper which has a specified pH value on final paper manufacture of not less than 7.5 and is therefore 'acid free'.

Contents

About the PEA

The Politics of Education Association (PEA) promotes the development and dissemination of research and debate on educational policy and politics. PEA brings together scholars, practitioners, and policy-makers interested in educational governance and politics; is affiliated as a Special Interest Group with the American Educational Research Association (AERA); and meets each spring in conjunction with AERA's annual meeting. The annual membership dues for PEA are $US25.00 (subject to change). Members receive a copy of the annual Yearbook and the *Politics of Education Bulletin*, which includes news on member activities and occasional short scholarly pieces. Membership dues should be sent to Robert Wimpelberg, PEA, College of Education, University of New Orleans, New Orleans, LA 70148, USA.

A List of Editors and Contributors

Kal Alston is Assistant Professor of Philosophy of Education in the Department of Educational Policy Studies at the University of Illinois at Champaign–Urbana. Her 1991 article in *Educational Theory* is entitled 'Teaching, Philosophy, and Eros: Love as a Relation to Truth', and she has forthcoming pieces on the pragmatics of difference and women and solitude. Her primary research interests revolve around philosophical, moral and aesthetic issues surrounding teaching practice, drawing from sources including gender theory, popular culture, classical philosophy and cultural studies.

Gary L. Anderson is an Assistant Professor and Director of Latin American Programs in Education at the University of New Mexico. Research interests include critical ethnography, action-oriented research and the micro-politics of schools.

Colleen Bell is Associate Professor and Gordon B. Sanders Chair in Education at Hamline University in St. Paul, Minnesota. Her research and teaching interests include gender and education, multicultural education policy and educational leadership. Since 1986 she has been collaborating with Susan Chase on a nationwide study of women's experience in the K–12 superintendency.

Jill Blackmore is a Senior Lecturer in the School of Administrative and Curriculum Studies, Deakin University (Geelong). Her research and publications include feminist critiques of educational administration and organizational theory; teachers' work and the notion of skill and competence; the history of parent and teacher organizations; and the implications of educational reform on women and girls. Her publications include *Making Educational History: A Feminist Perspective* (Deakin University Press) and a jointly edited collection with Jane Kenway (1993) *Gender Matters in Educational Administration and Policy: A Feminist Introduction* (London, Falmer Press).

Kathryn Borman is Professor of Education and Sociology at the University of Cincinnati where she also serves as Associate Dean of Research and Development. Her most recent book, *The First 'Real' Job* examines the experiences of young men and women following high school in manufacturing, clerical and in-person service jobs. Her ongoing research examines school district restructuring, the sources of gender inequities in schooling and career decision-making among adolescents.

Kevin Brown is an Associate Professor of Law at Indiana University in Bloomington, Indiana. His present research focuses on the intersection of law, race and public education. He has written numerous articles addressing issues related to race, law and public education including articles on school desegregation and school desegregation termination. Much of the substance of his chapter in this book is contained in a more expansive article entitled 'Do African-Americans Need Immersion Schools?: The Paradoxes Created by the Law's Conception of Race and Public Education' to be published in March 1993 in the *Iowa Law Review*.

Anthony S. Bryk is Professor in the Department of Education at the University of Chicago. He is also the Director of the Center for School Improvement and the Consortium on Chicago School Research. His current research is in three areas: the implementation of Chicago school reform; the social organization of schools; and the application of hierarchical linear models to educational research.

Louis Castenell is Professor of Education, with a joint appointment in Educational Foundations and School Psychology and Counselling, and Dean of the College of Education, University of Cincinnati. His research interests include race, class and gender equity in schooling. He is presently working on a text which will examine how women and minority leaders influence schools of education.

Susan Chase teaches sociology and women's studies courses at the University of Tulsa. Her research project with Colleen Bell on women in the superintendency led to her interest in professional women's stories about experiences of success and discrimination at work. Her book, *Stories of Power and Subjection; The Work Narratives of Women Educational Leaders*, examines how women narrate these contradictory experiences.

Michael Chen, Associate Professor of Educational Sciences at Tel Aviv University in Israel, specializes in educational policy and school organization. His studies deal with the implications of educational administration and school organization on gender, ethnicity, religion and class issues. He served on the Prime Minister's Commission on Disadvantaged Youth (1972), the Minister of Education's Committee on the Status of Teachers (1979), and other public capacities. He has published widely in the Israeli sociological journals. His international work has been published by *The American Journal of Education*, *The American Educational Research Journal* and *The International Journal of Sociology*.

Caroline B. Cody is an Associate Professor in educational administration in the Department of Educational Leadership, Counseling and Foundations at the University of New Orleans. In the early 1980s, she directed a project on the quality of textbooks for the National Association of State Boards of Education. Since that time, she has followed the various states through their reform efforts and written widely about political action of school boards and legislatures in the textbook area. She authored a chapter in the 1990 NSSE Yearbook, *Textbooks and Schooling in the United States* and has chapters in two recent books in the area of policy.

David L. Elliott is director of Educational Materials Associates in Berkeley, California. Previously, he served with the Educational Products Information Exchange Institute and on the education faculty at the University of California at Berkeley. He co-edited (with Arthur Woodward) the Eighty-ninth Yearbook of the National Society for the Study of Education (1990) Part I – *Textbooks and Schooling in the United States*, and has published many articles critiquing elementary-secondary textbooks.

Karen Gallagher is a professor of educational administration and the Associate Dean for Academic Affairs at the University of Cincinnati. She teaches courses in education policy and professional studies in teacher education. Her research interests include school reform and state education policymaking and the role of corporate and business leadership in school reform. From 1990 to 1991 she worked with the Commission on Education Improvement, an educational oversight agency established by the Ohio General Assembly. In 1992, she published *Shaping School Policy* through Corwin Press.

Charles L. Glenn is Professor and Chairman of the Department of Administration, Training and Policy Studies at the Boston University School of Education. He was previously for twenty-one years the Massachusetts state official responsible for urban education and equity. Glenn is author of *The Myth of the Common School* (1988) and *Choice of Schools in Six Nations* (1989). He is directing a study for the federally-funded Center on Families, Communities, Schools and Childrens' Learning, on how urban parents select schools under choice plans.

Ellen Goldring is Associate Professor of Educational Leadership at Vanderbilt University. Prior to this, she served as Chair of the Program in Educational Administration and Organization at Tel Aviv University in Israel. Her research focuses on the organization, governance and control of schools, and their impact on educational leadership and the principalship. In an international perspective, she has published in such journals as *Educational Administration Quarterly*, *Educational Policy* and *Urban Education*. She is co-author (with Sharon Rallis) (1993), *Principals of Dynamic Schools: Taking Charge of Change* (Corwin Press).

Kathryn Herr is a middle school social worker. Her research interests include soliciting stories of silenced voices, particularly those related to gender, class and race and understanding adolescent sexual scripts and decision-making.

Carolyn D. Herrington is an Associate Professor at Learning Systems Institute at Florida State University. She is the author of numerous articles and reports in the areas of politics of education, intergovernmental relations and the politics of integrating children's services. She has recently served as primary author of the *Condition of Education in Florida* and *Condition of Children in Florida* and is the editor of the *Politics of Education Bulletin*.

G. Alfred Hess, Jr. is the executive director of the Chicago Panel on Public School Policy and Finance, a coalition of twenty civic agencies dedicated to the improvement of public schooling. After a number of years in adult education and community organizing in the United States, Latin America, Europe and Asia, he was trained as an educational anthropologist. In addition to more than twenty studies of the Chicago school system, he is the author of *School Restructuring, Chicago Style* (1991) and recently edited a volume of studies of school restructuring across the country, *Empowering Teachers and Parents, School Restructuring through the Eyes of Anthropologists* (1992).

Jane Kenway is a Senior Lecturer in the School of Administration and Curriculum Studies, Faculty of Education, Deakin University (Geelong). Her research interests and publications concentrate on the connections between education and social inequality. Two current federally funded research projects focus on the reception of gender reform in schools and educational marketing. Jane works as a policy adviser to state and federal governments and with teacher networks. Her recent publications include *Gender and Educational Policy* (Deakin University Press, Geelong).

Catherine Marshall is Professor in the Department of Educational Leadership at the University of North Carolina, Chapel Hill. The ongoing goal of her teaching and research has been to use an interdisciplinary approach to analyze cultures – of schools, state policy systems, and the professional development of adults working in organizations. She has published extensively about politics of education (from state to micro-level), qualitative methodology, women's access to careers and about the socialization, language and values in educational leadership. She is author of *Culture and Education Policy in the American States*, *The Assistant Principal: Leadership Choices and Challenges* and *Designing Qualitative Research* and past President of the Politics of Education Association.

David Jude Ortiz is a 1992 graduate of the University of California, Riverside, graduating with honors in Political Science. He has presented a paper, entitled 'Superintending a Multifarious School District: A Case Study in Leadership Style', for the UCR Minority Summer Internship Program, and has been collaborating with Flora Ida Ortiz on a book chapter concerning knowledge base and superintendents. A Patricia Robert Harris Fellow, he is currently pursuing a Master of Public Administration Degree at California State University, Fullerton.

Flora Ida Ortiz is Professor of Educational Administration at the University of California at Riverside. Her recent work includes, *The Superintendent's Leadership in School Reform*, 'An Hispanic Female Superintendent's Leadership and School District Culture', and 'How Gender and Ethnicity Interact in the Practice of Educational Administration: The Case of Hispanic Female Superintendents'. These works relate superintendency leadership to race and ethnicity. Her forthcoming book, *Schoolhousing: Planning and Designing Educational Facilities*, analyzes school district and state agencies' interorganizational and interpersonal relationships.

Leonie Rennie is an Associate Professor at the Key Centre for Teaching and Research in School Science and Mathematics at Curtin University of Technology. She comes from a background of teaching science at a secondary level, and is interested in the affective outcomes of education in science and technology, particularly as they relate to gender.

Fazal Rizvi is an Associate Professor in Education at the University of Queensland, Australia. He has written extensively in the areas of ethics and educational administration; critical perspectives on educational policy analysis; problems of democratic reforms in education; and multiculturalism and the grammar of racism in schools and society.

Sharon G. Rollow is assistant director of the Center for School Improvement at the University of Chicago. Her doctoral work focuses on the politics of Chicago school reform.

Dale Shimasaki is Director of Research and Governmental Affairs at City College of San Francisco. Upon completion of his MA in Public Policy at the University of California, Berkeley, he took a position as a budget and program analyst with the Office of the Legislative Analyst. He subsequently became educational consultant to Assembly Speaker Willie Brown. While in his current position, Mr. Shimasaki is pursuing doctoral studies in Educational Administration and Policy Studies at the University of California, Berkeley.

Thomas Timar is Associate Professor of Educational Policy at the University of California at Riverside. He has served as consultant to the California State Legislature, initially to a committee to conduct oversight studies of all categorically funded education programs and, subsequently, director of governmental affairs for the California community colleges. His principal research interests focus on the relationship between policy and organizational behavior. As senior researcher with the Law and Education Study at Stanford University, he co-authored a book with David Kirp entitled *Managing Educational Excellence*. It examines various state strategies for school reform. Currently, he has a National Academy of Education Spencer Fellowship and is working on theories of policy implementation.

James Gordon Ward is Associate Dean for Academic Affairs and Associate Professor in the College of Education, University of Illinois at Urbana–Champaign. He is a political economist with particular interests in issues of social justice in educational policy and political and legal aspects of school finance policy. His recent edited volume, *Who Pays for Student Diversity?*, explores the interrelationships between demography and school finance. He is a past president of the American Education Finance Association and a former director of research for the American Federation of Teachers.

Sue Willis is a Senior Lecturer in mathematics education at Murdoch University in Western Australia and a senior curriculum consultant with the Commonwealth's Department of Employment, Education and Training. Her research interests are concerned with gender and education and with social justice and 'informed' numeracy.

Arthur Woodward is Director of the Research, Development and Outreach Center of the Norman Howard School, Rochester, NY. He has written extensively on textbook design, content and policy issues. He recently co-edited the 89th NSSE Yearbook, *Textbooks and Schooling in the United States*, and *Learning from Textbooks*.

Phillip P. Zodhiates is Assistant Professor at the University of Illinois, Urbana. His research interests focus on racism and equity issues.

The new politics of race and gender

Catherine Marshall, with the assistance of Phillip P. Zodhiates

A diversity of voices

The politics of race and gender is characterized by a diversity of perspectives and profound disagreement about what the major problems are, their causes and solutions. Indeed, what defines the new politics of race and gender is dissatisfaction with conventional liberal solutions, the search for new policy alternatives, and the ensuing dissension over means and ends. The reason for this dissension and re-examination of old assumptions and solutions seems clear: the continuing failure of our school system to provide for females and minorities the educational opportunities that lead to successful and productive lives.

The multiplicity of perspectives and the emergence of new coalitions and policy alternatives made editing this volume a challenge. It was a struggle to bring order to the cacophony of debates on race and gender. At the same time, however, the volume presented an opportunity to take stock of the current political environment from a variety of disciplinary and theoretical perspectives concerning the politics of race and gender. Editorial decisions (for example, to include several chapters that provide an opportunity for international comparison, to not include the politics of homosexuality, even though it is about gender, to not include post-secondary race and gender issues, even though there are raging political debates at this level) were attempts to make the volume cohere. Philosophical, curricular and political clashes over 'multicultural' issues are not emphasized, although they emerge in the chapters on the trade-offs and clash of interests in curriculum (Cody *et al.*), student culture (Anderson and Herr) and special schools (Alston).

Finally, this volume goes to press just as a new regime considers initiatives in the United States. Is there a mandate for a return to liberal agendas for school politics? Will there be a new coalition of business, education professionals and liberals who protect the public school mission and demand that equity values be pursued? Will there be new initiatives with altered assumptions?

The origins of the new politics of race and gender

The diversity of voices on race and gender is due, in large part, to the decline of the liberal consensus favoring equity that shaped federal policy in the mid-1960s, and the rise of a new conservative consensus. The principal reasons for this philosophical and political sea change were threefold: the collapse of the welfare state because of economic stagnation and conflict over an expensive and unpopular war; the resultant inability of the federal government to 'buy off' contending parties, thus pitting them against each other in a new zero-sum game; and the ensuing white resentment of federal policies perceived to be preferential towards blacks and women. By the late 1970s, liberal policymakers had lost faith in the ability of compensatory programs to solve social and educational problems. In addition, the liberal social agenda was in disarray, with its leaders fighting over the meaning of equality of educational opportunity. Did equal educational opportunity mean access to equal inputs (equal school budgets, racially and economically mixed student bodies, teaching staffs of similar experience and education) or equality of results (similar test scores, comparable attainment of jobs and higher education)? Questions that once seemed settled resurfaced: Does a commitment to educational equity require racial integration in schools? Does support for equal opportunity necessitate the preferential treatment of blacks, other minorities and women? What is multiculturalism anyway? What should count as relevant in determining conditions deserving of preferential treatment? Should we give up on public schools as instruments for social equity?

The election of President Reagan in 1980 marked the political ascendance of a new conservative consensus, with its 'new federalism', the devolution of equity policy to the states, and in education, an emphasis on excellence and quality rather than equity. In this 'new politics' dominated by conservative ideology, school desegregation and affirmative action, as well as federal entitlement programs for the poor, Title IX, bilingual and multicultural education, have lost much of their original federal support and moral and intellectual impetus. The Bakke decision[1], as well as court cases (for example, Grove City College in 1984[2]) that have weakened Title IX, have undermined the push for equity. Affirmative action has lost the political support of a large segment of the white electorate, and has become the lightning rod for a resurgent racism in academia and in the workplace. Women's equity has nearly disappeared from education. Reform documents of the 1980s seldom mention gender equity and, in 1992, Diane Ravitch, the Assistant Secretary of Education, declared that gender equity problems had been solved.

The new politics of race

Recipient groups, for their part, have also become disillusioned with the liberal policy agenda. The black community, for example, is deeply divided over the issue of desegregation as dramatized by the Boston case, in which part of the black community in Boston has sought to end the federal court's receivership of the public school system, and to return to the concept of (segregated) neighborhood schools, while another part of the black community has called for continued involvement of the courts until genuine desegregation is achieved. Of course, dissension over desegregation policy is not new. The early years of the civil rights movement were also marked by deep cleavages between liberal integrationists and radical separatists (see the debate in Bell 1980).

Recently, black dissatisfaction with the ability of public schools to educate black children has given rise to proposals for schools for black boys, causing further fissures within the black community, to say nothing of the unease such initiatives provoke in liberal circles. School choice has also caused splits in the old liberal coalition. Today, it is being pushed primarily by conservatives, but also by some reformers on the left, as a panacea for resolving problems of both quality and equity.

The Chicago school reform offers yet another example of the abandonment of the traditional liberal goals of racial integration in favor of community (read black) control of local schools. All four examples – the Boston case, the current crop of proposals in favor of exclusively black schools, parental choice, and the Chicago reforms – represent a rejection of traditional liberal compensatory strategies.

The new politics of gender

Efforts to eliminate racial and gender inequities have met with quite different levels of success. The record on women in education during the past quarter century has been uneven at best. Gender equity was never a major part of the liberal consensus, and policies in favor of gender equity were never strongly financed, monitored or enforced. Perhaps one reason for the difference is that race is closely connected to social class while gender is not (see Wilson 1980, and the discussion his arguments have fostered).

Conventional liberal solutions have failed to eliminate gender inequality. Liberal policies for gender equity left it up to women to seek redress. Few women have successfully launched Equal Employment Opportunity (EEOC) challenges or class action suits to eradicate the overt and subtle sexism preventing their access to school leadership. The federal government has not even kept good records of the placements of women in school administration. Title IX is a federal law designed in 1972 to eliminate sex-role stereotyping in curricular offerings and to equalize enrollments in home economics, woodshop, and the like. However, Title IX received no funding and no effective support for implementing its agenda. Instead, schools and universities lobbied and sued to exempt themselves from the law. All programs aimed at gender equity – ranging from women's caucuses in professional associations, to efforts to recruit females into science and mathematics programs – depended for their implementation on systems that, by and large, are not sympathetic to women's demands for equality: the schools, local, state and federal agencies, and the courts. Funding for the Women's Educational Equity Act was to provide dollars for programs to promote sex equity. However, the program applicants had to demonstrate how the program benefited men as well as women. These sex-equity programs thus revealed three fundamental weaknesses in liberal politics: 1) systems that created and perpetuated inequalities cannot be relied on to implement equity policy; 2) ambiguous policies will be implemented ambiguously; and 3) weak policies unaccompanied by implementing strategies, effective leadership, and adequate incentives and sanctions will just fade away.

The old liberal politics of gender, paralleling the old politics of race, asserted that males and females are equal, should have equal access, and that stereotyping and discrimination should be eliminated. This liberal agenda dissolved and the token support for gender equity disappeared. However, in the hand-wringing over quality in the teaching profession, it cannot be ignored that, given the choice of exit, voice and loyalty, some women are leaving education, abandoning a field that persists in preferring male leaders. In the hand-wringing over 'at-risk' children, it cannot be ignored that some girls, confused by mixed messages, drop out, get pregnant, or flunk math. These girls are told they can become doctors and astronauts, but they can see in their schools that women who break sex-role stereotypes encounter barriers, lack of support, and marginalization. The subtle politics of denial, the mixed messages, and the informal curriculum prevail when ambiguous policy is ambiguously implemented.

Some feminists and researchers are suggesting that another problem with liberal solutions is the deficit model upon which they are based. Special policies and programs for boosting women into leadership assumes that the current kind of leadership is desirable. Some feminists argue that males and females are indeed different, and that

women's values, styles of collaboration, interaction and leadership may be preferable for
school leadership. Researchers on the psychology of women include Carol Gilligan
(1982) who argues for a view of women's intellectual and moral development as distinct
from that of men, and Belenky *et al.* (1986) who show that 'women's ways of knowing'
are different. Such insights have implications for how girls learn in school and for the
ways in which women school administrators lead. Research on gender difference may
also provide insights into what is likely to happen when a predominantly female teaching
force takes on a more active leadership role. Nel Noddings' (1984) work on caring could
support a reconceptualization of leadership and values that would give precedence to
women's styles. However, it's a long leap from feminist philosophy to the political fray
in education and school reform.

In sum, the new politics of race and gender are characterized by a multiplicity of
views: disillusionment with conventional liberal solutions; new political coalitions around
such issues as parental choice, racially exclusive, and single-sex schools that cross traditional liberal-conservative boundaries; a search for new strategies, most notably a
resurgence of a 'pull yourself up by your bootstraps' mentality that is hostile to compensatory strategies; and a view of equity as a zero-sum game that pits blacks against
whites, women against blacks, men against women. Policy initiatives that have abandoned the old compensatory model include schools for black boys, community control
(as in Chicago), and such diverse reform efforts as Henry Levin's 'Accelerated Schools',
Theodore Sizer's 'Essential Schools', and James Comer's efforts to invest community
resources in the education of poor black students. Gender equity policy initiatives have
simply been abandoned. The silence or, at best, token nod to gender equity in the policy
agendas laid out in reform documents, makes a loud pronouncement about the valuing
of gender equity.

Overview of the book

The chapters presented in this Yearbook speak to many of these issues. Part 1, 'Cutting
across race and gender', is a grouping of chapters which raise questions and issues
connected with both race and gender, ranging from the trends and meanings of population
shifts and the power of businessmen to shape education policy to the ways we distribute
monies, count children and shape the curriculum.

In 'Demographic politics and American schools', James Ward documents emerging
population trends and identifies the political pressures on education that flow from these
trends.

Will a centralized state school finance system guarantee equity? What kind of political
coalitions and strategies emerge in such state systems? Timar and Shimasaki, in 'Categorical wars: Zero-sum politics and school finance', examine the case of California,
asking about the new politics of ethnicity in such a centralized system.

In 'Accountability, invisibility, and the politics of numbers', Carolyn Herrington
documents the media's control of framing reactions to Florida's 'school report cards'.
Left unasked by the media are the important questions about schools' efficacy in
addressing race and gender inequities.

Diversity breeds diverse and conflicting demands in curriculum politics as illustrated in two case studies of school board politics in 'Race, ideology, and the battle over
curriculum', by Cody, Woodward and Elliot.

Anderson and Herr use a deeper meaning of 'politics' in 'The micro-politics of student voices'. By examining students' oral histories, they demonstrate the cultural politics the students see at work in their daily lives as they form identities that encompass schools' deeper messages about their proper place in society.

Equal opportunity is relatively low priority among the business leaders who involve themselves in education policy formulation, according to the analysis by Borman, Castenell and Gallagher, in 'Business involvement in school reform'.

Part 2, 'Issues of race in the midst of reform', encompasses analyses and critiques of reforms, raising questions about the strength, persistence and legitimacy of racial equity as a priority.

Fred Hess, in 'Race and liberal perspective in Chicago school reform', highlights the efforts to decentralize school governance, with a focus on ways of assessing whether this reformulation of politics will increase access and equity.

In 'Democratic politics and school improvement', Rollow and Bryk provide another portrait of Chicago reform, highlighting the emergence of new power bases.

In the two chapters addressing a very controversial policy initiative, each author's title ends with a question mark. In 'Do African American males need race and gender segregated education?: An educator's perspective and a legal perspective' Kevin Brown provides a legal analysis, and in 'Community politics and the education of African American males: Whose life is it anyway?' Kal Alston provides a philosophical and cultural analysis, forcing hard questions about how such schools abandon the philosophy behind integration and admit openly that boys' troubles take precedence.

The word 'choice' calls for the kinds of conflicting emotions, needs and traditions that excite the policy process. Charles Glenn's 'Creating an irresponsible school choice program' gives a blow-by-blow account of the conflict between the values of choice and of equity and the intermixing of the policy analysis and politics in the formulation of Massachusetts' policy for choice, noting how equity fared.

Part 3, 'Is there a new politics of gender?' includes chapters that allow the reader to look for answers ranging from the micro-political to the district level and to make comparisons cross-nationally.

Emphasizing the power of board and top administrative positions, Bell and Chase, in 'The underrepresentation of women in school leadership', present the persistent preference for white male leaders for schools. The authors' search for explanation raises questions that the remaining chapters begin to answer.

Ortiz and Ortiz, in 'Politicizing executive action', demonstrate how Hispanic women superintendents, managing leadership within the context of cultural political biases favoring white male leadership, must vigilantly monitor the symbols they project.

In 'Politics of denial', Catherine Marshall presents her research on minority and women site administrators, demonstrating how administrators suppress their differences and feelings of exclusion in a district where affirmative action and desegregation policies are treated as unpleasant memories.

Moving beyond the US, Goldring and Chen's analysis of 'The feminization of the principalship in Israel' provides an answer to the question – what happens when women attain a majority of the principalships? As that situation unfolds in Israel, their case reminds us that position without critical power and resources means nothing.

'What's working for girls?', by Blackmore, Kenway, Willis and Rennie, focuses on the cultural and political context which generated and received gender equity reform in Australia. Their case-studies of policy implementation are set up as a challenge for analysts of politics to make the needed expansions of theory to incorporate gender policy issues.

In Part 4, Fazal Rizvi's chapter, 'Race, gender and the cultural assumptions of schooling', takes on the large task of providing perspectives from critical policy analysis as he pulls out deeper meanings and overarching questions raised from the issues addressed in race/gender politics and policies.

This Yearbook is an integrated compilation of the work of a range of scholars, analysts, and activists who observe and comment on race and gender politics. The authors' varied methodological and conceptual frameworks add to the richness of the book. Marcia Huth and Jeanne Steele contributed a great deal of editing assistance. Phillip Zodhiates' work on the initial conceptualization and recruiting authors was an important contribution. The book's contributors all leave us asking, will we see crystallizing events, symbols, programs, coalitions and a politics that mark the emergence of new cultural assumptions about the value of race and gender equity? Will there be a *newer* politics of race and gender?

Notes

1. Bakke v. Regents of the University of California undermined the use of affirmative action and special consideration for minorities' admission to universities.
2. In Grove City College v. Bell, the Reagan administration successfully argued to the Supreme Court that Title IX's bans against sex discrimination could be enforced only on specific programs, not entire institutions, thus limiting the power of Title IX.

References

BELENKY, M. F., CLINCHY, B., GOLDBERGER, N. B. and TARULE, J. M. (1986) *Women's Ways of Knowing: The Development of Self, Voice, and Mind* (New York: Basic Books).

BELL, D. (1980) *Shades of Brown: New Perspectives on School Desegregation* (New York: Teachers College, Columbia University).

COMER, J. P. (1989) 'Racism and the Education of Young Children', *Teachers College Record*, 90 (3) pp. 352–61.

GILLIGAN, C. (1982) *In a Different Voice* (Cambridge, MA: Harvard University Press).

LEVIN, H. M. and HOPFENBERG, W. S. (1991) Don't Remediate, Accelerate! *Principal*, 70 (3) pp. 11–13.

NODDINGS, N. (1984) *Caring: A Feminine Approach to Ethics and Moral Education* (Berkeley: University of California Press).

SIZER, T. (1992) *Horace's School: Redesigning the American High-School* (Boston: Houghton Mifflin).

WILSON, W. J. (1980) *The Declining Significance of Race: Blacks and Changing American Institutions* (Chicago: University of Chicago Press).

1   *Demographic politics and American schools: Struggles for power and justice*

James Gordon Ward

Population changes, such as trends in births, immigration, and migration, affect schools in many ways. These population trends affect the internal organization and operations of schools, as well as relate to the larger political and economic context of schooling. Some key issues to be explored include the changing requirements for education of a global, information-based economy, political participation in educational decision-making, and effects of these on existing power relationships. Power, who holds power, and how the exercise of power in our society affects schools are important issues for consideration. Some important questions for making schools instruments of opportunity include exploration of broader political participation, community organizing, and unionization as agents of change.

It seems to be an American trait to see our own history as a history of individual events and not a product of long-term social trends which affect our economy, our politics and our daily lives. Yet, it is demographic forces and population trends that we scarcely recognize and little understand which have a profound impact on our lives. Historian E. A. Wrigley reminds us in the opening of his classic *Population and History* that when Immanuel Kant wanted to show the regularities of what seemed to be random and unpredictable occurrences in history, he did so through the study of population (Wrigley 1969: 8). The purpose of this chapter is to inquire into some of the recent population trends in the United States, to explore possible future trends, and to speculate on their impact on the politics of education. Of particular interest will be the effects of these population trends on the struggles of racial and cultural minorities for power and social justice. This inquiry will adopt the 'long view' of demographic trends, rather than a history of events.

    Schools are profoundly affected by population forces because trends in births, immigration and migration patterns determine the number of school children, the nature of the school population, and the characteristics of children in schools in different areas and regions of the nation. Population trends make a difference in the political realm because they affect political interests, voting patterns, and the spatial and temporal distribution of power. Population trends combine with the effects of international economic forces to change the demands upon schools and our expectations of education. Population trends partially explain, but transcend, short-term events like the school finance reform movement of the 1980s. If we are to construct a road map to the future, we must not only know what roads to traverse, but something about the topography we will encounter.

Recent population trends in the United States[1]

An examination of recent population trends in the United States will show certain notable trends which have had an effect on schools. As these trends continue, or change, schools will be affected by changing conditions in their internal and external environments. These trends include:

- The United States is becoming more diverse;
- The American population is aging;
- There are fewer traditional nuclear households and families;
- The rich are getting richer and the poor, poorer;
- The population is becoming more concentrated in the South and the West;
- The United States is becoming more suburban.

All these trends merit some discussion.

The American population is becoming more diverse. As Usdan (1984) observed, the United States is an anomaly among the countries of the world because it is one of the few major nations where the majority of the population is not of color. Only about one-fourth of the American population qualifies as being 'minority'. African Americans comprised 12 percent of the American population in 1990, while Hispanics totalled 8.4 percent, and the 'other races' category, largely Asian and Pacific Islander, comprised 3.6 percent (Waldrop and Exter 1991). During the 1980s, the Hispanic population grew at a rate of four times that of the total population and the African American and Asian and Pacific Islander populations grew faster than the white population (Waldrop and Exter 1991). Between 1990 and 1995, the number of children in the elementary school age cohort in the United States will decrease slightly and the number of high school age students will increase somewhat (Sternlieb and Hughes 1987). Over the same period, the number of African Americans of school age will increase over 10 percent and the number of Hispanics even more (Sternlieb and Hughes 1987). This will increase the racial and cultural diversity of the American school age population. These trends will likely be exacerbated by immigration to the United States from other nations which may experience political or economic instability.

The American population is maturing. The 'baby boom' generation, those born between 1946 and 1964, fueled the rapid growth of the American public school system in the 1950s and 1960s and it was their growing to adulthood that caused large declines in the American public school population beginning in the mid-1970s (Jones 1980). The age cohorts born after 1964 were smaller and even though the nation has experienced an upswing in births as the 'baby boomers' became parents, the number of live births in a given year has never reached the heights of the 1946–1964 period. As a consequence, the American population is becoming older. In the 1990s and beyond, the age cohorts over 35 years of age will grow faster than the younger cohorts. Education of children will be less important to the nation, as fewer adults have children in schools, and this older generation will be more interested in financial and personal security, recreation and cultural activities, and health care. This older generation will vote more often than the younger generation and exercise greater political power. They will be better organized politically and they will have money to spend on political activities. Younger generations will be more heavily minority, will be poorer, will not vote as frequently, will be less organized, and will have fewer discretionary dollars to contribute to political causes. In other words, the younger generations are likely to be less powerful than their older neighbors. This may also lead to cultural clashes in the workplace as the managers and supervisors tend to be older and less likely to be minorities and the new entrants and younger workers will be increasingly minority and culturally diverse.

There are fewer traditional nuclear families in the United States than there used to be. During the 1980s, the average family size fell from 3.29 to 3.17 and the average household size fell from 2.76 to 2.63 (Waldrop and Exter 1991). These statistics indicate an increase in the number of households and families with only one adult present. Therefore, there are increasing numbers of one-parent households and a shocking number of 'no parent' households with schoolchildren. On a cautionary note, one should not assume that such 'non-traditional' households are necessarily a source of social instability, but they are merely an indicator that family support for children in such households may be diminished. Also, the increasing number of two-income families, a phenomenon that grew tremendously during the 1980s, raises issues of before and after-school programs for children and issues of homework and home-based instructional support.

We are experiencing shifting income distributions in the United States. Between 1980 and 1987, the share of income earned by the top 20 percent of all households increased from 44 percent to 47 percent (Waldrop and Exter 1991). One analysis suggests that this figure reached 50 percent by 1991 (Reich 1991). This phenomenon of increasing disparities in income distribution in the United States has been attributed to more working women which results in more two-income families (Waldrop and Exter 1991), a stronger relationship between education and earnings potential (Reich 1991, Waldrop and Exter 1991), specific government policies creating income imbalances (Phillips 1990), and global economic trends (Reich 1991). Americans, both male and female, with more education have increased their economic position over the last decade when compared to those with less education. While this provides evidence of the importance of education to economic success, it also makes the job of ensuring equal educational opportunity more difficult as the well-off and the poor become increasingly segregated residentially.

After the Second World War, earlier population trends, such as the mass exodus of African Americans from the rural South to the industrial cities of the North, shifted and many more Americans began to relocate to the South and the West. Older, industrial and agricultural areas of the Northeast and the Midwest began to lose population. Northern cities became progressively African American and poor. Hispanic migration to those cities occurred later in the period. By 1990, over 55 percent of the us population resided in the South or West, and the Northeast was surpassed by the West as the third largest census region (Waldrop and Exter 1991). Nineteen of the twenty-five us counties with the highest projected growth rates in the 1990s are in the South or the West. The greatest number are in California, Florida and Texas (Exter 1991). A major source of growth in California results from a large increase in both the Hispanic and the Asian population and both Florida and Texas are experiencing an increase in the Hispanic proportion of their state populations. Immigration, lower average age of the population, and higher birth rates are contributing to the very rapid increase of both Hispanic and Asian populations in the United States.

During the 1980s, the urban population in the us stagnated and non-metropolitan areas in the Midwest, South and West actually declined (Waldrop and Exter 1991). Major growth occurred in the suburbs, where the proportion of the American population living there grew from 44 percent to 47.2 percent in the 1980s (Waldrop and Exter 1991). The 1970s saw large growth in the non-metropolitan areas of the country, but this trend reversed in the 1980s. The one constant in American population growth over the last four to five decades has been the relentless, steady growth of the suburbs (Jackson 1985).

There are many lessons for schools to be drawn from these demographic trends. First, the school clientele is becoming more racially and culturally diverse, and the

income distribution in the nation is contributing to economic diversity. These trends
are likely to continue in the foreseeable future. These trends also seem to be associated
with certain social problems such as lack of adult supervision of children before and
after school hours, drug and alcohol abuse, teenage pregnancy, welfare dependency, and
children living in violent environments. These social problems plague rural as well as
urban areas, and are increasingly evident in the suburbs. The schools not only need to
re-examine the curriculum to see if it is meeting the needs of a changing clientele, but
they also need to consider new modes of instruction and expanded social support programs, often in conjunction with other social agencies.

Second, there is ample evidence that education is becoming increasingly critical to
the financial and career success of students as they pass into adulthood (Reich 1991).
Those who are well-educated are much more likely to end up in the higher income
strata and to hold jobs that are both economically and personally attractive. Those with
a poor education seem far more likely to be relegated to low paying jobs with little
future and fringe benefits or to unemployment. In past generations, those with a poor
education could often gain and hold highly paid and high security unionized jobs in the
factory or on the railroad. Those jobs, and the opportunities that came with them, have
disappeared in many areas.

Third, there is a widening gap between those who pay for government programs
through taxation and those who benefit from such programs. Political power, if it ever
was truly held by the latter, seems to be shifting to the former. It seems to be true in
state after state that the news headlines accompanying the release of the 1990 US Census
data have been heralding a political shift in power away from the cities, farms and small
towns to the affluent suburbs. Those in the suburbs are often Republican, fiscally
conservative, protective of their own affluence, and highly unlikely to be sympathetic
to the classic beneficiaries of government social programs, including education.

These demographic trends and their implications deserve attention. Their precise
impact on individual schools may vary, but their overall impact on education in general
will be important. The Population Reference Bureau summarizes their analysis of these
population trends by admonishing:

> The problems of children and youth should be of immediate concern to the policy-making community. The rates
> of poverty among children are high; results of educational test scores are troubling; and far too many youths are
> dropping out of school, having children of their own, using drugs and engaging in criminal behavior. To be sure,
> not all of today's youth face such a bleak scenario. However, as a society we need to address the problems that
> threaten to leave a significant portion of tomorrow's work force ill prepared for the demands and responsibilities
> of life in the 21st century. (De Vita 1989: 23–24)

I would argue that the effects of such a scenario are not only economic, as the Population
Reference Bureau suggests, but are political and social as well.

The changing global economy and schools

The changing and more unequal income distribution in the United States, noted above,
is partially the result of a changing global economy (Phillips 1990, Reich 1991). One of
the reasons the rich are becoming richer and the poorer are becoming poorer is explained
by Reich (1991). What is no longer so important to our future well-being is the national
economy of any nation and as we move well into the information age characterized by
massive information exchange and world-wide electronic communications, the global
economy is the context for consideration of our future. Recent shifts in the global

economy have involved a greater dependence on information manipulation rather than factory production. These shifts have increased, in turn, the relative power that accompanies being able to analyze and manipulate verbal, numerical and visual symbols and images to engage in problem identification, problem solution and strategic brokering between the two (Reich 1991). Reich calls those who possess high proficiency in these tasks symbolic analysts.

In fact, Reich (1991) presents evidence that the top one-fifth of all wage and salary earners who earn up to one-half of all earned income in the United States is made up primarily of symbolic analysts. Symbolic analysts are engineers, lawyers, health care professionals, bankers, financial consultants, planners, scientists, computer systems analysts, high level managers and sometimes professors. The key to their economic success is their education. Symbolic analysts receive a high quality education and that level of education opens the doors to countless opportunities for earning power. Symbolic analysts also enjoy more satisfying personal lives and often hold political power greater than their numbers would seem to indicate. They are politically active, contribute both time and money to political causes, and are very adept at protecting the privilege they have gained through political as well as economic means.

They receive an education rich in experiences relating to abstract and critical thinking, systems thinking and complex relationships, risk-taking behavior and experimentation, and collaboration and group problem-solving. This kind of education is generally found in the best private schools and in the better public schools in the suburbs. It is less commonly found in large cities, small towns, and in rural schools. Not all children who are well-educated in symbolic analysis join the economically affluent stratum of society, but few reach this high income level if they are not symbolic analysts (Reich 1991).

The power of the symbolic analysts not only results from their superior education, but also comes from a changing global economy that places a higher premium on such skills than has ever been experienced before. Information processing, information analysis, and translating information into knowledge are more than ever forming the basis for economic success worldwide. It is not the production of our factories that counts, but the work of our minds.

Schools in contemporary America are denying certain children the access to the kind of education that is necessary for the needs and attributes of an information-based society and global economy. These schools are not prepared to produce symbolic analysts. In some cases, it is due to the lack of financial resources, but in many cases it is due to not understanding the demands of a global economy based on the analysis and manipulation of symbols and a lack of vision of the future. Too often, school policymakers, administrators, and other leaders project into the future an exact copy of yesterday. Unfortunately, far too many of those denied an education required of a symbolic analyst are children of color, children of immigrant families, children of the non-English proficient, and children of the poor, both urban and rural. In fact, many of the major policy disagreements in education revolve around how much those with power are willing to sacrifice in order to provide other children with the same kind of education they provide for their own children.

Demographics and political participation and power

Data from 1984 indicate that in the United States, 61 percent of whites claimed to have voted, 56 percent of African Americans claimed to have voted, and 33 percent of Hispanics claimed to have voted (Piven and Cloward 1988: 205). The same data show that the employed are one and a half times more likely to vote than the unemployed, that males and females vote in about the same proportion, that those in the North and the West are more likely to vote than those in the South, and that the more education one has, the more likely one is to vote (Piven and Cloward 1988: 205). In fact, the 1984 data show that of those with less than a high school education, only 44 percent reported they had voted, but that 79 percent of those with four or more years of college reported voting (Piven and Cloward 1988: 205). Yet, Piven and Cloward (1988) argue that,

> The right to vote is the core symbol of democratic political systems. Of course, the vote itself is meaningless unless citizens also have the right to speak, write and assemble; unless opposition parties can compete for power by offering alternative programs and leaders; and unless diverse interest groups can also compete for influence. And democratic arrangements that guarantee formal political equality through the universal franchise are inevitably compromised by sharp social and economic inequalities. (p. 3)

They also point out that the United States is the only major democratic country where those with less privilege are markedly under-represented in the electorate (Piven and Cloward 1988: 4).

The demographic trends show how American schools have and will continue to have a larger proportion of racial and cultural minorities than the population at large and show how many of the clients of schools are among the powerless and under-represented in society. At the same time, global economic and social trends require even greater educational skills in order to succeed and this trend is very likely to continue. The affluent in American society seem intent on holding onto the privilege they have gained and are particularly reluctant to fund schools properly that are heavily enrolled with minority children, with poor children, and which are located in cities or rural areas where the affluent do not live (Kozol 1991). What emerges is a pursuit of privilege and a politics of exclusion, focusing on taxes, schools and zoning, which results in a widening gap between the resources available for social programs, including schools, and the need for those resources (Harrigan 1989: 300–304).

The ability to break through this pursuit of privilege and politics of exclusion is severely hampered when those who are the victims of this process are profoundly handicapped in their ability to seek redress through the political process because they are under-represented among those registering to vote and among those who do vote. To make matters worse, the victims of exclusion, because they do tend to be poor, also lack the financial resources to become major players in political campaigns. The only resource the under-represented victims of exclusion have is the ability to organize themselves and engage in direct action to redress wrongs, but this is often interpreted as being anti-democratic. What results is tight control of the political process by the privileged who practice exclusion when it comes to good schools. As Piven and Cloward maintain, 'elites are confirmed structuralists' (1988: 254). Governmental structures have been designed to maintain the current situation and make it difficult for the non-elite to become more politically powerful and to change the political structures. The privileged maintain access for their own children to schools which produce symbolic analysts and the non-affluent are denied such access. Such schools have a much higher proportion of their graduates who attend four-year colleges, especially elite four-year colleges. As a number of economists have shown, evidence from the 1980s indicates a much stronger relationship between college attendance and graduation and earning power than has existed before in the US (Berryman and Bailey 1992; Reich 1991). As a result, the income distribution between the upper one-fifth of society and the lower one-fifth of society widens and widens. Attempts at meaningful school finance reform and curriculum reform are met with defeat after defeat. There is little evidence, for example, that school finance reform in the United States has materially affected those it was designed to help in any positive way (Ward 1990). It is not so much that the populace does not want reform, as it is that those in political control have what they want and they desire to deny it to others. The affluent can provide an acceptable mix of economic goods and services for themselves through a combination of private and public purchases as a result of their own economic power. Those in less fortunate circumstances must rely more heavily on public goods and services for such things as education, health care, recreation, housing and income security, which results in a situation where 'the fortunate in the polity find themselves paying through their taxes the public cost of the functional underclass, and this, in the most predictable of economic responses, they resist' (Galbraith 1992: 42). Such is the politics of resistance to taxes and exclusion.

Political and educational implications

How future political trends will affect this pattern is open to debate. However, past experience would indicate that the politics of exclusion is a powerful force and will not be overcome easily. The Population Reference Bureau has identified five possible political trends resulting from demographic changes:

- The aging of the population will increase the number of voters in middle and older age groups;
- The changing racial and ethnic composition of the population will result in more minority voters;
- The changing composition of households and families will place new demands on government services and alter the property tax base of many localities;
- Migration to the Sunbelt and the outer suburbs will affect political boundaries and political alignments; and
- The tightening of labor markets will affect the ability of government to attract and retain workers at a cost they can afford to pay. (O'Hare and De Vita 1990: 2)

These factors provide a mixed message. Some suggest that ending the politics of exclusion may become easier, while most indicate an opposite trend. There is little indication here that there will be major shifts in political power away from the social and economic elites toward those who traditionally have had little power.

Smith and O'Day have offered a set of policy priorities that they think will be necessary in order to deal with these demographic trends. They include:

- Ensure that low-income children are ready for school;
- Ensure that all children receive a high-quality, coherent educational program;
- Expand educational opportunity for low-income and otherwise educationally needy students beyond the school day. (pp. 86–88)

These prescriptions may not be so easy to attain. Smith and O'Day stress that public sector leadership and additional financial resources are necessary to implement these policies (p. 89). More than just leadership and funding may be required.

A new political economy of education?

There is nothing in these data or policy implications to suggest that historic patterns of
power have been sufficiently altered to allow greater attention to the education of the
most needy in our society. Educational historian Thomas James reminds us that education is still a contested good in our society (James 1991). Educational need will continue to be greatest among those children who come from homes in poverty, from
immigrant families, from families where English is not the first language, from families
where the parents are not well-educated, and who are children of color. Political power
remains in the hands of those who are more affluent, who are white, who are well-
educated, and who are male. It seems no accident, then, that schools in the affluent
suburbs and in other districts where relatively affluent, white, well-educated residents
are dominant are generally doing a good job and are well-funded. Schools in communities where a larger portion of the residents and children are poor, immigrant, non-
white, and poorly educated are not nearly as well-funded and are regarded as needing
major reform. Jonathan Kozol documents this condition well in *Savage Inequalities* and
ends the book with these words:

> It is a tragedy that these good things are not more widely shared. All of our children ought to be allowed a stake
> in the enormous richness of America. Whether they be born to poor white Appalachians or to wealthy Texans,
> to poor black people in the Bronx or to rich people in Manhasset or Winnetka, they are all quite wonderful and
> innocent when they are small. We soil them needlessly. (Kozol 1991: 233)

Soil them needlessly we do.

The prevailing view in the United States is that education is a zero-sum game
because so many people view education as a private consumption good rather than as
a public good. Peterson (1981) addresses this issue when he discusses whether the public
provision of education is a developmental policy or a redistributive policy (pp. 94–99).
The resulting mix of public education as developmental in suburbs but redistributive in
cities results often in a situation where suburban schools are well-funded and city schools
are under-funded. If we provide more to some children, we deny more to others.
People generally recognize the value of education as the instrument for achieving the
good things in life, however defined. As a result, the affluent believe, for the most part,
that to provide a better education to those who have been denied a good education is
to lessen the opportunities for their own children. This may be viewed as actually
providing fewer resources for the education of their own children or as increasing the
competition for their own children. As a society, we believe in competition sometimes,
especially when we think it benefits us, but at other times we find it not to be healthy.

Therefore the American education system can be an instrument of oppression as
much as an instrument of opportunity. The education system can be a source of liberation
and empowerment for some, but it also can serve to deny that liberation or empowerment to others. That denial is often based on the quality and nature of schooling and
the level of school funding.

Just as this may be an historic truth, there is also evidence that the situation may
be worsening. We may have entered a new political economy where the divisions in
our society are becoming greater and social separatism is increasing. Barber (1992) has
characterized this as a society where

> individuals regard themselves almost exclusively as private persons with responsibilities only to family and job,
> yet possessing endless rights against a distant and alien state in relationship to which they think of themselves,
> at best, as watchdogs and clients and, at worst, as adversaries and victims. (p. 232)

The sense of community, to the extent it formerly existed, is diminished and debased.

Income distribution in the United States is becoming more uneven and there has appeared a bifurcation in labor markets between very high-income jobs and very low-income jobs. Fewer jobs are available in the middle ranges. Poverty among children is increasing, as it is among many minority groups. Recessions in both the early 1980s and the early 1990s set back whatever economic progress African Americans, Hispanics and others may have been making prior to those times.

Federal social welfare programs were severely curtailed in the 1980s and then these programs were blamed for urban unrest in the 1990s. The social 'safety net' was removed and the victims of poverty were blamed by many national policymakers as the cause of their own plight.

After over two decades of school finance reform litigation and legislative efforts to equalize school funding across districts, there is scant evidence that equity has increased or that the poor have been provided more resources or better schools (Ward 1990). Equity indexes have not improved in states with or without reform and there are still massive resource disparities between urban and suburban schools (Kozol 1991). National educational reform movements, like school choice and the excellence movement, seem designed to hold this pattern in place and to deny many children the opportunity to hope for better schools. One of the most thorough and well-documented analyses of the current interest in school choice concludes that

> exit and choice will never work well to allocate that good [education] – unless working well means warehousing the poor, the less gifted, and the academically disinclined in educational facilities that make existing public schools look like the Institute for Advanced Studies, and that prepare young adults for no place in the social structure save the correctional facilities they would resemble. (Liebman 1991: 313)

Reich (1991) describes the 'secession of the successful' and the 'pursuit of privilege' that allows the affluent to enjoy the best of society and, at the same time, isolate themselves from those who are less affluent. As a nation, we seem not to be coming together, but to be accentuating our differences. Many examples of cultural isolationism can be found and this does not accrue to the benefit of the less affluent or the racial and cultural minorities. Few signs of educational progress are evident.

The new American political economy is based on the premise that those who have succeeded have the right to pass the fruits of success on to their children and that they owe nothing to those others in the community who have not achieved the same level of success (Barber 1992, Phillips 1990, Reich 1991). Our systems of school organization and finance, our system of taxation, and various other governmental institutions keep this new political economy in place.

Some policy mechanisms for change

There is no simple answer to what might alter these power arrangements, but three possible avenues for exploration include political participation, community organizing and unionization. Piven and Cloward (1988) hold out hope for the poor and the working classes in terms of increased voting and political participation. They argue that:

> Much about the current political situation in the United States is reminiscent of the closing years of the nineteenth century. A rapidly changing economy has once again made shifts in state policy inevitable. Now, as a century ago, the question is how government will intervene and who will benefit. Business has again mobilized on a huge scale to influence electoral politics; it has once again realigned in support of the Republican party; and it is again pressing for a series of radical changes in public policy that would depress working-class standards. (p. 249)

They argue that the major obstacles to greater political participation and voting by the poor are structural; the affluent, not confident of their own ability to sway the voters in important matters, have pursued public policies that have limited the franchise. This can be seen in bureaucratic restraints on voter registration and voting and in campaign financing laws which favor organized interest groups. Piven and Cloward conclude their study by saying that 'whether an enlarged electorate would transform American politics can only be known, finally, by obliterating the remaining obstacles to voting' (p. 255).

Increasing the franchise and limiting the obstacles to political participation are process rather than content approaches to reform. Steinberger (1985) confirms that increased access to the political system and greater political participation may need to be the emphasis for making major social changes. Barber (1992) sees 'voice' rather than 'exit' as the key to improving public education. Williams (1989) argues that 'the neighborhood organization is a political instrument whereby residents can make their educational and other public needs known and have them answered' (p. 148). Community organizing can become an instrument for achieving educational change by mobilizing local citizens to engage in active participation in working for better schools. This requires some consensus on what the failures of the school are and how these failures might be remedied. The policy instruments for seeking remedies might be electoral, legislative, judicial. Or, change may come by focusing public attention on intolerable circumstances. There is a long history in the US of community organizing for urban school reform, but the results have been mixed (Williams 1989). However, this does not mean that community organizing is not a potential route to social change. Current school reform efforts in Chicago, which have empowered local residents and given them greater voice in school decisions, is one example of how community organizing may bring positive change.

The role of teacher unions in achieving social change and in working toward social justice has been controversial. However, some hope has been suggested in the transformation of teacher unions from industrial unionism to professional unionism (Kerchner and Mitchell 1988). Murphy (1990) argues that,

As community organizers press for the divorce of politics from education, unionized teachers must take leadership in political battles lest power over education fall into the hands of real-estate speculators and tax conscious corporate interests. Teachers have always been in a bind over the issue of public school finance, but only in the age of collective bargaining have their demands been legitimized, not as luxuries, but as necessities in the overall bill of educational quality. (p. 268)

Interestingly, Murphy suggests that teacher unions have been more progressive and have better represented the interests of those who lack power in society when they have been led by women. Women leaders in teacher unions have been very assertive in addressing both gender inequalities and racial discrimination. Professionalism and the 'triumph of merit' have unified civil rights issues and gender issues, along with a general sense of concern for the oppressed (Murphy 1990: 261). Perhaps this will be true in the role played by teacher unions in eradicating social injustice for children.

Conclusion

The long-term demographic trends have supported economic and political conditions that create a social context where the gap between the 'haves' and the 'have nots' in the United States is widening and the political power of the 'haves' is increasing. Social justice is much discussed, but remains an elusive goal. It is likely an unwanted and repugnant goal for some. Many current public policies seem to support the political hegemony of the affluent in American society. Redistributive social policies are attacked as unworkable and too costly. The vast inequities in our educational system will not be erased until there is some real movement in altering current power relationships in favor of the less favored. The affluent have a clear stake in preventing any such change in political power structures. The improvement of education for all children may rest on the ability of the poor and working classes to organize politically to press for social justice. The chances of that happening, no matter how important, seem slim in the current public environment.

Note

1. Much of the material in this section is adapted from Ward, J. (1992) 'The Power of Demographic Change: Impact of Population Trends on Schools' in J. Ward and P. Anthony (eds) *Who Pays for Student Diversity? Population Changes and Educational Policy* (Newbury Park, CA: Corwin Press).

References

BARBER, B. (1992) *An Aristocracy of Everyone: The Politics of Education and the Future of America* (New York: Ballantine).

BERRYMAN, S. and BAILEY, T. (1992) *The Double Helix of Education and the Economy* (New York: Teachers College, Columbia University).

DE VITA, C. (1989) *America in the 21st Century: A Demographic Overview* (Washington, DC: Population Reference Bureau, Inc.).

EXTER, T. (1991) 'Booming Counties', *American Demographics*, 13 (1) p. 55.

GALBRAITH, J. (1992) *The Culture of Contentment* (Boston: Houghton Mifflin).

HARRIGAN, J. (1989) *Political Change in the Metropolis* (Glenview, IL: Scott-Foresman).

JACKSON, K. (1985) *Crabgrass Frontier: The Suburbanization of the United States* (New York: Oxford University Press).

JAMES, T. (1991) 'State Authority and the Politics of Educational Change,' in G. Grant (ed.) *Review of Research in Education*, 17 (Washington, DC: American Educational Research Association).

JONES, L. (1980) *Great Expectations: America and the Baby Boom Generation* (New York: Ballantine).

KERCHNER, C. and MITCHELL, D. (1988) *The Changing Idea of a Teachers' Union* (New York: Falmer Press).

KOZOL, J. (1991) *Savage Inequalities: Children in America's Schools* (New York: Crown Publishers, Inc.).

LIEBMAN, J. (1991) 'Voice, Not Choice', *Yale Law Journal*, 101 (1) pp. 259–314.

MURPHY, M. (1990) *Blackboard Unions: The AFT and the NEA, 1900–1980* (Ithaca, NY: Cornell University Press).

O'HARE, W. and DE VITA, C. (1990) *America in the 21st Century: Governance and Politics* (Washington, DC: Population Reference Bureau, Inc.).

PETERSON, P. (1981) *City Limits* (Chicago: University of Chicago Press).

PHILLIPS, K. (1990) *The Politics of Rich and Poor: Wealth and the American Electorate in the Reagan Aftermath* (New York: Random House).

PIVEN, F. and CLOWARD, R. (1988) *Why Americans Don't Vote* (New York: Pantheon).

REICH, R. (1991) *The Work of Nations: Preparing Ourselves for 21st Century Capitalism* (New York: Knopf).

SMITH, M. and O'DAY, J. (1991) 'Educational Equality: 1966 and Now', in D. VERSTEGEN and J. WARD (eds) *Spheres of Justice in Education* (New York: Harper Business).

STEINBERGER, P. (1985) *Ideology and the Urban Crisis* (Albany: State University of New York Press).

STERNLIEB, G. and HUGHES, J. (1987) 'The Demographic Long Wave: Population Trends and Economic Growth', *Economic Development Quarterly*, 1, pp. 307–22.

USDAN, M. (1984) 'New Trends in Urban Demography', *Education and Urban Society*, 16, pp. 399–414.

WALDROP, J. and EXTER, T. (1991) 'The Legacy of the 1980s', *American Demographics* 13 (3) pp. 33–38.

WARD, J. (1990) 'Implementation and Monitoring of Judicial Mandates: An Interpretive Analysis', in J.

UNDERWOOD and D. VERSTEGEN (eds) *The Impacts of Litigation and Legislation on Public School Finance: Adequacy, Equity, and Excellence* (New York: Harper and Row).

WILLIAMS, M. (1989) *Neighborhood Organizing for Urban School Reform* (New York: Teachers College Press).

WRIGLEY, E.A. (1969) *Population and History* (New York: McGraw-Hill).

2 Categorical wars: Zero-sum politics and school finance

Thomas Timar and Dale Shimasaki

Passage of Proposition 13 and the California Supreme Court's *Serrano* decision made California the first state to change from a locally funded to a centralized, state school finance system. The attraction of such a system to policymakers and school reformers was its assumed capacity to create a rational system of school finance – a system attuned to concepts of both vertical and horizontal equity. On the other hand, centralization created a new politics of school finance, as the decision-making arena shifted from local districts to the state legislature. Access to decision-making, mobilization of political coalitions and newly legitimated interests comprise the new political mix. This chapter examines how the new politics affects issues of ethnicity, manifested as tensions between urban, suburban and rural school districts. Demographic shifts threaten old political coalitions. This chapter examines the tensions in that change.

Introduction

In 1979, with voter enactment of Proposition 13[1], California created a state school finance system. In spite of the disruptions caused by the measure's fiscal restrictions, many – particularly advocates of school finance equalization reform – hailed the move toward full state assumption of school finance as a move toward greater equity. Certainly, the measure accelerated implementation of the California Supreme Court's *Serrano*[2] mandate to equalize spending among the state's 1043 school districts to within $100 of one another. California voters accomplished, albeit unwittingly, what the legislature, at best, could have accomplished only over a prolonged period.[3] (Elmore & McLaughlin 1982)

The allure of a centralized, state school finance system is the promise of a more equitable school finance scheme. Issues that are difficult to address in locally fragmented and diverse funding systems can be addressed, hypothetically at least, more rationally in centralized, state-funded systems. The textbook version of an ideal school finance system is one that balances horizontal and vertical equity interests. Such state school funding plans reduce overall fiscal disparities among the majority of students, while attending to the special learning needs of others. This policy ideal should be more easily attainable when funding is centralized.

Like nearly all states, California's prior school finance scheme relied principally on local property taxes. While advocates of such a system tout its virtues for local control, critics point to finance inequities as the price of such control. Had the state legislature been willing and capable, politically, of addressing issues of funding inequalities among districts, *Serrano* would not have been necessary, but *Serrano* in California and similar lawsuits in other states exist because the political system is not adroit at redistributive politics. Politicians are most successful when they have a growing revenue base. School finance politics prior to Proposition 13 was born of tensions between high and low wealth districts. The legislature's response was to encourage equalization through incentives to unify. Because larger districts created larger tax bases, some local funding disparities could be eliminated. A growing state tax revenue base made the strategy politically palatable as state tax revenue rose annually to the point where the state had a nearly $15 billion budget surplus just prior to Proposition 13. In spite of state revenue growth, however, the legislature's school finance equalization strategy addressed the problem obliquely. The issue of wealth redistribution was never addressed directly. However, even an indirect strategy could no longer work in the wake of *Serrano*, Proposition 13, and other fiscal constraints which turned school finance politics into a zero-sum game.

As California has complied with the *Serrano* mandate it is generally assumed by policymakers that the new school finance structure is more equitable and more rationally attuned to diverse district funding needs.[3] Yet there is evidence to suggest that centralization has created new kinds of inequalities among districts. For example, districts with nearly identical needs receive vastly differing levels of aid.[4] Berkeley school district, for example, receives $128 per student in compensatory aid while ABC school district with an identical need index receives $50 per student; San Francisco receives $204 per student, while Long Beach, with a higher need index, receives only $92 per student. Similarly, state categorical support for desegregation funding is $1725 per black and Hispanic student in the San Jose District, while it is $679 in Los Angeles, and $14 in Sacramento. From a rational policy perspective, the most puzzling among the state's panoply of categorical aids is supplemental aid. Some districts receive no funding in this category, while others receive a maximum of $94 per pupil. Its policy objective, which we discuss more fully below, is simply to provide categorical aid to districts which receive little in compensatory support. Consequently, districts like San Ramon, which have the lowest need index in our district sample (over 73 percent below the state average) receive the maximum $94. Compton, on the other hand, whose need index is more than 450 percent above the state average receives nothing.

This chapter examines the current system of school finance in California. We assess how a state system addresses politically polarizing issues such as municipal overburden and rural diseconomies of scale by balancing competing political and economic interests with the educational interests of children. Over the past ten years, school finance equalization in California has moved apace, and although base funding to districts is now equalized within an inflation-adjusted band, is the overall system more equitable? Or have the vagaries of a politically determined finance scheme replaced inequities caused by local property wealth? This chapter addresses three basic issues regarding California's system of school finance. First, do funding disparities among urban, suburban and rural districts still exist? Are there disproportionate resources flowing to predominantly white, middle-class suburbs? And, conversely, have urban and rural districts been financially starved because of white flight from the former and lack of political clout in the latter? Second, do urban, suburban and rural districts enroll demographically different student populations? Fnally, what is the consonance between student demographic characteristics and school funding? Does funding follow need?

The analysis is based on 1990–91 district revenue and student demographic data. The data set consists of ninety-one unified school districts, comprising approximately one-half of the state's 4.5 million students. Of the districts in the sample, fifteen were selected because they represent the core of urban districts; fifty-six are suburban districts which form a ring around the urban districts; Some suburban districts, like Newport-Mesa and Piedmont, are upper-middle class enclaves and twenty are rural districts, chosen randomly. Others, like Santa Ana, Hayward, Moreno Valley and Riverside are 'transitional' suburbs that are becoming increasingly less 'suburban' and more like urban centers. The sample represents both very small school districts with student enrollments under 100 as well as districts with larger enrollments but lower population densities. Unified districts were selected for comparability.

The post-Proposition 13 system of school finance

California's school finance system consists of two basic components: basic support revenues (called 'base revenue limits') and categorical aid. Revenue limits are the base allocations per pupil to each district; the level is determined annually in the state budget. Though the revenue limit is comprised of both local and state property taxes and state general support, district allocations are determined by a legislatively-defined formula. If a district's property tax revenues increase, its state support is decreased by an equivalent amount.[5] A district's property wealth has no significance for how much the district may spend per pupil. There is considerable variation among districts in their mix of state and local support. In Lynwood district, for example, local property tax revenues are only $156 per pupil while in Newport Mesa they are $3590. The difference in levels of state general fund support is politically significant, however, because it represents a redistribution of wealth. Newport-Mesa taxpayers probably pay as much or more in taxes as those in Lynwood. Yet, in school revenues, at least, they receive considerably less. In fact, Newport-Mesa receives $108 per pupil in state basic aid, while Lynwood receives $2830.

The categorical portion of the budget consists of four funding areas: support for school improvement, compensatory aid, variable cost equalization and auxiliary service revenues. As the name implies, allocations for school improvement aim at improving instructional quality. The rationale for this type of funding is to provide districts with fiscal incentives to promote state reform policies. Though district participation is voluntary, improvement funding tends to be broadly inclusive. Some programs have been in place for some time. The School Improvement Program (SIP), for example, was begun in the early 1970s. This general funding category has grown dramatically since 1983, with the onset of the latest national school reform movement. As state strategies to improve educational quality proliferated, so did categorical programs to implement and pay for them. Programs like the Mentor Teacher grew out of the state's major reform bill, SB 813, in 1983. Staff development grew as a category of finance from about $3 million in 1983 to over $100 million by 1986.

Unlike school improvement funding, compensatory aid is targeted narrowly to districts on the basis of various student characteristics. Historically, this type of funding is rooted in efforts to equalize the educational opportunities of poor, disadvantaged, handicapped or non-English speaking students. However, the special needs category has grown to include the Gifted and Talented program as well as Economic Impact Aid for low-income, minority students. Monies in these categories are targeted to specific student needs. Because funding sources for such programs are usually broadly based while program benefits are exclusive, they are politically vulnerable.

Variable cost revenues are allocated to districts to compensate them for extraordinary costs that lie outside of districts' control. Home-to-School Transportation, Year-Round Schools, and Court Ordered Desegregation are some of the programs in this funding stream. The final category, auxiliary service revenues, includes funding for adult education, food services, deferred maintenance, and the like.

The base revenue limits to districts and compensatory categorical aid have been politically the most controversial features of the state's school system. Early debates over court mandated equalization focused almost exclusively on differences among districts in base funding – specifically, over the size of the state local property tax 'buyout.' A particularly difficult issue centered on funding disparities among school districts. Political contention grew from the fact that local funding disparities reflected both differences in local capacity and willingness of school districts to tax themselves. Though capacity varied, controversy over state equalization was fueled by the fact that equalization failed to differentiate between capacity and effort. Districts in which voters favored low property taxes over higher educational expenditures would get a windfall from the state. While a state funding windfall could be justified on grounds of fiscal capacity, it could not be justified on the basis of effort. On the other hand, districts that had taxed themselves at a high rate would now be penalized. Districts which had placed a premium on education and were willing to tax themselves at high rates saw their efforts slip away as they were squeezed into the $100 funding band. The winners and losers, however, were not clearly differentiated according to urban, suburban or rural status. Property-rich industrial districts, like Emeryville in the San Francisco Bay Area, which enrolled mostly poor black children, stood, potentially, to lose as much as those districts with mainly affluent white students. Districts with high fixed costs – high teacher salaries, for instance – suffered the most.

Controversy over categorical funding tended to focus on several issues. Chief among them was, and continues to be, a deep ideological division between proponents and opponents of compensatory aid for low-income, disadvantaged students. Democrats in the state legislature regard such programs as entitlement and as part of a larger social policy agenda that promotes greater educational and, ultimately, social equality. Conservative Republicans (which comprise the majority of Republicans in the legislature), on the other hand, are 'philosophically opposed,' as one key Republican legislative staff member put it, 'to the concept of giving more money to students because they perform poorly in school.' Furthermore, suburban districts regard compensatory aid programs, inasmuch as they are targeted mainly to urban districts, as a redistribution of general tax revenues from suburban to urban districts. Moreover, as state revenues – and with it funding for schools – declined in a frenzy of fiscal retrenchment in the wake of Proposition 13, high spending districts wanted greater flexibility to spend categorical monies.[6]

Political pressure to 'deregulate' categorical funding led to a state budget stalemate in 1979. The Republicans in the legislature, who as a group represent predominantly suburban and rural areas, would not support Assembly Bill 8 – a school finance measure that restructured the state's school finance system after Proposition 13 and *Serrano* – unless regulations governing categorical programs were eliminated. A last-ditch, late-night compromise created the 'Sunset Review' of all existing categorical programs in education.[7]

Deregulation notwithstanding, categorical programs proliferated over the next ten years. In 1980, when the legislature established the 'sunset' committee, there were nineteen state-funded programs. By 1990–91, there were over seventy. Their proliferation is dramatically illustrated by the change in relative levels of general versus categorical support. In 1979–80, categorical aid (including federal aid) represented about 13 percent of total K–12 funding. In 1991–92 that ratio is just over 29 percent.[8]

Several explanations account for growth in categorical funding. During the 1980s, there was an ongoing struggle in Sacramento between the conservative governor, Assembly Republicans and Democrats. The former wanted to target money away from

urban districts toward suburban districts, which were generally represented by Republicans. Governor Dukmejian and Assembly Republicans opposed increased categorical funding for three reasons. Because funds were targeted for specific students (generally,
the disadvantaged), the lion's share of categorical monies went to urban districts (mostly
represented by Democrats), and not suburban or rural districts (mostly represented
by Republicans). Moreover, Assembly Republicans had argued that funding formulas
for categorical programs were unfair. Specifically, suburban districts which had similar
demographic populations as urban districts were ineligible for categorical funds. Finally,
Republicans argued that programs were too restrictive and created unnecessary bureaucracy and administrative overhead. As a result, increases in categorical education programs for workload adjustments and cost-of-living adjustments were not supported by
Assembly Republicans. When such increases were included in the state budget, they
were vetoed by the governor.[9]

Towards the end of the Dukmejian administration and the beginning of the Wilson
administration, the Republican strategy towards categorical funding had changed. In
his 1992–93 budget proposal, Governor Wilson had limited increases for general aid,
and instead, increased funding for new categorical education programs. Two reasons
account for his reversal of the Dukmejian trend. He wanted to keep as much money as
possible off the collective bargaining table,[10] and he wanted additional education funds
targeted to his education priorities which included increased funding for preschool and
health education programs. Thus, categorical funding became the battleground where
competing policy goals and political interests were fought. The contested boundaries of
school finance expanded from base versus categorical funding to types of categorical
funding.

On the surface, the Republican approaches to education funding appear contradictory;
during the Dukmejian years, funding for categoricals was avoided, during the Wilson
term, additional categorical programs were created. Yet the approaches share the common theme of targeting money to constituent districts. The funding strategy of both
Republicans and Democrats has been to target money toward their respective constituents. Insofar as Republicans represent largely suburban and rural districts, their strategy
has been to devise new categorical programs that would benefit their districts. Democrats,
on the other hand, have fought to keep their share of categorical funding to urban
constituencies from eroding.

While pressure to increase funding to schools has been quite intense over the past
ten years, there has been little agreement about how additional monies should be spent.
Unlike base revenues which come with no regulatory strings attached, categorical monies
can be targeted to state policy goals through accompanying regulations. Categorical
funding is also attractive to politicians because it associates individual politicians with
program benefits. Not only can politicians embody their favorite ideas about education
in specific programs, but they can also build political constituencies around the financial
benefits of those programs.[11]

Political conflict within the legislature mirrored conflicts between urban, suburban
and rural schools over competing funding schemes. Urban districts have pushed for
increasing compensatory aid since that benefits them directly. Suburban districts, on the
other hand, have tended to favor base revenue growth, because that benefits them. A
persistent conflict during state budget negotiations is over the mandatory cost-of-living-
adjustment (COLA) guaranteed by law to compensatory programs. Republicans, and
the suburban districts they represent, have been staunch opponents of COLAs. They
would prefer that funding increases to compensatory programs be included in funding

negotiations over K–12 apportionments. They believe that if compensatory aid is taken off the bargaining table, they lose negotiating leverage.

The question then, is how different are urban, suburban and rural districts in terms of level of funding, types of funding, and types of students whom they serve. Table 2.1 shows the different levels of funding to districts. The data show that base revenue limits to urban districts are $120 above that of suburban districts and $6 below that of rural districts. The difference fits comfortably within the inflation-adjusted band – now between $200 and $300 dollars – allowed by the court in *Serrano III*. On average, urban districts receive 2 percent more than the state average, rural districts 3 percent more (this is due to the state funding formula that compensates rural districts for diseconomies of scale), while suburban districts receive 2 percent less than the state average. The data also illustrate the state finance system's redistributive effects. While local property tax revenues for urban districts are at 15 percent below the state average, suburban districts are 9 percent above the state average. Though one interpretation of this imbalance argues that urban districts were allowed to keep less property tax money for schools (as more money was diverted into other municipal services) in the original local 'bailout' legislation after Proposition 13, suburban districts argue that they are paying for the cost of services that urban centers chose to provide to residents for no direct fees (for example, free garbage pick-up service) and for which suburban districts charge fees. They point out, further, that taxpayers of one area (suburbs) are being forced to bear the financial burden of choices made by taxpayers in another area (cities).

Although base revenue funding is equalized, the data show significant differences in funding levels among districts when categorical programs are entered into districts' total revenue calculations. (We exclude Special Education funding because analysis of differences among districts in this category is beyond the scope of this chapter.) On average, urban districts receive $696, suburban districts $449, and rural districts $519 per pupil in categorical funding. In total funding, children in urban schools receive $367 more than children in suburban schools and $171 more than children in rural schools. These differences are observable within the various categorical funding streams. Variable costs account for $164 per pupil in categorical aid for rural districts, compared to $92 and $76 for urban and suburban districts. Of the $164, about $130 is explainable by home-to-school transportation costs. Compensatory, Supplemental and Desegregation grants show considerable variation among the three types of districts. On the other hand, monies in the School Improvement category are quite evenly distributed among the three types of districts. This is understandable because school improvement funds, as noted earlier, are linked to state initiated reforms. The Mentor Teacher Program, for instance, is aimed at general, systemwide improvement. It is not targeted to a special population. Compensatory, Desegregation and Supplemental funding, on the other hand, are targeted to special populations.

Given the funding disparities, the question is how can differences among districts in compensatory, desegregation and supplemental funding be justified. Inequalities in categorical funding can be justified on grounds that districts have different needs and, therefore, should receive different amounts of money. As noted earlier, categorical funding for transportation costs are principally related to population sparsity in rural districts. Indeed, the major source of variation in variable costs can be *attributed to* transportation which comprises 66 percent of that cost category. Presumably, compensatory aid should be related to student needs, and hence differences in compensatory support among types of districts should reflect different student characteristics. As Table 2.1 shows, urban districts receive on average $71 more per pupil in compensatory aid than suburban districts

Table 2.1: District funding per student by type of district

Funding Category	All Districts			Urban			Suburban			Rural		
	% of Total	Amount	Ratio of Average	% of Total	Amount	Ratio of Average	% of Total	Amount	Ratio of Average	% of Total	Amount	Ratio of Average
Local Revenue Limit[1]	29	$903	1.0	24	$772	0.85	31	$949	1.05	27	$872	0.97
State Revenue Limit[1]	71	$2193	1.0	76	$2397	1.07	69	$2100	0.96	73	$2303	1.05
Total Revenue Limit[1]	86	$3096	1.0	77	$3169	1.02	87	$3049	0.98	86	$3175	1.03
State Categorical[2]	14	$506	1.0	23	$696	1.38	13	$449	0.89	14	$519	1.03
Variable Cost	19	$98	1.0	13	$92	0.94	17	$76	0.78	32	$164	1.67
Desegregation	7	$35	1.0	29	$205	5.86	0.5	$2	0.06	0	$0	0
Improvement	49	$248	1.0	36	$249	1.0	55	$249	1.0	47	$246	0.99
Compensatory	13	$68	1.0	18	$123	1.81	12	$52	0.76	13	$70	1.03
Supplemental	8.5	$43	1.0	2	$15	0.35	8.3	$57	1.33	4	$23	0.53
Vocational Ed	0.3	$2	1.0	0.1	$1	0.5	0.2	$1	0.5	1	$6	6.0
Other	1.6	$12	1.0	2	$11	0.92	3	$12	1.0	2	$10	0.83
Total State Funding[3]	100	$3602	1.0	100	$3865	1.07	100	$3498	0.97	100	$3694	1.03

Notes: *Data Source: California State Department of Education.*
1 *The Local Revenue Limit is the amount that districts receive in local property tax revenues; the State Revenue Limit is the amount of state support required to bring districts up to their statutorily determined Total Revenue Limit.*
2 *State Categorical does not include Special Education and Adult Education apportionments.*
3 *This represents the sum of 'Total Revenue Limit' and 'State Categorical'.*

Table 2.2:   Student demographic characteristics by type of district [1]

Demographic Characteristics	All Districts[2]	Urban Districts[2]	Suburban Districts[2]	Rural Districts[2]
Percent White	48.0	25.0	50.0	60.0
Percent Minority	52.0	75.0	50.0	40.0
Hispanic	30.0	29.0	31.0	28.0
Black	8.7	27.0	6.4	1.6
Asian	6.7	13.0	6.6	2.6
Filipino	2.0	3.5	2.0	0.7
Native American	1.0	0.3	0.1	4.7
Other	3.6	2.2	3.9	2.4
Percent AFDC	16.0	30.0	11.0	20.0
Percent LEP	16.0	21.0	16.0	12.0
Need Index[2]	1.0	2.57	0.73	0.57

Notes: 1 *Data Source: California State Department of Education*
       2 *Percentages represent mean values.*
       3 *Percentages may not add due to rounding.*

and $53 more than rural districts. In school desegregation aid, urban districts receive $203 more than suburban districts and $205 more than rural districts. We now address the rationality of differences in funding in light of differences in district characteristics.

District needs and categorical funding

Demographic differences among students in urban, suburban and rural districts are illustrated in Table 2.2. Districts clearly differ on the basis of racial composition, poverty and number of immigrants who have only limited or no English-speaking skills. While California schools are now 52 percent minority, minority enrollment in urban districts is 75 percent. Of those students, 29 percent are Hispanic, 27 percent Black, and 13 percent Asian. Interestingly, suburban districts enroll 50 percent minority students. Among those districts, however, the predominant majority are Hispanic. Urban districts also enroll a significantly larger portion of students with special needs. The percentage of urban students whose families receive welfare benefits (AFDC) exceeds the state average by 14 percent. The percentage of such students in urban districts exceeds the percentage of such students in suburban districts by 19 percent and in rural districts by 10 percent. In order to assess the multiplier effects of racial isolation, poverty and immigration, we constructed the Need Index to assess their combined effects. (Need Index = percent of minority students in a district × percent of students whose families are AFDC recipients × percent LEP–NEP students in a district). We then calculated an index for urban, suburban and rural districts based on the ratio of the mean district type to the state mean. We selected these factors because state compensatory funding formulas are based on them. Table 2.2 shows that the Need Index for urban districts is two and one-half times greater than the state average, while for suburban districts it is about three-quarters and rural districts somewhat over one-half of the state average.

    Clearly, urban districts have greater concentrations of minority, limited-English speaking and AFDC students, and it is also clear that levels of categorical funding among the three types of districts differs. It is not clear, however, to what extent need factors drive categorical funding to urban districts. The textbook view of school finance argues

Table 2.3: **Correlations of selected funding categories and selected student and district characteristics**

	Supplementary	*Compensatory*	*Desegregation*	*White*	*Minority*	ID	*Need*
Supplementary	1.00						
Compensatory	−.56**	1.00					
Desegregation	−.24	.27*	1.00				
White	.26*	−.65**	−.23	1.00			
Minority	−.26*	.65**	.23	−1.00	1.00		
ID	−.33**	.57**	.62**	−.43**	.44**	1.00	
Need	−.36**	.82**	.18	−.74**	.74**	.51**	1.00

*Note: N of cases = 91; *denotes 1-tailed significance at .01; **denotes 1-tailed significance at .001.*

that urban districts should receive more money because of the students whom they serve. Hence, vertical equity justifies higher levels of funding as urban students require higher levels of educational services than their suburban counterparts. A competing argument to the rational school finance model is that finance in a centralized system is driven by political clout, not by student need. Urban districts form a powerful voting block in the state legislature and also form the nucleus of the Democratic caucus in both the Senate and the Assembly. Moreover, the leadership in both houses represent urban districts. According to the political argument, categorical funds are a convenient way to funnel money to political constituencies. Categorical funding becomes a way of rewarding political allies, not student needs.

Categorical funding and need

The correlations among categorical revenue variables and student and district variables, shown in Table 2.3, support both views of categorical funding. There is significant correlation between each of the variables – compensatory aid ('Compensatory'), the percentage of minority students in a district ('Minority'), and 'Need' – suggesting that need and compensatory funding are, indeed, related. On the other hand, 'Compensatory' is also significantly correlated with 'ID', a categorical variable that identifies urban districts. The correlation (.5727) suggests that simply being an urban district – having political clout in the legislature – is also significant.

Examining the simple correlations among the variables does not allow us to disentangle the effects of the variables on one another. For example, they do not allow us to isolate the effects of Need on different levels of categorical funding. To disentangle and estimate the magnitude of effects of student characteristics on the one hand, and politics on the other, we propose three linear models. The first addresses the relationship between levels of compensatory aid and student characteristics. In the hypothetical model,

Compensatory = Need + ID

'Compensatory' is the amount of compensatory categorical aid to a district; 'Need' is a district's Need Index; and ID is 1 if the district is an urban district, and 0 if it is a suburban or rural district. The results of the estimated model are shown in Table 2.4. Need and ID together explain 71 percent of the variance in compensatory funding, but 67 percent of that is explainable by Need alone. The relative importance of ID in the equation is clarified by its partial correlation with the dependent variable. When we

Table 2.4[1]:   Estimated linear model of compensatory funding (N = 91)

Funding Category	Constant	Need	ID
Compensatory	42 (11.36**)	.11 (10.66**)	24 (3.16**)
Summary Statistics	R^2 = .71	F = 105.97	Sig F = .000

*Note: 1 T-values are shown in parentheses: *denotes significance at .01; **denotes significance at .00.*

Table 2.5:   Estimated linear model of desegregation funding (N = 91)

Funding Category	Constant	Minority	ID
Desegregation	13 (0.54)	0.25 (−0.53)	210 (6.9**)
Summary Statistics	R^2 = 0.38	F = 27.43	Sig F = .000

*Note: T-values are shown in parentheses: *denotes significance at .01; **denotes significance at .00.*

remove the linear effects of the other variables in the equation, the partial correlation between Compensatory and ID is .18, a significant reduction from the simple correlation, .57. This suggests that ID has an intervening effect on the dependent variable, but not a significant causal effect. Urban districts receive more in compensatory aid than other districts because of the higher level of need in those districts. The estimated average amount of funding to districts, according to our model, is $65, which is close to the actual average of $67 shown in Table 2.1. For urban districts average compensatory funding is estimated at $89, which is less than the $123 average for urban districts, but within the 95 percent confidence level.

The second equation hypothesizes the relationship between funding for desegregation and a district's minority population. Logically, one would expect categorical aid for desegregation to be associated with high percentages of minority students. However, the correlations in Table 2.3 indicate no significant relationship between Desegregation and Minority; on the other hand, desegregation funding and simply being an urban district are significantly correlated.

The linear association between desegregation funding on the one hand and minority concentration and political influence, on the other, is the following:

Desegregation = Minority + ID

'Desegregation' is the amount of desegregation aid to a district; 'Minority' is the percentage of minority students in a district; and 'ID' denotes an urban district. The estimated model is shown in Table 2.5. According to the model, funding for desegregation is totally unrelated to the percentage of minority students in a district. On the other hand, being an urban district is worth, on average, $210 in desegregation aid. Interpretations for this rather peculiar phenomenon will be discussed below.

The final source of categorical funding that shows considerable variation among the three types of districts is Supplemental Aid. This is a form of categorical equalization aid. While, to policy analysts, this seems a contradiction in terms, it is indeed intended to provide categorical support to those districts which receive none. Though we discuss this form of aid more fully below, for immediate purposes we are principally interested in determining the beneficiaries of this type of aid. Does the aid flow predominantly to certain types of districts? Is there any connection between supplemental

Table 2.6[1]: Estimated linear model of supplemental funding (N = 91)

Funding Category	Constant	White	ID	Need
Supplemental	25 (1.7)	0.07 (0.35)	33 (4.48**)	0.03 (0.11)
Summary Statistics	$R^2 = .20$	F = 11.98	Sig F = .000	

Note: 1 T-values are shown in parentheses: *denotes significance at .01; **denotes significance at .00.

aid and need? The correlation matrix in Table 2.3 shows that 'Supplemental' is highly associated with 'White,' the percentage of white students in a district; inversely associated with 'ID', suburban and rural districts; and inversely associated with 'Need'.

Questions regarding benefit from supplemental grants and the relationship of funding to need are addressed in the following linear model.

Supplemental = White + ID + Need

The estimated model results are shown in Table 2.6. Although the simple correlations suggest a relationship among several of the predictor variables with the dependent variable, it is clear that once the linear effects of the independent variables on one another have been removed, ID – whether a district is suburban or rural – is the only significant predictor of supplemental aid. Indeed, the partial correlation between Supplemental and White is 0.03, while for Supplemental and Need it is −0.14.

Policy, politics and categorical aid

The analysis suggests that categorical funding decisions are driven by politics as much as they are driven by policy. Although Variable costs and Compensatory aid are closely related to actual costs and student need, respectively, two other sources of district revenues, Supplemental and Desegregation aid, bear no demonstrable relationship to discernible policy ends. The model shows that Desegregation aid goes primarily to urban districts and it is unrelated to the number of black and Hispanic students in a district. Supplemental aid, on the other hand, flows predominantly to suburban districts. Clearly, in these two funding categories, educational interests are subordinated to political interests.

Supplemental grants

The California legislature created Supplemental Aid in response to intense pressure from the Assembly Republican caucus in 1989. Republicans argued that categorical funding to districts should be equalized – that is, brought within the *Serrano* standard. Moreover, they initially asked for $500 million to be used for equalization purposes. According to the equalization proposal, districts receiving below average amounts in categorical support would be eligible for funding. The compromise that was enacted into law provided for $185 million, with a maximum $95 per pupil allocation. This funding strategy sets a new standard for irrationality in public finance. There is no policy rationale justifying this type of revenue other than the desire to give more money to suburban districts at the expense of urban districts. Altbough it does make sense to equalize within funding categories so that similar school districts receive similar amounts of funding, it makes no policy sense to equalize across all categorical programs.

The net effect of the Supplemental grants is to disequalize funding among California school districts as money flows disproportionately to those districts that have the least need. Indeed, if compensatory funding were perfectly equalized on the basis of need, urban districts would receive 2.5 times the state average, or $170 per pupil, instead of the $123 which they currently receive. The fact that the money goes predominantly to suburban districts suggests that power politics plays a strong role in school finance decisions.

Desegregation aid[12]

Desegregation aid was intended to help schools offset the costs of either court-imposed or voluntary school desegregation efforts. Districts are reimbursed for actual costs. Reimbursements to districts for the 1990–91 school year were just over $500 million – $424.5 million for court-ordered desegregation and $76.2 million for voluntary desegregation. The lion's share, just under $320 million, went to Los Angeles Unified School District. Since 1982–83, desegregation funding has grown by 300 percent from $141 million to over $500 million.

Disparities in per pupil funding under the desegregation program are the result of three factors: the cost reimbursement formula, the type of desegregation fund and changing demographics.

Cost reimbursement

A factor in funding disparities is the unique formula on which desegregation aid is distributed. Desegregation funding is a cost reimbursement program; consequently, funds are not allocated on a per-pupil basis. To qualify for funds, districts are either under court order to desegregate or have established a voluntary desegregation effort to avoid a court order. Under this funding mechanism, districts submit a claim to the state and are reimbursed for costs approved by the State Controller's Office. Cost-reimbursement claims lead to wide disparities in per-pupil funding. These costs, moreover, go beyond home-to-school transportation costs (busing) which are costs traditionally associated with desegregation. For example, Los Angeles Unified School District was ordered by the federal judge to establish new programs in magnet schools, establish specific class size ratios, and provide additional stipends to teachers who are in racially isolated schools. These costs might be significantly different from a desegregation program offered by a judge in another district. Given the reimbursement scheme, desegregation funding may be dependent on the degree to which the district can persuade the court to approve an enriched program under the desegregation order and thereby increase the cost reimbursement from the state.

Type of desegregation funding

Related to the cost reimbursement issue is the level of appropriations dedicated to court-ordered versus voluntary programs. Originally, reimbursement for desegregation was restricted to court ordered programs. At that time, only four unified districts were eligible for funding: Los Angeles, San Bernardino, San Diego and Stockton. The rationale was that the districts did not have any control over court-ordered costs. This funding, however, created an unintended consequence – encouraging districts to get sued, go to court, and encourage the court to mandate enriched programs to qualify for state desegregation reimbursements. Consequently, other school districts went to the legislature requesting special legislation to reimburse their court-ordered claims. Four years after it authorized court-ordered reimbursements, the legislature established voluntary desegregation rates at much lower levels. The original four districts, however, were allowed to keep the funds, adjusted for workloads and inflation, already approved by the court.

Subsequent legislative activity has created a funding inequity among districts. If a district was fortunate enough to be one of the original four, its base funding was maintained and 'grandfathered' into the funding system. If a district entered the reimbursement process late, it could qualify for funding but at a lower rate because more districts had to share the fiscal pie.

Changing demographics

In the last decade, not only has the state's school population become increasingly non-white, but the racial composition of the non-white population has also changed dramatically. For example, Stockton Unified School District had a racial minority which was predominantly black and Hispanic when it qualified for desegregation money. Since then, Stockton's school population has changed significantly; the black population has declined, while the number of Southeast Asians has increased considerably. Desegregation funding to the district does not reflect that change.

Such demographic shifts point to two problems in the desegregation funding formula. On the one hand, the allocation mechanism for desegregation does not reflect the changing composition of the disadvantaged population among districts who receive funds and those who could qualify for funds. On the other hand, districts which currently receive desegregation funding, despite demographic shifts in their student populations, continue to receive funds to provide stability in their budgets. In essence, desegregation funding has become an institutionalized part of funding for some districts. Loss of those funds would cause major dislocations to those districts. Consequently, there is considerable political pressure to ensure the continued flow of those dollars, regardless of actual need.

In addition to the issue of reimbursable costs, the allocation of desegregation funding among districts raises serious equity issues. Districts with identical concentrations of minority students receive vastly different amounts of aid. Sacramento City Unified and Bernardino City Unified each have 65 percent minority populations. Sacramento receives $6 per pupil while San Bernardino receives $246. San Jose, with a 60 percent minority student population receives $791, while Hayward with 63 percent receives nothing. Funding disparities among districts receiving desegregation aid become even more pronounced if examined in relationship to the number of Hispanic or black students in a district: that is, if funding for desegregation is considered in light of minority concentration.

There is no rationally discernible basis for allocation of desegregation funding, certainly not one that is based on the number of students or any indicator of need. School districts that are nearly identical in their black and Hispanic enrollments receive vastly different amounts of support. San Jose Unified receives nearly twice as much money, per black and Hispanic student as San Diego City School District. It is hard to discern, too, on what basis San Francisco Unified, with a black and Hispanic student

Table 2.7: Desegregation funding to districts per black and Hispanic student

District	Funding per Black and Hispanic Student	Percent of Black and Hispanic Students
ABC Unified	$29	36
Berkeley Unified	$531	53
Fresno Unified	$85	45
Long Beach Unified	$145	50
Los Angeles Unified	$679	78
Monterey Peninsula Unified	$25	34
Pajaro Valley Joint Unified	$66	61
Pasadena Unified	$67	76
Richmond Unified	$271	50
Riverside Unified	$20	39
Sacramento City Unified	$15	43
San Bernardino City Unified	$417	57
San Francisco Unified	$1125	37
San Jose Unified	$1726	44
San Diego City Unified	$899	43
Stockton Unified	$187	48
Sweetwater Union Unified	$17	62
Ventura Unified	$9	24

population of 37 percent receives $1125 per black and Hispanic student while Riverside Unified with 39 percent receives only $20. Clearly, the present reimbursement scheme is highly irrational and results in significant inequities among districts.

The success of relatively few urban districts at capturing a disproportionate share of state school funding is attributable, in large measure, to benefits realized from the centralization of the state's finance system. Urban districts are better mobilized into coalitions and have more votes in the legislature than their suburban or rural counterparts. They are also better connected to the leadership in both houses of the legislature. The finance and policy committees of both houses are dominated by representatives of urban districts. The Speaker of the Assembly, the President pro tempore of the Senate, the Chair of the Assembly Ways and Means Committee – as well as its education subcommittees, and the Senate Appropriations Committee all represent urban districts. Since Proposition 13, categorical funding has come to serve a multiplicity of purposes for urban districts. They respond to pressures from politically well-connected, strong, mobilized teacher unions that seek higher levels of funding for their districts to pay for higher salaries.

The Supplemental grants, on the other hand, evidence the new political muscle of suburban districts. While Republicans have traditionally represented the state's suburban interests, demographic trends show a growing group of independent voters in the suburbs. (Schneider 1992) Moreover, the fastest growing areas in the state are the suburbs, particularly Riverside, San Bernardino and San Diego counties, in the south, and Contra Costa, Yolo, Sonoma, and Napa counties among a number of others in the north. (Kehew 1992) As a group, suburban districts are becoming a more powerful voting block in the legislature. It is noteworthy, for instance, that the chair of the Assembly Education Committee represents a suburban district. Prior to the current chair's appointment, it had been dominated by urban legislators.

Conclusion

School finance skirmishes in the legislature between urban and suburban interests may be harbingers of a more ominous trend in public finance. School finance has become a zero-sum game in California, but one in which all the shares are becoming relatively smaller. Reasons for this encompass two broad themes. According to Governor Wilson's policy analysts, at least, the ratio of individuals who use public services to those who pay for public services is increasing. Others argue that California voters have become tax evasive since Proposition 13; and while they may be willing to approve narrowly targeted tax increases, they are not willing to support broad, general purpose tax increases (Schneider 1992). As public sector costs increase, revenues to pay for them decrease. This is particularly evident in education. Though spending for K–12 as a percent of personal income has increased from 3.1 percent in 1981–82 (a recession year) to 4.0 percent in 1989–90, it remains below the national average of 4.6 percent (PACE 1992). By all measures – except teacher salaries where they are the second highest in the nation – California is in the bottom quartile, nationally, of K–12 funding (PACE 1992).

While both the limited-capacity-to-pay and the unwillingness-to-pay scenarios are plausible, the latter is more convincing, given the state's changing demographic and political climate. If, indeed, we are witnessing the demise of a century of urban political domination, as William Schneider suggests, in favor of the 'new century of suburbs', we may be witnessing a shift in the balance of political power from urban to suburban districts. The shift entails more, however, than just a shift in power with new winners and losers. What is likely to emerge is a new political consensus. What is unclear, however, is what that political consensus may be. Does suburbanization and the increasing privatization that attends it portend a new social consensus based also on privatization? If open communities are replaced by gated communities and public parks by private shopping malls and country clubs, what will that mean for schools? Will urban centers and those living in them become socially, politically and economically marginalized as economic power shifts away from them? Or, are we witnessing more modest adjustments that naturally attend demographic changes?

It still remains unclear how the balance of political power between cities and suburbs (and rural areas, for that matter, as they become suburbs themselves of existing suburbs) will be influenced by changes in the legislature. The majority that the Democrats have held in the legislature is as attributable to their ability to control reapportionment of state assembly, senate as well as congressional seats as it is to their appeal to voters. While reapportionment may not have an immediate impact on the balance of power, due to the advantage of incumbency, its combined effects with term limitations, which California voters enacted in 1990, may be significant. Yet even if Republicans fail to capture majorities in both houses of the state legislature and Democrats retain their majorities, it is likely that the political agendas of those Democrats will reflect suburban interests. While there is a strong urban bias among Democrats in the legislature now, it probably will not last much longer. Already, as a result of 1990 state reapportionments, cities have lost representation to suburbs. Potential changes in the balance of political power are further threatened by the implementaton of legislative term limits which go into effect in 1994.

If suburbs can eclipse cities in political and economic power, what happens to those who live in the cities? It is evident from our data that urban school districts have the largest concentrations of minority, poor, limited-English proficient children. Will suburban politicians embrace them as part of a larger social consensus? How far will suburbs extend the concept of community to embrace the cities, realizing that the future of children in cities defines their futures as well?

How these various scenarios play out may well raise new legal issues with regard to school finance. The *Serrano* standard may, in the long term, prove to be ineffective in the face of political pressures. It is possible that achieving the equity standard imposed by the state constitution and courts may necessitate new legal remedies to realize it. For instance, the relationship between categorical funding, school desegregation, and equity has not been challenged on legal grounds. If categorical funding is an entitlement, to what does it entitle students? Could, for instance, the same standard for entitlement to services that is used in education for the handicapped be used for educating those who are racially isolated or educationally and economically disadvantaged? Fairly predictably, as the old social and political consensus in California breaks down, the courts may again play a significant role in helping define the boundaries of a new consensus, much as they did for the New Deal and the Great Society.

Notes

1. Proposition 13, a state initiative enacted by California voters in 1978, reduced property taxes to 1974 levels, limits ad valorem tax on real property to 1 percent of full cash value, allows for reassessment only when there is a change in ownership, requires any local tax increases on property (other than ad valorem) be approved by a two-thirds majority.
2. In its 1979 *Serrano v. Priest* decision, the California Supreme Court ruled the state's system of school finance unconstitional. The Court declared that 'the quality of education may not be a function of wealth, other than the wealth of the state as a whole.' It did not say how the state should implement this standard, nor what differences in per pupil funding were justified and constitutionally tolerable.
3. *Serrano III*, in 1982 found the system to be generally in compliance with the equalization mandate.
4. The state determines need based on a variety of factors, but the formula's principal components are a district's percentage of minority students, students whose families receive AFDC, and who are limited- or non-English speaking. The data for this chapter are based on State Department of Education data for the 1990–91 school year.
5. The Legislature's intent in devising this formula was to implement the Serrano decision in the wake of Proposition 13. Because of Proposition 13, implementation of *Serrano* moved from unequal ability to raise local dollars (local tax effort) to unequal expenditures per pupil. This was because Proposition 13 severely curtailed the ability of local governments to raise local revenues. This movement shifted state policy from providing equal access to revenue, while allowing for differences in local per pupil spending, to a system which requires mandated equal spending. The California Supreme Court affirmed in the case of *Butt v. State of California* (1992), in which the central issue was whether the trial court had the authority to order the state to keep the Richmond school open after the district ran out of funds, that 'the equal protection clause precludes the state from maintaining its common school system in a manner that denies the students of one district an education basically equivalent to that provided elsewhere throughout the state. The Court further stated that 'the Constitution does not prohibit all disparities in educational quality or service.' While acknowledging that disparities are legally permissible, the decision gives little direction on which disparities are constitutionally tolerable and which are not.
6. The Office of the Legislative Analyst estimates in a June 16, 1988 briefing paper that the cumulative state and local tax relief benefits enacted by the legislature between 1977–78 and 1988–90 amounted to just under $190 billion. On an annual basis that is roughly the equivalent of the state's general fund support for all of K–12 education.
7. The compromise required the legislature to conduct a review of the state's categorically funded programs and established a five-year timeline for its completion. If no legislative action were taken on a particular program by a specified date, all regulations pertaining to the program would be voided. However, districts would still be required to comply with the program's 'legislative intent,' and funds for the program would have to be used for the general purposes of the program.

The legislature established a joint senate-assembly committee to oversee the sunset review. The principal author of this article was the committee's consultant.

8. This is potentially significant, particularly for equalization purposes, because it means a decline in the relative share of base revenues to categorical revenues.

9. State compensatory funding formulas did not recognize the major demographic shifts that occurred between 1980 and 1990. Suburbs, especially in Southern California, that had been largely white, middle-class enclaves came to resemble urban areas in their demographic characteristics. Democrats in the legislature, particularly the Assembly, had little interest, furthermore, in readjusting categorical aid formulas to benefit suburban districts, and, indirectly, Republican legislators.

10. In fact, Governor Wilson's budget proposal included language to prevent local school districts from using funding increases for increased employee compensation.

11. It should be noted that there is no legal obligation to equalize funding disparities for categorical aid. Both sides in *Serrano* agreed to limit equalization to general aid. On hindsight, the decision may not be surprising. At the time, categorical funding represented a small proportion of the total education budget and funding for categorical programs came largely from the federal government. Over time, however, the number of state-initiated and financed categorical programs comprises a much large portion of the state budget. In 1979–80, categorical funding represented about 13 percent of total K–12 funding. In 1990–91 that ratio was just over 29 percent. During fiscal stress, when dollars become scarce, the perceived funding disparities of categorical education programs among districts becomes more visible and controversial. See Timar, T., 'Urban Politics and State School Finance in the 1980s,' in Politics of Education Association Yearbook 1992, J. Cibulka, R. Reed, and K. Wong, eds (Philadelphia: Falmer) 1992.

12. *California State Education Code*, Sections 42243.6, 42247, and 42249. For amounts and controlling language, see Chapter 467, *Statutes of 1990*.

References

ELMORE, R. and MCLAUGHLIN, M. (1982) *Reform and Retrenchment: The Politics of California School Finance Reform* (Cambridge, MA: Ballinger).

KEHEW, D. (ed.) (1992) *County Factbook, 1991–92* (Sacramento, CA: California State Association of Counties).

KOZOL, J. (1991) *Savage Inequalities* (New York: Crown Publishing).

MOCKLER, J. (1989) 'A conceptual framework for K–12 district revenues: Testimony to the Ways and Means Subcommittee on Education', Sacramento, CA: Murdoch, Mockler, Associates, 21 February.

POLICY ANALYSIS FOR CALIFORNIA EDUCATION (1990) 'Conditions of education in California, 1990', (Berkeley, CA: Policy Analysis for California Education, Graduate School of Education).

SCHAASFMA, P. (1988) 'Major state and local tax relief benefits, 1977–78 through 1988–89: Testimony prepared for the Joint Legislative Budget Committee', (Sacramento, CA: Office of the Legislative Analyst).

SCHNEIDER, W. (1992) 'The suburban century begins', *The Atlantic Monthly*, July, pp. 33–44.

TIMAR, T. (1992) 'Urban politics and state school finance in the 1980s', in J. CIBULKA, R. REED, and K. Wong (eds) *The Politics of Urban education in the United States (The Politics of Education Association Yearbook, 1991)* (Philadelphia: Falmer).

Accountability, invisibility and the politics of numbers: School report cards and race

Carolyn D. Herrington

This chapter explores the use of school report cards as a mechanism to address one of the most persistent problems plaguing education, the continuing underachievement of minority students. Using data from Dade County Public Schools (Miami), the author argues that a numbers-based strategy designed to eliminate race or ethnicity-based institutional biases is fundamentally at odds with the environment conducive to school-level improvement.

Minority performance and school report cards[1]

This chapter focuses on school report cards as an accountability tool and how their use interacts with one of the most persistent problems plaguing the public education system, continuing underachievement of minority students. Despite three decades of attention to the issue, minority student school performance lags considerably behind that of majority students. Furthermore, the extent of the gap has often been masked by aggregate data.

Policymakers have turned to school-based performance data reporting requirements to help address the problem. Reporting student and school performance data by race and ethnicity, holds out the promise to redress the situation 1) by providing accurate data on the nature, extent and location of the problem and 2) by fomenting pressure by parents and other community members on school officials, motivating them to focus more energies on ameliorating inequities. However, there has been virtually no research on utilization or impact of school-based performance data reporting requirements (Gaines and Cornett, 1992, Mackett and McKeough 1992).

This chapter looks specifically at the issues concerning the desirability of reporting student performance by race and ethnicity at the school level. Would such a policy increase the likelihood of resources being targeted to students in greatest need, making them more visible? Or would the reporting of these disaggregated data reinforce negative stereotypes about the performance of minority students? Do school officials behave differently when these data are available? What is the impact on local school policy when these data are made available by race and ethnicity? These are important questions that go to the root of school-based accountability policies – their purposes and their effects on schools, teachers and students.

The search for accountability: School report cards

School-based performance data reporting requirements, or school report cards as they are commonly termed, are an increasingly popular mechanism by which policymakers hope to make schools more accountable for their actions. Currently, over one-half of all states require districts or schools to produce and disseminate some form of report to parents and the general community on educational performance (Education Commission of the States 1992). Information to be included on the reports generally includes data on enrollment, racial and ethnic background of students, student performance, teacher salaries, teacher length of service, and other such commonly agreed upon characteristics of school organization and performance. Claims made for the benefits of school report cards are substantial and reasonable. Gaines and Cornett (1992) summarizes the policymaker's presumed intentions in requiring the reporting of school data to parents and the community as follows:

> Behind all of these efforts is the understanding that information can shape public support for education – that parents and state leaders need to be kept up-to-date about what students know and can do. When schools report regularly and clearly on results, government, business, and community leaders are more willing to ease regulations and leave decisions in the hands of teachers and principals. Taxpayers also want a straightforward report card showing whether their major investment in public education is paying off.

The increasing popularity of report cards reflects a convergence of a number of different lines of research and development including a greater need for public accountability, positive research findings on the role of parental involvement in school performance, research on effective schools and, finally, increased data management capacity at the state and local levels.

Accountability

Policymakers' search for greater accountability in public school performance has been constant from the beginning of publicly funded schools. However, since the 1970s, the search has become more stringent, urgent and unrelenting. The fragmenting of the coalition of educational interest groups in the 1960s, resulting in, among other things, the establishment of teachers' unions, significantly reduced the credibility of professional educators and forced policymakers to seek alternative and presumably more objective sources of information for the purposes of evaluating school effectiveness. This interest led to data-based reporting and evaluating as a primary means of establishing accountability (Kirst 1990).

Parental involvement

Simultaneously, the research base supporting the effects of parental involvement on student achievement has become increasingly strong (Epstein 1987, Henderson 1987). However, it is worth noting that parental involvement takes two distinct forms. In one, parents may become more involved with their child's own schooling or, in the second form, they may function as 'outside' monitors and policymakers, observing and advising on school operations. School report card policies rest on the latter assumption, that parents, motivated by their interest in their own child's achievement, will seek greater involvement at the school level. However, the evidence supporting the positive effects of parents' involvement in their child's own academic development (that is, providing them a quiet place to do homework, reading to them, etc.) is much stronger than the research on the effects of parents as advisors on school policy (Rich 1987).

Effective schools research

Interest in formulating policies that focus on the school as the unit of accountability and school improvement has been bolstered by the effective schools movement. The effective schools research demonstrated positive impacts of schoolwide variables such as shared goals and vision, strong leadership and high expectations for student performance (Brookover *et al.* 1979, Edmonds 1979, 1986, Lezotte and Bancroft 1985, Purkey and Smith 1983).

Information management systems

Finally, through the stimulation of federal reporting requirements and the greater role of state-level offices in educational reform, there has been significant development in the technological capacity of states and districts to manage complex information systems, enabling them to produce educational performance data at increasingly disaggregated levels, including school-specific and student-specific data. The type of data on school and student performance laid out in school report cards has only recently been available to states and districts.

These lines of research and development which have been occurring over the last two decades – need for greater accountability, benefits of parental involvement, effective schools research and improved data management capacities – converged to produce a credible rationale and capacity for the use of school report cards as a tool for pursuing public accountability. In addition, as a policy instrument, it had a number of appeals to state policymakers. The approach philosophically reinforced the time-honored notion within the American polity of local control of public education, the neighborhood being the most local of all units. It had the added benefit of also situating responsibility for redressing whatever problems the information might reveal at the local level (a particularly attractive feature for state policymakers). Finally, it is a relatively low-cost strategy, basically relying on the voluntary contribution of parents, motivated by the desire to improve their child's education.

Reform context: Dade County public schools

A series of interviews were conducted with school, district and community-based officials knowledgeable about the role of parents, minorities and school improvement. The intent was to explore the intersection of state-mandated school-based performance reporting policies (school report cards) and their impact on increasing the visibility of minority students.

Dade County public schools in Florida were selected for a number of reasons. One, the state of Florida has mandated school report cards since 1976. Florida has a long tradition of legislative activism. In fact, it has been described as having the most active state legislature in the country in the area of education (Wise 1979). While it has been known most recently for its highly prescriptive reform acts of the early 1980s, it has a much longer history of pursuing accountability through deregulatory approaches, granting considerable fiscal and managerial flexibility to local schools. In the early 1970s, in the heyday of a national accountability movement, the state of Florida passed out a comprehensive and ambitious package of legislation dealing with accountability (Herrington, Johnson and O'Farrell 1992). One of the critical components of this state accountability strategy was the requirement that all schools provide reports to the community. These reports were to include information on student achievement, attitudinal data on teachers, and other school characteristics. In the late 1970s this legislation was amended specifically to require a school report card that provided data by race and ethnicity. Between 1976 and 1991, Florida has required schools to provide information on student attendance, dropouts, corporal punishment, suspensions and expulsions broken down by race and gender. Significantly, Florida does not require student achievement data to be reported by race and gender.

The public school system of Dade County was selected for its recent reform activities and diverse student population. It is the fourth largest school system in the US. It embraces large cities such as Miami, Miami Beach and Hialeah, a number of other smaller municipalities and a large unincorporated area. Like other large urban school districts, it has been struggling with high poverty rates, high numbers of non-English speaking and immigrant children, as well as with issues of school and community violence and high underemployment. The city of Miami has the fourth highest poverty rate in the US. The diversity in population is extreme; the school district reports the existence of 120 distinct cultures and fifty-four languages among its students. It experiences high inter-district and intra-district student mobility. Currently, 1000 students from other countries are entering the school district monthly. If one lists only its major population groups, its enrollment currently consists of 47 percent Hispanics, 34 percent African Americans, 18 percent non-Hispanic whites and 1 percent Asians and Native Americans. It has been particularly affected by the unstable political and economic environment of Caribbean and Central American countries, resulting in unanticipated numbers of immigrants with volatile political alignments and diverse social characteristics. It has also been experiencing extremely high rates of growth with the school population increasing by around 10,000 students a year for the last few years (Council of the Great City Schools 1991, Visiedo 1992).

Dade has responded to the situation with one of the most ambitious reform efforts in the country. For the last six years, it has been developing a school-based management/shared-decision-making approach that has focused on teacher professional development and school-based decision-making. One of the fundamental concepts of the Dade County school-based management initiative is to allow instructional reform responsibility to devolve to the school-level so schools can respond to the unique mix of their own students, staff and neighborhoods. The Dade County experiment has been considered one of the most promising and ambitious restructuring efforts around the country. Though outcome data on the success of these reforms are inconclusive at this point (Collins and Hanson 1991), it is clear that the level of activity and the glare of the national spotlight makes it a particularly interesting site in which to investigate school-based reform strategies and minority concerns.

Interviews with school and community officials

A broad cross-section of school and community officials, knowledgeable about community relations, minority performance and public schooling were interviewed. The respondents were asked the following: What are the arguments for and against reporting school performance data by race and ethnicity? Whose interests are being served by breaking down achievement data by race and ethnicity? Whose interests are being served by not reporting student data in a disaggregated form? What issues are involved in efforts to report student achievement data by race and ethnicity? What are the sources of resistance to such efforts? What are effective ways of making students who fail less invisible and schools more accountable for their failures?

The interviews were conducted in January 1992. A total of twenty-one individuals were interviewed in Dade County. The interviews lasted from between thirty minutes to an hour and a half, and, for the most part, were conducted by telephone. The length varied considerably according to the position of the individual being interviewed and the individuals' own interest or extent of opinions about the issues raised. Three distinct groups of individuals were interviewed. One group of respondents were principals of elementary and high schools. The principals and the schools were chosen to represent a mix of race and ethnicity among the principals and race, ethnicity and socio-economic status among the student population. A second group of respondents were officials at the district level and included senior officials from the following offices: public affairs, parental involvement, Chapter One, school board, student advocacy, a district-wide citizen's advisory committee and information technology. The final group of respondents were community-based and included the Urban League, a community action group established in response to race riots in 1983, a Cuban-American community group which operates two alternative schools in conjunction with the school district, the Chamber of Commerce and the education reporter for the major newspaper for the city. Parents were represented in the latter two groups. Members of all major racial and ethnic groups were included: African Americans, Haitians, Cubans and whites.

The politics of school report cards

Parents and school report cards

The most striking finding from the interviews was that though the state had been requiring the school report cards to be disseminated to parents since 1976, there was agreement among all interviewed that parents did not pay attention to the data on their children's school report cards. There was not one respondent who believed parents, on the whole, paid much attention to the reports. Parents, teachers, administrators and community-based advocacy groups all agreed that parents did not read the reports. Comments about parental attention were strongly stated, unqualified for the most part, and discouraging. Examples are: 'majority of all families totally entrust the process to school professionals'; 'my suspicion is that the reports are not very well read'; 'parents don't ever complain about anything except discipline', and 'nobody ever reads the reports'. The responses of community-based advocacy groups that work with parents to foster greater involvement were no different: 'parents aren't really aware of what's going on' and 'few people really pay attention to these reports'.

The only two reactions that differed slightly were from a school board member: 'very few parents are involved as they should be, but the few who are involved are very involved' and from a community advocacy professional who works to get parents more involved, 'while parents are not very involved, they are more involved than they used to be'.

Table 3.1: Impact of school report cards by role[1]

	Positive	Negative	Mixed	Irrelevant[2]
Principals	1	4	2	3
District Administrators	4	–	–	1
Community Advocates	5	1	–	–

Notes: 1 *It is important to note that no respondents believed the report cards had a significant impact on parents or the community either positively or negatively.*

2 *Respondents that indicated 'irrelevant' based their opinion on one of the following observations: 1) it doesn't matter because no one pays attention to the report cards and 2) Dade County is so racially conscious that everyone is used to having data broken down by race and ethnicity and no one pays attention to it.*

Principals and school report cards

In response to the question, does requiring schools to report performance data by race and ethnicity have a beneficial or detrimental impact on improving the educational system, all principals except one believed the impact was mixed, irrelevant or negative, with negative being the most common response (see Table 3.1).

The majority of principals believed that performance reporting by race and ethnicity was divisive and detrimental to the school community and emphasizing racial and ethnic performance differentials further increased racial tensions at the school. They saw their responsibility as treating each student fairly and equitably regardless of race in order to develop a cohesive, unified school culture.

The following comments from one high school principal were typical of those of principals:

> It was reported that 60 percent of the students we suspended were black, and we were questioned on it, but it doesn't change the way we deal with students. I deal with every case individually, regardless of the student's ethnicity. In my opinion there's no benefit in publishing it, because factors other than race are involved in performance.

Another principal argued that performance should be reported by race and ethnicity at the district level, so that problems can be identified and addressed; however, the same data should not be reported at the school level unless accompanied by substantial education on what the data mean, otherwise, it would stir up the community and create mistrust and resentment. Another principal from a high school with fairly affluent students asserted that all energies should be expended on improving kids' performance and nothing else; reporting by race and ethnicity is often used for political reasons and does not really help children. Another principal asserted that 'good teachers don't let kids fall through cracks, regardless of the kids' color'.

A number of principals said that reporting performance data by race and ethnicity perpetuated racial stereotypes. One principal gave an example of the potentially detrimental impact of reporting school performance data by race and ethnicity. Performance levels had declined as the percentage of minorities in one school had increased, resulting in the more affluent residents moving out of the school's enrollment area, thus further accelerating the decline in the school's performance levels. Another stated that reporting data broken down by race and ethnicity made no difference because, due to highly segregated residential patterns, everyone knew the racial composition of most schools anyway.

District administrators, community groups and school report cards

In contrast, district administrators and community-based individuals were of the opinion that reporting data by race and ethnicity was necessary to assure that minority populations received needed attention. When asked the advantages of reporting data by race and ethnicity, typical responses were: 'It helps us target resources at the students who need them the most' and 'helps us pinpoint where the deficiencies are and allows us to form strategies to address them'. Another one commented that 'schools got away with a lot of things against black children prior to it because schools didn't have to report everything. I have seen a trend of decreasing incidents against blacks'. Still another said,

> Breaking it down by race is good, so we can find out what kind of access all groups have to mainstream services. For example, reporting percentage of students on free lunch isn't putting anyone down, it's showing a need. I don't think objective knowledge hurts anyone. I have no reservations about it. It breaks the cycle of error and lack of opportunity.

While acknowledging that the data might serve to reinforce negative stereotypes, it was argued that objective data reporting was a critical safeguard for minority interests.

The same division between principals and other interviewees was found in respondents' replies to a related question: 'Does reporting student performance by race and ethnicity result in resources being better targeted to where they are needed the most?' While school principals insisted that school improvements occurred individually and internally to the school, those outside the school building responded that it was necessary to collect objective data analyzed by race and ethnicity in order to identify areas of need.

Another interesting finding in addition to the fact that responses broke down by principals versus the other two groups is that the responses did not differ between the other two groups: district administrators and community groups. The opinions of district administrators and community groups (most of whom were minority advocacy groups) on the impact of school report cards and the benefits of breaking data down by race were essentially the same.

School report cards and school improvement

The majority of the respondents, both school-based and other, did not believe that the data themselves were used at school level for planning purposes to effect school improvement (unless forced to by district offices). A common response was 'Only the experts at the district level pay attention to the data. School personnel locally don't pay attention to it and don't use it'. The same respondent also added, 'accountability cannot be done at the district level; local schools must take responsibility'.

A number of reasons were cited. First, in Dade County data are supplied by the school but the compilation and analysis of the data occur at the district office. While this provides better assurance of comparability across schools, a number of respondents noted this procedure had the unintended negative consequence of separating the data analysis from the school-based planning and improvement process. Second, the capacity for effective use of the data may not be sufficient at the school level. A district official charged with civil rights compliance stated: 'I have not seen a change in the data's impact as laws have required that the data be disaggregated more explicitly over the years. For one thing, the reports are too complex, not only for the general public, but sometimes even for school personnel as well'.

District office and school report cards

Almost all respondents, particularly district administrators and outside community groups and also some principals, believed the data were scrutinized carefully at the district level and served as an impetus to targeting new policies and resources to deficiencies that emerged. As one respondent stated, 'The reports probably have their greatest value at the district level, where disparities can be identified and change can be coordinated and implemented'.

The media and school report cards

In stark contrast to the respondents' views about the lack of parental involvement, the role of the media was seen as powerful. Though questions about the media were not on the interview protocol, over half of the respondents on their own brought up the media when queried about community reaction to issues about reporting performance data by race and ethnicity. These respondents stated that it was the media reporting on performance data by race and ethnicity that triggered community interest and response, not the school report cards. The ability of the media to stimulate public interest was considered virtually unlimited yet this power was not always used professionally or helpfully. A number of respondents noted that sensational stories dealing with sexual harassment, drugs and violence dominated media reporting. Also, schools were often pulled into a story when the school was not involved in the incident. The example given was a headline entitled 'North Miami High Student Arrested' even though neither the arrest nor alleged offense occurred on school grounds. Another respondent noted that stories about individuals or 'incidents' commanded media attention but not reports on data. The exception to this was the release of the annual Scholastic Aptitude Test (SAT) data. These were seen as being expertly released to the press, because the press was given a comparative analysis on which to peg the stories. One principal when asked who does benefit from performance reporting by race replied, 'Only those activist groups who are interested in perpetuating the differences so they can get press out of it.'

The respondents were split as to how positive an impact the media reporting had on school improvements. Some believed that media were too sensationalist, particularly the electronic media, exploiting incidents to generate reader/viewer interest; others believed the reporting to be a healthy stimulant to the educational system, making it more responsive. All agreed, however, that issues concerning performance and race were raised by the media (not by the school report card) and were successful in stimulating parent and community interest.

The author interviewed the journalist who covered the education beat for the city's major newspaper. She believed that mentioning race and ethnicity was important and cited cases in which her stories had resulted in reallocation of resources to meet the needs of minority students. Though noting that schools often do not like the publicity attendant to media coverage of racial disparities, she also claimed to have observed that the same schools who complained about performance data being reported in the media by race and ethnicity would take advantage of the resulting publicity to argue for more resources, citing the same data.

Limitations of school report cards

Even those who believed the impact of reporting school performance data by race and ethnicity to be positive, were quick to emphasize that data reporting in itself was of very little value and may even be misleading at times. Two examples were given. In the first, it was noted that parental involvement had different interpretations in different cultures. A district administrator related an issue involving Haitian parents. Repeated efforts by the district to involve Haitian parents in their children's education had not been successful. The reason turned out to be that in Haitian culture, to question a teacher about a child's educational progress was considered a sign of disrespect to the teachers. Another example cited of potentially misleading interpretations of data regarded the publication of corporal punishment data by race and ethnicity. Prior to the abolishment of corporal punishment in the district, data was published indicating that African American children were paddled disproportionately to white children. This created considerable hostile community reaction. Upon closer examination it was revealed that African American parents gave permission for corporal punishment much more frequently than white parents.

Another issue that surfaced was more practical in nature. The explosion of different racial, ethnic and cultural groups meant that much of the reporting by race and ethnicity lacked sensitivity to very substantial differences in subgroups. An official from a Cuban community advocacy group described as follows the racial composition of one school in which he is involved: 60 percent Native Nicaraguans, 17 percent American-born Hispanic, 12 percent Native Cuban, 10 percent Native Honduran and 1 percent white. As he said, 'the data we have even now is not getting analyzed. The registrars say it would be a record-keeping nightmare to have to report by Cuban, Honduran, whether native-born and so forth'.

Impact of school report cards on minority concerns

One may conclude from this research that some of the basic assumptions underlying the use of school report cards as an instrument for accountability for addressing race and ethnicity-based performance gaps may need to be rethought. The reports are presumably designed to serve two interrelated functions: they provide a mechanism for parents to become informed about the performance of the schools where their children attend and, if dissatisfied, apply pressure on school officials and, second, they provide the school-specific data necessary to diagnose the problem.

However, the interviews reported above suggest that the mechanism is ineffective. Parents are not reading the reports and the data are not being used by school officials for school improvement. It is thus unlikely that under current conditions, the report cards themselves are resulting in school improvement, at least not as a result of activity at the school or neighborhood level.

Principals reacted negatively to the very idea of categorizing students by race and ethnicity and linking it to their performance. Principals repeatedly emphasized that they saw their job as exactly the opposite; that is, to ignore students' race and ethnicity and to treat all students equally at all times. They insistently claimed that they spent their energies producing a school climate in which every child is treated as an individual and where expectations remain the same for all students. Their reaction to focusing on data which highlights the differential performance of subgroups within the school population was that such policies undermine their efforts to build a socially cohesive and color-blind environment.

On the other hand, district administrators and community-based advocates, while acknowledging the minimal or even negative impact of reporting data by race and ethnicity at the school-level to parents and the community, insisted that the data had to be reported. There was agreement that the use of disaggregated data by district officials did focus the attention of district officials and the media on disparities among racial and ethnic groups, sometimes resulting in targeting of additional resources.

It is notable that the lack of utilization of the data at the school level appears in a school system undergoing a dramatic experiment in school-based management. Considerable discretion over policy, personnel and budget is being relegated to school-level planning councils in select schools. Presumably utilization of school-level data at the school level would be greater in this district than in others.

School report cards, parents and the visibility of minorities

The discussion above suggests that there is an essential disjuncture between the environment conducive to school-level improvement strategies and numbers-based strategies designed to eliminate race or ethnicity-based institutional biases.[2] These analyses suggest that the historical advancement of the racial equality movement proceeding from an emphasis on equity to one emphasizing excellence may be at odds with itself. The very strategies that protect minorities from being invisible, such as public accounting and reporting, may be antithetical to the characteristics of a healthy school culture and environment which school-based management attempts to foster. The equity agenda requires confronting racial differences and holding up inequities for public inspection and redress. However, the excellence movement is best pursued through the development of trust and community among people involved in a shared enterprise. Unfortunately, the goals of the equity movement have yet to be achieved while there is a layering on of an excellence movement creating new and additional sets of expectations.

Dade County may be a harbinger of future urban communities in the multiplicity of races, ethnicities and languages represented in its population. There is no dominant minority group or even one or two dominant groups, but rather a complex diversity in which race, culture and language group in differing combinations. Stratifying strategies that attempt to define, categorize and respond separately may be insufficient and impractical as the numbers of groups multiply. Furthermore, the knowledge base upon which to base differential instructional approaches to meet the needs of different minority groups is underdeveloped and controversial in application (Weis 1988).[3]

Perhaps what seems to have evolved in Dade County, even if not by design, is a rational response to these conflicting streams of events. The development of a two-tiered strategy may be necessary to capture the benefits of school cohesiveness and community-building at the school level without losing the monitoring and oversight critical to identify and alert educators and others to continuing poor achievement among racial and ethnic subgroups of students.

Conclusion

There was no evidence in these interviews that the reporting of student performance data by race and ethnicity at the school level to parents and the community in and of itself assisted in improving the visibility of minority educational issues or addressing racial inequalities. (That did occur but it was due to the analysis of school-specific data by district administrators and the media, not because of the school report cards being disseminated to parents.) Because the parents did not themselves appear to read, much less use the data, the impact at the school level would be considered minimal. Within the school itself, school officials clearly believed that race-based analyses were divisive to the development of a healthy educational climate within the school and to positive community relations without the school.

What role does this leave for school report cards? The responses of the individuals interviewed seriously question the effectiveness of school report card strategies in terms of stimulating parental interest and pressure on school officials for reform. However, more research is needed to determine why. Is it due to design flaws in the content, organization, display or dissemination of the school data in school report cards? Comparative research varying type, level and socio-economic status of schools and their populations, district and state-level policies and requirements, and types of ethnic groups and neighborhoods is needed to test the preliminary findings in this chapter.

Another related question, however, is how realistic is it to assume that many parents, especially parents whose children are the least successful in school, have either the will, the resources or the understanding of the technology of teaching and learning to play an effective role as an outside monitor of school performance. Demographic and economic profiles of today's families suggest that parents have less time than ever to devote to nonessential activities beyond raising their children and maintaining their jobs. Or, even if through extensive parental education, the level of understanding and involvement of parents could be raised, policymakers would then be faced with an additional determination: at what level might those same resources be more effectively used on other reform strategies.

Notes

1. The author wishes to acknowledge Phillip Zodhiates' valuable assistance in framing the basic issues discussed in this chapter.
2. For discussion of a similar disjuncture between Congressional expectations regarding school improvement and the regulatory armature surrounding the Chapter One federally-funded programs, see Herrington and Orland 1992.
3. The New York State Department of Education, in reaction to public protests, had to withdraw a handbook that suggested that many black pupils do not easily respond to Anglo-American cultural learning styles. It noted, for example, that black children tended:

    to approximate space, number and time instead of aiming for complete accuracy;
    to focus on people and their activities rather than objects;
    to view things in their entirety and not in isolated parts.

    For a discussion of the incident, see Hacker, A. (1989) 'Affirmative Action: The New Look' in *The New York Review of Books*, 12 October, pp. 63–67.

References

BROOKOVER, W., BEADY, C., FLOOD, P., SCHWEITZER, J. and WISENBAKER, J. (1979) *School Social Systems and Student Achievement: Schools Can Make a Difference* (New York: Praeger).

COLLINS, R. A. and HANSON, M. K. (1991) *Summative Evaluation Report: School-Based Management/Shared Decision-Making Project: 1987–88 through 1989–90* (Miami, FL: Dade County Public Schools).

COUNCIL OF THE GREAT CITY SCHOOLS (1991) *The Condition of Education in the Great City Schools* (Washington, DC: Council of the Great City Schools).

EDMONDS, R. (1979) 'Effective schools for the urban poor', *Educational Leadership*, 37(1) pp. 15–24.

EDMONDS, R. (1986) 'Characteristics of effective schools,' in U. NEISSER (ed.) *The School Achievement of Minority Children: New Perspectives* (Hillsdale, NJ: Erlbaum).

EDUCATION COMMISSION OF THE STATES (1992) Personal conversation, November.

EPSTEIN, J. (1987) 'Parent Involvement: What the research says to administrators', *Education and Urban Society*, 19(2) pp. 119–36.

GAINES, G. F. (1991) *Report Cards for Education: Accountability Reporting in SREB States* (Atlanta, GA: Southern Regional Education Board).

GAINES, G. F. and CORNETT, L. M. (1992) *School Accountability Reports: Lessons Learned in SREB States* (Atlanta, GA: Southern Regional Education Board).

GREENE, M. (1993) 'The Passions of Pluralism: Multiculturalism and the Expanding Community', *Educational Researcher* (22)1, pp. 13–18.

HENDERSON, A. (1987) *The Evidence Continues to Grow: Parent Involvement Improves Student Achievement* (Columbia, MD: National Committee for Citizens in Education).

HERRINGTON, C. D., JOHNSON, R. and O'FARRELL, M. (1992) *A Legislative History of Accountability in Florida* (Tallahassee, FL: Learning Systems Institute).

HERRINGTON, C. D. and ORLAND, M. E. (1992) 'Politics and federal aid to urban school systems: The case of Chapter One', in J. CIBULKA, R. REED and K. WONG (eds) *The Politics of Urban Education in the United States* (London: Falmer).

KIRST, M. W. (1990) *Accountability: Implications for State and Local Policymakers* (Washinton, DC: US Department of Education).

LEZOTTE, L. and BANCROFT, B. A. (1985) 'Growing use of the effective schools model of school improvement', *Educational Leadership*, 42 (8) pp. 23–27.

MACKETT, M. and McKEOUGH, M. (1992) 'Accountability for Schools that Work For All Children: The Case of the Illinois School Report Card', a paper presented at the annual conference of the University Council for Educational Administration, Minneapolis, MN.

PURKEY, S. C. and SMITH, M. S. (1983) 'Effective schools: A review', *Elementary School Journal*, 83 (4) pp. 427–52.

RICH, D. R. (1987) *Schools and Families: Issues and Actions* (Washington, DC: National Education Association).

VISIEDO, O. (1992) 'Dade's Public Schools: A Success Story', *Miami Herald*, 5 April.

WEIS, L. (1988) *Class, Race and Gender in American Education* (Albany, NY: SUNY Press).

WISE, A. (1979) *Legislated Learning* (Berkeley, CA: University of California).

Caroline B. Cody, Arthur Woodward and David L. Elliott

Americans always have argued over the content of schooling. In the past, political power enabled majority Americans to win those arguments and to ensure that their values and perspectives dominated in schools and schoolbooks. As Americans have become more diverse and power more dispersed, special interest groups have increasingly challenged the consensus on the content of schooling. Two case-studies illustrate that ethnic groups are involved in ideological bargaining with other groups, and that school boards find themselves increasingly in conflicts that cannot be resolved.

Americans always have argued over the content of schooling

In the United States' system of governance of education, political power has enabled some Americans to decide what is taught in schools; the system, however, promises other Americans that they have the right to petition and complain – and they have. Throughout US history, all Americans – those with power and those who petition – have acted in the belief that what children are taught in school and, more specifically, that what children read in school, is what they will believe and therefore is worth arguing over. Controversies over curriculum and over textbooks, where the curriculum is made visible, have been the focus of many of those arguments. In this chapter, controversies over curriculum in New York and over textbooks in California illustrate that Americans are finding it harder and harder to agree, and that new political pressure on the process is coming from groups in the culture with newfound power and pride.

Historical analysts – revisionists and others – agree that our system of school governance has resulted in schools that reflect the dominant economic and political interests of the times. From the early days of the common school, because colonial communities recognized that schooling would be a powerful force in the socialization of children, early school committees ensured that the content taught in schools functioned to shape and control the minds of students (Finkelstein 1978).

Agreement about what values should be inculcated, however, has never been universal. Controversy over curriculum and complaints about schoolbooks are as characteristic of the system as the attention to American values. Those controversies have become more common and increasingly difficult to resolve as US society has become more diverse (Tyack 1974).

In her book, *America Revised*, Frances FitzGerald (1979) traces changes in history textbooks and describes the interaction between the majority culture and minorities over the content of those books and over curriculum issues. Although concern and complaints about books occurred in the mid-nineteenth century and increased as compulsory education was enforced early in the twentieth, those complaints met with responsive ears only when they originated with citizens perceived to have power and prestige in the community. For instance, suggested changes coming from patriotic concerns and economic interests often met with success (FitzGerald 1979) and, over the

decades, school boards and increasingly legislatures have enacted curricular requirements and specifications for textbooks designed to address the ideological issues of the
times and the fears of powerful Americans (Cody 1990).

The 1960s bring a new voice to curriculum decisions

FitzGerald (1979) found that history textbooks spoke as one voice until about the 1960s.
Then with desegregation and the civil rights movement, pressures on school curricula
began to come from new sources and to meet with success. School boards made up of
the white, male elite who had acted for the community to preserve stability and represent the public interest as they perceived it began to disappear. As boards began to
represent a broader range of community interests, the nature of board decision-making
changed (Lutz 1965). Differences came out into the public arena, and it became increasingly clear that Americans do not agree about a lot of things – including what is
in the public interest and what the content of schooling should be. Since the 1960s,
it has become increasingly evident that all differences cannot be resolved through the
pluralistic bargaining that seemed to work when policymaking boards and legislatures
worked out quiet agreements across the board table, granting small concessions to
minorities to keep the peace. As community stability lost its place as a central value and
as a majority position became increasingly difficult to establish, issues became increasingly
ideological and too basic to work out behind the closed doors of the board room
(Peterson 1976).

Progressives, fundamentalists, mandarins and ethnicity

FitzGerald (1979), from her analysis of history texts, believed that the pressures on
curricula came from three distinct groups: the progressives, the fundamentalists, and the
mandarins, and that the interaction in the public arena of these three ideological groups
explains what has occurred with history books. Since the late 1970s, however, a pressure
that FitzGerald did not recognize has evolved. The fourth ideological pressure is based
on ethnicity. As ideology has bred ideology, the interaction of the four ideologies –
progressive, fundamentalist, mandarin, and ethnic – explains much that has happened
in curriculum in the past decade.

Progressive thought has influenced education since the early days of the twentieth
century with ideas about the application of schooling in society and with a broad concept
of how learning takes place. The influence of this thinking in schools has often been
perceived by the public as threatening to traditional thinking and discipline, but the
influence of progressive thought brought us problem-centered curricula, inquiry approaches to learning, parental involvement, and textbooks mediated to be responsive
to the reading problems and interests of students.

Beginning in the 1960s, not only did African American voices speak from the
power of the school board table, but educators committed to equality and working in
the progressive tradition of Dewey tried from inside schools to change the curriculum
and the books to meet the educational needs of minority children. Research in cognitive
psychology convinced many educators that minority children should have the learning
advantage of reading about children like them. Pictures of and literature by African
Americans began to appear in schoolbooks.

The fundamentalists' ascendancy and influence on curricula and books was fueled by their reaction to these new books and their growing awareness that the content of schooling was open to political influence. Local fundamentalist groups coalesced around controversies over curricula and books – often around issues dear to the hearts of progressive educators – like independent thinking. National fundamentalist groups invested energy and resources in the studies of books and curricula that resulted in waves of complaints about books throughout the country, many of which met with success (Jenkinson 1986). Fundamentalist energies were fueled by their great success in their campaign against 'Man, A Course of Study', and their success resulted in a kind of ideological precensorship on the part of publishers (Cody 1990).

Other Americans who found problems with the process-based curriculum had some success in the 1950s (FitzGerald 1979), but their concern that US schools are short on content and low on standards grew very strong during the Reagan years. Textbooks became a particular interest of this mandarin community – many of whom are people of letters, well-educated in the classical tradition. They were moved to action by studies which said that books were too easy, that content had been replaced by pedagogical fads, and that the writing in books was contributing to students who could not or would not read (Woodward 1987).

The mandarin position was reinforced during the 1980s, when concerns about national economic competitiveness fostered a rash of critical reports on American education. The reports pointed to education and its lack of emphasis on content as central to the problems associated with a competitive work force. The 'excellence' movement and the waves of reform that followed focused on action by states where new interest in 'hard content' was made manifest in increased requirements for high school graduation and the use of testing to hold schools accountable for teaching the required curriculum (Porter, Archbold and Tyree 1991). Reform of textbooks specifically caught the attention of national policymakers such as secretaries of education Terrell Bell and William Bennett and California's chief state school officer Bill Honig. All three developed strategies to address the large issues as well as the specific issues associated with books and their content.

During the Reagan administration, an unspoken alliance between the fundamentalists and the mandarins resulted in support for tougher standards, traditional values, classical literature and history – all antithetical to the interests of a growing minority population in the country. It is not surprising that with progressive forces in the society scrambling to maintain their influence on education in reaction to the forces of the day, a new and fourth ideological pressure evolved. It was based on race and ethnicity.

In 1963, in their classic book, *Beyond the Melting Pot*, Glazer and Moynihan said, 'The ethnic group in American society became not a survival group . . . but a new social form' (p. 17). They went on to say that 'ties of interest' growing out of factors other than ethnicity resulted in ethnic groups that were also special interest groups. Explaining how race can become an ideology and to assert that time would not result in assimilation of such groups, Glazer and Moynihan wrote:

> Color marks off a group, regardless of time, and perhaps more significantly, the 'majority' group, to which assimilation should occur, has taken on the color of an ethnic group, too.

The use of the 'melting pot' metaphor has fostered many misconceptions about how US culture responds to ethnicity and ethnic groups. The concept of cultural pluralism provides a better conceptual framework for viewing US society and the many issues that surround diversity.

Cultural pluralism holds that this nation is a complex interlocking of ethnic and other groups whose members pursue their diverse interests through the medium of private associations, which in turn are coordinated, negotiated, encouraged, and guided by a federal system of representative democracy. (Tesconi 1975)

The ethnic group performs vital functions for individuals in society (Roback 1991). Ethnic groups not only provide social functions for individuals, they stand between the individual and the larger society. Through such groups, individuals have a stake in the larger culture and a mechanism for competing in the arena where differences are resolved (Dahl 1956).

A growing ethnic middle class would seem to be articulating an ideology which challenges the ideas of a common culture and the very nature of 'national identity' (Goodson 1991). Peterson's (1976) model of ideological bargaining anticipates that such groups would be involved in policymaking characterized by the following: 1) groups committed to broad objectives will become involved in a range of policy questions; 2) they will find like allies and enemies across those issues; 3) permanent alliances will form among these groups and political factions; 4) groups will find defeat preferable to compromise (p. 51).

Case-studies involving the adoption of a new curriculum in New York and new textbooks in California illustrate the way in which groups in ascending power in the 1990s, specifically the mandarins and racial and ethnic minorities – are playing out the ideological bargaining process over the content of schooling.

A case from New York

The appointment of Thomas Sobol as Commissioner of Education for New York in 1987 was not without controversy. He came to the job after a number of years as superintendent of the wealthy Westchester County school district of Scarsdale, NY. Doubts were raised about whether Mr. Sobol would be an appropriate and effective chief educational officer for a state whose population was so diverse. Perhaps in response to those concerns, soon after his appointment, Mr. Sobol created a number of committees to investigate minority issues in education. One such committee was 'The Commissioner's Task Force on Minorities: Equity and Excellence'. The report of this committee, titled, 'A Curriculum of Inclusion', was published in July, 1989. The report and its recommendations created an uproar that illustrates the forces at work in the culture.

The Commissioner's Task Force on Minorities consisted of seventeen members – school district heads, professors, representatives of minority groups – and was led by the highly respected president of the New York State Conference of the NAACP. Four consultants assisted the committee as representatives of different minority groups. The task of the committee was to investigate New York curriculum's responsiveness to the needs of the state's minority population.

At the same time, the state education department was concluding its revision of the state social studies curriculum, a tortuous process involving extensive study and consideration of recommendations by leading historians such as Christopher Lasch and social studies educators such as Hazel Hertzberg. The revised curriculum, while quite traditional in its approach and clearly in the progressive tradition, placed a much greater emphasis on global studies and the contributions of minorities than the previous curriculum and generally won high praise for its attempt to recognize and respond to the needs of a multicultural population. As events evolved, however, this new curriculum was held hostage to the controversies that grew out of Sobol's more visible Task Force and the public attention it received from the mandarins and ethnic forces.

'A Curriculum of Inclusion' was authored by Harry Hamilton, a professor of atmospheric science at SUNY Albany. Professor Hamilton was assisted in writing the report by Leonard Jeffries, professor of black studies at City College, New York and one of the consultants to the Task Force. Jeffries also wrote an appendix to the report in which he analyzed the state curriculum from an African American point of view.

The eighty-page report was initially well received by the Board of Regents and met with little interest in the state. However, in the ensuing months, a growing controversy developed and the early endorsement of the report's concepts became an embarrass-ment. The controversy focused on three issues: the polemical tone of the report and its derogatory treatment of whites; its view of multiculturalism and the implication of this view on established scholarship; and how well the recently revised social studies cur-riculum addressed the issues raised in the report.

The Task Force had found little evidence of systematic bias in the state curriculum, with Jeffries himself noting substantial progress in the curriculum in the ways in which it portrayed the multicultural nature of US society. Despite his positive review, the Task Force claimed that the curriculum was Euro-centered and that efforts to integrate multicultural perspectives were 'add-ons'. The report noted,

> The mere inclusion of materials on minority experience, no matter how extensive, cannot counteract deeply rooted racist traditions in American culture. Merely adding marginal examples of other cultures to an assumed dominant culture cannot reverse long established and entrenched policies and practices of that dominant culture . . .

The first sentence of the report's executive summary set the tone of the report and fueled the controversy,

> African Americans, Asian Americans, Puerto Ricans/Latinos, and Native Americans have all been the victims of an intellectual and educational oppression that has characterized the culture and institutions of the United States and the European American world for centuries.

In the appendix to the report, Leonard Jeffries stated that the public school curriculum of New York reflected 'deep-seated pathologies of racial hatred'.

While a number of scholars who would fit FitzGerald's definition of 'mandarin' became involved in attacking the report, two in particular – Diane Ravitch and Arthur Schlesinger, Jr – were particularly vocal. Historian Ravitch, an adjunct professor at Teachers College/Columbia University, took the lead in attacking the report, publishing numerous articles in newspapers and magazines as well as professional publications and scholarly journals. (Ravitch was also a Republican-appointed assistant secretary at the US Department of Education and an author of the California social studies/history curriculum framework.)

In mid-November 1989, in response to the ongoing controversy, Commissioner Sobol convened a meeting of representatives of the Task Force, the Regents, and state department of education staff to hear the comments of four consultants – Ravitch, Asa Hilliard, Virginia Sanchez–Korrol and Edmund Gordon. The meeting was reported as emotional, contentious and difficult. Later two members of the Task Force denounced Ravitch at a meeting of the Black and Hispanic Caucus of the New York State Legislature.

By the new year, Commissioner Sobol sought to distance himself from some parts of the report. *Education Week* (14 February 1990) reported that the Commissioner sent a letter to newspaper editors in which he said,

> The task force's report is purely advisory. I have not recommended, nor will I recommend, that the Board of Regents adopt the task force report. Nor have I recommended the adoption of a new curriculum.

In an interview in the *New York Times* (7 February 1990),

> the Commissioner said that he agreed with 'the central thrust of the report – namely that our curriculum ought to be more inclusionary of all the people who comprise American society today'. He said that he had 'disagreements' with some of the conclusions, although he declined to cite any, saying it would 'not be helpful' to do so.

In a letter to the Regents, Sobol stated that 'unfortunately, the report's language has offended some who, I think, would be inclined to agree with many of its recommendations, taken dispassionately'. He did not ask the Board to adopt the Task Force report, but instead asked them to direct him and his staff to implement a number of the report's recommendations. The Regents did so on 15 February 1990. Specifically, the recommendations included the following: further curriculum revision, implementation of requirements that school districts ensure their local outcomes are consistent with multicultural educational goals, encouragement to publishers to produce instructional materials reflecting a diverse population, and a requirement that teacher education programs in the state prepare potential teachers to work with diverse learners.

Sobol noted that curriculum revision would be done by a new ethnically diverse group made up of teachers and nationally recognized scholars. Since 1992, the committee is still deliberating and the controversy continues to find space in the media.

A case from California

The leadership of the California state superintendent of public instruction, Bill Honig, was very influential in ensuring that history content was the central feature in the 1988 revision of the history/social studies curriculum framework. History scholars in the mandarin tradition – Henry Chambers, Charlotte Crabtree, Matthew Downey, Paul Gagnon, David Kennedy and Diane Ravitch – were involved in the design which departs from the traditional social studies scope and sequence and places great stress not only on history, but on geography, other social sciences, and literature as important contributors to narrative history as a 'story well told'. The framers of the curriculum expected that this departure would be controversial. They were unprepared, however, for the issues raised over the degree to which textbooks designed to meet the requirements of the 'the framework would be found lacking in meeting the state's social content requirements for books concerning the representation of men and women and of a racial, religious' (p. 5).

To a large extent, the framework is the California specification list for textbooks. The departure from the traditional scope and sequence for social studies, therefore, was a challenge to publishers to create new programs just for the California market. This increased the risks associated with the adoption process for both the superintendent and publishers. Since California teachers depend heavily on commercial textbooks to implement the curriculum frameworks, as do most teachers in the United States, it was very important that commercial publishers respond to the new framework, or the schools of the state would be extremely hard pressed to maintain an instructional program in social studies, much less to bring about change or reform.

During the history/social science adoption cycle, after reviewing the very limited submissions, the Instructional Materials Evaluation Panel (IMEP) concluded that, in spite of state legislation which requires at least five adoptions per cycle, only one K–8 series and an additional eighth grade US history text fit the framework criteria adequately. The IMEP acted only after the textbooks had been found acceptable by the statewide legal compliance panels who analyze all submissions for 'social content', that is the proportion of representation given and the lack of stereotyping in treatment of large groups such as Asians and Native Americans, blacks, women, the disabled and the aged.

The IMEP recommendations were accepted by the eighteen-member Curriculum Commission, with three dissenting votes and were adopted unanimously by the State Board of Education, with the proviso that certain errors of fact be corrected before the books were printed and distributed. The action was taken in the face of vociferous opposition from spokespersons representing a number of California's 'minority' groups – African and Asian American, Hispanic, Native American and Jewish.

These opposition groups based their attacks on at least three sets of reasons:

1   The texts were seen as containing errors of fact, omissions and inadequate coverage. For example, the Association of Chinese Teachers in San Francisco complained that one text gives only token attention to Asian Americans and trivialized the brutality and discrimination Chinese workers suffered while building the trans-continental railroad; Jewish leaders requested that 'Hebrew Bible' be substituted for 'Old Testament' and that Judaism not be depicted as a crude antecedent of Christianity. The Japanese Citizens League asked for more detail on the internment of Japanese Americans during World War II. Project 21 demanded 'fair and accurate representation of gays and lesbians', including information on the sexual orientation of famous people in history. Smaller racial and ethnic groups wanted to be represented, such as for example Cambodians and Laotians and specific Native American nations. An African American spokeswoman described distortions, inaccuracies and 'justifications and trivialization of unethical and inhumane social practices, namely racial slavery'.

2   The social studies texts were also accused of containing misinterpretations of facts and obsolete theoretical structure for history. For example, they were criticized for an implicit emphasis on the 'immigration model', 'Euro-centrism' and concentration on 'dead, white European men' or DWEMS. African American spokeswoman Joyce King claimed the notion of the United States of America as a nation of immigrants 'barely fits Native Americans and it doesn't fit blacks at all'. Sylvia Wynter of Stanford University wrote a long critique of one book in which she argued that it tends to equate the prejudice once experienced by white immigrants with the racism suffered by people of color, thereby justifying their exclusion. What is needed, she said, is an entirely new framework that

> seeks to go beyond the model of a nation-state co-terminus only with European immigrant America, to one co-terminus as a 'world' civilization: and therefore, for the first time in recorded history, co-terminus (as a land that's not been yet but must be) with humankind.

3   Some attacks were characterized by proposals to substitute African American versions of history for more established mainstream scholarship. For example, Joyce King argued that

> It's not possible to produce a single perspective on history – that's simply an updating of the melting pot myth about common culture. The idea was to see everyone in a single great narrative, but the narrative itself is faulty. What we have here is a difference in perspective, and you can't get any

more fundamental than that. I'm less concerned about the survival of common culture than about the survival of African-American culture.

The arguments made by the opposition were covered extensively in the press. They were given voice at the state level by individuals such as Joyce King, a member of the Curriculum Commission, and Jackie Berman of the Jewish Community Relations Councils. Local leaders from Sacramento, Los Angeles, Oakland, San Francisco, Berkeley and other communities were also quoted in press accounts. More than seventy group representatives testified at a public hearing held by the State Board of Education on 26 July 1990. At the board's first press conference since 1983, the superior qualities of the adopted texts were extolled, and historian Gary Nash, an author of the adopted series, responded to over 100 pages of criticisms, agreeing to make some changes but rejecting most. Nash said the 'underlying, basic criticism is absolutely wrongheaded – that it [the series] is Eurocentric'.

Commenting on opposition arguments, Bill Honig is quoted in the *New York Times Magazine* (19 September 1991):

They do not like the idea of common democratic principles. It gets in the way of their left point of view that this country is corrupt. This country has been able to celebrate pluralism but keep some sense of the collective that holds us together. Everything is not race, gender or class. The whole world cannot be seen through just those glasses. Democracy has certain core ideas – freedom of speech, law, procedural rights, the way we deal with each other. If everything becomes hostile race and class warfare, we are going to lose this country. The issue is not multiculturalism. We agree with that. The question is, Are you also going to talk about the political and moral values that are essential for us to live together?

Defending California's adoption process, Honig argued that

This is part of a national agenda of reversing the 'dumbing down' of textbooks that occurred in the 1970s and moving forward so that the books are of higher quality, more complete, and more demanding of our students than ever before. The whole country has been talking about reforming the way history and geography is taught, and many of those same ideas are in these books.

Honig went on to predict that the approved textbooks will set a new standard for history and social studies across the country.

Discussion

Educators who are involved with curriculum and textbook adoption need to understand that two things are going on in the controversies over the content of US schooling. First, there are at least four strong pressures jockeying for influence on what children learn: the progressives, the fundamentalists, the mandarins, and ethnic groups. People representing these positions will be heard from in local communities when library books are an issue, in states when the adoption of books is due, and throughout the country when what schools should teach is discussed and debated.

Second, the conflicts that arise are more difficult to resolve because they are based on larger ideological issues (Peterson 1976). Although one could say that the issues in New York and California were the reverse of each other, the outcome could be said to be very much the same. In New York, the mandarins organized an attack on a report dominated by the ethnic point of view; in California, a mandarin-designed curriculum and books were attacked by ethnic groups. In both states, although the policymakers were able to reach consensus, the debate in the larger arena took on a life of its own, and there was no public resolution. There was no attempt by the parties in the conflict to reconcile in the interest of peace in the public eye. The historians continue to raise the issues in New York and, in California, minority spokespeople have continued their protest in the local book adoption process in several communities and eventually prevented the books from being purchased in at least two communities.

The most evident indicator of ideological bargaining – that defeat will be preferable to compromise (Peterson 1976) – is clearly present. Racial and ethnic groups – particularly African Americans – are moving away from negotiation within the system to open conflict in the larger arena where both victories and losses may be symbolic and where, therefore, losing may be more effective in defending the group's interests than quiet compromise. The African American community and the Asian community have become special interest groups with interests far beyond the issues of poverty and discrimination which helped to bind them together. Their growing middle class provides these groups with increasingly articulate voices. They speak from positions of prestige and with the power that comes from their growing voting strength. One could say that racial ethnic groups are defending their group cultures and are determined to ensure that their children will understand what it means to be a part of their group. Assimilation and acceptance into the common US culture are not the issues.

In the two cases reported, the negotiations do not take place on the board tables of the state agencies charged with making decisions about the content of schooling, although the parties to the controversy are represented there. Rather, the negotiations take place in the larger public arena of hearings, open letters, public magazines, and media pronouncements. State procedures for resolving conflict over the content of schooling in both California and New York were used in 1988; the state policymaking board supported their chiefs and committees which included representatives of minority communities studied the curriculum and served on the Task Force established specifically to evaluate its responsiveness to multicultural education. In California, the complex system of framework development, legal compliance review, Instructional Materials Evaluation, and the deliberations of the state board itself worked as it was designed to work, but the results did not satisfy those who petitioned, even after their specific complaints resulted in some response.

The systems did not produce resolution because the losers in the conflict – the mandarins in New York and the ethnic groups in California – are willing to live with the enemies made in the controversy. There was no attempt, in either case, to patch up the differences in expectation that today's enemies will be tomorrow's friends.

The winners were not particularly magnanimous either. As the conflicts progressed, both Sobol and Honig took the hard line – Sobol attacking the historian spokeswoman, Honig attacking the ethnic minority complainants. In both cases, it was clear that, as victors, both chiefs wanted to consolidate their positions and perceived it to be in their political interest not to seek peace with their adversaries, but to maintain the alliances already established and to justify the principles upon which those alliances were built.

The fundamentalists attacked progressive education; the mandarins also attacked and set out to reform an educational system by reclaiming the schools from progressive pedagogy in order to establish higher standards and reestablish in schools a responsibility for instilling common values and the traditions of our national identity. A fourth ideology, however, is growing in ethnic communities. The principles of cultural pluralism predict that policymakers will increasingly be in the position of referee between and among such ideologies. We can expect more differences and those differences will be settled though conflict and winning and losing; this will be the tradition Americans share.

References

Cody, C. B. (1990) 'The politics of textbook publishing, adoption, and use', in D. L. Elliott and A. Woodward (eds) *Textbooks and Schooling in the United States* (Chicago: National Society for the Study of Education).

Dahl, R. (1956) *A Preface to Democratic Theory* (Chicago: University of Chicago Press).

Finkelstein, B. (1978) 'Pedagogy as intrusion: Teaching values in in popular primary schools in nineteenth century America', in D. Warren, *History, Education, and Public Policy* (Berkeley CA: McCutcheon).

FitzGerald, F. (1979) *America Revised* (New York: Vintage Books).

Glazer, N. and Monihan, D. P. (1963) *Beyond the Melting Pot* (Cambridge MA: MIT Press).

Goodson, R. F. (1991) 'Nations at risk' and 'national curriculum': Ideology and identity', in S. H. Fuhrman and B. Malen, *The Politics of Curriculum and Testing* (London: Falmer).

Jenkinson, E. B. (1986) *The Schoolbook Protest Movement: Questions and Answers* (Bloomington IN: Phi Delta Kappa).

Lutz, F. W. (1965) 'Methods and conceptualizations of political power in education', In J. D. Scribner (ed.) *The Politics of Education* (Chicago: National Association for the Study of Education).

Peterson, P. E. (1976) *School Politics Chicago Style* (Chicago: University of Chicago Press).

Porter, A. C., Archbold, D. A. and Tyree, A. K. (1991) 'Reforming the curriculum: Will empowerment policies replace control?' in S. H. Fuhrman and B. Malen (eds) *The Politics of Curriculum and Testing* (London: Falmer).

Roback, J. (1991) 'Plural but equal: Group identity and voluntary integration', in E. F. Paul, F. D. Miller and J. Paul (eds) *Reassessing Civil Rights* (Cambridge, MA: Blackwell).

Tesconi, C. A. (1975) *Schooling the America: A Social Philosophical Perspective* (Boston: Houghton Mifflin).

Tyack, D. (1974) The One Best System (Cambridge, MA: Harvard University Press).

Woodward, A. (1987) 'Textbooks: Less than meets the eye', *Journal of Curriculum Studies*, 19 (6), pp. 511–26.

5

The micro-politics of student voices: Moving from diversity of bodies to diversity of voices in schools

Gary L. Anderson and Kathryn Herr

Traditional approaches to the politics of schooling have failed to examine students' struggles to construct an identity within the cultural politics of school life. This study describes how institutional silencing works to drive student voice inward, thus making their daily struggles invisible. Data from a study based on student oral histories are analyzed to illustrate the micro-politics of student voice. Mikhail Bakhtin's work on legitimated and non-legitimated voice is used to provide a conceptual framework for the data. The dysfunctionality of social myths like color-blindness, meritocracy, and equal opportunity, are discussed and recommendations for a deeper and more political conceptualization of multicultural education are provided.

The 1980s have left in their wake a neoconservative backlash against affirmative action, the cynical characterization of concern for poor and disenfranchised groups as 'political correctness', and a resegregation of the United States of America's schools. In spite of all of this, 'diversity' is still in vogue in most social institutions, and educational institutions generally support the notion of diversity and multiculturalism. As Sleeter (1991) points out, however, there is a generalized misunderstanding of what diversity and multiculturalism mean. Sleeter argues that too often it means curricular add-ons, or merely having a culturally diverse student body. Baptiste (1986) claims that multiculturalism must move beyond the mere addition of courses or formalization of certain experiences to 'a highly sophisticated *internalization* of the process of multiculturalism combined with a philosophical orientation that permeates all components of the educational entity' (p. 308).

This chapter will argue that, regardless of how well-meaning, educational institutions cannot move from 'soft' definitions of multiculturalism to more sophisticated ones without an understanding of the role the educational institution plays in the identity struggles of its students. The interface of dominant institutional norms and the struggle of students to form an identity constitute a micro-political stuggle which takes place under the noses, but outside the consciousness, of most educational institutions. In addition, the chapter argues that when various voices within the students are not legitimated by the larger institution, even the students themselves lose access to those parts of themselves that might challenge institutional assumptions and explanations, thereby effectively 'silencing' themselves. The oral history process utilized in the research works to legitimate voices that might otherwise fall silent.

The micro-political perspective

Traditionally the study of the politics of education has been about conflict over vested interests, ideological commitments, and material resources. Studies of these conflicts have tended to focus on state and federal legislatures, school boards, special interest groups, administrators and teachers. Although student achievement and well-being have always been the central concern – at least rhetorically – of educational politics, students themselves have generally been ignored as political actors.

More recently attention in education has turned to 'micro-politics' or the study of less visible, behind the scenes, negotiations of power, what Hoyle (1982) calls 'the dark side of organizational life' (p. 87). This work has provided the study of educational politics with accounts of the politics that occur within the organizational underworld of schools and school districts (Ball 1987, Blase 1991). In the hands of management-oriented researchers, however, studies of micro-politics are often little more than a listing of the strategies that various organizational stakeholders engage in to get what they want. In these studies, too, students tend to be absent.[1]

Because of its roots in functionalism and scientific management, the field of educational administration has tended to neglect the subjective reality of the clients of educational institutions and the 'core technology' of teaching and learning. The management perspective has tended to objectify students and to view educational institutions from a top-down perspective rather than from a bottom-up one. This top-down perspective often leads to well-intended, but unsuccessful, policies that lack a phenomenological understanding of the micro-politics of students' lives in schools. Accounts of schooling grounded in students' perspectives are needed so that teachers, administrators, and policy-makers can better understand the ways schools and classrooms funnel student diversity and idiosyncrasy into a narrow range of school-approved behavior (Herr 1993).

In this chapter, we are asking readers to broaden their notions of what constitutes 'politics'. We would argue that nothing is more political than the inner struggles of students to construct an identity in institutions that have the power to legitimate, de-legitimate, or simply ignore their voices. Much as feminists in the 1970s redefined the realm of the political to include the personal, so in education, we must begin to view students as political actors with grievances that are daily ignored in subtle ways.

This chapter, then, will describe a more empowering approach to micro-politics, and discuss how students do their identity-work in the context of the school's micro-politics. Data from a study based on student oral histories will be provided to illustrate the particular angle of vision through which students view the structure of opportunities and constraints of school life. We also will illustrate ways that those who work in educational institutions can tap into the subjective world of students and learn to be more responsive to their individual and social conflicts.

Invisible Students

Students are everywhere in schools, and yet they are too often invisible to the adults who work there. Their invisibility is not unlike that of Ralph Ellison's African American protagonist who laments, 'When they [whites] approach me they see only my surroundings, themselves, or figments of their imagination' (Ellison 1947: 3). The theme of student invisibility has become a popular metaphor in educational writing as more researchers are viewing schools as consisting of multiple realities in which some realities are 'defined out' of the dominant social construction (Anderson 1990, Philips 1982, Rist 1978, Stanlaw and Peshkin 1988). As we will illustrate later in this chapter, student 'acting out' is often an attempt on their part to force their visibility onto the consciousness of the institution that fails to 'see' them.

Fine (1991) uses a different metaphor to capture this phenomenon. She argues that schools actually engage in an active process of silencing students. She has documented the many ways that school policies and practices silence student voices so as to smooth over social and economic contradictions. She found time and again in the high school she studied a structural fear of *naming*.

> Naming involves those practices that facilitate critical conversation about social and economic arrangements, particularly about inequitable distributions of power and resources by which these [poor and minority] students and their kin suffer disproportionately. The practices of administration, the relationships between school and community, and the forms of pedagogy and curriculum applied were all scarred by the fear of naming, provoking the move to silence. (Fine 1991: 34)

There is, however, an even more insidious form of silencing that occurs *within* institutional clients themselves, and which ethnographic studies seldom probe. This form of inner silencing occurs in educational institutions as students censure their own inner dialogue which, in the case of adolescents and children, forms part of what Wexler (1988) calls their 'identity-work'.

Drawing on the work of Soviet literary critic Mikhail Bakhtin, Quantz and O'Connor (1988), suggest how inner voices are silenced before they even become vocalized in the public domain.

> In trying to understand human behavior, we must be cognizant that some voices are legitimated by the community and, therefore, vocalized, while others are nonlegitimated and, therefore, unspoken . . . Thus, as the multiple voices within the individual and within the community struggle to control the direction of the acceptable dialogue, ideological expressions may be reinforced, reinterpreted, or rejected . . . By recognizing and recording the multiple voices occurring within communities, we should be able to analyze the specific factors which affect the formation in historical situations of legitimated collusions and subsequent social actions. (pp. 98–99)

Aside from its micro-political implications, what makes the concepts of multivoicedness and legitimated and non-legitimated voice so powerful is Bakhtin's view that inward speech that becomes outwardly vocalized is probably that which is most compatible with the socially organized ideology. Thus, as students silence those inner voices that are not legitimated by the educational institution, conformity to the school's 'socially organized ideology' is achieved. Because of this dynamic of inner speech, then, student silencing need not be an overt form of oppression, but rather can be the result of institutional deafness, or the failure to elicit non-legitimated voice.

Just as students learn what behavior is institutionally sanctioned, they also learn to recognize institutionally sanctioned discourse. As Fine so well illustrates, issues of difference and inequality, be they based on class, race, gender or sexual orientation generally do not constitute legitimate discourse, except when they are dealt with abstractly, that is, not related to the students' own lives in their own schools and classrooms. Because one's class, race, gender and sexuality are key elements in how one constructs an identity, particularly in adolescence, non-legitimated voice must be driven inward and manifests itself as inward speech, and as we will see, 'acting out' behavior.

Ethnographic research methods have lately been the object of criticism by those who accuse educational ethnographers of 'voyeurism', in that they retain an objective, detached approach to their respondents' lives (Wexler 1987). Goodson (1980–81), Mischler (1986) and others claim that qualitative research methods as currently utilized neglect personal biography and historical background. Although there are strong oral history traditions in anthropology, history, sociology and clinical psychology, oral history methods have, until recently, been largely ignored by educational ethnographers. As students of the politics of education come to appreciate the importance of eliciting the multiple voices of micro-political actors, oral history methods will provide the phenomenological depth and complexity required of micro-political studies.

For the reasons stated above, oral history data were selected to illustrate the micro-politics of student voice. These data are part of a larger cross-national study of students' 'voices'. Oral history interviews were gathered from middle and high school students in Mexico and the Southwestern United States. In each country, three schools, stratified by social class, were chosen for student interviews. The following cases were chosen because they illustrate not only the micro-politics of voice, but also how this struggle for voice interfaces with well-meaning, but inadequate institutional attempts to cope with the micro-politics of student diversity.

Victor and Janice's inner dialogues

Interviews of two students will be used to illustrate the concept of 'identity-work' and the multiple voices struggling within the students for legitimation. Both are students at Markham Prep, a pseudonym for an elite private school in the Southwest, offering grades 6 through 12. Janice, a senior, the daughter of a white mother and African American father, and Victor, a Hispanic eighth grader, are two of a very few students of color in the predominantly Anglo student body. Both entered the school in the sixth grade.

Janice and Victor are struggling to understand who they are, as students of color in an Anglo school environment and as people of color in their own extended families. What seems evident in both interviews is that the strategies they adopt to survive in the school remove them further from their ethnic identities and impact negatively on their status as students.

The micro-politics of invisibility: Lost voices and lost identities

According to Bakhtin, one's identity is a product of an ongoing dialogical process with one's social environment. It is thus a socially constructed entity, a phenomenon which exists on the boundary between the individual and the social. Identity work is a constant struggle among multiple and competing voices seeking legitimation from the social world. Voices that are not legitimated by one's social context are silenced by either being forced underground or muted entirely. Thus silencing can be both an individual decision ('This is too painful, I'll set it aside until I'm ready to deal with it') and a socially imposed condition (the absence of social input that would affirm various aspects of the individual). In either case it results in the loss of voices and the silencing of whole dimensions of one's identity.

Much of Victor and Janice's identity-work involves them in an inner dialogue around how their race and ethnicity makes their experience at Markham different from that of other students. The following excerpt is from a flowing monologue Victor delivered in response to the question 'What's it like to be a student of color at Markham Prep?'

I don't label myself as the typical Hispanic person; I kind of label myself as the typical Anglo-Hispanic person. In other words, I have the education and the same opportunity right now as the Anglo person so I'm equal, I'm equal with them. I'm looking ahead, eye to eye; I'm looking eye to eye at them, and I'm stable. We're on a balance beam and it's balanced. And, I kind of look at myself as kind of an Anglo person in some ways. The way I speak sometimes, I really don't – Hispanic people really have a strong accent and black people have some strong accents, you know, and Vietnamese and Asian people and all that – you know, I really don't – if you look at it. I am Hispanic, you know, my blood, my color, my background but right now I'm turing into an Anglo. And hypothetically speaking again I've turned into an Anglo – the customs, the ways, but then again also, I do have my Hispanic background, my Christmas, my traditions, you know, the funerals, all that – I really have all that with me but right now I'm kind of seen as a stabilized person who has the best of a Hispanic world, who has the best of an Anglo world, who has the best of a poverty world, who has the best of a rich world. The best of the whole world, you know.

The balance beam is Victor's metaphor for his attempt to balance his own ethnicity and social class with that of his classmates at Markham Prep. Although the almost excessive bravado in his narrative betrays some insecurity about his future, he has an eighth grade optimism in being able to thrive in both worlds. Janice, a more seasoned African American senior, seems to feel that she belongs in neither world.

I think what I gave up – I came here at a young age and I think that was difficult because you want to fit in, you want to be what everybody else is . . . so, I think what I gave up was part of myself. I chose to, I guess, undermine what I was and undermine what I could do because I thought it would make me fit in or I thought that people would like me better for what I, for what I was.

All the influence I had, all the people I was around were white and I had a lot of white people resent me for that because I'm not white . . . it created a lot of problems, like with my relatives [black], because they go out and do things and I would try to imitate them but because I wasn't young or because it wasn't something that I was used to, it was very awkward for me. And then they would think I was making fun of them. So, I cannot act what is, quote 'black', you know? So, it's alienated me from a lot of people because they say, well, you're trying to be white; why can't you be more like us? And I don't know how to do that.

I think what hurts a lot for me is that what I grew up around most has no willingness to accept me. So the environment [white] that I have been around all my life is not supportive. And the other environment [black] is one that does not understand me and that does not choose to understand me. So I kind of don't, I still don't know where I am, because it's really hard for me to accept the fact that everything I grew up around is something that I can't be a part of. But I can't go back and try to be part of something that I don't know very much about on a cultural level.

Janice and Victor are engaged in a struggle for a sense of selfhood and they both are aware of and are articulate about this struggle. The politics of identity for Janice are more complex in some ways. She sees no way out of her dilemma. She cannot speak the legitimated voices of the African American world, and her culturally white voice is subtly rejected by the white world because of her race. Janice feels that she has become 'two separate people' and has shut down her identity work until she can figure a way out of this dilemma. She wistfully reflects, 'I just wish I could come out of all this knowing what and who I am'. After graduation, she has chosen to attend a small, elite, largely white, eastern college. Although this environment will be similar to Markham, one wonders if a black college or a more racially mixed university setting would be any less alienating for her.

Victor on the other hand, still sees his voices as legitimated by both worlds. Unlike Janice, who cannot seem to gain self-actualization in either world, Victor feels he can achieve an identity in both. The tensions, however, spill over into both of the students' academic lives and have had a negative impact on their academic achievement.

When Janice took the math entrance exam at Markham, she scored in the 95th percentile in math; now as she prepares to graduate, she contrasts her past student identity with the way she feels now: 'I had a lot of confidence in math before I came here and I leave this school not being necessarily illiterate but feeling illiterate.' She makes sense of this by underscoring that she is a female and a minority; 'I'm the cliche; I'm not supposed to be smart. You know, just look at me, I have every sort of thing that everyone puts down.' She goes on to stress that students read undercurrents, respond to putdowns even if they are subtle. As for her strategy in dealing with the low expectations people have of her, she says, 'I think I tended to become quiet in class . . . I chose not to fight.' She blames herself for not being 'strong enough in the first place to handle coming to this school' and says 'what I am here, I don't like.' She speculates that 'maybe people who are stronger can do better' than she has.

Although Victor insists that he is stable in his juggling of these multiple worlds he inhabits, another incident that he describes illustrates how unresolved the dilemma is. The situation arose in an Advanced Spanish class made up of native Spanish speaking students, like Victor, and Anglo students. At the time of the interview, Victor was failing the class. In describing his troubles in Spanish class, Victor made clear that one dilemma it brought to the forefront was his struggle over 'am I Anglo or am I Hispanic?'

> But being put in a position where – I have a friend named Eduardo Francisco Fernandez Gomez – you met him – from La Estrella – and he's Hispanic and I can relate to everything he's thinking and all that – and yet being put in a position also where I got to either decide where I'm going to sit during class; am I going to sit with my friends Jenny Barnard and Tara Reynolds or am I going to sit with Eduardo, you know. It's kind of frustrating, you know.
>
> But I just didn't like being put in that situation and having to cope with and deal with either distinguishing who I really was – cause that was really hard because I wanted to be proud of my heritage and Hispanic, and then I turn around and kick myself in the butt. I fell on my face because I wanted to be Hispanic and do the things that Hispanic people do and yet then again, I usually – what I do is I switch. I go to school, I'm school. Then I switch, I go home, with the neighborhood kids and I, then I switched to Hispanic . . . and then I'll turn around to being an Anglo and being that kind of person. It's like Dr. Jekyll and Mr. Hyde. I kind of didn't like being put in that situation because who was I, Dr. Jekyll or Mr. Hyde, you know. And I had to be Victor, and that's kind of hard for me to do, being Victor, just being the person I was . . . I just didn't like being put in that position.

The first description of himself as stable is Victor's official version of his life. It was unsolicited. It is the version legitimated by his school and by his immediate family. There is tremendous pressure to juggle multiple identities successfully, but there is no recognition by the school of its difficulty, and there is nowhere within Markham Prep a site where this identity work can be done in an open, legitimated manner. Janice's becoming 'quiet', choosing 'not to fight' and Victor's symbolic sabotaging of his Spanish class through his 'acting out' behavior, are perhaps their ways of portraying a dilemma that they cannot resolve themselves. Unfortunately, it does not seem to occur to the school to solicit these aspects of the students' school experiences, or acknowledge the cultural dilemmas in any way – both because of cultural insensitivity and because to legitimate their suffering would be to delegitimate the school as an institution that works at being 'culturally diverse'.

The micro-politics of silence: Institutional deafness

Both Janice and Victor acknowledged that they had been given a tremendous opportunity in coming to Markham; both felt that education was the path to future success and were interested in making something of the chances they had been given. Their daily reality, however, offset these feelings of opportunity and brought them face to face with the truth that, as Janice put it, 'This has not been a fostering environment. It hasn't been a supportive environment. And it hasn't been a comfortable environment.' Factors combined to make both Janice and Victor feel invisible and unappreciated in the school environment.

> . . . you have to give black students, you know, you have to make this school, in other words, make it seem like it's a part of them or they're a part of it . . . It's very easy for white children to feel that, because they have a lot of background and a lot of white areas. But, if you bring black children into something but you don't expose them

to what they are or you don't let them see what has happened with their history or with their culture, then in a way you're saying that their culture isn't important and in a way you're saying they're not as important because you don't stress what they are.

Bringing students in is not enough. You have to, you know, you have to accommodate them and you have to give them something to be able, to make them understand that they do belong. That they have done something good, that they have had some sort of influence; they have had something to do with anything. But you don't see anything of that, so everything that you see – all the accomplishments you see, all of the wonderful discoveries, everything that you see – has been done by somebody who was white. So what does that make you if you are black?

Not seeing yourself reflected in the curriculum or in the culture of the organization is only part of the problem. The 'acting out' behaviors of minority students are often misdiagnosed by an institution that does not make the unique issue of their identity-work part of its body of professional knowledge. For example, during the third quarter of the school year, Victor and his family were notified that he might not be offered a re-enrollment contract for the next school year because of the failing grade in Spanish; his particular grade was a 33 percent, with a low effort grade as well. Victor was told, by the eighth grade dean, that unless he brought up his grade in Spanish, particularly his effort grade, he would not be allowed to return to Markham. The dean made clear that he was particularly disappointed in Victor's 'lack of effort'. Input from the Spanish teacher (a female Hispanic) characterized Victor as a constant troublemaker, a clown who seemed uninterested in working. She would routinely resort to kicking him out of class and he would spend the remaining part of the period alone in the student commons, isolated from the classroom and class activities.

The task of reconciling his conflicting worlds, that of being Hispanic while functioning in an Anglo-dominated society, is left solely to Victor. The assumption is that it is Victor who has to change. In the case of the Spanish class, the dean would like to see 'better effort'; the teacher wants him to behave. The possible repercussions fall solely on Victor; he may not be invited to re-enroll if he does not bring up his Spanish grade. Discussions of a student is doing better work, the consequences of a failing grade or behaving poorly in a class, are all part of an institutionally sanctioned discourse; implications that the problem could lie other than within the student are not raised – even by Victor, until later solicited by the interviewer.

Victor accepts this analysis of his 'failure' and that he has 'goofed off'. Owning the responsibility for the flunking grade also implies that he alone is the one to rectify it.

All the high people [the administrators] – they've given me a million chances. I've looked at it now; this is my last chance. This is my last chance to make something out of my life, you know. I've been given chances since the day I was born. There comes a point, a time in your life where you get you last chance and that's it. That's the last chance you're going to get. That's it.

This classic 'privatizing and psychologizing of public and private issues' (Fine 1989) reinforces the institutionally sanctioned discourse and prevents other vantage points from being introduced for analysis. The institution remains safe from a call to change but is also buffered from the opportunity of becoming truly culturally diverse. Until students like Victor feel that an institution is open to a multiplicity of voices, their speech will continue to reflect the legitimated organizational reality.

Carlos: Soliciting non-legitimated voices and helping institutions hear

The documentation of the variety of inner voices of students like Janice and Victor could be a powerful first step in encouraging institutional change, should a school like

Markham Prep genuinely engage in the process of diversifying culturally. If students are more likely to vocalize the versions of their thoughts that are legitimated by society, however, adults in the institution will need to provide a variety of views of 'reality' that encourage students not only to take responsibility for their own struggles but also to translate their private trouble into social concerns. Typically in schools, students who are failing academically or who are a behavioral problem in the classroom, are referred to administrators, counselors or school social workers for intervention. The goal usually is one of 'fixing' the student, i.e. helping him or her raise the failing grade or learn to 'behave' in the classroom. While both are worthwhile goals in the school scheme of things, the behavioral messages of students, failing grades and 'acting out' behavior, can also be seen as opportunities for the institution to begin to hear the inner dialogues of students.

The following vignette illustrates the broadening of a behavioral message on the part of Carlos, another Hispanic student at Markham, translating it to the articulation of a social concern as experienced by that student. A teacher in the school reported Carlos, a seventh grader, to the dean, having witnessed an episode where Carlos hit another student with a baseball bat at recess. Since Carlos was already on probation because of prior 'acting out' behavior, he was at risk of not being allowed to remain in the school.

In an interview with the dean and another teacher, Carlos tearfully admitted that he had indeed hit the other student; he characterized it as an incident where a playful disagreement about whether or not someone was safe on first base had escalated into a full-fledged fight. The dean told Carlos that she could not allow someone to remain in the school community who was at risk of endangering other students and underscored to him that, since he was already on probation, the repercussions for him could be quite serious.

At that point, the dean was called out of the conference for a telephone call. In the intervening moments, the teacher, still puzzled by Carlos' outburst on the playing field, asked him once again just what had happened. Carlos replied that 'no one knew what it was like for him here' and related to the teacher the name-calling he endured on the playground as a Hispanic student in the school (for example, 'stupid spic'). He said that he tried to hold his anger in as much as he could, but sometimes he just erupted. He went on to disclose that a small group of Anglo male students constantly harassed him for being Hispanic. When asked why he had not told any adults in the school community about these incidents, he asked, 'What's the point?'

When the dean returned, the teacher asked Carlos to share with her this further aspect of the 'acting out' behavior on his part; in rather muffled tones, he hesitantly did just that. The dean acknowledged that the behavior of his peers was not right either, but that that did not give Carlos license to hit others. She reiterated that he was in major trouble and needed to learn to curb his acting out impulses. The teacher, at this point, echoed that she agreed that Carlos could not hit others but also amplified the message that he had been routinely racially harassed, creating a very frustrating situation for him in the school. The teacher suggested to the dean that the incidents Carlos related also needed to be investigated and, if verified, appropriate disciplinary measures needed to be taken against the cadre of Anglo students involved. The teacher amplified to Carlos that he had the right to a school environment where he 1) didn't experience racial harassment and 2) saw adults in the community as his advocates, should incidents occur.

Several things worked in this episode to translate it solely from Carlos' private problem to one with larger institutional implications. The teacher was willing to ask Carlos, again, to tell his story, to try to tap into some of his private experiences at

Markham. Carlos was willing to risk disclosing a version of his reality that was not one legitimated by the school. The teacher was willing to amplify and align herself with him; she legitimated Carlos' experience of school reality and helped him articulate it to someone in a position of authority. The teacher prodded the dean to action on Carlos' behalf and interpreted to her an alternate reality concerning Carlos' acting out behavior. She also reiterated to Carlos his rights as a full fledged member of the school community – that he was entitled to an environment free from harassment and that adults would be his advocates, should that occur – a promise of further legitimation should other incidents happen.

As Fine (1989) documents, the most effective means of silencing is to banish voices of dissent, routinely done through mechanisms of discipline. The baseball bat incident was at risk of following that very avenue; Carlos was on the verge of being expelled, without the school being given the benefit of the articulation of his private experiences there. In this case, the voice of dissent was invited to emerge and a more accurate story was conveyed, one with implications both for Carlos and the school; the issue moved from a purely private concern to a social and institutional issue.

The dysfunctionality of social myths: Color-blindness, meritocracy and equal opportunity

The ideals of color-blindness, meritocracy and equal opportunity presuppose a world in which race, gender, poverty and sexual orientation are not factors in one's life chances. They are in fact myths which describe an ideal world that does not currently exist. These myths are dysfunctional in that they blind members of dominant groups from understanding the very real dilemmas of minority groups.

Students like Janice, Victor and Carlos are daily confronted with the task of internally bridging the gap between their own cultural experiences and knowledge and that of the dominant culture of the school. As Victor put it, these students are constantly learning 'that works in our world but not in the world we're in right now.' Currently the burden is on individual students to learn the kind of constant translating of cultural rules that means survival for them. Many teachers, priding themselves on being 'color-blind' and therefore treating their students the same, may not realize the disservice involved in discounting the expertise required of students of color to accurately read cultural rules not their own. There is no equivalent burden on teachers and administrators to become equally expert in the students' cultural context. When teachers view students coming through the classroom door as equally invited to participate, without taking into account that some of these students have entered a foreign environment, their attempts at equal opportunity for all fall short of the goal. When students then do not perform as well as they could, the setting is ripe for head shaking by those saddened that students have not taken advantage of their educational opportunities.

In a stratified society, educational institutions, whether serving the oppressed or the elite, cannot maintain the legitimacy of official ideologies like color-blindness, equal opportunity and meritocracy and, at the same time, acknowledge their students' voices of institutional and social critique. Markham Prep needs Victor, Janice and Carlos at least as much as they need Markham Prep. They get upward social mobility at the price of their cultural identity; the institution gets students of color and a façade of social class and cultural diversity which legitimates it in the eyes of the larger community. In this way the *status quo* of structural inequality and the myths that help sustain it are maintained.

This trade-off of identity for institutional legitimacy benefits neither the student nor the institution in the long term. It dissolves the tensions that are a natural part of any society in which classism, racism, sexism and homophobia form part of the social fabric. Without embracing this social tension as a force for institutional learning and change, schools like Markham Prep force minority students into calling attention to themselves through violence (Carlos), acting out (Victor) and silence (Janice).

Student empowerment through the legitimation of inner voices of student critique will not alter the role of elite private educational institutions like Markham Prep in social stratification, but it may reduce the alienation of students like Victor, Janice and Carlos and ensure that those inner voices of social critique are nurtured and retained as part of their adult identities. This may help students of color better understand the legitimating function that minority students who 'make it' play, and render it less likely that Janice, Victor and Carlos as adults will view their 'success' as individual 'bootstrapping' accomplishments that any minority could and should achieve. For a few chosen minorities like Janice, Victor and Carlos, education is – at the cost of selfhood – the road to economic well-being. For the vast majority of their fellow minorities, it has led to very different outcomes.

Conclusion

In this chapter, we have attempted to suggest how the elicitation and analysis of student voices might help us understand how students construct their identities in the context provided by educational institutions. We further suggest ways that this attention to student voices might help educational institutions and educational reform movements better respond to students' needs. One of the reasons for choosing the Markham Prep data was to illustrate the fact that extra resources do not automatically guarantee a better environment for minority students. Markham Prep has all the resources on every educator's wish list – low student-teacher ratios, bright students, a large counseling staff, a huge professional development budget, etc. It also espouses an interest in promoting diversity, and because of a large endowment, has in fact been able to offer scholarships to low SES minority students. However, while a place is reserved for the minority bodies, there has yet to be a place for their voices. What this suggests is that the creation of an environment in which student voices are welcome involves more than professional development in multiculturalism or increased opportunities for student–teacher interaction. Markham Prep has those things and yet appears unable to elicit and then hear the voices of its minority students.[2]

If Markham Prep has not yet managed this with its resource base, it is even harder for the average public middle or high school to do so. As Baptiste (1986) reminds us, unless multiculturalism is internalized and forms a part of how things are done and thought about in a given school, student problems associated with cultural identity issues will be viewed as just that – the student's problem.

Notes

1. See Bloome and Willett (1991) and Opotow (1991) for a discussion of the micro-politics of students. We have chosen to use the term student 'micro-politics' here rather than student 'cultural politics' (Giroux 1991) because of our emphasis on the interface of student and institution.

2. See Stanlaw and Peshkin (1988) for a discussion of what constitutes an optimum critical mass of minority students in a school or community. At Markham Prep, Janice encountered too few other black students, and although there was a critical mass of Hispanic students, Victor and Carlos, being on scholarships, were distinguished from other Hispanics by their social class. For Victor and Carlos, their social class was, of course, an additional factor in their struggle at Markham, but it is interesting to note that Janice, although an upper-middle class student, shared their alienation with regard to racial and ethnic issues.

References

ANDERSON, G. L. (1990) 'Toward a critical constructivist approach to school administration: Invisibility, legitimation, and the study of non-events', *Educational Administration Quarterly*, 26, pp. 38–59.

BALL, S. (1987) *The Micro-politics of the School: Towards a Theory of School Organization*. New York: Methuen.

BAKHTIN, M. M. (1981) *The Dialogic Imagination: Four Essays in M.M. Bakhtin*, M. HOLQUIST (ed.) (trans. C. Emerson and M. Holquist) Austin: University of Texas Press.

BAPTISTE, H. P., JR. (1986) 'Multicultural education and urban schools from a sociohistorical perpective: Internalizing multiculturalism', *Journal of Educational Equity and Leadership*, 6(4) pp. 295–312.

BLASE, J. (ed.) (1991) *The Politics of Life in Schools* (Newbury Park, CA: Sage).

BLOOME, D. and WILLETT, J. (1991) 'Toward a micropolitics of classroom interaction, in J. BLASE (ed.) *The Politics of Life in Schools: Power. Conflict and Cooperation* (Newbury Park, CA: Sage) pp. 207–36.

ELLISON, R. (1947) *Invisible Man* (New York: Signet).

FINE, M. (1989) 'Silencing and nurturing voice in an improbable context: Urban adolescents in public school', in H. GIROUX and P. McLAREN (eds) *Critical Pedagogy, the State, and Cultural Struggle* (Albany: SUNY Press) pp. 152–73.

FINE, M. (1991) *Framing Dropouts: Notes on the Politics of an Urban Public High School* (Albany: SUNY Press)

GIROUX, H. (ed.) (1991) *Postmodernism Feminism, and Cultural Politics: Redrawing Educational Boundaries* (Albany: SUNY Press).

GOODSON, I. (1980–81) 'Life histories and the study of schooling', *Interchange*, 11 (4) pp. 62–76.

HERR, K. (1992) 'Portrait of a teen-age mother', in R. DONMOYER and KOS, R. (eds) *Students at Risk: Portraits and Policies* (Albany: SUNY Press).

HERR, K. (1993) ' "Something to keep the relationship holding": Victoria, A pregnant adolescent', in R. DONMOYER and R. KOS (eds) *At-risk Students: Portraits, Policies, Programs, and Practices* (Albany: SUNY Press) pp. 119–34.

HOYLE, E. (1982) 'Micropolitics of educational organizations', *Educational Management and Administration*, 10, pp. 87–98.

MISCHLER, E. (1986) *Research Interviewing: Context and Narrative* (Cambridge, MA: Harvard University Press).

OPOTOW, S. (1991) 'Adolescent peer conflicts: Implications for students and for schools', *Education and Urban Society*, 23 (4) pp. 416–41.

PHILIPS, S. (1982) *The Invisible Culture: Communication in Classroom and Community on the Warmsprings Indian Reservation* (New York: Longman).

QUANTZ, R. A. and O'CONNOR, T. W. (1988) 'Writing critical ethnography: Dialogue, multi-voicedness, and carnival in cultural texts', *Educational Theory*, 38, pp. 95–109.

RIST, R. (1978) *The Invisible Children: School Integration in American Society* (Cambridge MA: Harvard University Press).

SLEETER, C. E. (1991) *Empowerment through Multicultural Education* (Albany: SUNY Press).

STANLAW, J. and PESHKIN, A. (1988) 'Black visibility in a multi-ethnic high school', in L. WEIS (ed.) *Class, Race and Gender in American Education* (Albany: SUNY Press) pp. 209–29.

WEXLER, P. (1987) *Social Analysis of Education: After the New Sociology* (London: Routledge & Kegan Paul).

WEXLER, P. (1988) 'Symbolic economy of identity and denial of labor: Studies in high school number 1', in L. Weis (ed.) *Class, Race and Gender in American Education* (Albany: SUNY Press) pp. 302–11.

6

Business involvement in school reform: The rise of the Business Roundtable

Kathryn Borman, Louis Castenell and Karen Gallagher

During the 1980s and into the 1990s business in the United States has become increasingly involved in education reform. The Business Roundtable (BRT), a major actor in all 50 states, is dominated by white males, raising a number of issues related to the new politics of race and gender. Three issues are raised: the nature of business-related school and education reform contexts; political processes at the national, state, and local levels central to polities of the BRT and other formal and informal business groups; and future trends in business involvement in education reform. The evidence brought to bear on these issues consists of reports and newsletters published by the BRT and other business-dominated organizations. Overwhelmingly, business interest and involvement in education reform have been compelled by narrow business self interest, contradictory to the interests of women, people of color, and children and often at odds with business labor market practices. Little optimism for future business-led efforts to generate structural change in education can be expected unless these efforts become more collaborative with previously excluded constituencies.

The decade of the 1980s witnessed the development of highly visible and well organized business involvement in the schools of the United States that continues into the 1990s. Several formally constituted organizations of corporate leaders including the Business Roundtable (BRT) focused their attention on the nation's education problems. The BRT's agenda targets specifically the governance and organization of schools and school systems. Organized in all the fifty states, the BRT's membership until recently has been exclusively white and male, raising a number of issues central to the new politics of race and gender.

Although it is difficult to argue a direct causal relationship between the exclusion of particular voices and points of view and subsequent informal and formal policy emanating from the business community, we will attempt to show how outcomes in particular state and local contexts display a clear relationship to a conservative business ideology. According to Frederick Edelstein, until recently a policy analyst with the National Alliance of Business,

> There has not been a wealth of involvement in education by black business leadership (at least by the Black Business Council) nor by the National Association of Women Business Owners nor the US Hispanic Chamber of Commerce. (personal communication 1992)

Edelstein explains this lack of participation as a function of 'individual interest' rather than exclusion by white male corporate leaders: 'Involvement is more a function of interest in an issue, concern, understanding and knowledge of what one can do and be effective'. This explanation ignores the important gatekeeping function of traditional power brokers. We argue that in the face of the prevailing business school reform ideology of the 1980s display of 'interest' by itself is insufficient for most members of marginalized groups to gain seats around the table.

Background: The creation of a business school reform ideology

The questions addressed here are crucial to an understanding of a number of issues arising from the decline in the 1970s of a national liberal consensus in pursuit of racial and gender equity and an attendant loss of faith in compensatory programs. Considering the significance of school reform in the context of national, state and local agendas for addressing problems facing schools and school systems, we raise these concerns: What are the business-related school and education reform contexts? What political processes at the national, state and local levels are central to the organization and policies of the Business Roundtable and other business groups? What is the direction that business involvement is likely to take in the coming decades?

While such traits as 'problem-solving skills' and 'organizational effectiveness and leadership' are currently pushed forward in the recent report 'Learning a Living' developed by former Labor Secretary Lynn Martin's Commission on Achieving Necessary Skills (1992), the entire corpus of the business reform rhetoric: 1) ignores the current profile of low skill, low wage service sector jobs actually available to youth, 2) hurries past any consideration of the inclusion of citizens in formulating reforms, and 3) focuses on upgrading 'standards' and filling a 'skills gap' without recognizing business's role in eliminating and exporting jobs and building an involuntary part-time workforce.

Corporate efforts in changing schools did not develop in a vacuum but in fact were encouraged and actively supported under two conservative presidents. Under Reagan's presidency, corporate involvement in education willy-nilly responded to two pressures at the state and local levels: 1) To enhance the competitive edge of the workforce by improving students' basic skills and problem solving abilities and 2) to improve teachers' abilities to cope with the challenge of providing a more sophisticated curriculum to meet new workplace demands. The latter reforms were to occur through 'professionalizing' the calling, a process we will examine in the next section of this chapter. More recently, under President Bush's agenda, corporate involvement in influencing education policy has become institutionalized in such rubrics as Bush's Education Policy Advisory Committee (EPAC) and his New American Schools Development Corporation (NASDC), organized to spearhead widespread educational innovations in the nation's elementary and secondary schools. Given the constraints imposed here on the scope of our analysis, we will focus only on business activities late in the 1980s and early 1990s with special emphasis on the Business Roundtable, particularly since it is a force in state-level reform. However, these recent activities can be seen as an outcome of earlier business coalitions.

The development of the Business Roundtable's education public policy agenda and those of other business coalitions occurred in the context of pervasive business influence on reform efforts in the 1980s. Business and industry-sponsored attempts to reform schools both led and pushed several kinds of efforts. A number of reforms were aimed at teachers and teaching, state and local school policies, and school-to-work transition programs.

The contexts of Business Roundtable involvement in educational reform

Business and teaching reforms

The commitment of business, particularly during the late 1980s, to reforming both the conditions of teaching and restructuring teacher education took several forms. First, free enterprise and business-dominated policy forums such as the Carnegie Corporation drafted policy statements and established committees and agencies intended to have sweeping effects on teaching. In its policy statement, *A Nation Prepared*, released in 1986, the Carnegie Forum on Education and the Economy argued for the full participation of teachers in carrying out the management of the schools in which they teach. Drafters of the Carnegie Forum document, including most notably Marc Tucker, argued that teachers must be involved in all matters that touch upon their work, namely: 1) determining the curriculum, 2) hiring, firing and evaluating their own, and 3) steering the school budget. The development of a strong, five-year liberal arts and professional core for educating pre-service teachers with an emphasis on internships in 'professional development' schools was an additional hallmark of a comprehensive policy to professionalize teaching thoroughly. As a result of these reforms, Carnegie Forum members reasoned, an academically more able group of individuals would be recruited and retained in teaching.

The move to alter dramatically teacher preparation as well as the organization and structure of teaching as a career was also taken up by a network of college of education deans under the rubric of the Holmes Group (Schneider and Hood 1993). In addition, these reforms became a rallying point for teacher organizations as first Albert Shanker, long time President of the American Federation of Teachers (AFT) and later Mary Hatwood Futrell of the National Education Association (NEA) abandoned policies predicated upon strong distinctions between management and labor. Business, higher education and the two largest national teacher organizations centered enormous efforts on changing teacher education and teaching in the 1980s. These reform interests were occasionally acted upon in concert by these groups. For example, the Lilly Foundation supported Holmes Group colleges of education planning meetings. These meetings, in turn, included representatives from both higher education and the teacher organizations.

Because teaching is an overwhelmingly female-dominated occupation, the interest during the 1980s on 'reforming' and 'upgrading' teacher education and the occupation itself raises at least two questions from the perspective of a new politics of education based on an analysis of gender and ethnicity. First, as business leaders interested in making reforms correctly reasoned, teaching by the 1980s had become an occupation of last resort. In 1991, women made up 85.8 percent of all teachers in grades K–6 and 53.7 percent of teachers in grades 7–12 (*Education Daily* 1992). During the past twenty years, large percentages of women enrolled and graduated from academic programs other than education. Lott (1987) reports increases in the numbers of women studying medicine (10–15 percent), engineering (1–6 percent), law (4–15 percent), and business (19–37 percent). With a considerable proportion of academically talented females entering professions perceived to be more challenging, those students choosing education represented the least well prepared students.

Teaching became feminized in the late nineteenth century when men either abandoned the occupation for careers as school administrators in the expanding educational system or sought employment in other occupational spheres (Apple 1993). By the 1970s, highly academically qualified women, the usual pool from which teachers were drafted, were increasingly able to find access to more lucrative careers in law, medicine and business at least at the entry level and as a result abandoned relatively low status work in teaching. Thus, teaching was a particularly vulnerable occupation, an easy target for policies aimed at strengthening its professional core (Popkewitz 1993).

Second, while females continue to dominate all major fields of education, there is an additional worrisome trend for racial and ethnic minorities. For a variety of reasons including decreased financial aid and staggeringly high school dropout rates, fewer

minorities are graduating from college. A declining number of blacks major in education as undergraduates (Trent 1990). If current trends continue, the percentage of black
teachers available by the year 2000 will be a mere 5 percent of all those teaching. In
short, it is clear that future teachers are more likely to be female and white and many
are likely to be only marginally academically qualified.

Historically, whenever women have gained the most headway and made the most
substantial numerical impact on a profession, a professional backlash against women has
occurred (Lott 1987). Thus, although business-supported efforts to 'upgrade' teaching
and teacher education may be applauded for enhancing the status of the occupation and
raising appallingly low salaries, a number of demographic realities must not remain
overlooked. Programs such as the Ford Foundation's Teaching Leadership Consortium
in place in Alabama, California, Florida, Georgia, North and South Dakota, Louisiana,
Ohio, and Mississippi expressly recruit ethnic minority students into the calling. Such
programs partially offset the exodus from higher education by talented Hispanics and
African Americans. If business is still 'trying to figure out its role' in teacher education
as Edelstein asserts (1992), support of such initiatives by business groups with tangible
resources in the form of scholarships is an activity for business groups to pursue.

Business and state educational policy reforms

A second major area of reform activity in the 1980s was widespread political activity at
the state level aimed at refinancing and restructuring schools and reordering school
governance arrangements.

Business involvement in state level school reform is perhaps most clearly illustrated
in the case of reform efforts in California and Minnesota. The effort in California, the
first of the two states to undertake reforms, was, in fact very much dependent on the
leadership of the California Business Roundtable, organized in that state in 1976 to
consider and address a range of business-related issues including but certainly not limited to education. According to their analysis of both of these state reform movements,
Berman and Clugston (1988) conclude that in each case business activities developed in
four stages: '1) getting involved, 2) developing a reform agenda, 3) working to enact
the agenda, and 4) continuing the involvement' (p. 122). At each point, corporate
leaders carried out a sort of cost-benefit analysis to determine to what extent they
wished to continue to invest resources in the reform enterprise, how they might proceed
strategically, and which coalition of players to involve.

Each state had experienced a decline in the quality of formerly strong educational
programs. In the case of California, the press of new immigrant populations, constitut-
ing approximately a quarter of that state's school-aged population by 1980, exerted
uncommon stress on a system unprepared to work with enormous cultural differences
including unprecedented language diversity. In Los Angeles schools alone, more than
thirty distinct language populations were present during the 1980s. However, the most
overwhelming difficulty facing the state was the financial devastation brought about by
the passage of Proposition 13 in a taxpayers' revolt. According to Berman and Clugston:

> The combination of a robust economy and high inflation during the mid 1970s quadrupled state and property taxes.
> By 1978, the state government had compiled a $4 billion surplus. The value of real estate had greatly escalated,
> and property taxes, which were assessed according to market values, correspondingly rose to a point where they
> became a heavy burden on the state's home owners. Despite considerable wrangling, the legislature could not act
> either to redistribute the surplus or to reduce property taxes. A citizens group gathered signatures to place

Proposition 13, a tax rollback initiative on the 1978 ballot. California's voters supported this measure, thus severely slashing property taxes and limiting the level of taxation that could be raised by a property tax. (1988: 123)

As with other social, economic, and demographic trends, California's state-wide educational perils in the wake of Proposition 13 predicted similar difficulties nationally in virtually every state in such matters as declining test scores, reduced allocations to schools and inadequate textbooks and curricula. These problems, of course, were compounded by the financial woes besetting numbers of local school districts nationally, many of which declared bankruptcy or financial exigency during the 1980s.

The concerns of CEO's involved in assessing California's educational needs emerged as a reform agenda following an analysis undertaken by Berman, Weiler Associates (BW), an independent firm. The strategy of utilizing a team of outside experts to carry out such a study has become the norm. In its first newsletter, 'Change Agents in Education', the Business Roundtable and National Alliance of Business described the process of conducting a 'gap analysis'. This method is used by independent consultants such as BW and others to focus on public policy efforts at the state level addressing the Nine Essential Components of a Successful Education System[1] (also called the Nine Points), a current yardstick for measuring the strengths and weaknesses (or gaps) in a state's educational reform policies. At this writing, six states including Connecticut, Iowa, Missouri, Montana, New Jersey and Ohio were either carrying out or were poised to conduct such analyses. The strategy is similar to that used by BW in California in 1982 in that a diverse array of stakeholder groups including representatives of teacher associations, the governor's office and the business community are interviewed, and school sites are visited. What is new is the allegiance to the Nine Points, the codified list of components originally conceived by the National Governors Association and subsequently embraced by the business community.

Thus far, business backed state-wide education reform efforts have been extremely effective in ordering a reform agenda tailored to a given state's needs as perceived by reform-minded business interests including Business Roundtable members. California, Minnesota and, most recently, South Carolina have carried out plans to eliminate badly outdated curricula, reorder school governance and the like. Other states, notably Kentucky, have adopted major, comprehensive state-mandated school reform programs. These successes reflect the trend during the 1980s to a new federalism manifest in the creation at the state governor's level of a virtual mandate to beef up standards, create a climate of accountability in schools, and employ tough new chief state school officers to direct the operation.

Although businesses are urged by the BRT spokespersons to form coalitions with major elements of the establishment in a given state, business is to supply the 'leadership and support' to bring about reform via the channels just enumerated. To what extent these and other efforts will be derailed by the economic reversals US firms are currently experiencing is both unknown and problematic. The exclusion of interest groups reflecting the needs and concerns of ethnic groups, women and children is a manifestation of businesses' conviction that business-led and dominated coalitions alone can solve education's systemic problems.

Business and local school reform

In addition to their interest in teacher education reform and both state and federal level educational policy formulations, businesses have also taken up various issues confronting local schools, especially the school-to-work transition for so-called at-risk youth. These efforts, in fact, were among the earliest educational change concerns evoking the involvement of both individual firms and collectively organized business groups.

Among the most well-publicized of these efforts is the Boston Compact. Amid much fanfare, the Compact was announced publicly in September 1982 by members of the Compact's coalition of local area chief executive officers and school administrators. A formal arrangement signed by local representatives from business, trade unions, universities and colleges, and the school district, the Compact centered on the desire of businesses to have a well prepared local labor pool. The business community agreed to hire 400 June 1983 graduates in permanent positions and to employ as many as 1000 graduates over a two-year period, if, in fact, these graduates met entry level requirements (Farrar and Cipollone 1988). Working through the local Private Industry Council (PIC), the business co-signers also agreed to recruit additional companies, increase the number of summer jobs for youths (from 750 to 1000 by 1983), and strengthen summer employment opportunities for city youth.

The Boston Compact in its organization and its aims is similar to many school–business arrangements that have developed in a number of urban and other settings during the past ten to fifteen years. Initially these collaborative arrangements, as in the Boston case, targeted secondary school students and sought to provide tutoring services, job skills training and school-to-work transition experience through summer employment and placement following graduation. The emphasis has been on readiness for work for secondary school students, a focus that has been problematic in the Boston case and elsewhere because at least two issues tend to be overlooked: the low-level skills of students entering the ninth grade – academic problems have developed in the earlier grades and have been neglected or overlooked – and a lack of attention to teaching and teachers. Teachers' needs and desires to improve their skills and to change outdated curricula through staff development, training and collaboration have been consistently ignored despite business interests in restructuring teaching as a career. In sum, the Boston Compact and programs similar to it are not without flaws. Nonetheless, these business–school partnerships continue to be promoted by the Business Roundtable and National Alliance of Business.

Despite a number of shortcomings, the ingredients of the Boston Compact have found their way into arrangements that exist in an increasingly large number of locations. In the Boston case, as in mid-sized cities such as Cincinnati and large cities like New York, business interests had coalesced earlier to address school-related issues. In Cincinnati, for example, a coalition of some twenty-five CEOs working under the rubric of the Cincinnati Business Committee (CBC), subsequently became concerned about the school system's fiscal arrangements and had informally provided assistance to the district's financial office beginning in 1978. Similarly, in Boston, the Coordinating Committee, consisting of the twenty-five CEOs of Boston's largest firms had participated in programs to train and assist youth since the late 1970s. The involvement of the business community in the federally funded Youth Entitlement Program had been critical in directing the extraordinary sum of $40 million under the Youth Employment Demonstration Act to assist Boston's income-eligible in-school youths (Farrar and Cipollone 1988). This involvement prefigured the Boston Compact.

In fact, the pattern seen in the Boston case is discernible in virtually every community in which the schools and business interests have entered into arrangements of one kind or another. Thus, in Cincinnati, the CBC's original interest in assisting the district in its fiscal management of the schools prefigured CBC's articulation of a full-blown management plan for the district in its 1991 Buenger Commission Report. The Buenger Commission directed by Clement C. Buenger, CEO of Fifth Third Bank, put forward a plan to alter radically the administrative structure of the district's downtown offices by cutting back a central office administrative staff from 127 to sixty-two individuals. An additional seventy-seven support staff jobs were also subsequently cut. The district saw a savings of $16 million dollars in 1992–93 as a result of these actions and plans to use these funds to implement changes recommended by the Buenger Commission. Plans call for enhancing school site-based programs to retain students and to address student discipline. The makeover of the administrative hierarchy not only reflects prevailing business school reform ideology by embracing a 'lean and mean' corporate profile but also utilizes corporate titles: the superintendent is now the CEO; the chief of business operations is a 'vice president'. This latter position is occupied by an executive recruited from the petroleum industry.

The involvement of business in local school-matters historically has taken several forms in the US. The near-universal participation of representatives from the business community on local school boards led, for one thing, to the development of school system management structures that resemble the hierarchical ordering of management responsibilities in US firms. Cooperative education is another long-established arrangement, one that requires frequent and systematic interaction between the schools and specific firms which regularly serve as settings for youths pursuing vocational training. In fact, the majority of school–business alliances have been built around the issue of linking the school to the world of work. Businesses continued to show a preference for an investment of their resources in programs and policies that strengthen the workplace competencies of high school students and are typically less enthusiastic about early childhood education programs that prepare preschoolers for kindergarten (Berenbeim 1991).

The preference of business for involvement at the local level in programmatic efforts designed to prepare youths for entry level jobs following high school has implications for the groups we are concerned with in this chapter. One of the problems has to do with what the Educational Testing Service (ETS) has termed 'the wall between academic/general education and vocational education' (1990). An outcome of this division between academic subject matter and work-related skills has been the issue of providing information about those skills employers value. Reading and mathematics often mean different things as practiced in the classroom and on the job. Thus, a student engages in reading to answer a written or an oral question from the teacher about the content of the passage being read. In contrast, the employee on the job reads to gain information to alter conditions in the immediate environment. Likewise, problem-solving in mathematics takes one form in the classroom and quite another on the job. Because low-income and minority students are likely to be enrolled in high school vocational programs, it follows that they are faced with the problem of acquiring skills in their academic subject matter classes that have little applicability to job settings.

Moreover, these same academic subject-matter competencies are assessed by measures that do not provide data on skills employers desire. Although there is no uniform consensus among US employers, it is clear that at least a substantial number agree to a core set of desirable skills and behaviors. The ETS report (1990) summarizes findings from several recent surveys of employers including a report from the American Society for Training and Development that synthesizes information from several surveys on employers' needs. Employers desire their newly hired employees to display the following skills and abilities:

- Reading, writing and computation,
- Learning to learn,
- Creative thinking/Problem-solving,
- Interpersonal/Negotiation/Teamwork,
- Self-esteem, Goal-setting, Motivation/Personal and Career development,
- Organizational effectiveness/leadership.

These competencies do not appear on student report cards or in student records, perhaps explaining why employers often ignore student transcripts (ETS 1990). Although employers agree to a set of skills they value in new employees and despite recent efforts by the former Secretary of Labor to develop a new 'Learning a Living' vocational curriculum, entry-level positions occupied by recent high school graduates rarely demand that young workers display traits such as organizational effectiveness, creative thinking, and the like.

Both ETS and others, notably the T. Grant Foundation's Commission on Work, Family and Citizenship (1988) identify a second problem with far-reaching consequences, namely the deteriorating wage-earning position of high school graduates. While all workers have been affected during the last two decades by the decline in real wages, as noted by ETS:

> For the period from 1973 to 1986 . . . [there are] highly disparate trends in earnings for 20 to 24-year-old males according to the level of education received . . . Real annual earnings declined by 26 percent, on average, for this age group. This decline was suffered the most by those with the least education . . . [who experienced] a drop of 42 percent; the decline for high school graduates was 28 percent. (ETS 1990: 5)

At the same time that all male workers' incomes decreased in real dollars from 1973 to 1986, the severest impact on their earning power was experienced by black males. Those with a high school degree suffered a 44 percent loss while dropouts saw a decrease of 61 percent.

In fairness, it must be emphasized that business groups at the local level through programs such as the Boston Compact, tutoring arrangements, and a continuing commitment to Cooperative Education have addressed the important and consequential issue of the school-to-work transition. Furthermore, lessons are being learned and incorporated into such programs. For example, from the Boston Compact's history, we know that: 1) sufficient numbers of business employers must be committed to offering jobs to qualified graduates; 2) people at the school level must engage the full trust of employers and students through a full commitment to mentoring roles; and 3) program and individual student goals must be documented and evaluated.

However, as we see in disturbing trends showing declining earning power for young workers, their success in the workplace is a broad, macro-economic issue in at least two ways. First, national policies emanating from the business community and the federal government have resulted in the elimination of jobs in the manufacturing sector, overall reordering of occupational structures and alterations in those skills required by a newly reconstituted job market emphasizing service sector employment (Borman 1991). Second, corporate strategies such as technological changes in production and investment in foreign human capital designed to enhance US world market competitiveness erode opportunities for US high school students, many of whom attend schools targeted for reform by business. Unfortunately, those most affected by the elimination or transfer of jobs to foreign countries are poor and minority youths who have traditionally held these same low-skilled and semi-skilled jobs. While job creation in the service sector may, in fact, partially compensate for job loss in manufacturing, salaries and benefits in such jobs are hardly comparable, contributing to the real wage declines we have previously identified and discussed. Exacerbating this pattern of job loss and job creation is the increase in part-time positions, a business strategy aimed at reducing the size of business's investment in workers. According to the US Bureau of Labor Statistics, between 1970 to 1990, the number of involuntary part-time workers jumped 121 percent, to 4.9 million (Kilborn 1991). Up to this point, business leaders have not directly addressed these issues, issues having an overwhelming significance for the very school reforms business leaders desire.

Business-sponsored reforms have addressed three major agendas: teacher education and professionalization, state policy initiatives, and local school system reforms. While we would not maintain that business interests have ignored or, indeed, consciously exacerbated issues confronting women and minorities, we can conclude that business has been primarily motivated by its own self-interest in devising reform strategies. If we could in fact make this assertion and move on, our criticisms would be rather mild. However, when reform efforts are placed against a macro-economic background, it becomes difficult to understand the contradictions between business investment in narrow-gauge educational change and corporate strategies such as investment in foreign economic capital without making harsh judgments about businesses' motivation to direct energy toward educational reforms. We next turn to an analysis of the development of the most influential of organized business groups, the Business Roundtable.

The development of the Business Roundtable

In 1972, CEOs from the top 200 corporations in the Fortune 500 organized as the Business Roundtable. The primary purpose of this national organization was to lobby the President of the United States, the executive branch, and members of Congress for legislation and regulations more favorable to corporate interests. These men reasoned that they could do a more effective job than any lobbyist in talking directly with key national policymakers. The early efforts of the Business Roundtable focused on passage of legislation and the elimination of federal regulations that would be helpful to improve international trade.

Until the early 1980s, corporations were largely disinterested in school affairs. The 1970s represented an era that was disdainful and hostile to corporate and business practices and the people who ran corporations and businesses. Because a general attitude of distrust of business and businessmen prevailed among influential leaders, the participation of corporate leaders in public education was not often sought by educators.

Intensifying foreign competition, an increasingly demanding workplace in some labor market sectors, and the debilitating effects of the 1981–82 recession, however, changed the business community's attitude toward schools considerably. The first collective action by the business community to strengthen schools was the 1982 report issued by the US Chamber of Commerce, *American Education: An Economic Issue*. This report warned that Japanese industries worked at greater capacity than their United States counterparts because their educational system was vastly superior to the public schools of the United States. This theme was particularly popular with business and corporate leaders and politicians through the 1980s (Toch 1991).

The most dominant recurring theme emanating from the business and corporate communities was that US economic strength was tied to the education of workers. That is, if productivity and competitiveness were faltering in the private sector, then the public schools were to blame because they failed to educate students to be productive workers. This theme was first voiced at the turn of the twentieth century when public schools faced the prospect of educating millions of immigrants and the main economic threat to the US was Germany. Business leaders argued then that schools failed to provide the necessary training for the successful school-to-work transition of most high school graduates. In the 1980s, business returned to these themes, replacing the European immigrants with the growing number of minority students who also lived in poverty and replacing Germany with Japan as the main threat to US economic dominance in the world.

In 1989 two events reinforced the importance of educational reform to corporate and business leaders. First, eight leading national business organizations, including the Business Roundtable, the US Chamber of Commerce and the National Association of Manufacturers, established the Business Coalition for Education Reform to lobby for national achievement standards, improvements in the teaching profession, fairness in educational funding, and other reforms. At the same time, the Business Roundtable accepted President Bush's challenge to help produce systemic changes in the way teaching and learning are practiced in the nation's elementary and secondary schools.

The Roundtable executive committee members agreed to a ten-year commitment of personal time and company resources to aid in this effort. They chose to undertake a comprehensive approach that would utilize the knowledge and resources of broadly based partnerships in each of the fifty states. The 200 corporations composing the Business Roundtable were divided across the fifty states and individual Roundtable CEOS teamed up with governors in order to identify and achieve a public policy agenda to define the characteristics of a successful school system.

This was not the first direct contact between the Business Roundtable and the White House. In 1985, the then-chairman of the BRT, Robert Beck, who was also chairman of the Prudential Insurance Company, and a dozen of the top corporate leaders came to President Reagan to urge him to do something about the mounting federal budgetary deficits. When this plea appeared to have no effect, the BRT organized a million-dollar effort to rally public support for cuts in the defense budget and for holding the line on Social Security and health care costs.

In 1987, Vice-President George Bush chaired a task force on regulatory relief. The BRT sent a report to Bush claiming that, 'The regulatory areas identified in the paper . . . represent major obstacles to international competitiveness' (*The Nation*, 4 April 1987, p. 421). Among its recommendations, the BRT suggested that EPA back off on restrictions to the disposal of nuclear waste, that OSHA cease asking for regulations compelling construction firms to notify workers of exposure to hazardous substances, and that Congress repeal fuel-economy standards for cars to strengthen the competitive position of the American automobile industry. Perhaps the BRT's real agenda and motive for its school reform effort are clearest in this set of recommendations which at first blush appear not to be related to education at all. The point here is this: in a climate that witnessed the rise of special interests and influential lobbyists at all levels of government and an overarching business school reform ideology as described earlier, it is not surprising that an organization such as the BRT would have multiple agendas to push. However, as critics such as Jonathan Kozol (1991) eloquently argue, 'dead zones' surrounding and penetrating the nation's most ghettoized schools have grown increasingly hopeless during this same period. In addition, the voices of children and their advocates have remained missing from education summits, commissions, and business coalitions organized not to save American children but rather to enhance and protect US business interests.

Future directions for business involvement in educational change

In anticipating where organized business interest in educational change is likely to be directed in the next decade, we can look to the agendas put together by formally organized groups such as the Business Roundtable and the National Alliance of Business. However, it is also useful to review the plans of firms not necessarily aligned with these organizations. We examine both sets in this section.

The Roundtable has articulated an agenda for change in its statement, 'Essential Components of a Successful Education System' (otherwise know as the Nine Points; see 'Note' at the end of this chapter). Roundtable members define the Nine Points program as a bipartisan effort to be carried out 'in partnership with the nation's governors, state legislators, educators and other private sector partners'. Coalitions have formed in seventeen states and are gearing their efforts to 'changing public policy' rather than 'tinkering with a few schools here and there'. Moreover, Roundtable publications stress the need to focus on school reform over the 'long haul', with the guidance of corporate CEOs, to target 'systemic change'. By systemic change, the architects of the Roundtable plan envision 'rethinking every aspect of the way we organize and run schools – from the way we manage districts, schools and classrooms to the way we use time, measure student achievement and hold educators accountable'. The Nine Points, furthermore, are seen as a 'package', one that cannot be dismembered when it is convenient to do so.

The Roundtable's emphasis in pushing its change agenda forward has in large part centered on standards and student assessment. These points resonate well with businesses' particular concern with a well prepared, competitive work force that can 'function in the global economy of the twenty-first century'. It is likely that the Roundtable and other allied organizations, particularly the National Alliance of Business will continue to push for national standards of some kind, though these might vary from state to state. Whatever form student assessment might take, the stated interest of the Roundtable is in raising 'the performance of virtually all . . . students to global standards of mastery'. For the moment, the Roundtable is counting on the congressionally chartered National Council on Education Standards and Testing to move the development of standards and measures for assessment forward. Should Congress become sluggish or recalcitrant, it is fair to predict that Roundtable members will be moved to seek other avenues of support.

What of other business coalitions as well as unorganized business interests, namely individual firms? A revealing profile of 176 US companies prepared by Berenbeim (1991) illustrates both businesses' appraisal of the need for reform and the kinds of commitments businesses of various sizes and types are willing to make. On behalf of the Conference Board, an organization formed in 1916 to improve the business enterprise system and to enhance the contribution of business to society, Berenbeim (1991) undertook a survey of 1600 US firms. The questionnaire was mailed to each of these corporation's CEOs and was subsequently returned by 176 respondents including CEOs, and lower ranking executives in contributions, community relations, human resources and public affairs. The firms responding represented eight employment sectors including mining/extraction; construction; manufacturing; transportation; utilities; wholesale/retail trade; financial services, and other services as shown in Table 6.1.

The survey utilized the six national goals for education originally formulated by the National Governors' Association in 1990 following a mandate from the Bush administration to create a national education reform package. Berenbeim also solicited

Table 6.1: Responding companies (N = 176)

Dominant Business	Number	Percentage
Mining/Extraction	8	5
Construction	2	1
Manufacturing	85	48
Transportation	5	3
Utilities	29	16
Wholesale/Retail Trade	7	4
Financial Services	33	19
Other Services	7	4

information from respondents about their motives for desiring change including 1) work-force needs, 2) global economic competitiveness, and 3) community quality of life. Finally, Berenbeim's instrument allowed respondents to identify types of effort expended in carrying educational reform forward including financial (contribution of funds, facilities and materials), program (partnerships, advice and school assistance projects), and political (support for legislation at any and all governmental levels). Berenbeim's results varied according to both type and size of firm. Respondents were requested to indicate the level of support (heavy, moderate or minimal) that their firms were currently investing in projects addressing the various national goals. Over-whelmingly, the responding firms reported heavy support of all three types (financial, programmatic and political) for Goal 4, regarding achievement in mathematics and science. Goal 3, regarding student achievement and citizenship, ranked second followed by Goal 5, regarding adult literacy and lifelong learning. The three lowest rankings were given to Goal 2, regarding school completion, Goal 6, assuring safe, disciplined and drug-free schools, and Goal 1, regarding readiness for kindergarten.

With respect to the motive for reform, there were variations by firm type and size in results reported by Berenbeim. Thus, large businesses (more than 50,000 employees) and manufacturing firms rated global competition as a concern of equal importance to the individual firm's immediate workforce needs. Smaller firms (less than 5,000) and those with traditionally strong local ties such as utilities and financial services organiza-tions viewed the need to maintain high standards in their community's life as a more important factor than global competitiveness. Results overall are shown in Table 6.2 and indicate among other findings, no consensus around three survey items including a concern to 'foster equal opportunity and social mobility'. Indeed, taken together the results of this survey suggest a disdain on the part of business for issues related to the greater good of the community and its citizens. Businesses favor goals and priorities that further their own immediate desires and shun those such as early education pro-grams and policies emphasizing social mobility that are removed from their immediate self-interest.

Conclusions

Given both the concerns of formal groups such as the Roundtable and those of firms more generally, it is difficult to adopt anything but a cynical view of business-related interest in educational change. While US firms call for a better prepared workforce to withstand competition from abroad, they continue to invest in foreign capital. Further,

Table 6.2: Priorities that best describe companies' concerns in seeking public education improvements

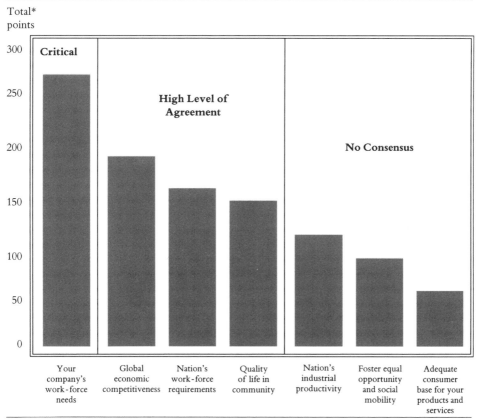

Note: *Participants (176 companies responding) were asked to indicate the degree (1 = heavy, 2 = moderate, or 3 = minimal) of their company's financial, program and political involvement in initiatives related to the National Educational Goals. Three points were awarded for a (1), two for a (2), and one for a (3). The total number of points represent the support levels for each program and type of assistance.

it seems clear that work-place practices discourage full application of anything more than routine, low-skill activities (Borman 1991). Indeed, ethnographic studies including Borman's (1991) study of job settings in factories and service sector businesses show the persistent requirement of tolerance for dull, routine tasks in most work-places employing recent high school graduates.

In businesses' agenda for school-to-work transition programs, employers urge a system that makes school work including academic subject matter coursework more applicable to work-place demands. Yet the National Center on Education and the Economy's Commission on the Skills of the American Workforce provides this dismal account:

> . . . only an estimated 5 percent of employers organize work so as to require a high level of skill among workers . . . this country's declining productivity is more the result of how employers organize work than a shortage of skilled workers. Although in surveys employers initially report such a shortage, the great majority consistently cite the need for a low skill work-force that would tolerate an ethic of obedience and a hierarchical organization. (Roditi 1992: 340)

Until businesses can honestly examine their own motives and practices it is difficult to see how those who are most endangered by businesses' continued reliance upon hierarchically organized systems and low-skilled, dutiful workers can benefit from businesses' interest in educational reform.

We must conclude that the exclusion of voices from traditionally disenfranchised groups has helped to create a climate of indifference as businesses collectively and individually pursue educational change strategies. While they espouse a deep commitment to reforming schools and school systems, businesses practice a number of strategies, namely investment in foreign capital, paternalistic approaches to teacher education reform, and a strong, persistent emphasis on hierarchical organizational arrangements and low-skill jobs, all of which run counter to real structural change. It is likely that in cities and towns with a strong local presence of utilities and other companies with traditionally strong commitments to the public weal, educational change may truly be systemic. The prognosis is bleak in other places unless we experience a change in the public will and a desire to include organizations representative of the interests of women, racial and ethnic minorities and children.

Note

1. The Nine Points, also termed the 'Essential Components of a Successful Education System' are as follows:

    1. The new system is committed to four operating assumptions:
        *   All students can learn at significantly higher levels.
        *   We know how to teach all students successfully.
        *   Curriculum content must reflect high expectations for all students, but instructional time and strategies may vary to assure success.
        *   Every child must have an advocate.
    2. The new system is performance or outcome based.
    3. Assessment strategies must be as strong and rich as the outcomes.
    4. School success is rewarded and school failure penalized.
    5. School-based staff have a major role in making instructional decisions.
    6. Major emphasis is placed on staff development.
    7. A high quality pre-kindergarten program is established, at least for all disadvantaged students.
    8. Health and other social services are sufficient to reduce significant barriers to learning.
    9. Technology is used to raise student and teacher productivity and to expand access to learning.

    Source: National Alliance of Business (1991) *The Business Roundtable Participation Guide: A Primer for Business on Education,* April (New York: The Business Roundtable).

References

America's Choice: High Skills or Low Wages (1990) (New York: Columbia University, Teachers College, National Center on Education and the Economy).

APPLE, M. (1989) 'American Realities: Poverty, Economy, and Education', in L. WEIS, E. FARRAR and H. G. PETRIE (eds) *Dropouts from School: Issues, Dilemmas, and Solutions* (Albany, NY: SUNY Press) pp. 205–55.

APPLE, M. (1993) 'Is Change Always Good for Teachers? Gender, Class and Teaching in History' in N. GREENMAN and K. BORMAN (eds) *Changing Education: Recapturing the Past or Inventing the Future?* (Albany, NY: SUNY Press).

BERENBEIM, R. E. (1991) *Corporate Support of National Education Goals*, Report No. 978, The Conference Board (New York, NY: The Conference Board, Inc.).

BERMAN, P. and CLUGSTON, R. (1988) 'A Tale of Two States: The Business Community and Educational Reform in California and Minnesota', in M. Levine and R. Trachtman (eds) *American Business and the Public Schools: Case Studies of Corporate Involvement in Public Education* (New York, NY: Teachers College Press) pp. 121–49.

BORMAN, K. M. (1991) *The First 'Real' Job: A Study of Young Workers* (Albany, NY: SUNY Press).

THE BUSINESS ROUNDTABLE AND THE NATIONAL ALLIANCE OF BUSINESS (1992) *Change Agents in Education*, 1, 1, pp. 3–4.

CARNEGIE FORUM ON EDUCATION AND THE ECONOMY (1986) *A Nation Prepared: Teachers for the 21st Century* (Washington, DC: The Forum).

CHUBB, J. E. and MOE, T. M. (1990) *Politics, Markets and America's Schools* (Washington, DC: The Brookings Institute).

BUSINESS COALITION FOR EDUCATION REFORM (1992) Correspondence, 18 March.

EDELSTEIN, F. (1992) Personal communication to Kathryn Borman.

Education Daily (1992) 16 January, p. 6.

EDUCATIONAL TESTING SERVICE (ETS) (1990) *From School to Work*, Policy Information Report (Princeton, NJ: Policy Information Center).

FARRAR, E. and CIPPOLONE, A. (1988) 'After the signing: The Boston Compact 1982 to 1985', in M. LEVINE and R. TRACHTMAN (eds) *American Business and the Public School* (New York: Teachers College Press) pp. 89–120.

HARE, B. (1987) 'Structural inequality and the endangered status of black youth', *Journal of Negro Education*, 50, 11, pp. 100–10.

HARRISON, B. and BLUESTONE, B. (1988) *The Great U-Turn: Corporate Restructuring and the Polarizing of America* (New York: Basic Books).

HENRY, W. (1990) 'Beyond the melting pot', *Time*, 9 April, pp. 28–31.

KANTROWITZ, B. and ROSADO, L. (1991) 'Falling further behind', *Newsweek*, 19 August, p. 60.

KEARNS, D. and DOYLE, D. P. (1988) *Winning the Brain Race: A Bold Plan to Make Our Schools Competitive* (San Francisco: Institute for Contemporary Studies).

KILBORN, P. (1991) 'More people forced into part-time work', *Chicago Tribune*, 1 September, Section 8, p. 1.

KOZOL, J. (1991) *Savage Inequalities: Children in America's Schools* (New York: Crown Publishers).

LOTT, B. (1987) *Women's Lives: Themes and Variations in Gender Learning* (Pacific Grove, CA: Brooks and Cole Publishing Co.).

NOBLE, D. D. (1992) 'New American Schools and the New World Order', paper presented at the Annual Meeting of the American Educational Research Association, April.

PETERS, T. and WATERMAN R. (1982) *In Search of Excellence* (New York: Harper and Row).

POPKEWITZ, T. (1993) 'Certification to Credentialing: Reconstructuring Control Mechanisms in Teacher Education', in K. M. BORMAN and N. GREENMAN (eds) *Changing Schools: Recapturing the Past or Inventing the Future* (Albany: SUNY Press).

RAY, C. and MICKELSON, R. (1993) 'Structuring Students for Restructured Work: The Economy, School Reform, and Non-college bound Youths', *Sociology of Education*, 66, 1.

REED, S. and SAUTTES, R. (1990) 'Children of poverty', *Phi Delta Kappan*, 71, 10, pp. K1–K12.

REICH, R. B. (1991) *The Work of Nations* (New York: Alfred A. Knopf).

RODITI, H. F. (1992) 'High School for Docile Workers', *The Nation*, 16 March, pp. 340–3.

SCHNEIDER, B. and HOOD, S. (1993) 'Pathways to Institutional Change: From the Dean's Network to the Holmes Group', in K. M. BORMAN and N. GREENMAN (eds) *Changing Schools: Recapturing the Past or Inventing the Future* (Albany: SUNY Press).

SECRETARY'S COMMISSION ON ACHIEVING NECESSARY SKILLS (1992) *Learning a Living: A Blueprint for High Performance* (Washington, DC: Department of Labor).

SIDNEY, H. (1985) 'Your leadership is demanded', *Time*, 24.

TOCH, T. (1991) *In the Name of Excellence* (New York: Oxford University Press).

TRENT, W. (1990) 'Race and ethnicity in the teacher education curriculum', *Teachers College Record*, 91, 3, pp. 361–9.

T. GRANT FOUNDATION COMMISSION on Work, Family and Citizenship (1988) (Washington, DC).

US CHAMBER OF COMMERCE (1982) *American Education: An Economic Issue* (Washington, DC: US Chamber of Commerce).

7   *Race and the liberal perspective in Chicago school reform*

G. Alfred Hess, Jr.

The traditional liberal perspective is characterized by egalitarian and compassionate concerns. Mid-twentieth century liberal strategies focused on the uses of centralized governmental authority to overcome local prejudice and nicely meshed with early century reforms towards a centralized, depoliticized professional bureaucratic governance structure. Chicago is symbolic of a new trend towards decentralized governance designed to address the continuing inequalities in education after decades of implementing ineffective centralized strategies. This chapter examines the conditions that gave rise to the Chicago reform approach and explores its relationship to traditional liberal perspectives.

With a few exceptional periods, the first eight decades of the twentieth century have been marked by policies reflecting the liberal perspective, particularly in the realm of public education. Matching the development of rationalized and depoliticized public management that saw the rise of town managers, public education developed a professionalized school bureaucracy and universities correspondingly developed departments of educational administration (Katz 1992). Later, at mid-century, school desegregation dominated the social issues of the 1950s and 1960s, as 'separate but equal' was overturned by *Brown v. Topeka Board of Education*. In the late 1960s, in line with the philosophy of the federal government's war on poverty, compensatory funding to offset the disadvantages of poverty or special conditions of children became an accepted mechanism to broaden access to equality of educational opportunity.

One of the central precepts of the liberal political strategies of the middle of the twentieth century was that local interests regularly denied the civil rights and equality of opportunity of minorities. From this perspective, perhaps founded in the perception that racial bias was far more virulent in the South than in other regions of the United States, it was a logical strategy to rely upon the imposition of directives (judicial, legislative and executive) from higher, more centralized jurisdictions to overcome local prejudices. From this mindset grew a massive civil rights strategy, rooted in the US Supreme Court decision in *Brown v. Topeka*, elements of which are still relevant in arenas such as securing finance equity among school districts in a state.[1] But, as the extent of Northern racial bias was revealed in Chicago and other cities in the late 1960s and as the national handles of power were assumed by those with less concern for equality for all Americans, the understanding that 'centralized' meant 'more progressive' and 'local' meant 'more unequal' was discarded by many who worked in America's cities.

The 1980s witnessed a turning of the political tide, as more conservative forces took control of federal policymaking in reaction to the perceived failures of the liberal social agenda. The success of public education was also called into question. The National Commission on Excellence in Education (1983) said we were 'a nation at risk' and bemoaned the 'rising tide of mediocrity' in our schools. The attack on the failures of the mid-century liberal strategies did not just come from the right, however. By the end of the decade, Jonathan Kozol, one of the dramatists of school failure in the 1960s

(Kozol 1968) was again investigating schools across the country and being startled by 'the remarkable degree of racial segregation that persisted almost everywhere' (Kozol 1991: 2). Kozol was particularly concerned that the nation seemed to have abandoned the moral implications of *Brown* in favor of seeking equal, if separate, education for minorities. He then went on to describe the 'savage inequalities' that give the lie to any claims of achieving equity.

School desegregation efforts in the us's major cities have not met with great success. Urban geography, demographic changes and court decisions, such as *Milliken I* and *II* in Detroit, have effectively eliminated the possibility of interdistrict school desegregation for most urban areas (Monti 1986, Tatel, Lanigan and Sneed 1986). While some scholars continue to document the benefits of individual student integration, where that can be accomplished (compare Crain and Strauss 1985, Rosenbaum, Kulieke and Rubinowitz 1987), the vast majority of urban minority students are more likely to be left in the racially isolated settings Kozol encountered (Monti 1986, Tatel, Lanigan and Sneed 1986). This was clearly the case in Chicago.

I first became aware of the disillusionment of community activists with the 'centralized' strategies for achieving equity as the Chicago public schools sought to adopt a plan for the desegregation of its schools in 1980–81. Having resisted the efforts of the 1960s and 1970s, desegregation then had quite different connotations for Chicagoans than it would have two decades earlier. By 1980, only 18 percent of the city's public school students were white and these white students overwhelmingly attended a few predominantly white schools. Similarly, three of five black students attended all minority schools, and another 35 percent attended schools with less than 30 percent white students.

When the newly installed minority-dominated board of education sought to fashion a desegregation plan, however, it had much more difficulty than it had anticipated. Black community leaders were reluctant to take visible positions on the desegregation issue and the five black board members eventually voted against the plan which was adopted. At one set of public hearings during the planning process, only one black leader forthrightly advocated busing. 'If it means my kids have to get on a bus to guarantee our civil rights, then my kids will be on the bus', he said,[2] but no others echoed his sentiments. Based on their testimony, black parents were far more interested in improving the quality of their neighborhood schools than in sending their kids off to other parts of the city to attend better schools or to attend schools with white kids.

Pierre van den Berghe's (1973) typology of pluralism provided insight into these events. I renamed the three categories he described 'stratified pluralism' (with caste-like characteristics), 'egalitarian pluralism' (a consociative model reflective of the Swiss cantons), and 'uniform incorporation' of diverse peoples in a 'color-blind' society (Hess 1984: 132). The advent of the Black Power movement of the 1960s and 1970s had revealed a disenchantment with pursuing 'individual integration' in favor of seeking 'equal access to power and economic resources'. To eliminate caste-like stratified pluralism in Chicago, minority leaders in 1980, I suggested, were pursuing strategies which would produce a society based on egalitarian pluralism rather than one built on uniform incorporation. But the desegregation effort was being driven by a legal interpretation more consistent with a society of individual integration. One lawyer from the Department of Justice, commenting upon the board's public hearings, complained, 'They weren't supposed to be running a referendum on the Constitution!' (Hess 1984: 138). It appeared that many black leaders, reluctant to openly break with the traditions and history of the civil rights movement of the 1950s and 1960s, were, by the late 1970s, pursuing objectives of equal access rather than those of individual integration. Their silence on the desegregation plan was indicative of their awareness of the difficulty of explaining that their goals had not changed, but their strategies had. It was this shift away from a strategy of individualized integration and towards egalitarian pluralism which was to puzzle Kozol only a few years later.

Chicago school reform: Left-over liberalism or neoconservative conspiracy?

Kozol, among others, is suspicious that reform efforts focused on restructuring are little more than the creation of 'a more "efficient" ghetto school' (Kozol 1991: 4). Other critics have other complaints. In fact, the Chicago School Reform Act has been lionized and vilified by commentators from both the left and the right. Chester Finn (Finn and Clements 1990) and Harold Howe (1988) have both lauded it as one of the most radical efforts to reform the us's schools. Meanwhile, Myron Lieberman (1988) and Gary Orfield (1991) deride it as not radical enough. Does the Chicago effort represent a rejection of liberalism and an embracing of more parochial neoconservative approaches of community control? Is it one more frantic effort to patch up the failed, massive bureaucratic solutions of the war on poverty which Chubb and Moe (1990) say is doomed to equal failure because it still relies on democratic control? Are the architects of the reform effort 'left-over liberals of the 1960s' as Bruce Cooper (1990) has suggested? Or are they misguided neoconservatives in liberal clothes, as Orfield has implied? Does it make any difference what label they wear?

In this chapter, I attempt to describe the conditions which led reform advocates in one major us city, Chicago, to champion the elements of the legislation enacted in 1988 and to examine the challenges to traditional liberal strategies this reform effort poses. As one of the several 'architects' to whom Cooper referred, I would assert that the intellectual roots of the reform effort in Chicago are clearly in the egalitarian and compassionate soil of the traditional liberal perspective. However, the solutions were fashioned more pragmatically than ideologically. They were directly connected to the analysis of the problems being experienced in the Chicago public schools during the 1980s. In that sense, perhaps it is fair to say the Chicago approach embodies a rejection of the failed, centralized strategies earlier liberals had designed to solve the problems of schooling for low-income and minority students. I would maintain, however, it is the strategies of liberalism which were unsuccessful in Chicago, not the philosophical perspective. The Chicago school reform effort was not an abandoning of the effort to assure equality of opportunity to all of the city's students, but it was an assertion that, under the then reigning liberal paradigm, such opportunity was still being systematically denied.

The failure of the liberal agenda in Chicago

When the outcomes of the 1981 desegregation plan were later examined (Hess and Warden 1988, Easton and Hess 1990), the results were disappointing from the perspective of disadvantaged minority youth. By 1986, the system had successfully eliminated all predominantly white (above 70 percent) schools and only a third of white students then attended majority white schools. For minority students, however, there was little benefit as only 3 percent more minority students attended desegregated settings in 1986 than had done so in 1981. Dollars and staff were disproportionately focused to new and continuing magnet schools, and white students were disproportionately enrolled in magnet schools. By the 1988–89 school year (the year in which reform legislation was finally enacted), white students made up only 12 percent of the public school enrollment and the percentage of minority students attending predominantly (above 85 percent) minority schools had actually increased from 58 to 63 percent! After a decade of centrally directed desegregation, minority students were no better off than they had been at the beginning of the effort, even though an increasing proportion of desegregation resources were devoted to predominantly minority schools in the later part of the 1980s.

In addition to the continuing and intensifying racial isolation, minority students were attending schools in which student achievement was very low. In 1985–86, eighth grade students attending magnet or desegregated schools (above 30 percent white enrollments) were achieving at the national norms or above on the Iowa Test of Basic Skills, while those in the 300 racially identifiable or racially isolated schools were from eight months to more than a year below the norm. In high schools, all students did less well. In desegregated and selective entrance schools, median students performed at the 42nd percentile (norm = 50th percentile), while in segregated schools the median was at the 24th percentile.

Our studies of the dropout phenomenon in Chicago (Hess and Lauber 1985) showed that 43 percent of entering ninth graders never graduated from a Chicago high school. Once again, segregated inner city schools (in aggregate, less than 6 percent white) had a cumulative dropout rate of 56 percent, while the mostly desegregated and selective high schools (together 25 percent white) had an aggregated dropout rate of 25 percent, slightly below the national average. We called this a system of educational triage (Hess 1986). A study by Designs for Change (1985a), another key organization in the Chicago school reform effort, came to similar achievement and dropout conclusions. But, we noted that some high schools, despite receiving high proportions of ill-prepared students, were more successful than others with similar enrollments. Our follow-up study (Hess et al. 1987) had findings similar to other effective schools research (compare Purkey and Smith 1983) that the quality of the principal, the type of discipline maintained, the clarity of the educational philosophy, and the degree of direct and interactive instruction in the classroom were all associated with schools with lower dropout rates. The Designs for Change study had also emphasized the findings of the effective schools literature.

In addition, we were also documenting the failures of the centralized administration of the school system to manage the system efficiently or to provide equitable resources to disadvantaged students, even when the system's chief administrators themselves were minorities. Our 1987 study was called 'Where's Room 185?' because it documented a widespread practice of shortchanging Chicago high school students of their instructional opportunities by scheduling them for excessive study halls which were either chaotic or, frequently, non-existent. Students at one high school with 'Room 185' (a supply closet) on their schedules knew they were to come to school late or leave early for that period.

The system's mismanagement also stretched to fiscal matters and the priorities these financial decisions reflected. In 1979–80, the school system had become bankrupt, and was unable to meet its payroll that December. An emergency bailout scheme was enacted by the state legislature which eventually forced the closing of more than 8,000 positions. A study of staffing changes (Hallet and Hess 1982) had shown that student contact staff, maintenance staff, and clerks were more sharply cut back than administrators and technical staff. As the system recovered from its fiscal collapse, the priority on increasing non-student contact staff was maintained. Between 1981 and 1988, the number of bureaucrats per 1,000 students grew from 6.3 to 8.6 (Hess 1991: 27). At about the same time, Designs for Change, led by Donald Moore, who was to become the chief of the 'architects' of the reform legislation, had shown that Chicago was engaged in a pattern of racial steering in special education classifications (Moore and Radford-Hill 1982).

The system's priorities were also askew for spending among schools. Not only were funds disproportionately directed to magnet schools, and thus, disproportionately to white students who were also generally more affluent, funds were directed away from those schools which were predominantly enrolling low-income students. Elementary schools with fewer than 30 percent low-income students were spending an average of $2350 per student, while schools with between 90 and 99 percent low-income were allocated only $1995 per pupil. Because of the concentration of federal compensatory funds in completely low-income schools, the 100 percent low-income schools averaged $2339 per pupil. This curvilinear pattern existed despite state compensatory funding which was to increase as the proportion of low-income students increased. Administrators for the board of education both illegally reallocated some of these targeted low-income funds and supplanted basic services with others, creating significant inequity, which the state, using straight-line correlations, had failed to detect.

By 1987, when a long school strike mobilized a broad movement for school reform in Chicago, this picture of failure and inequality was widely shared across the community. The studies of the Chicago Panel and Designs for Change had been widely covered in the news media and extensively discussed in editorial pronouncements. They were augmented by similar studies from business groups (Chicago United 1981, King 1987) and the media (Chicago Tribune 1988). In 1986, Mayor Harold Washington, the city's first black mayor, had convened an Education Summit to consider ways to improve the education of minority youth in the city, and the failings of the school system were widely discussed during that year-long effort (See Hess 1991, for a more detailed account of the shortcomings of the school system and the movement which led to the adoption of the Chicago School Reform Act). The people of Chicago were already convinced of the failures of centralized approaches to solving the educational problems of disadvantaged students, when the nineteen-day school strike created the chairotic moment.

The reform response

The school reform movement in Chicago, the solutions embodied in the agreements of the second year of the Mayor's Education Summit, and the Chicago School Reform Act (PA 85–1418) which developed out of these efforts were responses to the perceived failures of the Chicago public schools and of the strategies embodied in educational policies being enacted by the school system and the state. The reform movement was shaped by the acknowledged failures of the preceding decade, including the unwillingness and inability of the federal government to initiate metropolitan solutions to segregated schools, housing and job opportunities, as included in the 1980 Consent Decree between the Justice Department and the Chicago board of education. School activists left aside the possibility of changing the whole of society before attempting to improve the city's schools. The focus was on Chicago and its schools, not the whole society and its problems. The conviction, supported by the effective schools literature and similar local studies, was that Chicago's schools could do a *better* job of educating the city's children, no matter what disadvantages they brought with them to school.

This is a distinctly different conviction about the educability of disadvantaged inner-city youth than that embodied in typical metropolitan desegregation approaches that spread out low-achieving students into schools dominated by higher achieving majority students. In those schools, frequently, minority students achieve no better than they did in their inner city schools, but desegregation advocates suggest these students' goals are higher and their later life opportunities are enhanced (Orfield 1986). Such advocates focus on the 'escape opportunities' for a few minority students while consigning the remaining minority students (by far the larger number) to continued failure. This paternalistic posture has preempted the liberal perspective but seems harshly at variance with ensuring equality of opportunity for all. It, too, represents a posture of educational triage.

In line with the conviction that Chicago could offer better educational opportunities to all its disadvantaged students, the reform act included a set of goals which were designed to equalize opportunity in the city's schools and lift student achievement levels to the national norms. The law envisioned accomplishing a normal distribution of scores on standardized achievement tests within five years. Reformers recognized that this was a terribly optimistic goal, but felt that it was necessary to make it explicit in order to engender the required changes immediately, rather than with 'all deliberate speed'. Further, the effective schools literature had emphasized that one of the critical elements was a widespread conviction among a school's faculty that 'all kids can learn' (Designs for Change 1985b, Brookover 1991).

The second major component of the legislation is a mandate to reallocate the system's resources to remedy the inappropriate reallocation and supplanting of state compensatory funds (known as State Chapter I). This provision forced the closing of more than 500 positions in the central administration and the shifting of $40 million to the schools for their discretionary purposes during reform's first year. By the third budget year, the percentage of staff working in non-school locations had dropped from 12 to 8 percent, while discretionary spending at the school site had increased from virtually nothing to an average of about $340,000 per elementary school. Base level funding, while still not totally equitable, had begun to level out and total expenditures per pupil were more clearly correlated with the proportion of low income students enrolled. This accomplishment is in line with the traditional liberal equity goal in school finance circles of treating equals equally (horizontal equity) and unequals unequally (vertical equity) (see Berne and Stiefel 1984).

Still, it is the third component of the Chicago School Reform Act which is best known and around which the greatest controversy swirls. After listing the ten goals of the reform effort, the act says:

> To achieve these priority goals, the General Assembly intends to make the individual local school the essential unit for educational governance and improvement and to establish a process for placing the primary responsibility for school governance and improvement in furtherance of such goals in the hands of parents, community residents, teachers, and the school principal at the school level. (PA 85–1418, Sec 34.1.01B)

Thus, contrary to the mistaken characterization of the act as focused on 'community control' (Mirel 1990), responsibility is placed in the hands of actors at each school site. This makes the Chicago effort quite distinct from the decentralization efforts in New York and Detroit (Rogers and Chung 1983, Glass and Sanders 1978). In those cities, authority was devolved to large community subdistricts with populations of hundreds of thousands. Such a plan was introduced by Republican legislators as a competitor of the Chicago School Reform Act but lost in the House as the current school-site focused reform was enacted.

There are two separate types of authority shifts which have been propounded under the image of school-based decision-making or school-based management. The first involves a shifting of who is involved in making decisions at the school site. In the more widely adopted plans sponsored by the national teacher unions, decision-making is expanded to include teachers and occasionally token representatives of parents. Under these models, there is little new authority given to the school site; authority which was previously exercised by principals is now shared more widely (see Hanson, Morris and Collins 1992; Etheridge and Collins 1992). The second type of authority shift is a true devolution of authority from higher levels of the school system bureaucracy to the school level. Under this type of authority shift, the school site becomes the locus of a significantly increased range of decisions. The Chicago School Reform Act utilizes both types of authority shift, expanding the categories of persons making decisions at the school site and significantly expanding the arenas over which decisions can be made. In the Chicago case, decision-making is shared between parents, community residents, teachers and the principal.

Richard Elmore (1988) has suggested that giving parents primacy in school decision-making distinguishes the Chicago model from 'teacher professionalization' approaches. He suggests that such 'client empowerment' approaches have more in common with enrollment choice proposals which also vest primary authority in parents as they exercise enrollment options. The Local School Councils (LSC) created by the reform act are composed of six parents, two community representatives, two teachers, and the principal. In high schools, a student also serves on the council, though with a vote limited to non-personnel items. With a majority of votes in the hands of parents, LSCs are, theoretically, parent dominated.

However, there are some important limitations on parent power. Lscs have three primary responsibilities: to adopt a school improvement plan, to approve an expenditure plan for the school, and to select the school's principal. They do not have the authority to determine which students to enroll; that authority remains vested in the central board to protect the system's current student assignment commitment under the desegregation plan.

The principal is given primary responsibility to develop the improvement plan and the school budget. The principal is charged to work closely with a committee of teachers, the Professional Personnel Advisory Committee (PPAC), in developing the improvement plan and other curricular suggestions. Thus, the school site professional educators have a large say in shaping the instructional program of the school. In this way, the Chicago act incorporates the notions of participatory decision-making which the professionalization approaches to school restructuring emphasized. The notion had been copied from business efforts to improve quality (see Deming 1982). The full council reviews, debates and occasionally amends the school improvement plan; it does not, generally, initiate the planning process. Further, while the majority votes of parents are enough to terminate the incumbent principal when his or her term expires, it takes seven votes to select a new principal. Thus the parents alone cannot select a school's educational leader. In studying the implementation of reform in fourteen representative schools (Hess and Easton 1992), we found few examples of decisions made solely by the votes of parents. And, we discovered, teachers felt they had a major say in shaping the improvement plans in their schools (Easton 1991). The potential for parent dominance is always present, however; parents make up a majority of the LSC, the chair of the LSC must be a parent, and they have the potential to dominate principal selection. In our sample of representative schools, we found at least two cases in which the faculty recommended retention of the incumbent principal, but the LSC voted to select someone else.

The reform community did split apart over addressing the 'savage inequalities' Kozol (1991) so powerfully described. In April 1992, the Coalition for Educational Rights, whose membership includes the Chicago Urban League, the Chicago Panel, and the state League of Women Voters, worked with Senators Arthur Berman (Democrat of Chicago) and John Maitland (Republican of downstate Bloomington) to fashion an amendment to the Illinois Constitution which would have made education a fundamental right in the state. The amendment was approved by a 60 percent majority in each house and put on the November ballot for adoption by the citizens of Illinois. While most of the community and school-based reform advocates strongly supported the amendment, business leaders who had previously supported Chicago school reform, such as Lawrence Howe, executive director of the Civic Committee of the Commercial Club, and Ed Noa, Chairman of CNA Insurance and a board member of Leadership for Quality Education, led the opposition. This effort to create a binding mandate upon the state to fund its schools more adequately and to assure greater equity in the levels of funding between districts fell 3 percentage points short of the 60 percent majority needed for adoption in the general election.

Discussion

In this chapter I have attempted to describe the Chicago school reform effort in a way that will correct some widely held misapprehensions about what the Chicago program is. It is not an effort at community control such as decentralization efforts in New York and Detroit, though it does devolve authority away from centralized control. It is not an abandonment of efforts to provide an equal opportunity for all students to succeed. It is not an abandonment of the traditional liberal goals of integration (the limited success of the board's desegregation plan is protected in the legislation), though it recognizes the current legal restrictions on addressing the city-suburban racial segregation currently typical of metropolitan areas in the USA. Rather, it is an attempt to deal with the vast majority of minority students who continue in segregated or racially isolated settings in the nation's third largest school system. Further, the reform act significantly extends the compensatory approach which had been diluted and corrupted by both state and local policymakers of the 1970s and 1980s, even though many of those officials were themselves black or Hispanic. The educationally activist members of the reform movement were leaders in the effort to change the way state funding is provided to schools in Illinois. Reform in Chicago is an effort to deal with the failures of traditional liberal strategies in the changed demographic and political context of the end of the twentieth century, while still pursuing statewide remedies where available.

The Chicago reform effort does call into question the unthinking connection between the liberal philosophical perspective and the strategies adopted by liberals in the 1950s and 1960s, which were linked to the professionalized, rational governance strategies of the early decades of this century. From the Chicago perspective, the mid-century liberal solutions simply were not working for the city's disadvantaged kids. Chicago reformers were unwilling to allow those kids' needs to go unmet for the sake of allegiance to 'traditional liberal strategies' which were not working, and they were not willing to settle for providing a triage strategy of escape for a few while the needs of the majority were ignored.

Thus, in Chicago, the strategies were changed. In many ways, school reform was just one focus for the broader changes in the society. Predating the school reform effort, Chicago's community leaders had abandoned an effort to create an integrated society of uniform incorporation in favor of establishing an egalitarian pluralism of equal access to power and resources. I have already described this change during the desegregation planning period. Similar changes were occurring in the fields of housing and job development. To this extent, Kozol's (1991: 4) concern that we may be returning to the 'separate but equal' strategies of *Plessy v. Ferguson* may have some relevance.

While maintaining as many desegregated settings as possible, the school reform effort built upon the strategy of egalitarian pluralism. It added to that notion the 'traditional liberal' approach of providing compensatory resources to the most disadvantaged. At the same time, it recognized the legal and political constraints to creating metropolitan-wide solutions. 'Traditional' (that is, 1960s style) liberals such as Orfield and Kozol have criticized the Chicago reform effort for being willing to work within these constraints rather than focusing exclusively upon a quixotic attack upon those windmills. For critics such as Orfield (1991: 10), any effort operating within the recognition of existing constraints is 'preposterous' and doomed to failure. In this stance, he comes to a position identical to that of his protagonists on the right, Chubb and Moe (1990). As the educational amendment campaign showed, however, many of these Chicago reformers were willing to take on the statewide inequities as well.

Reformers in Chicago were simply unwilling to wait for a mid-century type liberal political resurgence, a new civil rights movement or a new war on poverty, to fix our whole society before trying to improve the educational opportunities available to the city's disadvantaged students. To agree, as most Chicago reformers do, that school reform cannot deal with all the disadvantages kids bring to the schools is not the same thing as saying there is nothing the schools can do to improve the educational opportunities they are now providing students. The 'either/or' perspective adopted by defenders of liberal political correctness such as Orfield alienates others with a liberal perspective who have to deal with the failed results of the mid-century liberal 'so-called' solutions. If 'liberals' are unwilling to recognize the failures of their own attempts at solutions, how liberal are they?

However, there is another dimension to the Chicago reform effort which is outside the purview of the typical liberal–conservative debate. The Chicago school reform effort shifts the boundaries of what is traditionally thought of as 'schooling'. Under this reform effort, schooling in urban centers is re-established in the context of local community, from which it had been extracted as part of the rationalizing, bureaucratic reforms of the early decades of this century.[3]

In most communities in the us, schools represent at least half of the local political life through elections to the school board and referenda votes on educational resources. School funding typically represents more than 60 percent of the tax bills of Illinois' property owners. Schools represent one of the major focuses for discussions about the nature and future of local communities. In the urban us, this discussion has been stripped away from city residents and neighborhood organizations. Under Chicago school reform, with biannual elections of Local School Council members, this political discussion is re-emerging. Designs for Change (1991) reported that the number of elected black and Hispanic school board members nationally nearly doubled after the first LSC elections. A new level of political leadership is being developed, the ramifications of which are not yet fully clear (see Poinsett 1990).

Second, neither traditional liberals nor traditional conservatives take seriously the energy that is released when local communities are empowered to address their own identified problems. As Don Moore (1992) has pointed out, when parents are involved in school improvement planning, the problems which are identified are frequently very different from the problems identified by school professionals. Consequently, the resources available to address problems are also far broader. When schools are part of an inaccessible, encapsulated system, they are both protected from and unable to utilize the vitality of the communities in which they are set.

Finally, by loosening the bureaucratic control, the opportunities for innovation are multiplied. Innovation ceases to be a top-down policy initiative accompanying each change in superintendent, innovations notorious for their ineffective implementation. Instead, each local entity becomes a potential innovation site. Already in Chicago, more than 170 schools have been identified (Hess 1992) where new national reform efforts have been established, ranging from curricular innovation such as the Algebra Project or the Illinois Writing Project, to pedagogical changes implicit in the Accelerated Schools approach or cooperative learning, to organizational reorientation through projects in Total Quality Management.

It is not clear that the Chicago reforms will be successful. At the midway point in the initial five-year focus of the reform act, progress was exciting from an organizational development perspective. The system's resources had been redirected. Authority had begun to shift. New leadership had been installed in nearly half of the newly semi-autonomous subunits of the system. Plans for improvement had been adopted at all units, with varying likelihood of producing significant change.

But, from the perspective of whether the changes that had occurred would impact the way students learn in Chicago's schools, and therefore have a significant effect on student achievement levels, the picture was less encouraging. In less than a quarter of the schools had LSCS adopted plans which would dramatically change the instructional program of the schools. Many schools had 'added-on' new programs and extra assistance for lower performing students. Few had fundamentally altered the way in which students would encounter teachers in Chicago's school buildings, however. As critics of the left (Sizer 1988) and right (Finn and Clements 1990) have noted, unless really radical change is undertaken, it may not be enough. The question for Chicago is whether the school councils which have attacked important non-instructional problems like overcrowding, gang influences and disruption, discipline, deteriorating facilities and low attendance can begin to focus on the instructional programs of the schools in their next stage of development. For it is only then that we might expect to see the new strategy at the heart of Chicago's school reform effort produce the radical change called for by the critics of both left and right.

Notes

1. As president of the Coalition for Educational Rights Under the Constitution, a coalition of progressive groups supporting the more than sixty school districts in Illinois suing to prove the current state school finance system is unconstitutional, I expect this strategy to continue to be quite beneficial in some circumstances.
2. Observation recorded in field notes of author's postdoctoral study (Hess 1984) supported by Northwestern University Program in Ethnography and Public Policy (NUPEPP). Much of the data included in this chapter is drawn from similar participant-observer field notes compiled during the past twelve years.
3. I am indebted to Stanley J. Hallett for stimulating these observations.

References

BERNE, R. and STIEFEL, L. (1984) *The Measurement of Equity in School Finance* (Baltimore: The Johns Hopkins University Press).

BROOKOVER, W. B. (1991) 'So Far, Reform not so Good', *Catalyst*, III (3) pp. 15–17.

CHICAGO TRIBUNE (1988) *Chicago's Schools: 'Worst in America'* (Chicago: Author).

CHICAGO UNITED (1981) *Report of the Special Task Force on Education* (Chicago: Author).

CHUBB, J. E. and MOE, T. M. (1990) *Politics, Markets, and America's Schools* (Washington, DC: Brookings Institution).

COOPER, B. S. (1990) 'A Tale of Two Cities: Radical School Reform in Chicago and London', an unpublished paper presented to the American Educational Research Association, Boston.

CRAIN, R. L. and STRAUSS, J. (1985) *Student Desegregation and Black Occupational Attainment: Results from a Long Term Experiment* (Baltimore: The Center for Social Organization of Schools, Johns Hopkins University).

DEMING, W. E. (1982) *Quality, Productivity and Competitive Position* (Cambridge, MA: MIT Press).

DESIGNS FOR CHANGE (1985a) *The Bottom Line: Chicago's Failing Schools and How to Save Them* (Chicago: Author).

DESIGNS FOR CHANGE (1985b) *All Our Kids Can Learn to Read* (Chicago: Author).

DESIGNS FOR CHANGE (1991) *Closer Look*, 1, February (Chicago: Author).

EASTON, J. Q. (ed.) (1991) *Decision Making and School Improvement: Local School Councils During the Second Year of School Reform* (Chicago: Chicago Panel on Public School Policy and Finance).

EASTON, J. Q. and HESS, G. A., JR (1990) *The Changing Racial Enrollment Patterns in Chicago's Schools* (Chicago: Chicago Panel on Public School Policy and Finance).

ELMORE, R. E. (1988) 'Models of Restructuring Schools', unpublished paper presented at the American Educational Research Association, New Orleans.

ETHERIDGE, C. P. and COLLINS, T. W. (1992) 'Conflict in Restructuring the Principal-Teacher Relationship in Memphis', in G. A. HESS, Jr (ed.) *Empowering Teachers and Parents: School Restructuring Through the Eyes of Anthropologists* (New York: Bergin & Garvey).

FINN, C. and CLEMENTS, S. K. (1990) 'Complacency Could Blow "Grand Opportunity"', *Catalyst*, 1 (4) pp. 2–6.

GLASS, T. E. and SANDERS, W. D. (1978) *Community Control in Education: A Study in Power Transition* (Midland, MI: Pendell).

HALLETT, A. C. and HESS, G. A., JR (1982) *Budget Cuts at the Board of Education* (Chicago: Chicago Panel on Public School Finances).

HANSON, M. K., MORRIS, D. R. and COLLINS, R. A. (1992) 'Empowerment of Teachers in Dade County's School-Based Management Pilot', in G. A. HESS, JR (ed.) *Empowering Teachers and Parents: School Restructuring Through the Eyes of Anthropologists* (New York: Bergin & Garvey).

HESS, G. A., JR (1984) 'Renegotiating a Multicultural Society: Participation in Desegregation Planning in Chicago', *The Journal of Negro Education*, 53 (2) pp. 132–46.

HESS, G. A., JR (1986) 'Educational Triage in an Urban School Setting', *Metropolitan EDUCATION*, 2, Fall pp. 39–52.

HESS, G. A., JR (1991) *School Restructuring, Chicago Style* (Newbury Park, CA: Corwin Press).

HESS, G. A., JR (1992) *School Restructuring, Chicago Style: A Midway Report* (Chicago: Chicago Panel on Public School Policy and Finance).

HESS, G. A., JR and EASTON, J. Q. (1992) 'Who's Making What Decisions: Monitoring Authority Shifts in Chicago School Reform', in G. A. HESS, JR (ed.) *Empowering Teachers and Parents: School Restructuring Through the Eyes of Anthropologists* (New York: Bergin & Garvey).

HESS, G. A., JR and LAUBER, D. (1985) *Dropouts from the Chicago Public Schools* (Chicago: Chicago Panel on Public School Finances).

HESS, G. A., JR and WARDEN, C. (1988) 'Who Benefits from Desegregation Now?' *The Journal of Negro Education*, 57 (4) pp. 536–51.

HESS, G. A., JR, WELLS, E., PRINDLE, C., KAPLAN, B. and LIFFMAN, P. (1987) *'Where's Room 185?' How Schools Can Reduce Their Dropout Problem* (Chicago: Chicago Panel on Public School Policy and Finance).

HOWE, H. (1988) cited in *Update*, a 30 November release from Designs for Change (Chicago: Author).

KATZ, M. B. (1992) 'Chicago School Reform as History', *Teachers College Record*, 94 (1) pp. 56–72.

KING, T. (1987) *Reassessment of the Report of 1981 Special Task Force on Education* (Chicago: Chicago United).

KOZOL, J. (1968) *Death at an Early Age* (Boston: Houghton Mifflin Company).

Kozol, J. (1991) *Savage Inequalities* (New York: Crown Publishers, Inc).

Lieberman, M. (1988) 'A Brief Analysis of the Illinois Education Reform Act', *Government Union Review*, 10 (2) pp. 23–30.

Mirel, J. (1990) 'What History Can Teach Us about School Decentralization', *Network News & Views*, 9 (8) pp. 40–47.

Monti, D. J. (1986) '*Brown's* Velvet Cushion: Metropolitan Desegregation and the Politics of Illusion', *Metropolitan EDUCATION*, 1, Spring, pp. 52–67.

Moore, D. R. (1992) 'The Case for Parent and Community Involvement', in G. A. Hess, Jr (ed.) *Empowering Teachers and Parents: School Restructuring Through the Eyes of Anthropologists* (New York: Bergin & Garvey).

Moore, D. R. and Radford-Hill, S. (1982) *Caught in the Web: Misplaced Children in Chicago's Classes for the Mentally Retarded* (Chicago: Designs for Change).

Muncey, D. E. and McQuillan, P. J. (1992) 'The Dangers of Assuming a Consensus for Change: Some Examples from the Coalition of Essential Schools', in G. A. Hess, Jr (ed.) *Empowering Teachers and Parents: School Restructuring Through the Eyes of Anthropologists* (New York: Bergin & Garvey).

National Commission on Excellence in Education (1983) *A Nation at Risk: The Imperative for Educational Reform* (Washington, DC: Government Printing Office).

Orfield, G. (1986) 'Knowledge, Ideology, and School Desegregation: Views Through Different Prisms', *Metropolitan EDUCATION*, 1 (Spring) pp. 92–99.

Orfield, G. (1991) 'Forward', in P. Scheirer, *Poverty, Not Bureaucracy: Poverty, Segregation, and Inequality in Metropolitan Chicago Schools* (Chicago: Metropolitan Opportunities Project, University of Chicago).

Poinsett, A. (1990) 'School Reform, Black Leaders: Their Impact on Each Other', *Catalyst*, 1 (4) pp. 7–11, 43.

Purkey, S. C. and Smith, M. S. (1983) 'Effective Schools: A Review', *The Elementary School Journal*, 81 (1) pp. 426–52.

Rogers, D. and Chung, N. H. (1983) *110 Livingston Street Revisited: Decentralization in Action* (New York: New York University Press).

Rosenbaum, J. E., Kulieke, M. J. and Rubinowitz, L. S. (1987) 'Low-income Black Children in White Suburban Schools: A Study of School and Student Responses', *Journal of Negro Education*, 56 (1) pp. 35–43.

Sizer, T. (1988) 'Letter to All Coalition Schools', quoted in Muncey, D. McQuillan, P. J. (1992) 'The Dangers of Assuming a Consensus for Change: Some Examples from the Coalition of Essential Schools', in G. A. Hess, Jr (ed.) *Empowering Teachers and Parents: School Restructuring Through the Eyes of Anthropologists* (New York: Bergin & Garvey).

Tatel, D. S., Lanigan, K. J. and Sneed, M. F. (1986) 'The Fourth Decade of *Brown*: Metropolitan Desegregation and Quality Education', *Metropolitan EDUCATION*, Spring, pp. 15–35.

van den Berghe, P. L. (1973) 'Pluralism' in J. Honigman (ed.) *Handbook of Social and Cultural Anthropology* (Chicago: Rand, McNally & Company).

8

Democratic politics and school improvement: The potential of Chicago school reform

Sharon G. Rollow and Anthony S. Bryk

Chicago school reform is often misrepresented on the national scene where it tends to be described as anti-professional and a hearkening back to community control. Based on our research and involvement with Chicago school reform, we, like Hess, find that neither label adequately captures the subtlety of the political dynamics now at work in Chicago's schools. The reform created three distinct sites of power – parents and community, teachers, and the principal – each of which has new legitimacy and potential to challenge the status quo. We focus on the complex nature of Chicago's governance reform, and the politics that it has engendered in local schools during its early implementation. This democratic localism taxes traditional frameworks for studying school micro-politics. We also explore the largely ignored potential embedded in this reform to revitalize urban communities by enhancing their democratic life. This essay offers a commentary on 'Race and the Liberal Perspective in Chicago School Reform' by G. Alfred Hess, Jr. It draws on our own research and involvement with Chicago School Reform.

In 'Race and the Liberal Perspective in Chicago School Reform', Hess argues that the liberal strategies of the 1960s – centralization of responsibility and bureaucratization of service delivery – failed to produce a quality education for Chicago's students. Instead of advancing equality of opportunity, these strategies were used by professionals at the central office and school level to promote a variety of interests other than serving children. By the late 1980s, the Chicago Public Schools (CPS) had lost its agency. Despite a decade of efforts with desegregation, the system had failed to improve the education of minority youth. Low achievement levels, high dropout rates and racial isolation were pervasive. Entitlement funds were misused, and a bloated central office and bureaucratized teachers' union squelched initiative and resulted in a system where innovative principals had to be 'creatively insubordinant'. Parents' voices had been silenced and reform-minded teachers were equally disenfranchised.

According to Hess, Chicago reformers sought in Public Act 85–1418 a pragmatic redress to these abuses. Grounded in the repeated failures of the school bureaucracy to initiate constructive action, the reform movement came to accept the idea that fundamental governance change was a prerequisite to school improvement in Chicago. The existing power structure maintained dysfunctional schools. A strong shock to destabilize this status quo was necessary before meaningful improvements could occur.

We applaud the mobilization effort for Chicago school reform and the important role played by key organizations, such as the Chicago Panel on Public School Policy and Finance which Hess directs. During the mobilization stage, the reform movement catalyzed a diverse constituency among business, community-based organizations (CBOs), and advocacy groups. The dialogue among these various individuals and groups was broadly participatory and democratic, and culminated in Chicago's unique approach to school change (Moore 1990, Rollow 1990, Hess 1991, O'Connell, 1991).

We also agree with Hess that Chicago school reform is often misrepresented on the national scene where it tends to be described as anti-professional and as a hearkening back to community control. In our view, neither of these labels adequately captures the complexity and subtlety of the political dynamics now at work in Chicago's schools. Real authority and new resources have devolved to individual schools, and many principals, teachers, parents and community members are at work trying to solve local problems. Although it is still too early to judge the effects of these efforts on student learning, it appears that many of the old ways of conducting school business have been shattered and a restructured system, including a new role for the central office, is likely to emerge.

In trying to redress the misunderstandings about Chicago's school reform, Hess's chapter emphasizes the practical character of the reform, in particular, how it draws on understandings about effective schools and efforts to improve organizational performance through decentralization. Both sets of ideas were frequently cited during the mobilization phase for reform, and continue as a part of the public rhetoric shaping efforts in the city (Wong and Rollow 1990). PA 85–1418 also has, however, a more profound side than these instrumentalist arguments convey. It represents a direct assault on 'big government' and the vested interests that interlock with such government. As an alternative, however, it does not offer the currently touted panacea of 'choice and markets', but rather an enhanced democratic localism (Katz 1987). Although its specific aim is to improve student achievement, it also represents a new form of institutional arrangements potentially applicable to a wide range of human services.

In attempting to complement and build on the observations offered by Hess, we step back a bit to focus on some larger issues concerning school politics embedded in PA 85–1418 and what we are learning about them from the early implementation of the legislation. Our reflections derive from several sources: a case study project that has enabled us to be participant-observers in twelve diverse Chicago elementary school communities for the past two years; an intensive multi-year involvement in a school development project where we seek to support the comprehensive restructuring efforts of a small number of Chicago elementary schools; and two major citywide surveys of teachers and principals in which we have collaborated under the umbrella of the Consortium on Chicago School Research.[1]

Our remarks focus on the complex nature of Chicago's governance reform, specifically how understanding the political activity that has developed during its early implementation taxes traditional frameworks for studying school micro-politics. We also explore the largely ignored potential embedded in this reform to revitalize urban communities by enhancing their democratic life. While we are intrigued by these possibilities, we are also sanguine about the difficulties that can be encountered in realizing these aims in truly disadvantaged urban neighborhoods.

A complex system of school governance

In our view, PA 85–1418 involves both a more radical and a more sophisticated conception of school reform than most of its critics and even advocates acknowledge. In response to the entrenched, dysfunctional power relations that had calcified in the CPS, PA 85–1418 sought to do three things. First, it replaced traditional bureaucratic control of schools with a complex local school politics. The vertical 'problem-solution path', where local school officials looked up into the system for guidance, was rebalanced toward a greater engagement of school professionals with their local communities.

Similarly, parents and community members no longer had to fight with a distant central authority over local school issues. Rather, Local School Councils (LSC) were established to make schools more responsive and accountable to their students and community (Rollow 1990, Hess 1991, O'Connell 1991).

Second, at the school level, the Act legitimated new roles for teachers, parents and community members and the principal, and in so doing promoted three distinct 'sites of power' (Bowles and Gintis 1987). The powers afforded the LSC gave parents and community members explicit authority to influence decision-making in schools. Less often acknowledged, however, are the new opportunities for principals and teachers to participate in school decision-making, initiate activity and take responsibility for school improvement. Hess enumerates the new authority that devolved to school principals under reform, and he also explains that teachers, through the Professional Personnel Advisory Committee (PPAC), have an opportunity now to shape directly the instructional program of their school. Perhaps even more important in terms of school micro-politics is the fact that the faculty can now influence the choice of their principal by virtue of their two votes on the LSC. This change is both highly significant and potentially problematic. It creates a unique dynamic whereby principals are charged with evaluating annually a faculty which in turn has an opportunity every four years to influence whether that principal's contract will be renewed.

Thus, Chicago reform both encourages and legitimates greater engagement, not only by parents and community members, but also by principals and teachers. In essence it rebalances relations at the school level such that parents and community, teachers and the principal each become a significant 'site of power' with potential to challenge established relations and organizational practices. Moreover, the legislation creates a complex system of checks and balances across the three sites of power. Ineffective representatives on the LSC and PPAC can be voted out of office by their constituents. The contract of a non-responsive principal may not be renewed by an LSC. School faculties can organize to press on the principal and LSC for their own visions of school improvement.

Third, to counterbalance the emphasis on local empowerment, accountability provisions were also enacted to pull all schools toward educational improvement and high standards of achievement. As Hess notes, these consisted of explicit educational goals for children, and an extended set of school objectives. The Act also mandated a School Improvement Plan in an attempt to introduce elements of strategic planning and to rationalize local school decision-making. As part of this process, the school system is required to report annually on each school's progress toward these goals and non-improving schools are then subject to a variety of increasingly severe sanctions. In essence, this combination of provisions and sanctions was intended to create another form of checks and balances. In this case, a restructured central office would stimulate local accountability and serve as another check on dysfunctioning schools.[2]

In general terms, then, the legislation attacked the failures of the Chicago school system by weakening central control and by turning over to parents and community members, teachers and the principal some real authority and resources to solve local problems. To guide these developments toward valued ends, however, the legislation also added specific goals, objectives, and an accountability and strategic planning process. The aim was to create an overall environment in the CPS that would promote local change.

Moving beyond the formal legislative provisions, it is also important to note the substantial expansion of institutional activity focused on educational improvement that has been precipitated by PA 85-1418. Over the last four years, numerous associations among the city's business and professional leaders have emerged to provide technical and financial assistance to individual schools and to advocate for them. Education has been a sustained focus of activity among existing civic groups and CBOs. The local philanthropic community has committed substantial new funds. Individual faculty members from colleges and universities in the metropolitan area have become more active in Chicago's schools, and several new research, development and professional education centers have emerged. In the past, many of these individuals and institutions felt discouraged by their encounters with a seemingly disinterested school bureaucracy. Now, taken as a group, these various organizations constitute another external site of power, complementing the efforts of the central office to stimulate school innovation and to exhort continued local efforts at improvement.

At this point it is clear that the CPS is in the midst of a major organizational re-structuring. Neither the Board of Education, nor the central office, nor any other single entity is controlling this change process; rather, power is broadly diffused with extensive conversations about school improvement being sustained throughout the city. Moreover, the content of this conversation is evolving and these changing understandings are influencing policy. In 1989, when the reform was first implemented, attention focused almost exclusively on the formation and training of LSCs. Now conversations have shifted to the kinds of additional resources and institutional supports needed by local schools to effect substantive changes in classrooms.

Traditional views of school politics

Much of what provokes unease in external audiences about Chicago school reform is that the conception of local democratic activity which undergirds it, is quite different from traditional conceptions of school politics which offer a rather cynical and unflat-tering picture of a 'jungle' where individuals and groups compete to advance their particular interests.[3] Marginal changes may be affected by this competition but the basic structure of the system, and expecially the power relations within it, remain unchallenged.[4]

To be sure, we have observed interest politics in individual Chicago school com-munities. PA 85-1418 opened school doors to the neighborhood and, not surprisingly, pressing community issues have found their way into the school. In one of our field site communities, for example, gentrification is occurring. Correspondingly, the LSC is factionalized between the interests of the developers (and the affluent residents they are bringing into the neighborhood) and an older CBO which advocates for the low-income families who are being forced out. The allocation of discretionary monies in this school has become a main arena for political contest. While the low-income community group wants to encourage a greater involvement of poor parent and community members by hiring some of these individuals as tutors, the school staff, along with some of the newer community residents, prefer to use the funds to create additional certified positions.

Such activities are consistent with accounts of the earlier school decentralization in New York, where the basic elements of 'big city' politics – fights over contracts and jobs – were largely transferred from the citywide Board of Education to district-level boards. Although the context shifted, the basic nature of political activity did not (Fantini and Gittell 1973). Nonetheless, there is an important difference between the Chicago decentralization and that in New York. The fundamental governance unit in Chicago is the individual school, not a district-level board. As a result, the distance between the site of political activity and its consequences have been radically reduced. Individual accountability for political activity is now more sharply drawn.

The introduction of parents and community members into this new local school politics also appears to have changed the nature of this activity, at least in some schools. As Ball (1987) notes, educational decision-making is typically dominated by professionals and involves a deliberate attempt to depoliticize local problems. Public choices about common affairs are viewed as technical issues requiring experts and other managers to solve them. This professionalization of the public realm displaces more fundamental discussions among citizens about their schools including the 'opportunity to debate the definition of the school' (Ball 1987: 268). In contrast, in those Chicago schools where parents are actively involved, we have seen LSC members press a more personal and particularistic perspective about what 'our school' must do to meet the needs of 'our children'.[5]

A politics of school community enablement

In short, the full breadth of the political activity occurring in Chicago's schools is not adequately captured by a conception of school politics which reduces all activities to a competition among individuals and groups over scarce resources. In expanding on this pluralist bargaining frame, we have turned to the writings of Mansbridge (1980), Barber (1984), Evans and Boyte (1986), Bowles and Gintis (1987), Katz (1987), Lindblom (1990) and Bellah *et al.* (1991). These authors maintain that a renewed democratic politics, rooted in sustained local participation, is the necessary antidote to unresponsive societal institutions – like the CPS. They remind us of the importance of public discussion about common affairs, of the educational opportunities inherent in such conversations, and how over the long term, this activity can help institutions become more self-guided. Such enhanced democratic localism holds potential for enabling school communities to create an alternative vision of education for their children, or in Hess's words to 're-establish schools in the context of local community' (see p. 93, this volume).

This conception of school politics encourages us to attend to the nature of political discourse in school communities. Who is involved, what concepts appear salient and how are they being advanced? Do parents and community members bring forth new interests that challenge existing ones? Now that individual principals and teachers are free to express views that are distinct from the central office, what issues do they introduce? Of key concern is whether the definition of the school – its mission, goals, organization, operations, and relationship to the broader community – is subject to challenge.

The spirit of the reform legislation and the broader discussions about schooling that are occurring across the city can play an important role in this regard. This rhetoric challenges each school community to create an institution that is sensitive to the needs of its specific population and one where 'all children' will succeed and no child will fail. If taken seriously at a local school, these ideas can act as a powerful counterforce to a politics of private interests. In such a school, the efforts of an LSC parent seeking to improve educational opportunities for his or her own child can evolve into a concern for advancing the welfare of all children. Similarly, efforts by teachers to improve their work conditions can motivate a re-examination of school organization and operations to see how students' needs can be better served.

Places where such activity is occurring are marked by sustained debate over the key ideas that vie for moral authority and what these ideas mean in terms of specific school improvement plans. To be sure, individuals disagree and conflicts can be intense. But when these debates are about matters of broad concern, rather than narrow personal gains, differences in perspective can often be transformed into common interests. This is different from pluralist bargaining, which at its best produces a compromise among fixed interests, and at its worst creates winners and losers and leaves participants in an apprehensive stance toward each other. In contrast, when a participatory, democratic politics is successfully engaged, the base of shared understandings grows, positive sentiments and trust among participants rise, and the capacity of the school community to tackle even larger problems expands. Over time, a detailed scrutiny of existing organizational practices becomes possible.

On balance, the road to an effective democratic localism is neither easy nor assured and it is not without its own distinctive problems. Parochialism and an intolerance toward strangers and new ideas are potential pitfalls (Barber 1984). Moreover, many Chicago school communities suffer from high student and family mobility, a history of hostility between parents and school professionals, and a neighborhood context plagued by poverty and violence and a consequent overriding concern for personal safety and survival. When combined with a cynical view that politics means 'taking care of your own', these are not favorable conditions for the emergence of democratic localism.

These concerns notwithstanding, the idea of school communities as sites of strong democratic practice (Barber 1984) remains appealing. This seems especially so when we acknowledge that in this instance the aim of political activity – school improvement – is not a quick fix. Rather, school change necessitates the development of trusting personal relationships among parents and community, teachers and the principal, and requires that these relationships be sustained if stakeholders are to take risks, work together and stay committed for the long haul. That is, a systemic change process demands a strong democratic practice.

An important role for normative understandings

At the core of strong democratic practice is sustained conversation. Chicago school reform substantially expanded the scope of this activity in individual schools and the dialogue that has ensued is highly specific to local context. Many basic school practices (for example, should students march between classrooms in orderly lines, or be required to wear uniforms?) which were simply taken for granted in the past or decided by administrative fiat are now subject to debate among parents, community members, teachers and the school principal. Each participant brings to these discussions his or her own personal views about what is 'good', 'proper' and 'right' for their school. Different normative ideas built up out of past family, school and work experiences are now transported into these deliberations and can become sources of conflict among those now responsible for their school. These disagreements can be particularly sharp in some schools because of the highly varied backgrounds among the participants.

Included here are assumptions about: what is a good school (a place that has the programs and resources of a suburban school versus one that may need to be structured differently to meet the needs of particular students and families); about what children should learn (specific knowledge and skills to be acquired versus a view of students as active learners); about how children and parents should be treated, and how, in turn, children and parents should treat teachers; and especially in disadvantaged neighborhoods, about the school's responsibility to engage in adult education, parent education and a myriad of other activities intended to strengthen families and communities. In addition, since politics is the lever for school change in Chicago, individuals' understandings about the nature and purposes of political participation also come into play.

Although rooted in personal background and experience, normative understandings are not static. Rather they can be reshaped through social interaction in settings where different expectations and ideas prevail. The LSC holds potential as a context for such human development. Here parents, teachers and the principal can learn about each other, and in the course of the work that they are obligated to do together, forge a common interest. Through such interactions, basic understandings about roles, authority and domains of practice and responsibility can be recast and the institution itself renormed.

Ultimately, if such activity is maintained for a period of time, a more unitary form of politics (Mansbridge 1980) may emerge. Now matters of importance are regularly discussed, and conflict is less threatening because when it does occur there are avenues for resolution. The institution benefits from a substantial social resource formed out of both a set of principles held in common and the trusting face-to-face relationships built up within the small confines of a single school community.

The transition from governance change to school improvement: A need for technical knowledge and expertise

Currently, Chicago is awash with 'Christmas tree' schools where large amounts of discretionary money have combined with private gifts to add new programs and more equipment, a bit like hanging dazzling ornaments on a tree. Unfortunately, the tree itself and its basic needs have gone unattended.[6] Awareness of this problem, however, is growing across the city and a new wisdom is emerging that the core of schooling – teachers' knowledge and classroom practices – must be substantially improved.

This development, however, points to a major unresolved issue: How can technical expertise be drawn into enhanced local democratic activity? Schools are relatively complex entities where efficiency is highly valued. Past experiences with most educational innovations leaves us less than sanguine about how well most schools will fare at developing their own strategic plans. While some may do fine on their own, many will need to engage sustained outside assistance if the end result of the social participation occurring in schools is improvement in student learning.

How these new relationships are to be forged remains unclear. Instructional guidance in the form of top-down mandates from the central office were rarely effective in the past and seem highly inappropriate now. Similarly, the experiences of the last three years where schools have had increased freedom to purchase their own goods and services are not very encouraging (although some individual schools are notable exceptions).[7] In short, neither the command authority of a school bureaucracy nor the contractual relationship of the marketplace seems particularly well-suited for this purpose.

Interestingly, the new literature on enhanced democratic participation cited earlier is largely silent on the question of how local political practice might engage effectively with outside expertise. In our view, new forms of cooperative relationships between local schools and outside assistance appear necessary. The external expert as supervisor or as service provider will not suffice. Rather, these individuals must become more fully engaged in the political practice of a school community and share a stake in the outcomes of their efforts. These lessons gleaned here from Chicago's experiences should be of broad interest as they touch on larger, enduring concerns about the proper role of technical expertise in a democratic society.[8]

Effective local initiative depends upon a broad base of resources

In his discussion, Hess suggests that Chicago's school reform has potential not only to change schools but also their communities: 'to re-establish schools in the context of local community' and in so doing to develop a new generation of political leadership. This leadership will in turn be able to sustain political discussion 'about the nature and future of local communities' (p. 93). That school reform might stimulate this kind of activity represents an important side benefit of reform, arguably as important to the future and revitalization of our cities as it is to the improvement of local schools. The opportunities afforded here for individuals to develop public skills of citizenship, leadership and political discourse are essential to a revitalized democratic life. They resonate well with Lindblom's (1990) discussion of a need for a more self-guided society, Barber's (1984) considerations of the features of a strong democracy, Bowles and Gintis's (1987) analysis of the link between adult learning and political practice, and Evans and Boyte's (1986) notion of the educative function of 'free spaces'.

The emergence of 'truly disadvantaged' urban communities (Wilson 1987), however, raises questions about the viability of these aims and more generally about the efficacy of the reform itself in some neighborhoods. It can be very difficult to assemble and maintain the personal human connections on which democratic localism depends in places where residents are overwhelmed by poverty, violence, and social isolation.

A recent case study of 'Alexander school' (Moultrie 1992, see also Rollow and Bryk 1993) details these difficulties in the context of a highly impoverished and racially isolated African American neighborhood. The distrust, mobility and social malaise that characterizes this community also permeates the school. Despite efforts by the principal, some teachers and a few parents, none of these sites of power has been able to catalyze and sustain the level of activity needed to promote school change. Interestingly, considerable external expertise was available to this school, but it was not used consistently and effectively. Ironically, while Chicago school reform can enhance the human capabilities of individuals and promote social solidarity among groups, the reform also makes demands on these same human and social resources for its initiation and growth.

Some recent survey evidence allows us to generalize a bit from these case study findings. Many school principals reported in Bennett et al. (1992) that a diverse range of innovative practices had been catalyzed in their schools by reform. In a subset of perhaps 15 to 20 percent of the schools in the CPS, however, little has changed. Like Alexander, these schools 'left behind by reform' tend to be racially isolated, serve almost exclusively low-income students and have very low achievement levels. Interestingly, there is another subset of perhaps 10 to 15 percent of the schools with virtually identical demographic characteristics as the schools left behind, but where reform instead has catalyzed a broad upsurge of human activity and innovative educational practices. Three factors appear to distinguish between these 'recently restructuring' schools and those left behind. The restructuring schools have more positive social relations with their school communities, most have recently hired an efficacious principal, and they make more extensive use of outside technical expertise.

It is important to note that no single demographic or other descriptive characteristic of schools discriminates between those that appear to be embracing restructuring and those that are not. Thus, like the reform itself, its initial effects are not simple. Even so, these early findings do raise questions about the ability of *all* schools to become the 'potential innovation sites' that Hess (p. 94) and others (see for example Moore 1992) advocate. Without a base of social and human resources in at least one of the three sites of power in a school community, the status quo seems unlikely to be challenged. Moreover, just as Hess asserts that there may need to be a variety of strategies to accomplish equity goals when it comes to finance (e.g. treating equals equally and unequals unequally, p. 90), so too schools may need a mix of resources – human, intellectual and social as well as fiscal – to fully realize the goals of reform. Finally, when these resources are not present in a school community, it becomes imperative that external sources fill this void. Creating a mechanism for this external initiative and support for school development remains a challenge for Chicago school reform.

Notes

1. The Consortium on Chicago School Research is an independent federation of Chicago area organizations which have come together to undertake a range of research activities designed to assist school improvement in the city and assess its progress. Both the Center for School Improvement and the Chicago Panel on Public School Policy and Finance are members of the Consortium. (For a further discussion of the scope of work and organization of the Consortium see Bryk and Sebring, 1991).
2. The accountability and intervention functions described here have yet to be fully implemented by the CPS. Increasingly, reformers are focusing attention on the need to restructure the central office so functions such as these can be better accomplished in the future. Our intent is simply to describe part of the role envisioned under PA 85-1418 for a central office in a radically decentralized system.
3. See, for example, Bolman and Deal (1990).
4. The vast majority of past studies of educational politics have taken their lead from Peterson (1976) who focused on the pluralist bargaining that occurred among interest groups on Chicago's school board. More recently, this pluralist perspective has been used in investigations of the interactions between principals and teachers. See, for example, Ball (1987).
5. Hess cites Moore (1992) to make a similar point about the consequences of parent involvement in school governance.
6. Especially popular are computer systems that are now sold directly to schools and promise to help children on standardized tests like the Iowa Test of Basic Skills, but in fact deliver computerized drill sheets that directly mimic the tests. In fact, under decentralization, local schools have become a new market for an expanding network of entrepreneurs.
7. See, for example, Bennett *et al.* (1992) for information about principals' efforts to seek outside expertise from the central office as well as a variety of advocacy and educational institutions, and other organizations.
8. To be sure, these concerns are not new, although they may appear more pressing now than ever. For a prescient account see Dewey (1926) in *The Public and Its Problems*.

References

BALL, S. J. (1987) *The Micro-Politics of the School: Towards a Theory of School Organization* (London: Methuen and Co., Ltd).

BARBER, B. B. (1984) *Strong Democracy: Participatory Politics for a New Age* (Berkeley: University of California Press).

BELLAH, R. M., MADSEN, R., SULLIVAN, W. M., SWIDLER, A. and TIPTON, S. M. (1991) *The Good Society* (New York: Knopf, Inc.)

BENNETT, A. L. *et al.* (1992) *Charting Reform: The Principals' Perspective* (Chicago: Consortium on Chicago School Research).

BOLMAN, L. B. and DEAL, T. C. (1990) *Reframing Organizations* (San Francisco: Jossey Bass).

BOWLES, S. and GINTIS, H. (1987) *Democracy and Capitalism: Property, Community and the Contradictions of Modern Social Thought* (New York: Basic Books, Inc.).

BRYK A. S and SEBRING, P. (1991) *Achieving School Reform in Chicago: What We Need to Know* (Chicago: Consortium on Chicago School Research).

CHICAGO SCHOOL REFORM (1989) Public Act 85-1418 (General Assembly of the State of Illinois, Springfield, IL).

DEWEY, J. (1926) *The Public and Its Problems* (Chicago: The University of Chicago Press).

EVANS, S. M. and BOYTE, H. C. (1986) *Free Spaces: The Sources of Democratic Change in America* (Chicago: University of Chicago Press).

FANTINI, M. and GITTELL, M. (1973) *Decentralization: Achieving Reform* (New York: Praeger Press).

HESS, G. A. (1991) *School Restructuring, Chicago Style* (Newbury Park: Corwin Press, Inc.).

HESS, G. A. (1992) *School Restructuring, Chicago Style: A Midway Report* (Chicago: Chicago Panel on Public School Finance).

KATZ, M. B. (1987) *Reconstructing American Education* (Cambridge, MA: Harvard University Press).

LINDBLOM, C. E. (1990) *Inquiry and Change* (New Haven: Yale University Press).

MANSBRIDGE, J. J. (1980) *Beyond Adversary Democracy* (Chicago: The University of Chicago Press).

MOORE, D. R. (1990) 'Voice and choice in Chicago', in CLUNE, W. H. and WITTE, J. F. (eds) *Choice and Control in American Education* (London: Falmer Press).

MOORE, D. R. (1992) 'The case for parent and community involvement', in HESS, A. G. (ed.) *Empowering Teachers and Parents: School Restructuring through the Eyes of Anthropologists* (New York: Bergin & Garvey).

MOULTRIE, L. (1992) 'The school reform left behind', MA thesis (Chicago: University of Chicago).

O'CONNELL, M. (1991) 'School reform Chicago style: How citizens organized to change public policy', *The Neighborhood Works* (Chicago: The Center for Neighborhood Technology).

PETERSON, P. E. (1976) *School Politics Chicago Style* (Chicago: The University of Chicago Press).

ROLLOW, S. G. (1990) 'Populism and professionalsim: School reform in Chicago', unpublished paper (Chicago: University of Chicago).

ROLLOW, S. and BRYK, A. S. (1993) 'Implementing Chicago school reform: Micro-politics in two Chicago elementary schools', in HELEEN, O. and THOMPSON, S. (eds) *Equity and Choice* (Newbury Park: Corwin Press).

WILSON, W. J. (1987) *The Truly Disadvantaged: The Inner City, the Underclass, and Public Policy* (Chicago: The University of Chicago Press).

WONG, K. and ROLLOW, S. (1990) *From Mobilization to Legislation: A Case Study of Chicago School Reform* (Chicago: University of Chicago, The Administrator's Notebook).

9

Do African American males need race and gender segregated education?: An educator's perspective and a legal perspective

Kevin Brown

With the waning of the commitment to desegregation, many in the African American community are beginning to advocate separate education, especially for African American males, as a way to respond to the 'crisis' in the black community. Educational justifications for separate education recognizes that dominant us culture and African American culture exert an inevitable, unique and negative influence on the social environment of African American males which should be incorporated into the teaching techniques and strategies developed for their education. The legal system, in contrast, sees individuals as primarily responsible for determining the influences of culture on their lives. as a result, the best justifications for separate education for black males requires the acceptance by the legal system of an influence it does not recognize.

In a special issue of *Ebony* magazine published in August 1983, the African American community was introduced to a provocative question posed by Walter Leavy: is the black male an endangered species?[1] To emphasize the deteriorating condition of the African American male, Leavy pointed to a number of statistics regarding the condition of the African American male, including homicide rates, rates of imprisonment, increases in the rates of suicides and infant mortality and a decrease in life expectancy.[2] The debate about the endangered black male has been carried into mainstream us society with proposals by a few public school systems to establish African American male classrooms or academies. These proposals have been one of the most controversial educational issues of the 1990s. Proposals for such education have surfaced in a number of cities, including Miami, Baltimore, Detroit, Milwaukee and New York.

Unlike segregationists of the 1950s and 1960s, the champions for these academies display a genuine concern for the interests of black male students. Supporters of these schools, taking their lead from Leavy, have generally argued that these schools are necessary to respond to the crisis facing black males both within and outside of educational institutions.[3] To demonstrate the existence of the crisis within educational institutions proponents point to dropout rates, low grade point averages, suspensions and expulsions and the numbers of African American males placed in remedial educational courses. As a group, they are at the top of the negative educational categories and at the bottom of the positive ones. To demonstrate the crisis facing African American males outside of educational institutions statistics regarding unemployment, homicides and the numbers of black males involved with the criminal justice system are typically cited.

Despite educational justifications, the legality of race and gender-segregated education for African American males is open to serious questions. For example, in *Garrett v. Board of Education*[4] a federal district court in August of 1991 granted a preliminary injunction against the Detroit school board's proposal for male academies. The litigation in the case was structured by the American Civil Liberties Union of Michigan and the National Organization of Women Legal Defense and Education Fund. The plaintiffs ignored the racially motivated decision-making by school officials involved in the decision to establish and operate male academies. They only presented the district court with a challenge to the gender-based exclusion of girls. The district court enjoined the implementation of the African American male academies, concluding that the Detroit plan would violate state law as well as Title IX, the Equal Educational Opportunities Act and the Fourteenth Amendment. The Detroit School Board has decided not to appeal the decision.[5]

Miami abandoned its plan to establish experimental classrooms for African American males after receiving a letter from the Department of Education indicating that it was the Department's position that the operation of such classrooms were illegal.[6] The Milwaukee School System, on advice of counsel, established immersion schools that are open to males and females.[7] These subsequent developments have prevented the operation of separate schools for African American males.[8]

This chapter will explore why some educators see separate education for African American males as necessary and why the legal system views such proposals with suspicion. The actual dispute about the educational necessity and the legality of separate education for African American males involves a fundamental clash of world views that cannot easily be harmonized. The legal obstacles faced by proponents of race and gender-segregated education for black males stem from a fundamentally different understanding about the role of culture in influencing the lives of individuals. Educational justifications for separate education recognizes that dominant US culture and African American culture exert an inevitable, unique and negative influence on the social environment of African American males which should be incorporated into the teaching techniques and strategies developed for their education.[9] The legal system, in contrast, sees individuals as primarily responsible for determining the influences of culture on their lives. As a result, the best justifications for separate education for black males requires the acceptance by the legal system of an influence it does not recognize.

Cultural justifications for African American male academies

Since education is primarily a socializing process, it is only natural that educators would be concerned about the influence of culture on the social environment of black males. African American males are socially embedded in two different cultures, dominant American culture and African American culture. The underlying assumption supporting racial and gender-segregated education for African American males is: their educational needs should not be divorced from the influence that significant cultural systems will exert on the attitudes, opinions and beliefs they hold, as well as the social experiences they will encounter when they interact with dominant culture.

Social construction of African American males in our dominant American culture

Becoming an individual in US society, or any other society, is done under the guidance of historically developed cultural systems of meanings. None of us are free agents who independently come to our own unique understanding of the world. Individual consciousness is always conditioned and influenced by the various cultural systems of meanings. These cultural systems of meanings provide a patterned system of knowledge and conceptions which a given group has evolved from its collective past and progressively modifies and augments to give meaning to and cope with the problems of its existence.[10] Cultural systems of meaning therefore provide the thought patterns which various groups use to interpret their reality.

In the United States, as in any given society, there is a dominant cultural system of meanings. Among the knowledge contained in the dominant US cultural system of meanings will be common knowledge related to the pragmatic competence in routine matters of individuals falling into various social categories. Significant social classifications in US society include the individual's occupation, academic credentials, race, gender, sexual orientation, socio-economic status and religion. Within the dominant culture each of the subcategories under these classifications carries with it certain pragmatic knowledge about the presumed personality traits of people who inhabit those subcategories.

Individuals acculturated into the dominant US cultural system of meaning will rely upon this pragmatic knowledge to interpret their interactions with others. This is often done without being aware of the fact that the individual is drawing upon these dominant cultural ideas. As a result the minds of most – if not at least at times all – people, will think with the aid of this pragmatic knowledge. It will ascribe personality characteristics to individuals that are consistent with those generally believed to be possessed by people who inhabit the particular social categories they inhabit. Individuals will experience such judgments of another's personality characteristics as a reflection of their rational deduction from their own objective observations. In this way the attitudes, opinions and beliefs about the personal characteristics of individuals that inhabit given social categories become initially ascribed to those individuals irregardless of whether they possess such qualities.[11]

The cultural knowledge of pragmatic competence attached to various social categories individuals inhabit will often form the presumed natural backdrop of social interactions. This is not to say that individuals are always automatically fixed, programmed or interpreted by the norms and expectations that flow from various social categories they are known to inhabit at any given moment. Individual actors may, and often do, choose to abide by or reject the dominant social norms and expectations attached to the social categories they or others inhabit at any given moment. The choice and the interpretation of their actions, however, are not made in a vacuum. They are made against a background of expectations flowing from those social categories.[12]

In the United States, individuals can both influence whether they inhabit most social categories and when they let others know that they inhabit those categories. For example, individuals have some control over their occupation, religion, educational credentials or marital status. In addition, most social categories which individuals inhabit, including those just mentioned, are generally not apparent. Many social categories that an individual inhabits will not enter into a given social situation unless the individual decides to interject them. As a result, Americans have a considerable amount of control over whether the judgments attached to most social categories that they inhabit will be introduced.

Race and gender are unlike almost any other social category. They are obviously not chosen and are also generally visible characteristics. As a result, these features of the individual will be presented when they are present. Therefore the individual cannot control when the dominant culture's socially constructed meanings for these categories asserts itself. The dominant American racial and gender attitudes and beliefs are the products of the United States' particular socio-historical racial and gender experience and heritage. Racial attitudes have played a central role in the US socio-historical experience, predating the establishment of the political union itself.[13] While the dominant social meanings about black people have changed over time, what it means to be black in the dominant American culture has always been defined in derogatory terms.

What sets African American males (and females) apart from the rest of those in US society is the fact that race and gender places them in a social category with a particularly negative social connotation. African Americans, particularly males, continue to be described as lazy, lustful, ignorant and prone to aggressive and criminal behavior. No matter how much an individual black male resists, these notions will exert a tremendous influence on their lives. As a result, to be a black male is to be classified in our dominant culture in such a way as to place one at a consistent disadvantage. These background conditions are not transitory, but will form the natural backdrop of many of their social relations throughout their entire lives.

Influence of cultural conflict in public education

Traditionally, public education in US society – even when formally referred to as multicultural – has employed an assimilation model.[14] Even though most Americans would view this model as culturally neutral or reflecting the appropriate culture, it nevertheless embodies the Anglo-American cultural bias of the dominant American culture. Despite this bias, this model has generally been successful when applied to voluntary immigrants from non-Anglo Europe, Central America and Asia. That success, however, has not been replicated by other racial and ethnic groups whose ancestors were not voluntary immigrants to the United States. Recent comparative work by educational anthropologists such as John Ogbu and Margaret Gibson has begun to document how involuntary minorities throughout the world respond to their educational experience differently from voluntary immigrants.[15] The poor academic performance in public schools by African Americans is replicated by other involuntary minorities throughout the world and in the United States like the Koreans and Burakumin in Japan, the Maoris in New Zealand, the Aborigines in Australia, and the American Indians and certain Latino groups in the United States.[16]

The success or failure of the traditional assimilation model of public education may, therefore, have a lot to do with the respective cultures of various ethnic groups. As ethnic groups approach public education, these groups tend to have their own cultural system of meanings that provides them with an alternative understanding from that of the dominant culture of how their host society works and their cultural group's place in that order. Their understanding of public education is a part of this overall understanding. The following is a brief summary of John Ogbu's distinction between how the cultures of voluntary immigrants and involuntary minorities, such as African Americans in the United States, interpret their group's experience in their host country.[17]

Voluntarily immigrating to a country in search of a better life provides the culture of immigrants with a very different reference point for understanding their economic, social, political and educational experience in that country. Ethnic groups coming to the United States, for example, generally immigrate because they believe that it will result in greater economic opportunities and more political freedom than existed at home. The culture of voluntary immigrants tends to compare their economic, social, political and educational situation to what they left behind. This comparison generally allows them to develop a positive comparative framework for interpreting their conditions in their new country. If voluntary immigrants did not generally believe they were better off in their host country, many of them could – and some of them do – exercise the option of returning to their native land.

Voluntary immigrants also come with their native culture intact. Their native culture is, therefore, not structured around the discrimination that they experience in their host country. Voluntary immigrants also see the cultural differences between themselves and dominant group members as something that they must overcome in order to achieve their goals for a better life. This after all, is what brought them to their host country originally. As a result, cultural and language differences enshrined in public schools are not generally perceived as oppositional nor as threats to the identity that they wished to maintain.

Voluntary immigrants can, and often do, face prejudice and discrimination in US society and public education. When confronted with this discrimination, the cultures of voluntary immigrants tend to interpret the economic, political and social barriers against them as temporary problems which can be overcome with the passage of time, hard work and more education. Their positive comparative framework provides them with a good deal of evidence to prove that despite the discrimination they face, they are still better off in their host country. By viewing the obstacles they face as flowing from their lack of knowledge about their host country, education becomes an important element in their strategy of getting ahead. Even though voluntary immigrants know their children may suffer from prejudice and discrimination and their culture is often disrespected by public schools, voluntary immigrants tend to view this as the price for the benefit derived from being in the new country. Their positive comparative framework is also aided by the fact that their view of public education is shaped by the condition of education in their homeland. Since opportunities for education in the United States generally far exceed opportunities provided for most immigrants in their native lands, it is even easier to maintain a favorable view of education despite prejudice and discrimination that may be encountered.

While voluntary immigrants come to their host country to improve their condition, involuntary minorities are brought into their present society through slavery, conquest or colonization. Their cultural experience of incorporation into their host society does not include the voluntary aspect of attempting to improve their lives that exists for voluntary immigrants. As a result, involuntary minorities differ from immigrants in their perceptions, interpretations and responses to their social, political, economic and educational situation. Involuntary minorities do not have a homeland in the same sense that voluntary immigrants do in which to make a comparative assessment of their condition. Their comparative reference tends to be the dominant group. Since the dominant group is generally better off, their comparative framework leads to a negative interpretation of their condition. Their cultural interpretation tends to lead toward resentment, perceiving themselves as victimized by institutionalized discrimination perpetuated against them by dominant group members and the institutions, such as public schools, that they control. As a result, involuntary minorities tend to distrust members of the dominant group and the societal institutions, including public schools, which they control.

The response of involuntary minorities to prejudice and discrimination is also very different. Unlike voluntary immigrants, they can not point to the fact that they are foreigners as a means in which to explain the prejudice or discrimination they encounter. They tend to understand the prejudice or discrimination that they experience in society and school as related to the fact that they are members of a victimized group. Unlike foreigners who view their condition in this society as temporary, involuntary minorities tend to view their condition as more or less permanent.

As an involuntary minority group, the culture of African Americans stands in a very different relational position to dominant US culture from that of the cultures of voluntary immigrants. As with other involuntary minorities, the cultural interaction between African Americans and the dominant group arose after the former became an involuntary minority. In order to live with subordination, the culture of African Americans developed coping responses. These responses are often perceived by African Americans as oppositional to that of the dominant-group. African American culture is therefore more at odds with that of the dominant American culture enshrined in public schools than the native culture brought to the United States by voluntary immigrants.

These cultural differences also function as boundary-maintaining mechanisms that differentiate involuntary minorities from their oppressors – dominant group members. They give involuntary minorities a sense of a social identity and self-worth. As a result – unlike voluntary immigrants – involuntary minorities interpret cultural differences as differences of identity to be maintained, not overcome. Accepting certain ideas and beliefs and learning certain aspects of the dominant group's culture is perceived as detrimental to their social identity.

I do not argue that African American culture is somehow better or worse than dominant US culture, only that it exists and that it is different. It provides those accul- turated into it with access to an alternative explanation for many social phenomena which African Americans individually and collectively encounter. This reference to culture does not rest upon the essentialist claim that all African American schoolchildren share an undifferentiated black culture. Certainly there are geographic, religious, class and color variations that affect the attitudes and behaviors of individual blacks. The proposals for separate education for black males are also based upon the belief that there are important gender variations that should be addressed separately.

I also do not mean to argue that all African American children react to their indi- vidual educational situation the same way. The fact that children will react differently does not deny the fact that ethnic groups develop a cultural response that influences the collective interpretation of the group's – and hence the individual's interpretation of the – educational experience. The group's cultural interpretation will influence the success or failure of members of that community in public schools. When public schools ignore or undervalue the culture of involuntary minorities, such as African Americans, it is likely to have far more negative consequences for their education than it has or will have for voluntary immigrant groups.[18]

The twin purposes of race and gender-segregated education for African American males

Separate education for black males provides educators with the opportunity to restructure their education to take account of the deficiencies and shortcomings of the USA's dominant cultural beliefs about them. Educators can teach strategies and techniques to assist black males in successfully overcoming the racial obstacles that these beliefs will place in their path. Separate education for African American males also provides educa- tors with the opportunity to reduce the cultural conflicts that exist between the Anglo- American culture embodied in the traditional educational program and that of their black male students, thereby eliminating a primary cause of the poor performance of African American males in public schools.

Legal framework for the analysis of race and gender-segregated education for African American males

The United States Constitution is the supreme law of the US and as a result, its interpretation is the primary document that American society uses to justify its most important normative choices.[19] The equal protection clause of the Fourteenth Amendment is the applicable provision of the Constitution to consult when matters of racial and gender discrimination are involved. Both the interpretation of and the arguments related to the equal protection clause which are considered acceptable as adequate legal justifications are structured around a certain conception of social reality. It is this conception of social reality that is at the crux of the dispute regarding the constitutionality of race and gender-segregated education for African American males.

The role of government in the vision of society implicit in the equal protection clause

The vision of society implicit in the Supreme Court's interpretation of the equal protection clause generally conceives of society as a collection of knowing individuals.[20] These 'knowing individuals' are viewed as self-directed, coherent, self-determining, free-willed, integrated and rational individuals.[21] Because these knowing individuals are self-determining and free willed, their attitudes, opinions and beliefs are not seen as products of various cultural systems of meaning, but rather as freely chosen by these individuals. The effect of the social action of these knowing individuals is presumed to be controlled by their intent. These knowing individuals are in this way seen as the authors of their own thoughts, the captains of their respective ships, the ruler of their respective empires and the stewards of their behavior.

This conceptual structure of society contains its own cultural system of meaning for interpreting social events and, particularly for purposes of this chapter, the role of government. The role of government within this conception of society is to mediate the conduct of these knowing individuals so as allow them to pursue their own desires and to prevent them from unjustly interfering with the rights of their fellow persons. Government must therefore strive to achieve a sort of neutrality, respecting equally every knowing individual's pursuit of their various objectives. In order for government to maintain that balance it can neither seek to advance the parochial interest of a particular group, nor fail to treat people as self-directing and self-determining individuals.

The legal system does recognize that some characteristics of individuals such as race, gender and ethnicity are not the result of choice. Unlike educators who propose race and gender-segregated education for black males, the interpretation of the equal protection clause by the Supreme Court generally considers that the proper resolution of problems related to these characteristics is for government to transcend those characteristics in favor of treating everyone the same. For government to treat knowing individuals the same, requires that government treat them as if they are devoid of unchosen characteristics such as gender, race and ethnicity. For government to treat people as members of a racial or gender group is initially considered wrong and will require extremely important justifications.[22]

Even though children do not fit the ontological premise of knowing individuals presupposed by law's conception of social life, public education is a governmental function. As a consequence, public educators must also maintain the requirement of governmental neutrality that flows from the conception of society as a collection of knowing individuals. Public education must treat students as individuals and not as members of racial, ethnic or gender groups entitled to special treatment. Any argument surrounding the legality of race and gender-segregated education for black males that is not sensitive to this conception of society will have a difficult time surviving an equal protection challenge. In fact, referring to such programs as 'race and gender-segregated education for African American males' is an obvious affront to these requirements.

Conceptualization of race and gender-segregated education for African American males for purposes of constitutional analysis

Proposals to establish separate education for black males violates the requirement of governmental neutrality in two different ways. First, government is advancing the parochial interest of African American males by providing them a benefit that it is not providing to other groups. Second, by classifying students based on race and gender, public educators are no longer treating students as individuals. Government is treating students as members of racial and gender groups and thereby making decisions based on characteristics which individuals do not choose.

The best way to improve the chances of surviving a constitutional test is for public educators to be sensitive to the legal culture's conception of society as knowing individuals. Many school systems operate 'magnet schools', with a special emphasis on certain subjects, such as foreign languages, math, science or vocational programs. Enrollment in magnet schools is left up to the discretion of parents who wish to choose a particular educational concentration for their child. School officials in the exercise of their expertise determine the kinds of magnet schools to operate. School officials should not propose race and gender-segregated education, but rather should develop schools which black males happen to choose to attend along the same guidelines as magnet schools.

To do this school officials could seek to provide gender-segregated schools located in both predominantly black and white residential neighborhoods for both males and females. *These schools should not be based on a crisis plaguing African American males. Rather they should be firmly grounded in the benefits to be derived by both girls and boys from gender segregated education.* Gender-separate, but equal schools, provides all students with the option of choosing either coeducational or gender-segregated public education. By presenting all students with a gender-segregated option which they may exercise on their own, public schools are in a much better position to argue that they are being true to the constitutional requirement of treating all students as individuals and not advancing the parochial interest of a given group.

Notes

1. Leavy, W. (1983) *Ebony*, August, p. 41. Since that time the survivability and viability of the African American male has been debated and discussed at length. See, for example, Gibbs, J. (ed.) (1988) *Young, Black, and Male in America: An Endangered Species*; see also Gray, L. E. (ed.) (1981) *Black Men*.

2. Leavy (1983) The overall homicide rate for black males is 60 per 100,000, a rate higher than that for white males, white females and black females combined. Homicide is the leading cause of death of black males between the ages of 15 and 24. Of the 345,960 people in state prisons around the country, black men represent almost half, 170,452. 'Due to a number of societal stresses, experts say, the suicide rate among black males has more than doubled in the past ten years'. Black male infant mortality rate is double that of white males. The life expectancy of black males is five years less than that of white males, nine years less than that of black females and thirteen years less than that of white females.

3. *Garrett v. Board of Education* 775 Federal Supplement 1004, 1006 (Eastern District Federal Michigan, 1991).

4. 775 Federal Supplement 1004.

5. Kunjufu, J. (1991) 'Detroit's Male Academies: What the Real Issue Is', *Education Week*, 29, 20 November.

6. Letter dated 31 August 1988, addressed to Dr. Joseph A. Fernandez, Superintendent of Schools, Dade County Public Schools, from Jesse L. High, Regional Civil Rights Director, US Department of Education Office of Civil Rights.

7. Letter dated 23 July 1990, addressed to Dr. Robert S. Peterkin. Superintendent of Schools, Milwaukee Public Schools, from David Tatel and Bethany E. Lorenz of Hogan & Hartson. Milwaukee opened two African-American immersion schools. In one school, half the student population is composed of neighborhood girls. The faculty is two-thirds white with only two African-American male teachers. *Chicago Tribune*, 1 December 1991.

8. Baltimore, however, does operate three separate classrooms for African American male students in otherwise coeducational schools; *ibid.*, Detroit, New York and Milwaukee have all gone forward with their proposals to operate schools with a focus on the culture and heritage of African Americans. Enrollment at these schools is not limited to males, but rather is formally open to anyone in the respective school system who wishes to apply.

9. Given the justifications for these academies a significant question can and should be raised about the exclusion of African American females or their failure to also develop concurrent academies for them.

10. Bullivant, B. (1981) *The Pluralist Dilemma in Education* (Sydney, Allen and Unwin); see also Nobles, W. W. (1990) 'The infusion of African and African American content: A question of content and intent', in Hillard, A. G., Payton-Stewart, L. and Williams, L. O. (eds) *Infusion of African and American Content in the School Curriculum* (Morristown, NJ, Aaron Press).

11. Sandel, M. (1982) *Liberalism and the Limits of Justice* (New York, Cambridge University Press) p. 150.

12. Post, R. (1989) 'The social foundations of privacy; Community and self in the common law tort', *California Law Review*, 77, pp. 957, 972–4.

13. See, for example, *Dred Scott v. Sanford* 60 US 393 (1856) (noting that the founders of the US believed that people of African descent were considered so far inferior that they had no rights that a white man need respect.

14. Bank, J. A. (1988) *Multiethnic Education; Theory and Practice*, second edition, Boston, MA. Allyn and Bacon.

15. Ogbu, J. U. and Gibson, M.A. (eds) (1991) *Minority Status and Schooling; A Comparative Study of Immigrant and Involuntary Minorities*, New York, Garland, pp. 5–6.

16. *Ibid.*

17. Ogbu, J. U. (1991) 'Immigrant and involuntary minorities in comparative perspectives', in OGBU, J. U. and Gibson, M. A. (eds) *op. cit.*

18. See, for example, Fordham, S. (1988) 'Racelessness as a factor in black students' school success: Pragmatic strategy or pyrrhic victory?' *Harvard Educational Review*, 58, p. 54, which discusses the impact of race on high-achieving black students.

19. Race and gender-separate education for African American students will also call into question other federal laws such as Title IX of the Education Act Amendments of 1972, the Equal Educational Opportunities Act and possibly state antidiscrimination statutes. Space limitations, however, keep me from addressing these issues separately.

20. *City of Richmond v. Croson* 488 US 469 (1989); *FCC v. Metro Broadcasting* 110 S. Ct. 2997, 3028 (O'Connor, J. Dissenting).

21. See, for example, Schlag, P. (1990) 'Normative and no where to go', *Standford Law Review*, 43, pp. 167, 181; Benhabib, S. (1990) 'Critical theory and postmodernism; On the interplay of ethics, aesthetics and utopia in critical theory', *Cardozo Law Review*, 11, p. 1435.

22. Government is not prohibited from classifying people based on race or gender. When racial classifications are used courts will apply what is called strict scrutiny. In order to survive the test, government must supply a compelling state interest and adopt a scheme that is narrowly tailored to meet the interest. See *City of Richmond v. Croson* 488 US 469, pp. 493–4. The test has been called 'strict in appearance but fatal in fact'. Gunter, G. (1972) 'The Supreme Court, 1971 Term-Foreword: In search of evolving doctrine on a changing court: A model for a newer equal protection', *Harvard Law Review*, 86, pp. 1, 8. The standard of gender classifications is considered less strict. Requiring government to supply an important interest and developing a scheme that is substantially related to advancing that interest. See *Mississippi University for Women v. Hogan* 458 US 718 (1982). Both tests, however, embody a significant distrust of government actions based on race and gender classifications.

10

Community politics and the education of African American males: Whose life is it anyway?

Kal Alston

School restructuring and reform is always undertaken with implicit and explicit values guiding the formation of questions, problems, and policy. In the case of the various articulations of policies regarding the schooling of African American males, illuminating these values is important in assessing the success of the programs' consequences – intended and unintended. This chapter sketches the possibilities and problematics of separate schooling experiences for African American males in the contexts of individual, community, and State interests and power.[1]

In the aftermath of proposals for all-male African American academies in cities such as New York, Detroit and Milwaukee, among others, many voices immediately expressed grave reservations. The NAACP and the Urban League as well as feminist analysts were concerned that the proposals represented an abandonment of hope in a changing society (Ascher 1991: 14). They also feared that there would be legal ramifications on both racial and gender lines, namely the potential violation of Title VI of the Civil Rights Act of 1964 and Title IX, both of which curtail the rights of public institutions to provide differential resource allocation on the basis of race or gender. Further, there was concern that the proposals could be used to reinforce the *de facto* segregation of African American children in general (and boys in particular) already resulting in injurious differential treatment of those students in school. This chapter will be an attempt to contextualize those concerns as salvos in ongoing battles over the ownership and leadership of various communities. A look at the Milwaukee public schools' plan and programs in other parts of the country suggests that the disagreements that separate the sides on the issue of such academies have legal, educational, and social bases as well as consequences.

Is there life after desegregation?

In her 1985 monograph *Thirty Years After Brown*, Jennifer Hochschild paints a not-altogether-positive picture of the programmatic and systematic changes resulting from the 1954 *Brown* decision. There are changes to be sure: In 1968, 77 percent of black students attended schools with more than 50 percent black enrollment and 67 percent attended schools with 90 to 100 percent black enrollment. By 1980, 63 percent of blacks were in schools above 50 percent, but only 33 percent attended 90 to 100 percent black-enrolled schools. The national figures mask many things, however. Most of the changes took place in the South, and almost all court-ordered desegregation took place between 1968 and 1976. The five largest cities (New York, Los Angeles, Chicago, Philadelphia and Houston) have no mandatory desegregation plans, and only one out of the ten largest cities has more than 33 percent white public school enrollment. In the last decade, support for mandatory desegregation plans has eroded for many reasons: among them the growing significance of Latino interests, and the erosion of black support for desegregation (Ascher 1991: 11).[2] Coupled with the erosion of political support are concerns about the implementation strategies most often employed – strategies that result in plans most politically acceptable to whites (desegregation in upper grades; reassignment primarily of black children; the development of magnet schools) and least educationally beneficial to blacks. For example, no major city except St. Louis has used metropolitan-wide busing (i.e., busing beyond city limits) to share out the burdens and benefits of busing.

Hochschild offers three potential interpretations of *Brown*: the color-blind Constitution; desegregation first; and educational quality first (1985: 4). In the color-blind Constitutional interpretation that guided policy from 1954 to 1968, rigid scrutiny of any law distinguishing by race plays a conservative role – ending state-supported segregation, but limiting the possibilities for remediation. This interpretation is highly juridical and takes no stock of historical, economic and social barriers to equality. This is the formalist approach that ends *de jure* segregation, but is not proactive in looking more deeply into the long-term effects of segregation.

The most active era of court-enforced desegregation (1968–76) was guided by the second interpretation of *Brown* in which the central principle is the ending of racial isolation. The interpretation follows the assertion by the NAACP legal group that *Brown* was not about education but about race. The centrality of the concern for racial integration informed busing plans, which sometimes led to an overriding of concerns about preferences and effects. The plans articulated and implemented under this interpretation have been criticized for reassigning students without changing schools – leading to secondary segregation within school (tracking, differential sanctions) and the dispersion of black communities.

The third interpretation of *Brown* critiques the failures of forced desegregation, positing that desegregation alone is insufficient to abolish racism. Three possible alternatives evolve from this position: the state should limit its efforts to enforce equity in the allocation of tangible resources; the state should promote compensatory allocation of resources; and control of black schools should be returned to black educators and communities. Inherent in this last view is the belief that development of strong school programs within a student's community eliminates distribution of rewards and punishment by race and external barriers to academic and personal achievement. So, for example, secondary segregation by race in areas such as discipline and tracking are less likely in schools in which the population is all African American. The shift of emphasis in this interpretation marginalizes considerations about social integration and the development of economic and social networks across racial lines.

Returning to (grass)roots

Consequences of educational failure

In the third postulate of this last interpretive possibility of *Brown* can be found the intents and purposes of the proposals for separate schools for African American males. Advocates for the radical restructuring of public schooling for a population failed so miserably by public institutions seek to re-examine the supposed consensus about the social goods of racial integration and to hold schools, educators, and policymakers accountable for the intended and unintended consequences of their prior efforts.

The call for action for African American males comes in the face of daunting statistics. Economically, the state of black men is worsening: In 1973, 8 percent of African American males 20–24 years old reported no income; in 1984, 20 percent reported the same. Forty-three percent of these men were high school dropouts. In every racial and ethnic group the female-headed household is significantly more likely to be poor. One-half of black and Hispanic children live in female-headed households, and over 65 percent of children from those households live in poverty (*Digest of Education Statistics*: Table 18). Socially and politically, black men are increasingly deprived of franchise and freedom. Forty-three percent of federal and state prisoners are black men although black men comprise only 6 percent of the population. Twenty-three percent of black men (aged 20–29) are in jail, on probation or parole. Thirty-three percent of homicide victims are black males (higher in urban areas). Homicide is the fifth leading cause of death for black males (and second for young men, aged 15–19) (US Department of Health, Education and Welfare 1979: 15–16).

Educationally, as a group, African American men fare no better. The secondary segregation effects result in differential rates of non-promotions, suspensions, expulsions and dropouts. In New Orleans, for example, black males (43 percent of the total school population) make up 58 percent of non-promotions, 65 percent of suspensions, 80 percent of expulsions and 45 percent of dropouts (Garibaldi 1991). In school districts with more equal racial composition, the differentials are even more stark. Large urban school districts, which are largely *de facto* segregated, enroll larger numbers of poorer children, employ more poorly prepared teachers, provide less diverse curricula, house larger class sizes, draw support from parents who themselves have fewer years of education, and lack adequate material support. In states like Texas, where teachers are required to take achievement tests of basic verbal skills, there is a concentration of lower test scores among teachers who teach black and Latino kids. These lower test scores are more highly correlated to the race of the student than the race of the teacher. Teachers' weakness in verbal skill accounts for 25 percent of the variance between black and white *student* scores in math and reading and 20 percent of the variance between white and Latino students (Ferguson 1991). The number of black males enrolled in college and the percentage they represent in the college-enrolled population dropped sharply between 1976 to 1986. All of the increases in black students' college attendance are female.

In light of these devastating trends embodied in the most disadvantaged students, educators must own up to their complicity, although not sole responsibility. With the full acknowledgment that schools are limited in their ability to ameliorate broad economic and social problems, the plans for separate schools bring home the cost of avoiding the critical assessment of school organization and practices.

Plans for separate schools/schooling

In many cities, plans call for enrichment programs outside of the school structure – after school, Saturdays, and during the summer. East Cleveland's program for example, incorporates all three in a cultural enrichment program. Both boys and girls in grades 5 through 8 are admitted to the program which is based on the seven principles of Kwansaa,[3] but instruction is gender-segregated under the assumption that 'two halves are being prepared in order to create a whole'. The program culminates in a rites of passage ceremony. This program is privately funded. In Raleigh, North Carolina, an after school program pairs 11 and 12-year-old boys with African American school district employees who are paid by the district for their participation in a mentoring program in which the adult contracts to spend twenty hours a month with eight to ten boys (Ascher, 1991: 17–19). These and other beyond school programs focus primarily on the realignment of social groups, the decentering of drug and gang culture, and the improvement of academic, social and sexual responsibility by use of mentors, male role models, cultural education, and ritual.

The in-school programs are of two general kinds: those that seek to address general issues of educational equity,[4] and those that are more narrowly tailored to change values and achievement patterns. Strategies for the latter include introducing teaching methods that fit so-called African American 'learning styles' (Hale-Benson 1986), mobilizing school counseling services to raise self-esteem and provide information regarding employment options; involvement in parent training; employing African American male teachers and all-male classes to redefine maleness; and introducing more 'Afrocentric' curricula and rites. Most of the programs are aimed at African American boys between third and ninth grades, although there are several high school programs. The central and unifying themes of these diverse programs include:

1   Male bonding,
2   Building identity and self-esteem,
3   Developing academic values and social skills,
4   Strengthening parental and community participation,
5   Dignifying the transition to manhood,
6   Providing a safe haven from the temptations and pressures of the peer culture.

The Milwaukee Plan – Whose interests?

The Milwaukee Plan incorporates these goals in a clear and focused proposal for the restructuring of district policy and schools. The plan incorporates changes in district policy and staff development strategies. The plan is a critique of desegregation activities that result in counterproductive conditions for students who are already educationally at risk. District policy changes include:

1   A re-articulation of working policy and philosophy to state and support the belief that *all* students can learn;
2   The introduction of an Afro-centered curriculum K–12;
3   Emphasis on language development skills and mathematical skill (including ethnomathematics) with regard for the learning styles of African Americans;
4   The improvement of support for course selection, promotion, and math enrichment;
5   Increased access to after school and summer programs;
6   The development of a homework policy and increase of parent/student accountability.

Staff development strategies include:

1   Training to enhance multicultural awareness of faculty and staff regarding diverse student bodies and curriculum;
2   Diversification of instructional strategies;
3   An increase in the number of African American male teachers;
4   An increase in communication between parents and teachers;
5   Establishment of a Professional Development Model School at an African

American school site with a 90 percent African American student population (Milwaukee Public Schools 1990).

Milwaukee is proposing comprehensive changes in district policy with an eye to the legal problems encountered by Florida schools.[5] The school district has made the African-American immersion academies open to admission of females and non-African Americans although the programs therein are geared toward the needs of the target population.

In general, criticisms of the African American immersion academies have been aimed at a few specific areas. On the part of traditional black leadership as well as the liberal education establishment there is a not unjustified fear that these schools and their creation mark a turning point in United States education – potentially on the scale of *Brown*. The public school, since the days of Horace Mann, has carried with it the myth of being the great equalizer, the gateway to the American Dream. Indeed *Brown* (as well as many other education cases) could be conceptualized as being centrally about the power of public schools to normalize, to socialize, and to 'Americanize' children and to prepare them for the opportunities made available to them by virtue of having been schooled. The demand that 'separate but equal' schooling be abolished was at least in part a cry for blacks to be included in and given access to the American Dream. The question that worries the traditional Left is what the full consequences could be of resuming an explicit mandate for separate *and* equal schooling. Will it be seen as an admission that African Americans are the 'unassimilables'? That efforts at integration were failures, or worse, wrong-headed from the start? That the 'color-blind' Constitution cannot work because blacks (and black males in particular) are a deviant population? These are not unwarranted fears – especially given the potential legal consequences for *Brown* and its heirs. The traditional civil rights leadership is quite right to be uneasy about the consequences of this rejection of law and schooling as protectors and providers of social goods.

The teachers and community members advocating these schools in Milwaukee, Detroit and New York City have acknowledged the failure of the dream for their children; the promise of social integration, the eradication of racism, and economic and educational advancement has not been fulfilled. The immediate and proximate motivation for the inception of these radical programs is connected to perceptions of alienated children, institutions and communities, and the imminent loss of them as resources. These communities are no longer satisfied with promises of wholesale educational reform – the reform that would redress endemic inequities, transform US schools, and ensure increased access and success for all children. Instead, in the face of criticism from many sources and uncertainty about legal problems and resources, many communities have mounted different species of campaigns against the increasingly probable destruction of the community. Whatever the feeling about the long-term prospects for and benefits of racial *rapprochement*, there is a recognition that those communities which lose the vitality and contribution of their youth lose the capacity to replenish, reconstitute and reproduce themselves. Here and now, these communities assert, is the place and time for attending to the needs of the least and last. In the long run, perhaps integration would be a social good;[6] in the short run, the insistence on educational integration by the law is having the effect of crippling communities' capacity for self-maintenance and self-governance, and undermining access to broader educational goods.

The *racial* issues raised legally and in terms of *de facto* resegregation by a plan to separate African American males for educational purposes can be salved at least partially by understanding that the schools which the students are attending now are in fact segregated – not by law, but nonetheless racially isolated. In Detroit and Milwaukee, the plan calls primarily (although not exclusively) for a realignment of resources rather than racially determined student reassignment. The high school data included in the Milwaukee Plan suggest that the general quality of the school has more effect on student achievement than racial composition – achievement tests do not differ significantly on the basis of racial composition, but the best scores for black students are in the same schools as the best scores for white students (Milwaukee Public Schools 1990: Appendix I).

Further, the argument over the value of integration itself as an end for schools is not simply a contemporary one. W. E. B. Du Bois suggests in a 1936 essay that while there are limiting conditions for the education of African Americans, the mixture of black and white students is not to be viewed as an achievement in and of itself.

> Theoretically, the Negro needs neither segregated nor mixed schools. What he [sic] needs is education. What he must remember is that there is no magic, either in mixed schools or in integrated schools. A mixed school with poor and unsympathetic teachers, with hostile public opinion, and no teaching concerning black folk is bad.[7]

Subsequent history has borne Du Bois out on this point, and the Milwaukee Plan seeks to redress the balance of goods associated with schools on this argument. Racial balance is not, by this account, to be purchased with the futures of children. The shift in emphasis elevates the social goods of educational success and achievement above the social goods of racial *rapprochement*. Consequently, while Milwaukee and other communities may have stopped waiting for the American Dream to be handed to them at the schoolhouse gate, they are not abandoning hope for social change, but instead are mobilizing their love for community, self, and children – demanding that the stakes of that social change be transformed and rearticulated.

Shortfalls of crisis management strategies

Several things are true about the Milwaukee Plan: it is true that the plan is the product of serious deliberation on the part of teachers, students, administrators, parents and other community members – facing what look to be unsurmountable obstacles – looking at a grim present for these children that would most likely become an even grimmer future. It is true that community mobilization has been and will be a vital part of these programs, and that energy has the potential to bring in more material and human resources. It is also arguably true that if the people who will be implementing the programs remain attuned to both goals and possibilities, they will see improvement in academic and perhaps social achievement.[8] It makes sense that single-minded concentration of time, money and attention will yield positive results – just as they do in parochial schools and military academies.

If the integrationist/separatist concerns of the educational establishment are bracketed and the rights (and goods) of community sovereignty are granted, there remain two deep worries articulated from within as well as from without. The first is a concern about girls and community maintenance, and the second is a concern about the *long-term* costs of the benefits derived from a short-term, expedient vision of political/communal solidarity and unity. If one reads the Milwaukee Plan without any knowledge of US race relations or statistics on attainment, one might believe that African American boys are the lone outliers on the plain of success in school. Interestingly enough, however, in the published version of the Milwaukee Plan, the data are primarily disaggregated by race and not by gender. When they are, the achievement of girls is not significantly above that of the boys. So, on the one hand, there is a legitimate fear that in the mood of crisis, in this siege mentality, it will be forgotten that many of the students in those discouraging statistics are female, and that although girls may leave the system in different ways and numbers and for different reasons, their access to the corridors of power is just as problematic. On the other hand, a sense of competition between black men and women about the levels and manifestations of oppression cannot be positive – morally, socially, educationally or politically.

These are children whose life chances are conditioned on the same material circumstances: the same homes, the same poverty, the same cultural temptations and difficulties – as well as the same potential for hope. To suggest, even implicitly, that schooling as currently constituted is healthier for girls, or that the success of girls is conditioned on the failure of boys, is unconscionable. Further, to suggest that mothers, grandmothers and other women, such as teachers, who are responsible for the raising of these children are insufficient role models for males potentially creates a schism that school cannot heal.

There is an appropriateness to the resistance to the perceived interference of outsiders into this battle. In Detroit, African American teachers were justifiably infuriated by the intervention of the National Organization of Women's (NOW) Legal Defense and Education Fund, which charged that the schools violated Title IX intentions. The school board yielded and granted access to girls, albeit with the hope that they would not go to the academies. The perception of NOW as a primarily white, middle-class organization that was putting its own agenda (gender equality) above the interests of the community (preserving the educational and social futures of its own children) helped to undercut the reasonableness of discussion on gender. However, despite those perceptions[9] the discussion of gender separation and its consequences is fundamental to the possibility of these schools contributing to the sustenance of community. As Judge George Woods ruled in Detroit, 'There is no evidence the school system is failing males because girls attend schools with them. Girls fail too' (Walters 1991b: 8). Parents in the black community nevertheless protested the court decision to include 136 girls, decrying it as racist intervention.

Those cautionary voices *within* the community have not fared much better than those from outside. Rather than charges of interference, those African American women – mothers and teachers, as well as others – sensitive to gender issues in their communities were silenced or muted with charges of cooptation and betrayal.[10] Nathan Hare, whose educational writings (some with his wife, Julia) are often quoted in academy literature, has charged that black feminists are generally 'tools of white feminists'.[11] This sort of counterattack has served to silence women's criticisms. The women self-censor or are intimidated in order to avoid the public airing of (confidential) dirty linen, to avoid the appearance of disunity and disloyalty. As Nathan Hare, among others, argues, black men face extraordinary obstacles and hostility in their confrontations with mainstream (read white) male society and need support and low friction from 'their' women.

Negotiating gender relations requires the participation of both sexes in order to combat the historical and cultural pressures that separate or partialize the interests of the genders.[12] In the written materials and the press surrounding these programs there is, implicitly, elevation of claims of race over all other claims and the partialization of the voices of half a community. Even if the short-term goal of more and better educational opportunities for African American boys is realized, black communities cannot afford any further alienation between African American males and females if they are to survive.

The second fear has to do with univocality. In part this is a continuation of the previous worry: that there will be a univocal construction of black maleness into which the participants will be inducted – without any reassurance that the construction will allow for different approaches and embodiments of this 'new' cultural stance – towards maleness, manhood, and women. The encouragement of sexual responsibility and the realignment of peer group culture is positive, but they are offered in a context of male exclusivity that is worrisome, not only on behalf of the women in their lives, but for boys who may have a differing view of themselves from the norms of these new groupings. The same problem holds true for the question of race.

On the curricular side, the invocation of 'Afrocentricity' (a term which the legal counsel in Milwaukee advised against) is problematic as it seeks to replace one 'centricity' with another. The basic curriculum and instructional methods need to be changed and expanded – Eurocentric, partialized history is bad history; any single method of instruction is bound to be better for some kids than others. Partializing, however, even if by the previously marginalized, is still deleterious to some group of children in any classroom. To teach bad history in the name of love and the building of self-esteem is at the very least pedagogically suspect, if not morally indefensible. And to assume that all African American students have one learning style is more anecdotally than empirically supportable. Molefi Kete Asante, a scholarly proponent of Afrocentricity, himself cautions about the replacement of one orthodoxy for another. That was not the goal of Afrocentricity as he envisions it. Instead:

> It means treating African people as subjects instead of objects, putting them in the middle of their own historical context as active human agents. It is not the implementation of a particular world view as if it is universal. (Marriott 1991a: A18)

Asante's efforts to reposition Africa without advocating separatism have not always been successful. While efforts at 'multiculturalism' have been halting, fraught with conflict, and derided as 'ethnic cheerleading', Afrocentricity in its more radical guises – as a replacement for traditional curricula – is potentially disempowering for children already alienated from the culture of power. Correctives need not take the form of providing a distinct (and inwardly gazing) curriculum to children for whom it is continued to be hoped that they will contribute positively to their own immediate and wider communities.

The question of self-esteem is also more complex than academy proponents often admit. Research since the 1970s has shown that black children's scores on self-esteem measures are often quite high in relation to measures of academic success (Madhere 1991). Rather than concentrating solely on enhancing ethnic pride, it perhaps is reasonable to look for strategies to enhance school success and then connect that success with a positive self-image.

Conclusion

Aside from the educational problems of univocality, I am certain there are political costs to forcing unity out of fear. Julius Lester suggests that 'Only the weak need to be agreed with. (Real) unity comes from respect for difference and love of dissent.' Without the possibility of difference and dissent there can be no community with true respect for persons and relationships. The faces of the many are obliterated; the voices of the many are silenced; the power of the many is eviscerated – and the power of the black community can only be strengthened through resistance to an articulation of an identity that is fixed in time or space. Care must be taken with our children that they are given the same opportunity to resist univocality and insist on unity with difference and dissent. It is possible that separate schools for African American males will not impair their capacities for participation in future deliberations about the shape and ends of their communities or the articulation of common goods, but this cannot, this may not be left to chance or hope for the best possible unintended consequences. The jury is still out on the educational and social benefits of these programs, but out of the sense of obligation that the best kind of love engenders, all voices must be allowed to be heard, even voices of conflict and dissent. The lives, in school and out of school, of these children depend on their communities' capacities to be self-assertive, radical, tenacious, and willing to continue debate.

Notes

1. This project was begun for a conference, 'Race Consciousness and the Law', held at the University of Illinois in February 1992. The author wishes to thank Tony Taibi, Liora Bresler, James Anderson, William Trent, Shari Ellis, David Oakes and Philip Zodhiates for their comments and assistance.
2. In 1964, 78 percent of African Americans supported school desegregation; by 1978, their support had dropped to 55 percent.
3. The seven principles, created by Molefi Kete Asante, form the basis for African American family life and spirituality, embracing the African part of black American heritage.
4. Such as in Prince Georges County, where the plan entails increased funding to relieve inequities between Prince Georges County and neighboring Maryland counties as well as inequities within the county, the recruitment of African American male teachers and administrators, adding a multicultural component to the curriculum, re-evaluation of the mechanics of school placement, and strengthening the ties between school and community.
5. In particular, Pine Villa Elementary School – in which the all-male classes were judged to be in violation of Title IX.
6. Urban underclass communities are already racially stratified; many middle-class blacks are opting to leave integrationism behind and form race-conscious enclaves for professional and managerial class African Americans. See Dent, D. (1992) 'The New Black Suburbs', The New York Times Magazine, (14 June, pp. 18–25).
7. Du Bois, W. E. B. (1936) 'Does the Negro Need Separate Schools?' quoted in Woodson, G. C. (1977) The Miseducation of the Negro, 2nd edn) (New York: AMS Press) in the introduction by C. H. Nilon.
8. In fact, in Pine Villa, Florida, before the program shut down, reading test scores had improved.
9. They mirrored those of the ACLU which also began litigation against the school board in Detroit.
10. One of the mothers who was a named plaintiff in the Detroit case has withdrawn because of threats to her and her children.
11. He has used this argument both as a general defense against any criticisms of his educational goals and his principle of manhood as well as in a specific indictment of Anita Hill.
12. There is a problem with the claim made by Detroit schools superintendent, Deborah McGriff, and others, that these single-sex schools will have the same benefits as all-female colleges. At the very least the deep differences between the clienteles suggest that educating white, elite women with the purpose of preparing either well-bred wives and mothers, or women with limited public access but unlimited private access to the power structure, is a very different project from educating boys to survive the absence of economic and social power in their home communities. The anti-female strain heard by these strategists is de-emphasizing female contributions to community life, echoing concerns heard at the turn of the century about the pernicious effects of increasing numbers of female public school teachers. Female weakness and natural motherliness, it was argued, was not an appropriate model for boys, even at a young age. This strain cannot be remedied even with the last-minute opening of a female academy (Mae C. Jemison) for preschoolers and kindergarten.

References

ADLER, J. (1991) 'African dreams', *Newsweek*, 23 September, pp. 42–44.

ASANTE, M. K. (1991) 'Putting Africa at the center', *Newsweek*, 23 September, p. 46.

ASCHER, C. (1991) 'School programs for African American male students', ERIC *Clearinghouse on Urban Education*, May, pp. 11, 14.

BECK, J. (1990) 'Self-Esteem comes from achievement, not rhetoric', *Chicago Tribune*, 8 November, sec. 1, p. 25.

BEGLEY, S. (1991) 'Out of Egypt, Greece', *Newsweek*, 23 September, pp. 49–50.

CALDWELL, J. (1990) 'Summer program is targeted at keeping black males in school', *Boston Globe*, 5 September, p. 37X.

CAMPBELL, L. P. (1990) 'High court may tell schools just what desegregation is', *Chicago Tribune*, 30 September sec. 1, p. 13.

CHICAGO TRIBUNE (1991) 'A Special Need, a Precious Value', 10 August sec. 1, p. 16.

CLARK, J. (1988) 'It is time for blacks to take charge of their fate', *Ebony*, August, pp. 120, 122.

CLARK, M. L. (1991) 'Social identity, peer relations, and academic competence of African-American adolescents', *Education and Urban Society*, November, pp. 41–52.

DENT, D. (1992) 'The New Black Suburbs', *The New York Times Magazine*, 14 June, pp. 18–25.

DIGEST OF EDUCATION STATISTICS (1988) National Center for Education Statistics, Washington, DC.

ENTWISLE, D. R. (1987) 'The emergent academic self-image of first graders: Its response to social structure', *Child Development*, 58, pp. 1190–206.

FERGUSON, R. F. (1991) 'Racial patterns in how school and teacher quality affect achievement', *Challenge: A Journal of Research on Black Men*, 2, 1.

FORDHAM, S. (1988) 'Racelessness as a factor in black students' school success: Pragmatic strategy or pyrrhic victory?' *Harvard Educational Review*, pp. 54–83.

FOWLER, S. (1991) 'Forces of change may strengthen single-sex schools', *Chicago Tribune*, 2 June, sec. 6, p. 1.

GARIBALDI, A. (1991) 'The educational experiences of black males: The early years', *Challenge: A Journal of Research on Black Men*, 2 (1) May, pp. 36–49.

GATES, H. L. JR. (1991) 'Beware of the new pharos', *Newsweek*, 23 September, p. 47.

GLANTON, A. D. (1990) 'An Afrocentric school breaks from the norm', *Chicago Tribune*, 9 October, sec. 2, p. 1.

GOODMAN, E. (1991) 'Another form of segregation that's doomed to fail', *Boston Globe*, 5 September, p. 17.

HALE-BENSON, J. (1986) *Black Children: Their Roots, Culture and Learning Styles* (Baltimore: Johns Hopkins University Press).

HANCOCK, L. (1990) 'Ujamaa means controversy', *Village Voice*, 6 November, pp. 11–16.

HARMON, A. (1991) '300 rally in support of all-male schools', *Los Angeles Times*, 22 August, p. A4.

HOCHSCHILD, J. (1985) *Thirty Years After Brown* (Washington, DC: Joint Center for Political Studies).

HOUPPERT, K. (1992) 'Separatist but equal?', *Village Voice*, 19 May, pp. 27–31.

KANTROWITZ, B. (1991) 'A is for Ashanti, B is for Black', *Newsweek*, 23 September, pp. 45–48.

KEENAN, M. (1991) 'Detroit schools; Chief defends the one-gender format', *Chicago Tribune*, 8 September, sec. 6, pp. 1, 11.

LEE, V. E., WINFIELD, L. F. and WILSON, T. C. (1991) 'Academic behaviors among high-achieving African American students', *Education and Urban Society*, November, pp. 65–86.

LESTER, J. (1991) 'What Price Unity', *Village Voice*, 17 September, pp. 39–40.

MADHERE, S. (1991) 'Self-esteem of African American preadolescents: Theoretical and practical considerations', *Journal of Negro Education*, 60 (1) pp. 47–61.

MARRIOTT, M. (1991a) 'Afrocentrism: Balancing or skewing history?' *New York Times*, 11 August, pp. A1, A18.

MARRIOTT, M. (1991b) 'As a discipline advances, a debate on scholarship', *New York Times*, 11 August, p. A18.

MEYERS, M. (1991) 'Black racism at taxpayer expense', *Wall Street Journal*, 30 July, p. A16.

MILLER, K. (1991) 'Church-backed schools inspire Detroiters', *Wall Street Journal*, 29 August, p. B1.

MILWAUKEE PUBLIC SCHOOLS, AFRICAN AMERICAN MALE TASK FORCE (1990) *Educating African American Males: A Dream Deferred*, May.

NAVARRO, M. (1991) 'Segregation or a solution? Students ponder a school plan', *New York Times*, 18 January, pp. B1, B3.

NEW YORK TIMES 'US judge blocks plan for all-male public schools in Detroit', 16 August, (1991) p. A1.
NEW YORK TIMES (1991) 'Bush's backing of all-male schools is criticized', 11 September, p. B11.
RASBERRY, W. (1990) 'Afrocentrism (cont'd.)', *Washington Post*, 17 October, p. A25.
RIBADENETRA, D. (1991) 'Diverse curriculum urged for schools', *Boston Globe*, 28 April, p. 25, 30.
TRAUB, J. (1991) 'Ghetto blasters', *New Republic*, 15 April, pp. 21–22.
US DEPARTMENT OF HEALTH, EDUCATION AND WELFARE (1979) *The Urban Schools Reform Initiative Report: Final Report*, Government Printing Office, Washington DC.
WALTERS, L. S. (1991a) 'African-American immersion schools aim to help failing students', *Christian Science Monitor*, 14 June, p. 10.
WALTERS, L. S. (1991b) 'The plight of black male schools', *Christian Science Monitor*, 9 September, p. 8.
WHITE, B. (1991) 'Schools for black males have "merit," Bush says', *The Atlanta Constitution*, 10 September, p. E4.
WOODSON, G. C. (1977) *The Miseducation of the Negro* (New York: AMS Press).
YARDLEY, J. (1990) 'Afrocentrism and the prospects of change', *Washington Post*, 2 April, p. B2.

11 Creating an irresponsible school choice program

Charles L. Glenn

Massachusetts implemented, in the 1991–92 school year, an interdistrict choice policy that has been widely criticized as inequitable to poor and minority pupils and to urban school systems, as well as unconnected to school improvement. This chapter provides an insider's recounting of the effort to obtain support for an interdistrict policy that would be equitable and responsible, and of the political and practical consequences of the Massachusetts policy.

Supporting parental choice of schools does not mean supporting everything done in its name. When Massachusetts implemented a program to promote interdistrict school choice, strong supporters of school choice opposed it as irresponsible and incapable of achieving its stated goals of school reform and expanded opportunity. As more and more states and local communities implement school choice policies, it is essential that we think carefully about essential *design* considerations, such as those developed in Massachusetts over the past dozen years but ignored in pushing through the interdistrict program in 1991.

Of course, parents have always made choices about the education of their children for reasons that seem good to them. They clearly have a right to do so in a free society, a right confirmed by the Supreme Court's 1925 decision in *Pierce v. Society of Sisters* and by the international treaties to protect human rights. By deciding where they will live or whether to pay tuition to a private school, they make decisions which may serve the common good as well as their private interests. It is only as we begin to make public policy to *encourage* and *support* parental choice of schools, and thus seek to influence to some degree the private choices parents make, that fundamental principles such as equal access and the common good must guide the shape those policies take.

There are three reasons why I support well-crafted policies that encourage and support parental choice of schools. First, allowing parents to make decisions about how their children will be educated, within a framework that protects the interests of the children, is essential in a democratic society. Second, *all* parents should, as a matter of simple justice, be enabled to make these decisions; the United States is almost unique among Western nations in *not* providing public funding to allow poor parents to exercise the same rights that wealthier (but not necessarily wiser or more concerned) parents possess as a matter of course. Third, after twenty-one years attempting to reform urban schools from the top down, through enforcement and extra funding, I've grown convinced that the present structures are essentially unreformable and only break the hearts of fine teachers and administrators. Parental choice, *if organized right*, can create the climate, the freedom, and the incentives for schools to become effective.

The interdistrict choice program adopted and implemented during the first months of the administration of Massachusetts Governor William Weld has satisfied the first of these goals for a handful of parents, but it has no prospect of satisfying the second or third. It is important that we understand why.

The development of this program must be seen against the background of the previous administration of Governor Michael Dukakis. As Dukakis prepared to go to the 1988 Democratic National Convention, he faced a difficult decision. He needed to decide whether to sign or veto language placed in the state budget by Senate President William Bulger, expanding the opportunity for parents to choose a public school, at public expense, in communities other than that of their residence. Public education and civil rights groups were deeply opposed to the measure. Their opposition had the potential of creating a major controversy at the Democratic Convention, where the National Education Association and the American Federation of Teachers would be strongly represented. On the other hand, Senator Bulger – whose power was virtually unlimited in the Massachusetts Senate, and was not balanced by a strong leader in the House – felt strongly about this measure, and he was not a man to cross lightly.

Response to the initiative from suburban superintendents was mixed. Some pointed out that they could indeed accommodate additional transfer students, and would welcome them for financial reasons, but they expressed caution that such transfers 'would tend to have a negative effect on the people who are most needy'. Brookline already enrolled more than 100 students from Boston whose parents paid tuition of about $4800, and another 300 through the state-funded Metco program for urban/suburban desegregation; however, no more space was available at the elementary level. At the same time, enrollment declines in suburban communities like Avon were having a severe impact on the ability to operate a full high school program. Several days earlier it had been reported that the first-year class in Avon's high school would enroll only twelve to fifteen pupils unless an out-of-district recruitment effort already underway was successful in attracting pupils whose parents would pay tuition.

Before Dukakis left for the convention, he signed the state budget but vetoed the school choice language. He also signed a letter to Chairman James Crain of the Massachusetts Board of Education and Commissioner of Education Harold (Ron) Raynolds, requesting that the board develop a pilot program and legislation that would expand parent choice without harm to integration or to urban schools. Crain and Raynolds, Dukakis told the press, had agreed to set up a pilot program, with full public review. 'It's got to be done right,' the governor insisted.

Dukakis had resolved to veto the Bulger bill, he wrote, because of 'a number of unresolved issues and questions' and because 'there has been limited opportunity for public input'. This was not, he stressed, 'a rejection of the underlying idea of increasing parental choice in public education'.

Crafting a responsible choice program

The governor's letter called for design and implementation of an interdistrict choice program beginning in January 1989 after public hearings by the board. Such a plan should

1   ensure open, fair and equitable student admissions procedures;
2   allow the participation of bilingual and special needs students;
3   establish appropriate family income limits;
4   ensure no adverse impact on school desegregation;
5   provide transportation costs, especially for low-income students;
6   encourage transfer in both directions, not just from city to suburbs.

Some people within the Department of Education suggested that the most prudent course would be to go through the motions of complying with the Governor's request, while making sure that nothing came of the idea of expanded parent choice, which they regarded as without merit. Crain and Raynolds made clear, however, that they had promised the Governor to give the effort their best shot. At the same time, they stressed that no compromises would be made on equity and desegregation concerns. I was assigned to manage the process of developing draft legislation. Over the next four months, draft legislation for interdistrict school choice was hammered out through dozens of meetings and hearings across the state. The main elements follow:

[*Preamble*]
'It is the purpose of this legislation (a) to assure that the right of access, by any child in the Commonwealth, to a free and appropriate public education is not limited by his or her place of residence, (b) to provide to parents, so far as practicable, the opportunity to select the public schools their children will attend, and (c) to encourage improvements in the quality and diversity of the educational options available.'

[*Part A*]
[in summary] Any school committee could file a plan with the state by 1 November of any year to enroll out-of-district students the following year; the Commissioner of Education would publish, each February, a list of spaces available, and parents would apply by 1 May through a regional collaborative or office of the Department of Education (thus, individual schools would not decide upon admissions); districts with racial balance plans would amend those plans to assure that the net impact of transfers in and out would be neutral racially; the state would pay to the receiving district $2000 per pupil transferred; transportation for students entitled to free or reduced-price lunch would be funded by the state.

[*Part B*]
The Board of Education would make grants to urban magnet schools seeking to attract pupils from suburban communities. These could be used for parent information, programs, portable classrooms, and other purposes.

[*Part C*]
Collaborative arrangements among school systems to develop distinctive program specialties would be encouraged by funding pilot projects.

[*Part D*]
Teacher-initiated programs of choice, such as charter schools, would also be encouraged by funding pilot projects.

The most difficult issue was to devise an equitable and adequate funding system, in view of the unusually heavy reliance of Massachusetts public school systems upon the local property tax. The budget language initiated by Senator Bulger had been very simple: it amended the section of the statutes permitting school districts to accept tuitioned students, with tuition paid by parents or by the sending district, by adding language providing that the state would pay this tuition. It also amended the sections providing state aid to local schools by providing that the amount paid for tuition would be subtracted from the aid to the sending district.

Senator Bulger's program did not take into account the fact that state aid was, for most districts, less than half of the local expenditures for education and thus withholding it from one district would not cover the tuition to another district. Boston's deputy superintendent for planning and business affairs pointed out (*The Boston Globe*, 12 July 1988) that under the new open-enrollment plan, Boston would lose $5000 in state money for every student who leaves the system.

Simply having state aid follow the student would not, by itself, be sufficient. In fact, we concluded that the system of state aid to education was so arbitrary and inequitable that there was *no* sound way to peg the funding of this program to the present aid formula. It would be simpler and cleaner we reasoned, simply to pick an arbitrary figure and say that the state would pay that much for each student transferring, in lieu of local aid.

Having set a base figure, it was important to adjust it for bilingual and other students for whom the state stipulates a higher level of funding. Thus the draft legislation provided that 'this payment shall be adjusted for other categories of students in accordance with the pupil weights provided under' the relevant state laws.

In order to make an interdistrict choice plan two-way, and to avoid draining the cities of their most motivated or talented students – a concern expressed frequently throughout the process – we modeled the program directly on the Commonwealth's extensive experience with urban magnet schools. The impetus for developing magnet schools in Massachusetts has come largely from the state, which has provided funding since 1974. While racial balance has been a consideration, and sometimes the primary one, in districts with magnet schools, there has also been a strong emphasis upon overall educational improvement. The focus of this effort is most clearly revealed in the cities which have moved beyond magnet schools to making every school a 'school of choice', while abolishing school attendance zones altogether. The development of schools of choice and a framework for equitable student assignments had become a preferred method of upgrading urban education.

The draft legislation authorized the board of education to provide funding under the magnet school legislation adopted in 1974 to encourage program development and parent information necessary to attract students from suburban to urban communities. It also allowed the state to pay all transportation costs 'for out-of-district students whose attendance at urban magnet schools promotes racial balance, without limitation based upon income.' The intention was to remove any barrier to attracting students into city schools with substantial minority enrollments.

Another provision in the draft was that an urban magnet school could be developed 'in cooperation with any public or private organization, such as a cultural or higher education institution, or a major employer'. We had in mind the creation of 'work-site' schools, magnet schools operated on the premises of or in proximity to a major employer, which would serve not only students living in the vicinity but also others whose parents chose to bring their children with them to attend school near the workplace. We hoped that employers would offer to pay part of the cost of a good after school program for the children of their employees. Schools in Denver, Miami and elsewhere have already implemented such programs, and urban magnet schools in several Massachusetts cities were offering after school care, though not on an interdistrict basis. The approach seemed to offer a powerful means of encouraging suburban to urban choices.

Most of the public attention in this process was directed toward the possibility of increased movement of students between cities and suburbs. Less noticed was the interest, in some quarters, in providing for collaborative programs among several school systems to offer educational options that no one of them could support on its own.

The final substantive section of the draft legislation permitted grants to

> any school system that has indicated an intention of serving out-of-district students under an interdistrict transfer plan approved by the board, for the purpose of encouraging development of teacher-initiated educational alternatives, with shared decision-making and professional working conditions and accountability.

This provision reflected the interest of education reformers in new forms of school-level autonomy, based upon increased teacher professionalism. The Massachusetts Federation of Teachers was strongly interested in teacher-initiated programs like those in New York City's District 4 in East Harlem. There was some indication that the Massachusetts Teachers' Association, while more reserved, would also encourage such initiatives.

Several sessions were held during the planning process for representatives of teacher union locals. While none of these sessions led to unequivocal support for a choice bill, there was substantial interest in measures that would give teachers more opportunity to shape their working conditions and to use their professional judgment. What was needed above all, the teachers agreed, was *time* to plan and to communicate. Including in the draft legislation a provision for planning grants seemed the best way to get at these concerns.

On 22 December 1988, the board of education discussed the proposed legislation at length. My presentation stressed that

> The statewide process of discussion of interdistrict choice has revealed with dramatic force how *unequal* are the educational opportunities available in different communities. The attempt to grapple with these acknowledged inequities has been the most striking feature of this policy-development process. Is it right that many students in Massachusetts attend schools in which parents with other options would not willingly put their children? Is it right that per pupil expenditures on education in one city in Massachusetts are more than twice as high as those in another, that the public schools attended by children living on one side of a street (and town boundary) may spend a thousand dollars more on each student than the schools serving children who live across the street?

> At the start of this process it seemed to many that the unresolvable problem would be to make the movement of students two-way, from suburbs to city as well as the other way around. Urban educators have insisted that they already offer a variety of educational options – as a result of the magnet school development process of recent years – that cannot be matched by their surrounding towns. The draft legislation makes provision for building upon these successes, in confidence that the movement can indeed be two-way. It stresses urban program development, to expand the quality and variety of what is available to parents as they make choices, and also vigorous parent information efforts targeted to those who most need encouragement to be involved in the education of their children.

The legislation was filed by the governor the following month, only to be caught in the backlash of his unsuccessful presidential campaign. Senator Bulger showed no enthusiasm for the proposal, and liberals were in general responsive to the opposition of the Massachusetts Teachers' Association to any form of school choice, despite our earlier efforts to respond to their concerns. The support of the Massachusetts Federation of Teachers was not enough to advance a bill that carried a substantial price tag at a time when state expenditures were facing massive cuts, and it languished and died in committee.

Sequel: An irresponsible choice program

Republican William Weld was elected to succeed Michael Dukakis in November 1990 after a campaign that included attacks on Senate President Bulger, a strong supporter of Democratic nominee John Silber of Boston University. Weld and Bulger needed to patch over the wounds of the campaign and work together to resolve the state's fiscal crisis, and it was probably not coincidental that interdistrict school choice – in Senator Bulger's original form – would soon be revived with the strong support of the new governor. The fact that choice was a favorite cause of the national Republican administration facilitated this reconciliation.

The Weld Administration did not consult in any way with the state's education officials nor (apparently) review the work that had been done in late 1988 to develop interdistrict choice legislation. After some initial maneuvering, a bill was filed in the House and (as in 1988) as outside language in an emergency budget to amend the statute under which school committees could *choose* to admit non-resident pupils, with tuition usually paid by parents, so that

> the tuition required . . . for schoolchildren residing in the cities of Boston or Worcester but attending public schools outside their own school district shall be paid by the Commonwealth and if any schoolchild from a district

admitting schoolchildren from the cities of Boston or Worcester attends a public school within said cities the
Commonwealth shall also pay the required tuition; . . . the state treasurer shall deduct said amounts from the
distribution to be made to each city and town [of residence]. (H. 5231 section 156)

Even as the Joint Committee on Education and the Arts held a hearing on the
Governor's bill to require school systems to pay tuition for out-of-district pupils, the
House language was enacted in the supplemental budget (Chapter 6, An Act Establishing
Emergency Fiscal Controls for Fiscal Year 1991, effective 22 March 1991).

Since this budget expired on 30 June, no school system would be able to enroll out-
of-district pupils for the 1991–92 school year with confidence that tuition would be
paid by the state. Similar language, with two highly significant differences, was therefore included as outside language in the proposed FY 1992 (1991–92) budget: 'The
Commonwealth shall pay tuition to the host community'. Under this language, the
state would be obligated to pay tuition and could recoup a part of the cost by not paying
state aid for the pupil to the community of residence, but was not authorized (as in the
earlier language) to deduct the full out-of-district tuition cost. As we had advised the
Education Committee in February, charging the full cost would be highly inequitable
given the low proportion (less than 25 percent on average) of the costs of education paid
by the state in Massachusetts. Boston would lose state aid for six pupils to pay for one
attending a suburban school, even if that pupil was not previously in a public school in
Boston. And the limitation to pupils from Boston and Worcester was dropped.

Our efforts to convince Governor Weld's staff to consider more carefully the design of an interdistrict choice policy were in vain; indeed, in a letter to the Legislature
announcing his approval of the FY 1991 emergency budget, the governor made a point
that the costs of interdistrict tuition would be recovered in full from the community of
residence, 'as a stimulus . . . to take a hard look at their curriculum, their hiring practices and their policies and to take some bold initiatives to improve their districts and
make them competitive with other public schools'.

In order to answer many questions about implementation for September 1991, the
governor issued an executive order establishing an advisory committee chaired by a
suburban superintendent, John Barranco. The committee was heavily weighted toward
supporters of the choice initiative. Of the ten members, only the Commissioner and the
nominee of the House Speaker were likely to be critical of the program.

The committee, however unrepresentative, provided the first opportunity for the
State Department of Education to gain a hearing for our concerns about the deficiencies
of the interdistrict choice program as enacted in the budget. As we told the committee,
the most serious concerns had to do with a) *assuring equal access* and b) *tuition costs*. We
asserted:

We have a great deal of experience, in Massachusetts, with designing and implementing school choice programs
that are equitable. These programs have always required substantial additional funding for parent information and
for transportation to ensure that children of families with limited means have an equal chance to participate. A
sound interdistrict choice plan will need to find a way to provide this support, or it will function to benefit only
those who already enjoy advantages.

We also made strong assertions about the devastating effects of the tuition plan.

In order to help the committee understand the complexities of funding interdistrict
choice under Massachusetts school finance arrangements, I developed a number of
simulations based on differing assumptions about who would transfer and how tuitions
would be paid. We had to assume, I advised the committee, that many pupils who were
already in out-of-district schools would now be charged to the new program, since it
would provide full tuition payments. We pointed out that, in October 1989: 11,648 public

school students attended out-of-district (or out-of-region) schools. Of these 1115 were state wards and 410 lived out-of-state, leaving 10,126 who might have been eligible for the [new inter-district] program'.

We pointed out several other considerations:

a) The budget language could be read to require an appropriation before implementation, especially in view of the possibility that a cost is imposed on local communities. This was the position taken by the board of education with respect to an earlier legislative proposal for interdistrict school choice, filed in early 1989.

b) The funds could be simply taken 'off the top' of the . . . state aid to education, reducing the funds available for general distribution under the formula.

c) The funds could be taken from the [state aid] entitlement that would otherwise be received by the community where the transferring student lives. This was the arrangement in the original version of interdistrict choice in the FY 91 budget, which was *not* enacted but replaced by the present language. It would create problems for at least three reasons:

   1) The per pupil state aid to the sending community will in almost all cases fall *far* short of the per pupil expenditures in the host community. Thus the sending community would lose its state aid for a number of pupils who are *not* transferring in order to support one who is . . .

       The impact on Boston, if the 3200 Metco pupils were converted to a tuition basis, would be particularly devastating. Including another 300 Boston residents already tuitioned, and assuming that another 500 might find suburban places under this program, the city would lose over $20 million or half of its projected [state] aid, leaving another 55,000 high-need pupils with less than $400 per pupil [of state aid].

   2) In FY 92 there will presumably be many communities receiving no . . . state aid or so little that the amount needed to offset tuition costs could quickly be exhausted.

   3) A substantial number of the students participating will presumably never have attended the public schools of the sending community, which would therefore not have been receiving state aid for them. The state aid lost would thus be that 'earned' by pupils who are still in the schools of the sending community.

d) The host community could be allowed to count the incoming pupil for purposes of state aid, and the sending community not allowed to do so. This would be simple and logical, but it would in no case produce the level of payment to the host community projected in the four scenarios, and it seems unlikely that many would participate.

e) In order to even out the disparities in the amount of per pupil state aid received by different communities (which would otherwise make students living in some communities more fiscally 'desirable' than those living in other communities), the host community could receive the amount of state aid that the student would have earned in the sending community, *or* the amount the student would earn in the host community, *whichever* is higher, either through the [state aid] distribution or as a state grant. . . . This would not produce sufficient support for each student to serve as an incentive, without additional state funding.

We had concluded, in 1988, after much discussion by a committee with more than fifty members representing business, labor, school systems and community groups, and hearings across the state, was that the present system of state aid to education *cannot* be used as the basis for a program of inter-district school choice.

After hearing and discussing these points, the committee decided to advise Governor Weld that the legislation authorizing the interdistrict choice program should be changed in several important ways before implementation. Most importantly, Chairman Barranco wrote to Governor Weld on 19 June advising that the legislation should not go forward without a state appropriation (which, in the fiscal climate of the moment, meant that it probably would not go forward at all), and the tuition should not 'be provided by deducting the tuition costs from the sending school district'. Further, the program should be implemented on a pilot basis only in 1991–92, with costs – including transportation – paid by the Commonwealth on a needs-tested basis.

Although the letter to the governor concluded by expressing the committee's eagerness to continue their work, their advice was so unwelcome that the committee was not called upon again. The attorney advising the governor in this area gave an early press interview (*The Boston Globe* 23 June 1991) that seemed to indicate Weld would follow at least some of the recommendations in order to make it possible for low-income pupils to participate, but it soon became clear that the Weld administration was determined to go ahead with its original model of unconstrained, unfunded choice.

To this end, the language in the FY 1992 budget was amended to make clear that the full cost of tuition would be deducted from the state aid that would otherwise go to the sending community. At that, I broke bureaucratic discretion and told reporters that the program would be 'a disaster' for urban school systems and their children, and would leave the door open to a new desegregation suit (*The Boston Herald* 12 July 1991).

I repeated this prediction to the Joint Education Committee in testimony on 12 November, saying that

> the present Massachusetts program, in my judgment, will place the Commonwealth in severe jeopardy of contributing to and being found guilty of *de jure* segregation of schools in Brockton and other cities. This could in turn readily lead to imposition of *metropolitan desegregation* plans in several parts of Massachusetts, involving mandatory reassignment of urban and suburban pupils to correct a condition created by actions of the Commonwealth and of suburban school committees . . .

Since it was not until late August that the administration made it clear that the interdistrict choice program would go ahead, few school committees ventured to offer spaces for the 1991–92 school year. The strong opposition of the statewide association of school superintendents to the program also helped to limit – or at least to delay – participation. Commissioner Raynolds met with representatives of this association and issued a circular that I drafted clarifying, to the extent possible at that time, what the new legislation would mean for existing and future out-of-district pupils. 'No School Committee is required to accept non-resident students,' he wrote, and 'no School Committee may prevent its students from attending school in another community under this program'.

> The Treasurer will *deduct* any tuition payments made to the community where the child attends school from the state aid that would otherwise be paid to the community where the child lives, and credit that amount to the receiving community. . . . The sending community will have funds deducted from its state aid to pay for resident students enrolled in another community under the School Choice program even if they did not previously attend the local public schools. (Harold Raynolds, Jr, 'School Choice', 22 July 1991)

Although the interdistrict choice program got off to a slow start, by November there were twenty-eight school systems participating and enrolling 834 out-of-district pupils altogether. Of these, only 341 (41 percent) had previously attended the public schools of the communities where they lived. Nearly as many (318, or 38 percent) had already been attending the host school, generally with tuition paid by their parents, while 85 (10 percent) had been enrolled in non-public schools, 57 (7 percent) had not yet started school, and 33 (4 percent) had been in other public schools. Only fifty-seven (less than 7 percent) of the pupils participating were non-white or Hispanic, contrasting with more than 19 percent of the total public school enrollment in Massachusetts.

The largest number of transfers between two communities, 114 pupils, was from the city of Brockton to Avon. While over 40 percent of Brockton's pupils are members of minority groups, this was true of only 18 percent of those going to Avon, according to an analysis made for Senator Arthur Chase (R, Worcester); 24 percent of all Brockton pupils were from families eligible for AFDC, but this was true of only 4 percent of those going to Avon.

It was Brockton that I had in mind when I suggested that the effect of the state-sponsored transfer program would be to exacerbate the isolation of minority pupils and thus could lead to a successful desegregation suit requiring a metropolitan remedy. Between October 1990 and October 1991 (when the interdistrict choice plan was first in effect) the minority proportion in Brockton's K–8 enrollment increased from 37 to 41 percent, and several schools became substantially more identifiable as 'minority schools'. Alone among Massachusetts cities with a substantial minority population, Brockton had never adopted a racial balance plan, relying upon informal measures to prevent minority isolation. The interdistrict program – lacking, as it does, any provisions to protect racial integration – may make this approach impossible in the future.

Parental decisions to transfer children from Brockton to Avon were by no means unjustified educationally. Avon spent $10,239 on each high school pupil in 1990–91, contrasted with Brockton's expenditure of $4780, a figure which the city was forced to cut severely in 1991–92. Class sizes in Brockton rose to thirty-five or forty, while Avon promised that no class would have more than twenty pupils. Avon had been an active recruiter of out-of-district high school pupils for several years, charging them only $1500 in 1990–91 compared with $10,239 charged to Brockton for each Brockton-resident high school pupil enrolled in Avon in 1991–92. The state's interdistrict choice program meant a loss of $933,563 from Brockton's state aid, or the salaries of forty-five teachers.

Another severely impacted city was Gloucester, required to lose over $400,000 (salaries for twenty-two teachers) in state aid for seventy pupils enrolled in Manchester-by-the-Sea; forty-eight of these pupils had already been enrolled in Manchester, paying $1500 in private tuition. Manchester's per-pupil high school expenditure was $7777 in 1990–91, compared with $4426 in Gloucester. The state aid to Gloucester was $288 per pupil, so the city lost state funding for twenty-seven pupils for each Gloucester pupil enrolled in Manchester.[1]

It is obvious that the loss of perhaps twenty pupils (in addition to those already attending Manchester schools) did not save the Gloucester schools $400,000, nor is it likely to have permitted the consolidation of classes to save even one teaching position; the pupils who left were not so neatly grouped. The financial loss to Gloucester, as to Brockton, required cutting services to hundreds of pupils who remained in the local schools, in general the less middle-class pupils, and disproportionately racial and linguistic minority pupils.

Eventually the outcry against the fiscal impact of this program on certain communities grew so strong that the Administration and Legislature agreed to provide $2.7 million in emergency assistance to these communities, provided that they filed plans showing how they would improve their schools to prevent a recurrence of the loss of pupils. Thus the school system was required, in effect, to confess that its own failures – not, for example, its lack of resources or its concentration of poor and minority children – were responsible for the desire of some parents to remove their children. The affected school systems were given three weeks to develop and submit

an educational corrective action plan containing information, recommendations and suggestions relative to 1) areas needing improvement within the school system of the applicant, 2) methods of improvement to be employed, 3) goals and objectives of said improvement, 4) evaluation and control methods to be used, 5) personnel to be engaged in such improvement, 6) results intended to be accomplished within one year from the date of application, and 7) methods of increasing parental involvement to be employed.

The funding was contingent upon approval of this plan by the state's Secretary of Education. Of course, this timeline precluded any process of real involvement of school staff and parents in assessing the problems or finding solutions.

Assistance was limited to 50 percent of their actual loss of state aid, except in cases where that loss was 2 percent or more of the total school system budget, in which case the assistance would be 75 percent of the loss. Funds left over would be used to offset the out-of-district tuition costs of pupils from communities receiving no aid at all from the state.

Rather than laying out state funds in advance to stimulate informed choice and to promote new educational programs, as proposed in the legislation we drafted for Governor Dukakis, the Weld Administration was eventually forced to spend as much to bail out the most impacted cities, without creating the dynamic changes we had hoped for.

Conclusions

Urban school systems in Massachusetts have found parent choice a powerful means of driving school reform and increasing educational opportunities for families who cannot afford to live in suburban communities or to pay for non-public schooling. Nearly 25 percent of the public school pupils in the state attend school in communities that have made a strong commitment to school choice plans, developed in consultation with and funded through the state's Office of Educational Equity. I described the nature of these plans in *The Public Interest* (1991 Spring, 103, pp. 91–92)

Controlled choice is intended to accomplish four objectives:

1) to give all pupils in a community (or in a geographical section of a larger city) equal access to every public school, regardless of where their families can afford to live;
2) to involve all parents (not just the most sophisticated) in making informed decisions about where their children will go to school;
3) to create pressure for the improvement, over time, of every school through eliminating guaranteed enrollment on the basis of residence; and
4) where necessary, to achieve racial desegregation of every school with as few mandatory assignments as possible.

Parent choice can be a very powerful element in a reform strategy, but experience in Massachusetts has made clear that choice does not function *by itself* to produce the benefits frequently claimed. The 'invisible hand' is not enough. A well-designed

strategy for putting choice to work for educational reform should include three
elements:

a)   procedures to assure equal access unlimited by race, wealth or influence, to
     maintain confidence in the fairness of the admission process, and (where re-
     quired by law or sought as a matter of policy) to promote the racial integration
     of each school;
b)   effective outreach and individual counseling to assure that as high a proportion
     as possible of parents make conscious, informed decisions about the schools
     that will serve their children well, and that schools are providing accurate and
     useful information about what they offer; and
c)   measures to assure that there are real educational choices available, including 1)
     removal of bureaucratic requirements that limit new approaches desired by
     parents and teachers, 2) help to schools that are not able to attract applications,
     3) leadership and other changes if such schools do not change over time, and
     4) opportunities for groups of teachers, parents, or others to initiate additional
     alternatives within or outside existing structures.

The Massachusetts experiment with unregulated interdistrict choice has in no sense
been a fair test of the potential of choice to drive school reform or to increase opportunities
for urban children, those whose parents are most eager for expanded choice. Instead,
the interdistrict choice program *serves only a highly self-selected group of families*; nearly half
of the pupils were already attending schools other than those of their community of
residence. This contrasts with the programs in sixteen Massachusetts cities, where *all*
parents are involved in the choice process and all schools seek to attract and retain pupils
through the quality and distinctiveness of their educational offerings.

The program *does nothing to collect or provide information about what schools can provide
or the distinctive ways in which they challenge and support pupils*. This contrasts with the
programs in sixteen Massachusetts cities, where *all* parents receive information in a
systematic way (and in several languages) and have the opportunity for counseling
about the educational options available.

Finally, the Massachusetts interdistrict choice program rewards the schools and
communities which are already perceived as more desirable, and reduces the resources
available to improve the schools that most poor and minority children attend. Thus it
*does nothing to stimulate the supply side through encouraging and supporting development of new
educational models*. This contrasts with the programs in sixteen Massachusetts cities,
where *all* schools are challenged to become distinctively effective because no school has
a guaranteed enrollment based upon residential attendance areas.

We have not yet succeeded, however, in these cities, in bringing the full power of
choice to bear for fundamental educational reform. Crowded facilities, the result of new
Hispanic and Asian immigration, make it necessary to assign pupils even to schools that
few request. Bureaucratic structures remain in place, and – as in any monopoly system
– there are strong pressures to protect weaker participants from the consequences of
their incompetence.

School choice programs that have not been planned and implemented in a responsible manner do harm not only to the children who are left behind in impoverished
schools but to the positive momentum that the idea of parental choice has been developing
over recent years. This has created the impression that choice is inimical to the interests
of poor and minority children. Well-designed choice policies, to the contrary, can help

to bring new educational opportunities into existence, while providing more equal access to children who are now warehoused in school systems incapable of change.

Note

1. Analyses based upon a memorandum by William Crowley and Thomas Collins, Massachusetts Department of Education, November 19, 1991, and fact sheets prepared by the staff of Senator Arthur Chase, November 1991.

12   The underrepresentation of women in school leadership[1]

Colleen Bell and Susan Chase

Using national data on students, faculty, educational leaders and board members, Bell and Chase demonstrate how the US educational system, from elementary through postsecondary levels, is stratified by gender and by race and ethnicity. The authors examine women's underrepresentation in the superintendency specifically and the persistence of that pattern since 1899. In 1992, 5.6 percent of the United States' K–12 superintendents were women, the highest proportion to date. In their conclusion, Bell and Chase review explanations for the continuing underrepresentation of women and of people of color in school administration.

Any understanding of the significance of race and gender in the educational system in the United States needs to be based on information about where boys, girls, men and women of various racial and ethnic backgrounds are located in that system. In this chapter we begin by examining the numerical representation by gender and race of students, faculty, leaders and board members. We then take a closer look at the numbers of women in the public school superintendency. In the final section, we offer an overview of explanations for the continued and persistent underrepresentation of women in school leadership.

Let us acknowledge at the outset that by narrowing our focus to gender and racial stratification, we are *not* addressing differences in the kinds of experiences various groups have even when they occupy the same position within the educational system. For example, as students, boys and girls, men and women, are present in roughly even proportions across levels of the system. However, a number of studies have demonstrated that the sexes do not have similar educational experiences. As a recent AAUW (1992) report demonstrates, schools shortchange girls and women in multiple ways. Bernice Sandler (1987) and Yolanda Moses (1989) point out that higher education provides 'a chilly climate' for women, especially women of color. Hence, readers should remember that our close look at numbers ignores curriculum, pedagogy and other powerful contextual factors.

Gender and racial/ethnic stratification

The educational system in the United States consists of a hierarchy of levels of schooling: preschool, elementary, middle, high school, and higher education (including college and postgraduate study). For students, movement between these levels is marked by promotion from one grade to the next and by the earning of diplomas and degrees. For teachers and administrators, the hierarchical structure of these levels is marked by different certification requirements and by the greater prestige and salaries accorded to those at the higher levels.

Tables 12.1 and 12.2 present data that show how our educational system is strati-

Table 12.1: **Percentages of female students, faculty, leaders and board members at various levels in the us education system[10]**

	Students	Faculty	Leaders	Board Members
Postsecondary Level	54.5[1]	27.3[2]	11.3[3]	20[4]
Secondary Level	48.8[7]	52[8]	5.6[5] (sup'ts) 7.6[9] (principals)	34.7[6]
Middle Level	48.6[7]	57[8]	23[9]	
Elementary Level		87[8]	37[9]	

Notes: 1 *Almanac (1992, p. 11) 1990 data.*
  2 *Almanac (1992, p. 28) 1989–90 data.*
  3 *cupa (1991) 1991 data.*
  4 *Chamberlain (1988) 1985 data.*
  5 *Bell and Chase survey (1992) 1991–92 data.*
  6 *'Leadership' (1991) 1991 data.*
  7 *us Bureau of the Census (1991) 1989 data.*
  8 *ers (1988) 1987 data.*
  9 American School Board Journal *(December 1991) 1991 data.*
  10 *Data for K–12 schools refer to public institutions only; data for postsecondary schooling include public and private institutions.*

fied by race and ethnicity and by gender. Table 12.1 focuses on proportions of girls and women as students, faculty, leaders and policymakers at various levels of the educational system in the United States; Table 12.2 examines proportions of persons of color as students, faculty, leaders and policymakers. In these tables, the leadership column includes principals at three levels – elementary, middle school and high school – as well as superintendents and college presidents.

While the sexes are distributed more or less equally among students across educational levels, among faculty, women are concentrated at the elementary level and decrease in number as we look at middle school, secondary and postsecondary teachers. Although women comprise a majority of the nation's public school teaching force (70 percent of all elementary, middle school and secondary teachers are women according to a 1992 nces report), most school administrators are men. This is the case even though administrators are drawn from the ranks of teachers and in spite of the fact that women have made up at least half of enrollments in the nation's educational administration preparation programs since the mid-1980s (Miller 1986). Moreover, school administration at the highest level in public schools – the superintendency – is particularly resistant to the integration of women. It is noteworthy that in 1986 only 12 percent of faculty in educational administration preparation programs were women (McCarthy, Kuh, Newell and Iacona 1988) compared to the 27 percent of college faculty who are women overall. Interestingly, the percentage of women college presidents is higher than that of women in the superintendency, even though one of the major pools from which college presidents emerge – college faculty – is only 27 percent women.

Table 12.2 demonstrates that faculty, educational leaders, and board members do not closely reflect the racial and ethnic diversity of the student body, particularly in

Table 12.2: Percentages of students, faculty, leaders and board members at various levels in the US education system by race/ethnicity[8]

	Students	Faculty	Leaders	Board Members
Postsecondary Level	.75% American Indian[1] 4.0% Asian 8.9% Black 5.5% Hispanic 77.8% White	.3% American Indian[2] 4.7% Asian 4.5% Black 2.0% Hispanic 88.5% White	8% 'minority'[3] 92% 'nonminority'	6.3% Black[4] .6% Hispanic 3.0% other minority 90.0% White
Secondary Level	.9% American Indian 2.8% Asian 16.1% Black 9.9% Hispanic 70.4% White		.8% American Indian[5] .3% Asian 2.5% Black .6% Hispanic 95.8% White (sup'ts) 3.1% Black[5] 1.5% Hispanic 94.7% White (principals)	.3% American Indian .3% Asian 2.2% Black .8% Hispanic 96.5% White
Middle Level		8.2% Black[7] 2.9% Hispanic 88.8% White	9.3% Black[5] 2.1% Hispanic 88.7% White	
Elementary Level			1.0% American Indian 1.5% Asian 7.8% Black 1.5% Hispanic 87.9% White	

Notes:
1. Almanac (1992, p. 11) 1990 data.
2. Almanac (1992, p. 16) 1989–90 data.
3. CUPA (1991) 1991 data. Respondents indicated whether they were members of a minority group but were not asked to identify their race/ethnicity.
4. Chamberlain (1988) 1985 data.
5. 'Leadership' (1991) 1991 data.
6. NCES (1991) 1986 data.
7. NCES (1992) 1988 data.
8. Data for K–12 schools refers to public institutions only; data for postsecondary schooling includes both public and private institutions. Because of rounding, figures in this table may not add up to 100 percent. It should also be noted that Hispanics can be of any race.

K–12 schooling. While 16 percent of elementary, middle and secondary students are black, just 8 percent of teachers are black. The nearly 10 percent of learners who are Hispanic study in a system where less than 3 percent of teachers are Hispanic. Similarly at the postsecondary level, blacks, Hispanics, and American Indians are smaller proportions of faculty (as well as presidents and board members) than they are of students. Asians, who comprise 4 percent of students in colleges and universities and 4.7 percent of faculty, are an exception to this pattern.

Among administrators, the middle school level has the highest representation of black principals (9.3 percent) and of Hispanic principals (2.1 percent). At the highest levels of school administration and policymaking, positions are even more likely to be filled by whites. At the high school level 95 percent of principals are white; in the superintendency 96 percent are white; and among the nation's school board members 96.5 percent are white.

Persistent underrepresentation: The superintendency

The underrepresentation of women in school administration has a well-documented history (Hansot and Tyack 1981, Jones and Montenegro 1983, Schmuck 1975, Shakeshaft 1989, Strober and Tyack 1980). Because the superintendency has been particularly resistant to the integration of women, we examine it in more depth here. In this section we begin by looking closely at women's representation in the contemporary superintendency and then cast this picture into historical perspective.

A contemporary picture

In 1986 we began a study of women in the K–12 superintendency, a study based primarily on in-depth interviews with women superintendents about their work experiences. In order to determine the number of women superintendents in the United States' K–12 public school districts, we also conducted a survey of all fifty state departments of education, a survey that we repeated in 1989 and in 1991. Our primary reason for conducting these surveys lay in our need for more exact information about women's numerical representation than that provided by other surveys. Most surveys of the numbers of women occupying public school superintendencies rely on general categories in the collection and reporting of data. Recent surveys from professional organizations such as the American Association of School Administrators do not distinguish, for example, top leadership positions by district type; they count in the category 'superintendent' the top administrators in such varied sites as elementary districts, high school districts, K–12 districts, and vocational school districts. For some purposes this level of generality is acceptable, but when an inclusive category encompasses many specific subgroups it may be misleading. Furthermore, states vary in school district organization and structure, and so it is important to evaluate comparability of positions (rather than only official titles) across state contexts.

Table 12.3 is based on our surveys of state departments of education and reports the number of women in the K–12 superintendency by state, in 1986, 1989 and 1991. Fluctuations in states' data across years are due to changes in data collection and reporting as well as to consolidation and reorganization of districts. The proportions of women in the K–12 superintendency were 2.8 percent in 1986–87, 4.2 percent in 1989–90, and 5.6 percent in 1991–92.

Table 12.4 provides the breakdown of women K–12 superintendents by race and ethnicity in 1989 and 1991 from those state departments that collect such data. In 1989 only twenty-six state departments reported race *and* gender figures for the superintendency, compared with thirty-nine in 1991.

The overall picture of school administration is one of white dominance (96.6 percent of superintendents are white) as well as male dominance (94.4 percent of superintendents are men). According to a 1990 report from the American Association of School Administrators, just 3.4 percent of all superintendents in the nation in 1989–90 were African American, American Indian, Hispanic or Asian American (Jones and Montengro 1990).

Historical perspective

Table 12.5 adapts a format employed by a number of other scholars (Jones and Montenegro 1983, Hansot and Tyack 1981) to summarize results of selected studies of women's numerical representation in the superintendency between 1899 and 1992. It is important to interpret these percentages carefully for several reasons. Definitions of 'superintendency' are not consistent across these studies, as we have noted. Data reported by Bell and Chase (1987, 1990, 1992) in this table are for K–12 superintendencies only, whereas the AASA surveys (Jones and Montenegro 1983, 1985) include superintendents who lead K–8, county, and vocational-technical districts as well as K–12 districts. Further, composition and size of study samples vary. Some surveys rely upon individual superintendent reports and others gather data from state departments of education or chief state school officers. The data summarized in this table show that although women are present in the superintendency in greater proportions than ever before, the change in women's representation in the past century has been quite small.

Explanations for the underrepresentation of women

In the past twenty years, scholars have proposed and examined multiple explanations for the continuing underrepresentation of women and people of color in school administration. In what follows we will summarize these explanations with a focus on women, both white women and women of color.

Interestingly, explanations of women's underrepresentation have changed very little since Suzanne Estler's important article, 'Women as leaders in public education' (1975). Estler and those following her have emphasized enduring structural and cultural barriers to women's integration. Perhaps the major difference between the earlier and later studies is the confidence with which commentators reject the notion that women's 'internal barriers' – particularly women's lack of aspiration – explain women's absence from leadership positions. Following Kanter (1977), most researchers now interpret the presence or absence of aspiration in light of the structure of opportunities women face in occupational fields. In other words, they explain what appears at first to be an internal barrier as an external barrier. Shakeshaft (1989) offers an extensive overview of various structural and cultural explanations and their development in numerous studies of school administration. She also places her discussion within the broader context of male dominance of positions of power in Western societies. Ortiz and Marshall's (1988) analysis of the opportunity structure and culture of school administration and Sadker,

Table 12.3: Number of women in K–12 superintendencies by state, 1986–1991

State	1986–87 K–12 Sup'ts	1986–87 Women K–12 Sup'ts	1989–90 K–12 Sup'ts	1989–90 Women K–12 Sup'ts	1991–92 K–12 Sup'ts	1991–92 Women K–12 Sup'ts
AL	128	6	128	6	129	6
AK	54	4	54	5	54	5
AR	329	2	329	8	321	10
AZ	83	3	84	17	87	14[1]
CA	263	7	275	16[2]	289	24[1]
CO	173	4	172	8	176	13
CT	110	6	110	7	110	9
DE	16	0	16	1	16	1
FL	67	6	67	4	67	7
GA	178	11	179	13	176	15
HI[3]	7	4	7	5	7	3
ID[4]	106	2	106	1	111	3
IL	443	2	427	0	413	6
IN	290	6	289	7	238	6
IA	422	9	394	8	344	11
KS	304	2	303	3	303	3
KY	173	3	177	6	176	4
LA	66	0	66	3	66	4
MA	233	10	286	25	208	26
MD	24	1	24	1	24	2
ME	123	6	114	8	124	13
MI	527	9	522	17	524	32
MN	401	9	348[4]	15	322[4]	10
MO	452	7	453	11	453	14
MS	153	3	151	4	154[4]	6
MT[5]	159	6	155	9	155	21
NC	140	5	134	7	132	9
ND	270	3	217	3	198	2
NE	278	1	260	2	248	3
NH	59	1	63	2	65	6
NJ	226	11	210	16	222	24
NM	88	6	88	13	88	12
NV	16	0	16	0	17	1
NY	655	21	651	29	650	45
OH	615	25	612	25	612	31
OK	456	7	453	10	442	18
OR	155	7	165	7	155	6
PA	499	26	499	27	498	29
RI	30	2	30	2	31	4
SC	92	7	91	4	91	7
SD	175	0	139[4]	1	168	2
TN	122	8	137	14	121	11
TX	911	22	1068	37	1017	57
UT	40	0	40	1	40	1
VA	131	4	133	6	133	7
VT	4	0	4	0	4	0
WA	245	8	246	25	245	24

Table 12.3: (Cont.)

State	1986–87		1989–90		1991–92	
	K–12 Sup'ts	Women K–12 Sup'ts	K–12 Sup'ts	Women K–12 Sup'ts	K–12 Sup'ts	Women K–12 Sup'ts
WV	55	4	55	4	55	6
WI	367	10	382	13	357	20
WY	47	1	47	2	47	1
TOTAL	10960	307	11007	459	10683	594

Notes: 1 1990–91 data.
2 One of these women was a 'cosuperintendent'.
3 Hawaii is organized as a single statewide system with one board of education and state school officer. There are seven district superintendents who report to the state superintendent, each of whom is responsible for students in all grade levels K–12. These seven positions were treated as K–12 superintendencies in this survey because their work situations were comparable to those of K–12 superintendents in other states.
4 Figures reflect fulltime equivalents rather than persons.
5 While Montana districts are not organized as K–12 districts, there are superintendents who head high school as well as elementary districts. Because their work situations are comparable to those of K–12 superintendents in other states, these positions were included as K–12 superintendencies for the purposes of this survey.

Sadker and Klein's (1991) review of the significance of gender in K–12 education also provide important discussions of structural and cultural barriers.

Generally, researchers have pointed to several interrelated processes that impede women's integration into educational administration. First, gender stratification in schools is maintained by differential access to opportunities for advancement. While administrators emerge from the ranks of teachers, elementary teachers (87 percent women) are less likely than secondary teachers (52 percent women) to have access to opportunities through which vertical promotion occurs. Opportunities to perform extracurricular duties and entry-level administrative tasks such as directing special programs, coaching, and chairing departments exist primarily at the secondary level where male teachers are concentrated (Wheatley 1981). While the elementary principalship (37 percent women) is the administrative position that women are most likely to occupy, this position rarely leads to further promotion. By contrast, the high school principalship (7.6 percent women) is often a stepping stone to higher positions, including the district superintendency (Gaertner 1981).

Second, gatekeepers – those who have influence in the hiring and evaluation of school administrators – are predominantly white men. In the case of the superintendency, gatekeepers include established superintendents who have clout at local, state and national levels; consultants who are hired by school boards to conduct superintendency searches; professors of educational administration who establish internships for future administrators and introduce people to informal networks; and school board members who are responsible for hiring and evaluating superintendents.

Career opportunities for women and particularly for women of color are further limited by a form of occupational segregation in which desirable schools or 'plum' districts are seen as the province of experienced white males (Edson 1988, Doughty 1980). Valverde and Brown (1988) identify a pattern in which administrators of color

Table 12.4: **Number of women in K–12 superintendencies by race/ethnicity and state, 1989 and 1991**

State	1989–90						1991–92					
	American Indian	Asian	Black	Hispanic	White	All	American Indian	Asian	Black	Hispanic	White	All
AL			1		5	6			1		5	6
AK											4	5
AR			2		6	8			1		9	10
AZ	1	1		2	13	17	1				13	14[1]
CA									2	2	20	24[1]
CO			1		7	8			1		12	13
CT					7	7					9	9
DE									1			1
FL											7	7
GA									1		14	15
HI								2			1	3
ID					1	1					3	3
IL									1		5	6
IN			1		6	7					6	6
IA					8	8					11	11
KS											3	3
MA				1	24	25			1		25	26
MD					1	1					2	2
ME											13	13
MI			2		13	17[2]			4		28	32
MS					4	4					6	6
MT					9	9					20	21[3]
NC			1		6	7			1		8	9
ND					3	3					2	2
NE											3	3
NJ		1	3		12	16		1	3	1	19	24
NV											1	1
OH			1		24	25					31	31

OK					10	10					18	18
OR					7	7					6	6
PA		1			26	27						
RI					3	3						
SC					4	4					7	7
SD			1		1	1					2	2
TN				1					1		10	11
TX					37	37				5	52	57
UT					1	1					1	1
VA											7	7
WA	1	1	1	1			1		1			
WI					21	25		1	1	1	21	24
WY				1					1		19	20
											1	1
TOTAL	2	3	14	4	259	284	3	4	19	9	424	460

Notes:

1 1990–91 data.

2 This 1989–90 state total includes two women whose race/ethnicity was designated as 'other'.

3 This 1991–92 state total includes one women of unknown race/ethnicity.

Table 12.5:   Women in the US public school superintendency, 1899–1992

Year	Percentage of Superintendents Who Were Women*	Composition and Size of Study Samples	Source
1899	0.9	113 cities of 10,000+ population	Tyack (1976)
1928	1.6	not specified	Shakeshaft (1989)
1950	2.1	not specified	Shakeshaft (1989)
1972–73	0.1	N = 13,037 sup'ts	NEA (cited in Hansot and Tyack, 1981)
1982	1.8	N = 13,715 in 50 states & DC	Jones and Montenegro (1983)
1984–85	2.67	N = 11,055 in 41 states & DC	Jones and Montenegro (1985)
1986–87	2.8	50 state depts of education	Bell, Chase and Livingston (1987)
1989–90	4.2	50 state depts of education	Bell and Chase (1990)
1991–92	5.6	50 state depts of education	Bell and Chase (1992)

Note: * These percentages must be interpreted with care because of differences among the surveys in definition of 'superintendent' and in methodology.

are assigned to special programs and schools with large concentrations of students of color. Research on African American administrators has shown that black superintendents are often appointed to systems with inadequate financial resources (Scott 1980, 1990, Revere 1987, Sizemore 1986), districts with large concentrations of students of color and economically disadvantaged students, and low achievement test scores (Moody 1983, Townsel and Banks 1975). Black women are much more likely than their white counterparts to be clustered in and around cities (Revere 1987, Sizemore 1986). As Scott (1980) predicted over a decade ago: '[E]xpansion in the ranks of black superintendents will be related to whites not wanting to deal with the engrossing problems of cities' (p. 188).

Third, researchers point to the persistence of subtle and blatant forms of sex discrimination and racial/ethnic discrimination and impediments to women's integration into the occupation. Instances of discrimination range from the relatively benign neglect of not receiving help in finding internships or being ignored during their graduate education, to blatantly sexist or racist attitudes and overt discrimination in hiring. Even when they have hired women superintendents, school board members report that their deliberations included discussion about whether their communities would accept a woman as leader, and whether women could assert the authority necessary for the job. In addition, school boards sometimes evaluate negatively the decisiveness and assertiveness of the women they hire. Women superintendents are not always aware of these gender-related concerns because they are usually raised behind closed doors (Bell 1988). While these forms of subtle discrimination are often discussed in the literature, there is another important factor that is rarely addressed. Even when school board members and consultants express acceptance of women in positions of educational leadership, they explain women's actions in ways that conceal relations of dominance in the contexts in which women superintendents work. In particular, the ideological discourses of individual achievement and gender neutrality turn attention away from inequalities structured into the occupation and onto the woman's successful performance as an individual (Chase and Bell 1990). In other words, seemingly neutral language also contributes to the persistence of male dominance in positions of power.

This focus on structural and cultural barriers to women's integration into positions in educational administration is supported by the broader sociological literature on women in white and male-dominated professions. Many social scientists emphasize men's control of the formal and informal sites of hiring, decision making, power brokering and sponsorship, and argue that women – especially women of color – are rarely members of the inner circles that provide these resources and opportunities (Lorber 1984, Epstein 1983, Clark and Corcoran 1986, Fullbright 1986). Others point to the particular pressures that women experience when most or all of their colleagues are either men or white: greater performance expectations, exclusion from collegial groups and stereotypical interpretations of their actions (Kanter 1977, Dumas 1980, Benjamin 1991). Even when white women and women of color are among the gatekeepers, they are usually a numerical minority and thus subject to the same kinds of exclusion and isolation that women in leadership positions are subject to. Some scholars show that men's higher gender status and whites' higher race status reinforce the identification of masculinity and whiteness with highly valued professional traits (Kaufman 1989, Reskin 1978, Leggon 1980). Moreover, the timing of professional careers around men's life cycles fortifies the persistent assumption that women who have children are not committed professionals (Bourne and Wikler 1982).

A fourth set of explanations for the continuing underrepresentation of white women and women of color as leaders in educational systems centers around public policy trends and their effects on equity. In a study of the scope of change in federal education policy during the Reagan administration, Clark and Astuto (1986) pointed out that after 1980 attention to equity was replaced by a focus on 'excellence'. The title and substance of *A Nation at Risk*, a 1983 report of the National Commission on Excellence in Education, exemplifies this shift through its emphasis on establishing and enforcing performance standards and by its silence on equity policies and standards (Clark and Astuto 1986, Sadker, Sadker and Klein 1991). This federal policy shift set the stage for state and local policy action as well as the debate about education reform in the mid-1980s, a debate that virtually ignored equity issues. Sadker, Sadker and Steindam's (1989) content analysis of 138 articles on reform during this period reveals that less than 1 percent of the space they occupied in prominent education journals was devoted to gender equity.

Even though federal, state and local affirmative action and equal employment opportunity policies such as the 1964 Civil Rights Act remained in place during this period, attention to the new excellence agenda displaced monitoring and enforcement of extant equity policies. The shift of attention away from equity carried over into the 1990s and continues to shape girls' and women's access to and experiences in the US educational system.

Concluding observations

This broad look at trends in women's numerical representation in the US educational system, and at explanations for their underrepresentation, describes the context within which women lead schools. In two of the following chapters, Ortiz and Ortiz and Marshall go beyond the numbers and focus on experiences of educational leaders. Their chapters demonstrate that in a context of white and male-dominance, white women and men and women of color develop strategies for dealing with their differences from the majority of school leaders. These strategies de-emphasize difference, allowing administrators who are essentially 'outsiders within' (Collins 1990) to focus on what is expected of insiders. In a third chapter, Goldring and Chen show that even when women are numerically dominant at one level in a system, if they are isolated from influential networks, they remain underrepresented in national education policy. Thus while it is important to recognize patterns of segregation and stratification in educational systems, it is crucial to examine how social and political relationships are enacted within those structures.

Note

1. Research for this chapter was funded by the US Department of Education's Office of Educational Research and Improvement, the University of Tulsa, and Hamline University. We would like to acknowledge the work of Martina Thompson, who served as our research assistant in 1990 and 1992.

References

ALMANAC [Special issue] (1992) *Chronicle of Higher Education*, 39 (1) 26 August.
AMERICAN ASSOCIATION OF UNIVERSITY WOMEN (AAUW) (1992) *How Schools Shortchange Girls* (Washington DC: AAUW).
BELL, C. S. (1988) 'Organizational influences on women's experience in the superintendency', *Peabody Journal of Education*, 65 (4) pp. 31–59.
BELL, C. S. and CHASE, S. E. (1990) 'Women's numerical representation in the K–12 superintendency, 1989–90', unpublished raw data.
BELL, C. S. and CHASE, S. E. (1992) 'Women's numerical representation in the K–12 superintendency, 1991–92', unpublished raw data.
BELL, C. S., CHASE, S. E., and LIVINGSTON, M. (1987) 'Women in the superintendency: Their views on opportunities, barriers, and choices', in M. COMBS (ed.) *Proceedings of the Oklahoma Education Research Symposium IV: Reflecting on Our Past to Inform Future Practice* (Stillwater, OK: Oklahoma State University) pp. 73–77.
BENJAMIN, L. (1991) *The Black Elite: Facing the Color Line in the Twilight of the Twentieth Century* (Chicago: Nelson-Hall Publishers).
BOURNE, P. G. and WIKLER, N. J. (1982) 'Commitment and the cultural mandate: Women in medicine', in R. KAHN-HUT, A. K. DANIELS and R. COLVARD (eds) *Women and Work: Problems and Perspectives* (New York: Oxford University Press) pp. 111–2.
CHAMBERLAIN, M. K. (ed.) (1988) *Women in Academe: Progress and Prospects* (New York: Russell Sage Foundation).
CHASE, S. E. and BELL, C. S. (1990) 'Ideology, discourse, and gender: How gatekeepers talk about women school superintendents', *Social Problems*, 37 (2) pp. 163–77.
CLARK, D. L. and ASTUTO, T. A. (1986) 'The significance and permanence to changes in federal education policy', *Educational Researcher*, 15 (8) pp. 4–13.
CLARK, S. M. and CORCORAN, M. (1986) Perspectives on the professional socialization of women faculty: A case of accumulative disadvantage?', *Journal of Higher Education*, 57 (1) pp. 20–43.
COLLEGE AND UNIVERSITY PERSONNEL ASSOCIATION (CUPA) (1991) *Compensation, Benefits, and Conditions of Employment for College and University Chief Executives* (Washington DC: CUPA).
COLLINS, P. H. (1990) *Black Feminist Thought: Knowledge, Consciousness, and the Politics of Empowerment* (Boston: Unwin Hyman).
DOUGHTY, R. (1980) 'The Black female administrator: Woman in a double bind', in S. K. BIKLEN and M. B. BRANNIGAN (eds) *Women and Educational Leadership* (Lexington, MA: D. C. Heath).
DUMAS, R. G. (1980) 'Dilemmas of Black females in leadership', in L. F. RODGERS-ROSE (ed.) *The Black Woman* (Beverly Hills: Sage) pp. 203–15.

EDSON, S. K. (1988) *Pushing the Limits: The Female Administrative Aspirant* (Albany, NY: SUNY Press).

EDUCATIONAL RESEARCH SERVICE (ERS) (1988) *Men and Women in Public Elementary and Secondary Education* (Arlington, VA: Educational Research Service).

EPSTEIN, C. F. (1983) *Women in Law* (New York: Anchor/Doubleday).

ESTLER, S. E. (1975) 'Women as leaders in public education', Signs, 1 (2) pp. 363–86.

FULLBRIGHT, K. (1986) 'The myth of the double-advantage: Black female managers', in M. SIMMS and J. MALVEAUX (eds) *Slipping through the Cracks: The Status of Black Women* (New Brunswick, NJ: Transaction Books) pp. 33–45.

GAERTNER, K. N. (1981) 'Administrative careers in public school organizations', in P. A. SCHMUCK, W. W. CHARTERS, Jr and R. O. CARLSON (eds) *Educational Policy and Management: Sex Differentials* (New York: Academic Press) pp. 199–217.

HANSOT, E. and TYACK, D. B. (1981) *The Dream Deferred: A Golden Age for Women School Administrators* (Policy Paper no. 81-C2) (Stanford: Institute for Research on Educational Finance and Governance, Stanford University).

JONES, E. H. and MONTENEGRO, X. P. (1983) *Women and Minorities in School Administration: Strategies for Making a Difference* (ERIC/CUE Urban Diversity Series No. 85) (Washington DC: National Institute of Education; ERIC Document Reproduction Service No. ED 237 607).

JONES, E. H. and MONTENEGRO, X. P. (1985) *Women and Minorities in School Administration* (Arlington, VA: American Association of School Administrators).

JONES, E. H. and MONTENEGRO, X. P. (1990) *Women and Minorities in School Administration* (Arlington, VA: American Association of School Administrators).

KANTER, R. M. (1977) *Men and Women of the Corporation* (New York: Basic Books).

KAUFMAN, D. R. (1989) 'Professional women: How real are recent gains?', in J. FREEMAN (ed.) *Women: A Feminist Perspective*, 4th edn (Mountain View, CA: Mayfield Publishing Company) pp. 329–46.

'LEADERSHIP' (1991) *Education Vital Signs* [supplement to *American School Board Journal* and *The Executive Educator*], 178 (12) December, pp. A10–A12.

LEGGON, C. B. (1980) 'Black female professionals: Dilemmas and contradictions of status', in L. F. RODGERS-ROSE (ed.) *The Black Woman* (Beverly Hills: Sage) pp. 189–202.

LORBER, J. (1984) *Women Physicians: Career, Status, and Power* (New York: Tavistock Publications).

McCARTHY, M. M., KUH, G. D., NEWELL, L. J. and IACONA, C. (1988) *Under Scrutiny: The Educational Administration Professoriate* (Tempe, AZ: University Council for Educational Administration).

MILLER, J. Y. (1986) 'Lonely at the top', *School & Community*, 72, pp. 9–11.

MOODY, C. D., SR (1983) 'On becoming a superintendent: Contest or sponsored mobility?', *Journal of Negro Education*, 52 (4) pp. 383–97.

MOSES, Y. T. (1989) *Black Women in Academe: Issues and Strategies* (Washington DC: Project on the Status and Education of Women, Association of American Colleges).

NATIONAL CENTER FOR EDUCATION STATISTICS (NCES) (1991) *Digest of Education Statistics* (Washington DC: US Department of Education).

NATIONAL CENTER FOR EDUCATIONAL STATISTICS (NCES) (1992) *American Education at a Glance* (Washington DC: US Department of Education).

NATIONAL COMMISSION ON EXCELLENCE IN EDUCATION (1983) *A Nation at Risk* (Washington DC: US Government Printing Office).

ORTIZ, F. I. and MARSHALL, C. (1988) 'Women in educational administration', in N. K. BOYAN (ed.) *Handbook of Research on Educational Administration* (White Plains, NY: Longman) pp. 123–41.

RESKIN, B. F. (1978) 'Sex differentiation and the social organization of science', *Sociological Inquiry*, 48 (3–4) pp. 6–37.

REVERE, A. B. (1987) 'Black women superintendents in the United States: 1984–85', *Journal of Negro Education*, 56 (4) pp. 510–20.

SADKER, M., SADKER, D. and KLEIN, S. (1991) 'The issue of gender in elementary and secondary education', in G. GRANT (ed.) *Review of Research in Education*, 17, pp. 285–94.

SADKER, M., SADKER, D. and STEINDAM, S. (1989) 'Gender equity and educational reform', *Educational Leadership*, 46, pp. 44–47.

SANDLER, B. R. (1987) 'The classroom climate: Still a chilly one for women', in C. LASSER (ed.) *Educating Men and Women Together* (Urbana: University of Illinois Press) pp. 113–23.

SCHMUCK, P. A. (1975) 'Deterrents to women's careers in school management', *Sex Roles*, 1 (4) pp. 339–353.

SCOTT, H. J. (1980) *The Black Superintendent: Messiah or Scapegoat?* (Washington DC: Howard University Press).

SCOTT, H. J. (1990) 'Views of Black school superintendents on Black consciousness and professionalism', *Journal of Negro Education*, 59 (2) pp. 165–172.

SHAKESHAFT, C. (1989) *Women in Educational Administration*, 2nd edn (Newbury Park, CA: Sage).

SIZEMORE, B. A. (1986) 'The limits of the Black superintendency', *Journal of Educational Equity and Leadership*, 6 (3) pp. 180–208.

STROBER, M. H. and TYACK, D. B. (1980) 'Why do women teach and men manage?', *Signs*, 5, pp. 494–503.

TOWNSEL, C. W. and BANKS, L. A. (1975) 'The urban school administrator: A Black perspective', *Journal of Negro Education*, 44 (3) pp. 421–31.

TYACK, D. B. (1976) 'Pilgrim's progress: Toward a social history of the school superintendency, 1860–1960', *History of Education Quarterly*, 32, pp. 257–300.

US BUREAU OF THE CENSUS (1991) *Statistical Abstract of the United States*, 111th ed, (Washington DC: US Government Printing Office).

VALVERDE, L. A. and BROWN, F. (1988) 'Influences in leadership development among racial and ethnic minorities', in N. K. BOYAN (ed.) *Handbook of Research on Educational Administration* (New York: Longman).

WHEATLEY, M. (1981) 'The effects of organizational structures on sex equity in education', in P. A. SCHMUCK, W. W. CHARTERS, JR and R. O. CARLSON (eds) *Educational Policy and Management: Sex Differentials* (New York: Academic Press) pp. 255–71.

13   Politicizing executive action: The case of Hispanic female superintendents

Flora Ida Ortiz and David Jude Ortiz

The dramatic demographic changes taking place in US society are being mirrored in our public schools. Minority students representing diverse groups are outnumbering white students. This diversity is, however, not reflected at the superintendency level. Thus, the position of the superintendent is affected in two major ways when it is assumed by a Hispanic female. First, it serves as a symbol for the school board and community and second, it challenges the existing school organization structure. The challenge means that the Hispanic female superintendent conceptualizes her role and actions in fulfilling organizational ends with particular emphasis on uniformity and equity.

This chapter is a comparison of two Hispanic female superintendents' use of executive and political responsibility. The report is based on two separate studies that yielded many interesting and useful theoretical points that are addressed elsewhere (Ortiz 1991, Ortiz and Ortiz 1992). The present report is limited to a discussion about executive and political responsibility at the superintendency level as enacted by Hispanic females. As has been reported in the literature, (Blumberg and Blumberg 1985, 1991, Boyd 1974, Burlingame 1981, Hess 1977) superintendents' relationships with their school boards and communities are very often political. The two Hispanic female superintendents who are being examined here struggle to maintain an executive relationship while social, community and organizational forces impose political stress. The objective of this report is to display the distinction between executive and political responsibility, to examine how that distinction is related to gender and ethnicity, to demonstrate how Hispanic females maintain the distinction, and finally to show the process by which executive actions are challenged and politicized.

The reason that it is important to make these distinctions is because unlike the appointment of white males to the superintendency, the appointment of Hispanic females has symbolic and political overtones. However, as shall be seen, the superintendent's executive legitimacy is not granted for fulfilling the symbolic function or special group interests, but for adhering to the tenets of traditional executive action, that is, providing procedural order and resource allocation.

The dramatic demographic changes taking place in US society are being mirrored in our public schools. Minority students representing diverse groups are outnumbering the white students. However, the public school hierarchy remains predominantly white. Diversity is more common in the support services, but rare in the school boards and administrative ranks. Thus, the position of the superintendent is affected in two major ways when it is assumed by a Hispanic female. First, it serves as a symbol for the school board and community and second, it challenges the existing school organization structure.

The superintendents

School superintendents obtain their positions through sponsorship. They normally come to the job with extensive experience and organizational support. Most superintendents are promoted from within their own districts, those who are not come with established reputations and regional or statewide networks.

Dr. Singer obtained the superintendency with all of the traditional support systems, having established a regional and statewide reputation as a school administrator who had worked her way up the ranks. Being an associate superintendent for personnel for several years in a school district requiring extensive union negotiation, her successful resolution of both classified and certificated union conflicts was well known.

Dr. Zagala, on the other hand, was less experienced and younger. Support systems and networks were not extensively developed. There is some evidence of sponsorship from a university professor and the board president during the time when she was hired. The university professor provided some advice regarding the structure of the central office and the board president had known Dr. Zagala when they were both state school board members.

Dr. Singer from Willow Creek Unified School District was unanimously supported in her appointment to the superintendency. The district had been in desperate instability since 1974, for example, a dozen different superintendents had served in the last seven years. School administrator turnover was equally high. Instability was also reflected in the bankrupt financial state of the district.

Willow Creek Unified School District is one of the largest school districts in the state with an enrollment of over 33,000. The student population served by Willow Creek Unified School District is among the most diverse in the United States serving Anglo, black, Hispanic, American Indian, Korean, Cambodian, Taiwanese, Vietnamese, Indian, Japanese, Laotian, Filipino, and Central and South American students. The major issues faced by the district were finances, personnel morale, student performance, overcrowding and aging school buildings. Dr. Singer was expected to provide stability to the school district. There was no residence requirement for her; nonetheless, she resides in a local apartment while maintaining a permanent residence elsewhere.

Dr. Zagala was also unanimously supported when she was hired by the Arena Unified School District which serves five communities with approximately 15,250 students enrolled. The student body represents Hispanic, Anglo, black, Asian, American Indian, and Filipino ethnic groups. The district lies amidst a multifarious community. Disparities in socio-economic and cultural backgrounds are some of the most extreme of any area in the country. Further, tension exists in these communities as the long-established agricultural industry is driven out by powerful tourist and housing industries.

Dr. Zagala was hired during a 'very troublesome time' following a terminally ill superintendent and a year and a half period in which the district was without a full-time superintendent. Nevertheless when the superintendent was hired she 'did not come to fix anything up'. Instead the community perceived the school district as stable; however, the increasing proportion (55 percent) of Hispanic children in the district called for some attention. The community and the board agreed that one of the key requirements for the new superintendent would be bilingualism, the ability to speak in Spanish. Associated with that requirement, was the expectation that the new superintendent would live in the community and become involved in local affairs.

Because the community has been growing steadily, a school facilities building program was underway and the new superintendent was expected to complete it. In brief, the incoming superintendent was asked to develop an accountability system throughout the district, to develop techniques and strategies to address those populations identified as 'getting short-shrift', to deal with the school construction program, and to focus on the fiscal situation.

Aside from obtaining their doctorate degrees from prestigious universities and having experience in public education, as stated previously, both women differ markedly in their background and experience. Dr. Singer's experience was extensive and traditional, proceeding from teaching to school site administration and central office management to the superintendency. Dr. Zagala's teaching experience was brief, followed by experience as a school board member where she not only participated locally, but was actively involved at the state level. She then accepted a superintendency in a small school district where, as she explains, she had an opportunity to learn everything about a school district by being in charge of custodial, transportation, personnel, curriculum and evaluation services. It was from this position that she was hired by the Arena Unified School District.

Both women perceive the school district as an organization for which they are responsible. Both assume that organizations are instruments and that 'leadership is a willful act where one person attempts to construct the social world for others' (Greenfield 1984: 142). Both superintendents also view administration as profiting 'from ordinary competence and a recognition of the ways in which organizations change by modest modification of routines rather than by massive mucking around' (March 1984: 22).

Executive and political responsibility

In analyzing how these women provide leadership in their respective organizations, it is important to establish the distinction between executive responsibility and political responsibility. In regard to political responsibility, Easton (1965) defines a political system as

> patterns of interaction through which values are allocated for a society and these allocations are accepted as authoritative by most persons in the society most of the time. It is through the presence of activities that fulfill these two basic functions that a society can commit the resources and energies of its members in the settlement of differences that cannot be autonomously resolved (p. 57).

Political leadership is, then, concerned with the allocation of values for the community or society and with assuring their acceptance as authoritative. Political activity involves attempts to affect the allocation and assurance of values for a community and society.

According to Kaufman (1956: 1064), executive leadership ensures an organization that coordination systems and service operations are capable of critical task performance in a timely and cost efficient manner. The executive assumes responsibility for the organization's affairs through activities such as coordination of policies across fields and agencies, designation of jurisdictional spheres, determination of areas of service and regulation, and supervision of activities across areas. The executive is the person having administrative or managerial authority in an organization.

Most would agree that the school board's responsibility is a political one, because it refers to the allocation of values for the district community and assures their acceptance as authoritative. As elected officials, the role of board members is to determine the ends toward which the resources and energies of the district shall be directed. The superintendent is subsequently responsible for managing and coordinating these resources toward the prescribed ends. Conflict arises when either party does not adhere to its responsibilities or when the expectations of responsibilities are contrary to roles. That is, a Hispanic female superintendent, though regarded as a symbolic and political actor, cannot be a successful leader by fulfilling only that expectation. The position itself is an executive one whose legitimacy is not based on symbolism or politics.

Dr. Singer assumed a position which appeared undesirable in a district known to be in disarray. Arena Unified School District, in contrast, faced problems, but the district appeared stable. In order to ensure enough time to make the necessary changes, Dr. Singer locked her position by requesting a completely new cabinet and including a buy-out clause for all of them in her contract. On the other hand, because of her inexperience and because the school district was in better shape, Dr. Zagala's contract contained none of these conditions. Thus, the women differ in the political symbolism to which each is attached and the manner by which they assumed their positions.

Superintendents' executive responsibility retention

Organizational and personal interests

Dr. Singer's first major confrontation with the dilemma of executive versus political responsibility arose when she realized that the motivations of two school board members were personal rather than organizational. Her proposals regarding personnel appointments, programmatic emphases, and resource allocations were met with resistance by two of the board members. Because of Singer's careful presentation of her proposals as directly linked to organizational ends, the public, through its community leaders, became convinced that the replacement of the board members was necessary. Dr. Singer explained it this way:

> Holding an executive position in an organization implies competence and confidence that that person can bring about organizational improvement. Not all board members appreciate the complexity and not all board members are personally motivated to act in the organization's interest. My proposed actions and decisions which were opposed by the defeated board members highlighted for the community the distinction between personal and organizational intentions. I am grateful the community rallied and elected officials who are genuinely supportive of school district improvement.

The data indicate that community leaders emerged who systematically informed the community about the two school board members' challenges to the superintendent's proposed actions. The community leaders argued that the superintendent offered an opportunity for the district's improvement, and were successful in demonstrating how the two board members' actions reflected self-interest rather than institutional improvement. The executive action which was instrumental in bringing about this outcome was the assumption of responsibility for the organization's affairs through coordination of policies across fields and agencies.

Procedural order and allocation of resources

The executive provides procedural order and allocation of resources. Personnel assignments are part of the resource allocation, and often an area of contention between the board and the superintendent. Procedural order is often conceived of as a communication and coordination issue; for school superintendents it also means integration and provision of stability. Executive actions must, therefore, address these areas, and it is by examining issues related to these areas that one can distinguish between executive and political responsibility on the part of the superintendent.

The hiring of the cabinet was the first major personnel decision Dr. Singer made. Because she was heading a widely diversified school district, she hired what she refers to as a rainbow cabinet consisting of two outsiders and one insider. One of the members is a Chinese female, the businessman is a white male, the personnel woman is black. Each of the women represents more than one culture. The superintendent said,

No one can claim any of these individuals. They claim what they can, but they can't get it all. That is what I call softening the racial tension. Let me explain. The Chinese woman has blue eyes. The black woman's mother is American Indian. My mother is half Asian. We do not fit any stereotypical profile. We are, nevertheless, identifiable more with one group than with any other. The Hispanics do come to me. But by the same token, my husband is Jewish, so they know I cannot possibly have total allegiance to the Hispanics. The Chinese woman's fiancé is white. We are not exclusive to a group personally. So that, I believe, serves to permit people to act more neutrally. While we are claimed by any one group, there is not a way to depend absolutely on our inclination to lean towards that group. For example, the white male feels that whites expect him to speak for them. He cannot do that too freely while he is being watched by the three of us!

What Dr. Singer means by softening the racial tension by this action is that no one group's interest is being preferentially addressed. Political forces were restrained by hiring nationally recognized competent individuals and ensuring that the composition of the cabinet represented the community's diverse groups.

There is another consequence to the superintendent's personnel decision that bears directly on the relationship between her and the board. Because the team which Dr. Singer has constituted positively represents the district by being personable and professional, and because its members' reputations for competence in their areas and experience serve to justify their rightness for their posts, the board has learned to perceive them in a different way and has come to understand executive direction. Witnessing this highly diverse and competent team working towards a common goal has fascinated the board members. Their previous experience was with administrators who responded to personal and/or group interests. The present team responds solely to the school district's organizational needs, that is, the instruction of children. An associated consideration is that the district can lay claim to the cabinet and its accomplishments. The superintendent found the members but they do not owe her any allegiance from prior work with her. They all share her vision for the district and are willing to do what is required to fulfill that vision. This has allowed them to have a certain independence and display of self-confidence without the fear of being fired.

Interdependence among the members has also enabled the board members and district to experience executive direction. The cabinet, by virtue of its composition and its differentiated responsibilities, could demonstrate across the district how interdependence works. As mentioned before, the formal means by which interdependence of the cabinet could be ensured was through very good 'buy out' clauses in their contracts. It would be very expensive for the district to fire a member. Informally, actions and decisions are coordinated and synchronized among the four persons so school board members cannot possibly pit them against each other. School staff cannot bypass them. Procedures are agreed upon and adhered to across the district. March (1984) explains that 'much of the job of an administrator involves making bureaucracy work . . . and responding to the little irritants of organizational life' (p. 22). When the nature of the administrative task is understood and assumed, the results of organizational efforts may be spectacular. In light of the history of this school district, much of what the board perceived as outstanding cooperation and results was teamwork between the cabinet members.

How does the superintendent deal with personnel assignments when school board members object? A particular incident is used as an example. A board member opposing a proposed hiring said, 'We have layers and layers of administrative crud. Hiring any more offends me.' The superintendent objected to the remark and at the end of the

meeting asked the board to meet in closed session. The audience expected the superintendent to resign. The superintendent explained to the board members how a remark
from one of them has an effect. She said,

> The thing that is going around here about this administrative crud is creating rumors or jokes like, where are you?
> Are you a top layer or bottom? Are you a thin layer or a fat one? Are you a hard layer or a soft layer? It is not
> funny around here. The board has no right to talk that way.

The nature of the incident and the potential consequences demonstrate how fragile
superintendent–board relationships are and how executive direction may be diverted
into a personal or political one. Felicia Singer explained,

> They do not always mean to be bad but they are. Sometimes we go faster than we should and do not communicate
> as well as we need to. We know we do not have a lot of time to make an impact. If we dare stop, something comes
> in to fill the vacuum and creates a wedge. It becomes real hard to get it together again. The board is our boss and
> we appreciate that very much. They asked us to come. We are working very hard. People can see some things
> are changing. They are hopeful. We believe that we are making an impact.

The superintendent instructs the board to realize the impact of its members'
statements. The board can tell the administrators what they want but they have to allow
them to figure out how to do it. The superintendent assumes responsibility for seeing
that the distinction is retained. By identifying the issue, as one of a careless remark by
a member of the board, and immediately addressing the consequences, the superintendent is able to avoid conflict and is able to retain executive direction.

In providing procedural order and resource allocation to the various school sites,
the superintendent is again engaging in executive action. Sometimes that requires assignments, socialization activities, and expectations of uniformity. In dealing with the
principals, Dr. Singer engaged in 'executing a large number of little things' (March 1984:
22). The intent was to create a working group among the principals and to attach the
principals to the central office. These 'little things' included written communication,
acknowledgments of a principal's efforts, central office reports and scheduled meetings
of various sorts. Principals were encouraged to work together in the improvements of
their schools. They were encouraged to utilize the services of the central office and they
were expected to run their schools consistent with Dr. Singer's vision. The central office
staff, directed by the cabinet members, facilitated these working relationships. The
consequence of this effort was that improvements among schools could be cited across
the district. All district personnel and the total community could feel the impact of the
superintendent's intentions. Particular neighborhoods could not charge district inaction.
Dr. Singer explains,

> School site management is imperative, but principals' efforts must be consistent with my vision of school district
> productivity. I do not want a favorite school. I do not want abandoned or slighted schools in this district. If
> uniformity across the district is going to take place, I am the person who has to ensure that. Thus, I have to develop
> an intensive relationship with principals. A system of communication is necessary.

The consequences of superintendent/principal intensive interpersonal relationships is that because all schools are projected to be equally excellent, principals do not
have to compete for the allocation of resources. Resource allocation to each of them is
designed to improve their schools. Status differentiation among them due to school
assignment is virtually wiped out. Most principals are pleased. The uniformity maintained among the principals serves to avoid conflict with principals or groups of principals. This strategy serves to keep principals cooperating with each other and the
central office rather than seeking advice or support from the school board.

The erosion of executive responsibility

Now we turn to Dr. Zagala who also understands the dilemma arising from executive versus political responsibility. Unlike Dr. Singer who faced a unified, though diversified school district, Dr. Zagala's symbolic appointment as a bilingual superintendent raised expectations and mobilized the Hispanic community, while suspicion and apprehension increased in the non-Hispanic community. Neither the board nor the superintendent were prepared for the reactions. Within approximately three months' time in office, a parent's group led by one Anglo male, publicly approached the school board expressing a lack of faith in the district. Complaints and accusations, directed primarily toward Dr. Zagala, were later found by the board to be unwarranted and a public apology by the group was made. Yet the episode created much controversy and the effect was dramatic and lasting. The symbolic nature of the appointment would continue to induce political responses from within the organization and the community, becoming a detriment to executive action. The superintendent believed she was hired to be an executive and because the expectations from the board were so explicitly presented – 'We were looking for one who would be a rising star. We specifically advertised as desirable in our superintendent, bilinguality in the Spanish language and willingness to live and be involved in local affairs' – she proceeded to act out the expectations. As was later stated by the current school board president, 'Our move was too bold and forward'. As will be shown, the school board members did not fully realize how bold and forward Dr. Zagala's appointment was for the non-Hispanic community.

Political challenges faced Dr. Zagala from the moment she was hired. At the time of her appointment the board president was a Hispanic male, Mr. Martinez. She was highly visible and famous as the first Hispanic female executive in that region. The presence of two Hispanics in the top ranks raised suspicions within the organization and the non-Hispanic community causing the establishment of an executive relationship with the president of the school board to become problematic. Even though all of the board members supported and approved the appointment, Mr. Martinez provided what Dr. Zagala refers to as 'more direct communication and protection for my decisions'. She said, 'We spent a lot of time together and we were criticized for it. I felt we did spend a lot of time together, but it was pretty valuable. The decisions were buffered more than they are now.' Dr. Zagala was referring to the district practice of changing board presidents every year and the fact that the current president is a white male whose support is not as secure. Dr. Zagala describes the present situation: 'Under the current president, you are the administrator. You can do your thing, but then the decisions can be questioned or someone may raise a question or be asked why did you do that?'

Another challenge faced by the superintendent was creating a supportive cabinet. Since its selection was not part of her contract, she inherited the cabinet created by the former superintendent. The cabinet opposed Dr. Zagala's appointment and viewed her as a symbol rather than an executive, enabling them to ignore her decisions and actions. Instead of obtaining a small cadre of loyal, committed individuals who represented the community and shared the superintendent's vision, the cabinet was expanded to include the former members and newcomers. The rationale was that the size would diffuse the hostility. The result of the expanded structure was a further loss of control of individuals. With the exception of one black female, the other two males and five females were white, serving to accentuate the symbolic rather than the professional significance of these positions. Moreover, the superintendent was still serving with little support from her cabinet.

School site improvement meant hiring new principals. Dr. Zagala described how she went about hiring a principal.

> I hired a Hispanic principal for a key position in the district and I think that for the good old boys in the system the expectation is that the next duck in line takes the swim and I did not choose the next duck in line. I chose who I thought would be the best person for that particular school. The person applied and went through the process as did all others. It wasn't that I said, 'I want that candidate' and ignored the process.

Her action was not perceived as executive and legitimate, however. She explained,

> I knew that that was going to eventually come back and bite me. But I have always kept the board informed. I informed them this was going to come back. I said, 'Somebody isn't going to like this. They wanted this person, but I hired this other one.'

Principals complained and reported their grievances to the board. One of the principals' opinions follows:

> Her mistakes are lodged in her lack of experience. I call them scars that you have to develop as you work your way up. You develop scar tissue as you make mistakes and go up the ladder. In comparing her to the other superintendents I have worked for and worked under, the mistakes she makes appear to be those from an individual who isn't properly prepared at the various lower levels.

What is meant by 'properly prepared at the various lower levels' is the appreciation of the sponsorship system in educational administration. Educational administration literature (Griffiths *et al.* 1965, Ortiz 1982, Valverde 1974, MacCarthy and Zent 1981) shows that promotion and access to administrative posts is a sponsored process. The 'good old boys' refers to this practice. Hispanic individuals are less likely to be part of such a system, and access to administration would require intervention. Dr. Zagala's decision was based on trying to place the best person for that particular school, whereas it was expected that the personnel decision would be based on who has been sponsored and prepared for the next vacancy in the district and that Dr. Zagala would honor that norm. Dr. Zagala described how executive actions are questioned and become politicized:

> The ideal thing would be that when the question comes up, 'Did you know that Dr. Zagala hired someone that . . . ?' the board should say, 'Yes, the gentleman was selected through a process and we support the superintendent. We need someone bilingual there.' Instead, the board member remarks, 'Gee, let's look into it.' It is the remark, let's look into it, that gives a detractor an automatic opportunity of a window of saying something is wrong.

And it is the 'something is wrong', that becomes political rather than executive.

Dr. Zagala was hired to improve the condition of the Hispanic population in the district. One of her responsibilities is to provide services to the growing Hispanic student population. One way to improve the condition for Hispanics in Arena is to hire and place more Hispanic principals. The district does not presently have a proportion of Hispanic principals equal to the proportion of Hispanics in the population at large. Thus, the appointment could not be viewed as being problematic because of too many Hispanic principals, but it could be viewed that this superintendent might replace present principals with Hispanic principals.

Another aspect of this is that the procedural order for hiring principals traditionally has been through sponsorship. In order to mask the political nature of this process, white males, perceived to be equally capable of being principals, line up for the next vacancy. Dr. Zagala's neglecting to follow the sponsorship procedural order challenged white males' opportunities. The tension created among the principals is that now no one knows who will be promoted when, and the uncertainty created through this action placed the sponsorship practice in jeopardy. The reader is reminded that the traditional structure of school administration already has been altered by the presence of a Hispanic female superintendent.

The superintendent followed a procedural order which is public and agreed to by the school board. She explained the process by which decisions are made:

> If I make a decision, I'll write it up in the Friday letter. This is to ensure that three months later one of the principals or someone else may not like the decision and behind the scenes call a board member and say, 'I don't like that decision.' If it is a very difficult decision that might carry a lot of resistance or public outcry, I will touch bases with the president. He or she will call the board members or we will write about it, or say, 'Okay, are we ready?' And then we will go with the decision. Major decisions are packaged. Emergency decisions are the only ones which are not. For example, shall we close the schools or not? I don't have time to call for those kinds of decisions. After the decision is made I will call the board members and tell them. Most of the decisions we make are not emergency. They are more or less routine.

The former president of the board confirmed the process and he added,

> What I do is that I keep every Friday letter because I know somewhere along the line there is an issue she wrote us about and regardless of whether she agrees or disagrees, she will have that down in the letter. And that way we, the board members, can't say, 'No, we were not aware.' This letter shows we are aware.

The process by which Dr. Zagala is allocating resources or, as in this case, making personnel assignments becomes an occasion for assessing self and/or group interest. Her actions are interpreted in light of the formal procedure and the support she has received from the Hispanic male school board member in validating the procedure. Furthermore, this process has placed her at odds with the principals, eroding organizational support. The superintendent elaborates how political and executive responsibilities become blurred:

> From my perspective, ideally the situation would be being hired with something specific in mind and being supported throughout the process. It is probably the ideal way. I think what happens, not only in Arena, but in many organizations, is being hired with the understanding of the specific purpose but people go about their business and forget about the reason why somebody was brought in and then you do something. In the meantime, you cannot change values, and there are still people who know, but are saying, 'What the hell are we doing with a Hispanic superintendent here? She doesn't know what she's talking about'. People look for any little slipping of decisions or error and I think that is where there has to be consistency.

Several stages to this process have been identified. First, there is the suspicion that the group the superintendent represents will be preferred. Second, hiring outside of the group which has been informally 'lined up' or 'sponsored' reinforces the suspicion. Third, since the individual who was hired, in fact, does represent the same group the superintendent does, the situation is exacerbated. Fourth, the superintendent's front person, the board president, detaches himself from the decision, after having approved it, by publicly saying, 'Let's look into it'. Fifth, the superintendent and the action become vulnerable. The sixth step in the process, the creation of adversary parties, heightens the potential for political action.

As the adversarial relationships increase, invalidating executive action takes place through the different interpretations by the various groups. Mrs. Miraloma, an elementary principal, explains that the uneasiness between the superintendent and principals may be due to a communication problem:

> I suppose it is the feeling of communication. To be a person that they feel they can communicate with and that when they get a no it is justifiable. I don't think principals think there is that sense of sincerity of communication.

A principal explains why communication with this superintendent is an issue:

> She is from Mexico originally . . . I think that puts her at a disadvantage because you don't understand the innuendos. I mean, she picks them up quickly, but still if you have someone to ask the question or don't know what question to ask, that does block communication. It is hard to distinguish if that is blocking communication or if it is just a personal understanding. But the result is the same. Her Hispanic background and the fact that she speaks another language certainly helps the Hispanic here.

Another principal expresses the same apprehension in this way.

> She has raised the conscious level of the Mexican American, the bilingual. Again, I don't know if that is positive. In my opinion, it is tending to be negative. You got backlash that is coming. I am concerned that if we take one step forward, we might have to take three steps back because of the backlash.

In contrast to Dr. Singer, who arranged a variety of means to communicate with principals, to work with them, and to involve them with the central office, Dr. Zagala has tended to adhere to procedural order without much consultation. The antecedents to this response are related by Dr. Zagala.

> One of the board members told me, 'You have to be like the previous superintendent. He was very jovial, very social with his managers [principals].' So I started being very social and we talked. They said jokes. I said jokes. We had a good time. Well, in the meantime, they were documenting everything. They came back to the board saying that I had said this, that I had said that. . . . So I dropped the curtain on me.

'Dropping the curtain' in this case means following procedural order and becoming formal. In contrast to Dr. Singer's engagement in 'executing a large number of little things' (March 1984: 22) with principals, Dr. Zagala's social behavior, a reaction to political controversy and attacks based on suspicions, turned to a reduction in communication and interpersonal interaction open to a number of interpretations. A principal put it this way.

> It is not so much what, it is how it is being done. It is not what is being said, it is how it is being said. It is almost being done in a way that seems that all of us who were here weren't working hard enough or fast enough, and therefore we are part of the problem. It is like putting blame on us.

The process for invalidation of executive action and decision is to begin by faulting procedural order and proceed to blaming the superintendent. One of the principals states:

> I have come to believe there is some dissatisfaction. Some want to make it racial. In my opinion, it is not racial. It has to do with competency and qualifications. I also feel that those who are supporting her are doing so on the basis of race. But there is another thing going on, and I don't think it is racial at all. It has to do with qualifications, and competency and experience. It goes hand in hand with the bilingual issue and her being hired for that reason.

The implication is that the superintendent is engaging in reverse racism. There is an appearance of backlash.

In describing the superintendent, the board president said,

> She was accepted, I think, in some sectors of the community, very well. In other sectors of the community, I would suspect, and this is the sort of thing one surmises rather than being told, that hiring her was feared as being a rather bold move on our part. So, there was mixed, probably still are some mixed signals out there. People will continue to be shaken, and sometimes, are going to react negatively in terms of ethnicity and gender.

Providing procedural order and acting on personnel assignments enabled the superintendent to address two mandates presented to her when she was hired. The development of an accountability system and a system to improve the delivery of educational services to all was meant to be addressed through personnel assignments. In dealing with the fiscal situation, the superintendent reduced the travel budget for school site personnel. This meant that teachers and principals could not attend conferences as freely as before. It affected schools in varying degrees. One of the principals described his situation.

> We are not better off in the development of our teachers and the different kinds of teaching strategies because we are not able to send more than one of them to a conference. You need to send three or four people to a particular conference for them to come back and make some kind of impact.

These final actions and interpretations serve to highlight how the superintendent and executive action is invalidated. The action is shown to penalize the organization and to prevent it from fulfilling its purpose. This has the effect of immobilizing the superintendent, which results in having the school board and the community initiating a replacement process.

Conclusion

When Hispanic females are hired for symbolic reasons, their actions are more likely to become politicized. Dr. Singer's mandates were clearly executive; she was given the leeway to carry them out in a diversified community and school district. Dr. Zagala, on the other hand, was hired because she was bilingual in Spanish and was willing to live in the community and become involved in local affairs. Her executive decisions were perceived to be inseparable from her ethnicity and gender.

Dr. Singer maintained the distinction between political and executive responsibility by acknowledging the issue of representation within the community without preferring any group. She was able to make personnel decisions among principals by engaging in activities designed to communicate and include. She also was able to maintain an executive role with the board by immediately confronting the situation that jeopardized that relationship.

Dr. Zagala, in contrast, could not maintain the distinction. A dilemma existed for Dr. Zagala in being a symbol and also an executive of the district. Dr. Zagala's mandate from the school board included attending to a 'short shrift population' in the district that was predominantly Hispanic. Dr. Zagala's actions toward fulfilling this directive of the board were surrounded by political controversy. The symbolism which triggered suspicions of preferential treatment prevented actions by the executive to deal with an organizational problem. Dr. Zagala was hindered in her attempts to be responsive to a portion of the student population and so establish equity and uniformity in the provision of services throughout the district. The executive actions presented here are common ones in every school district, but the process is more easily politicized for Hispanic females because the interpretations of their actions can be conveniently placed in the context of gender and ethnicity. Both women viewed their job primarily as that of the executive of an organization rather than as a symbolic representative for any one group. They attempted to retain that role. Dr. Singer did so successfully, whereas Dr. Zagala did not. An understanding of the process by which executive actions become politicized is instructive.

This study of two Hispanic female superintendents serves to highlight the distinction between executive and political decisions and actions. There are eight steps associated with this process by which executive actions were eroded:

1. The symbolic appointment and the resultant suspicion that the superintendent will act to prefer members of her own group particularly when the board president is also a member of that group.
2. The superintendent does not have a supportive cabinet.
3. The superintendent hires a person who is not being sponsored within the organization.
4. The new hiree represents the superintendent's group.

5. The board president detaches him/herself from the superintendent and questions the action and decision.
6. The superintendent and decisions become vulnerable.
7. The superintendent is at odds with the group affected.
8. The creation of adversarial parties begins.
9. The process for invalidating the executive action begins.

The process by which the executive action is invalidated begins by providing different interpretations of the action. It takes place without adequate communication and the lack of communication, in this case, is based on the superintendent's command of another language. The second step in the process is the creation of adversary groups who react by claiming reverse racism. The final step is when the adversary groups link the organizational instability with incompetent and/or immobilized leadership.

In contrast, the process by which the executive actions are maintained has similarly been identified. The following represent steps in this process:

1. While the female Hispanic superintendent assumes the position with the symbolic significance of representing both women and the Hispanic community, a reputation and support system developed in acquiring extensive and traditional experience serves to establish credibility and validity within the district.
2. The suspicion and symbolism attached that the superintendent will favor members of her group is then minimized.
3. The manner in which the superintendent locks into the position, for example, the buy-out clause, promotes an interdependence between the superintendent and the school board.
4. Cooperation and a shared understanding of board–superintendent roles and relationship develop through open and direct communication.
5. Steps 2 and 3 avoid detachment by the board from the superintendent, and the actions of the superintendent are not vulnerable.
6. The hiring of a small number of diverse individuals, well-recognized as competent and unified in the pursuit of organizational ends as the executive cabinet transmits a symbolic statement and further restrains political forces.
7. An intensive interpersonal relationship between superintendent and principals creates close ties to the central office through which uniformity, trust and cooperation is maintained.
8. Consequently, improvements are made in all schools.
9. District personnel and the total community feel the impact of the superintendent's intentions.
10. The executive actions are thus validated.

In conclusion, this study shows that the Hispanic female superintendent must minimize her association with symbolic and political expectations. She must be keenly aware of political forces and actors in order to avoid and diffuse situations which deter or prevent executive action. Moreover, the Hispanic female superintendent must conceptualize her role and actions in fulfilling organizational ends with particular emphasis on uniformity and equity. Consequently, others within the district will adopt the superintendent's vision and work under her guidance. This course of action presents the only potential for success. For the Hispanic female superintendent, politicizing executive action is a perilous venture.

References

BLUMBERG, A. and BLUMBERG, P. (1985) *The School Superintendent: Living with Conflict* (New York: Teachers College Press).

BLUMBERG, A. and BLUMBERG, P. (1991) 'The superintendency and politics', in N. WYNER (ed.) *Current Perspectives on the Culture of Schools* (New York: Brookline Books) pp. 13–28.

BOYD, W. (1974) 'The school superintendent: Educational statesman or political strategist?' *Administrator's Notebook*, August, 22, p. 9.

BURLINGAME, M. (1981) 'Superintendent power retention', in *Organizational Behavior in Schools and School Districts* (New York: Praeger).

EASTON, D. (1965) *A Framework for Political Analysis* (Englewood Cliffs, NJ: Prentice-Hall, Inc.).

GREENFIELD, T. B. (1984) 'Leaders and schools: Willfulness and nonnatural order in organizations', in T. J. SERGIOVANNI and J. E. CORBALLY (eds) *Leadership and Organizational Culture: New Perspectives on Administrative Theory and Practice* (Urbana and Chicago: University of Illinois Press) pp. 142–69.

GRIFFITHS, D. E., GOLDMAN, S. and McFARLAND, W. J. (1965) 'Teacher Mobility in New York City', *Educational Administration Quarterly*, 1, pp. 15–31.

HESS, F. (1977) The political dimension of local school superintendency, *Council Journal*, New York State Council of School District Administrators, 1, pp. 125–137.

KAUFMAN, H. (1956) 'Emerging conflicts in the doctrine of public administration', *American Political Science Review*, 50 (4) pp. 1057–1073.

McCARTHY, M. and ZENT, A. (1981) 'School administrators: 1980 profile', *Planning and Changing*, 12 (2) pp. 144–161.

MARCH, J. G. (1984) 'How we talk and how we act: Administrative theory and administrative life', in T. J. SERGIOVANNI and J. E. CORBALLY (eds) *Leadership and Organizational Culture: Perspectives on Administrative Theory and Practice*, (Urbana and Chicago: University of Illinois Press) pp. 318–51.

ORTIZ, F. I. (1982) *Career Patterns in Education* (New York: Praeger).

ORTIZ, F. I. (1991) 'An Hispanic female superintendent's leadership and school district culture', in N. WYNER (ed.) *Current Perspectives on the Culture of Schools* (New York: Brookline Books) pp. 29–43.

ORTIZ, F. I. and ORTIZ, D. J. (in press) 'How gender and ethnicity interact in the practice of educational administration: The case of Hispanic female superintendents', in *Knowledge Base in Educational Administration: Multiple Perspectives*, Albany, NY: State University of New York Press.

VALVERDE, L. A. (1974) *Succession, Socialization: Its Influences on School Administration Candidates and its Implication to the Exclusion of Minorities from Administration* (Washington, DC: National Institute of Education, Project 3-0813).

Catherine Marshall

This micro-political analysis of administrators' careers demonstrates what happens with token compliance with affirmative action. While learning the norms of the administrative career, women and minority site administrators learn to deny and suppress the discomforts, struggles, exclusionary and different treatments they experience. In a traditionalistic political culture, in a southern urban district whose school leadership positions remained white male-dominated through the eras of desegregation and affirmative action, women and minorities who attained administrative positions learned to keep a low profile.

When women or minority administrators enter a career sensing that affirmative action is a low priority, how do they manage? Using case-studies of the recruitment and early career experiences of principals and assistant principals, this chapter presents research identifying a pattern of women and minority administrators' denial and belittlement of the impact of exclusion and tokenism in their careers.

Moving beyond administrator socialization theory

Most studies of administrators' careers emphasize socialization, looking at managerial role functions, mobility and career stages (Blood 1966, Bridges 1965, Brim and Wheeler 1966, Greenfield 1985, Gross and Trask 1976, Mascaro 1973, McCabe 1972, Mintzberg 1973, Peterson 1984, Van Maanan and Schein 1979). Ethnographic studies and case-studies emphasize the cultural press on administrators (for example, Wolcott's *The Man in the Principal's Office*, 1973, and Blumberg and Greenfield's *The Effective Principal: Perspectives on School Leadership*, 1980). Concepts like 'organizational space' (Katz and Kahn 1978, Ortiz 1982) and 'career-role strain' (Marshall 1979) have been used to organize thinking about the salient influences on school administrators' role formulation. Career decision-making and mobility studies add important concepts such as 'anticipatory socialization' (Merton 1964); the importance of being in an 'opportunity position' (Kanter 1977), career stages; and the different kinds of boundaries in organizational careers (Schein 1978, Van Maanan and Schein 1979).

However, these theoretical models have not responded to challenges to the bureaucratic model (Clark and Meloy 1988, Ferguson 1984), feminist theory and research (Belenky, Clinchy, Goldberger and Tarule 1986, Dunlap 1989, Gilligan 1982), and recent criticisms of organization and leadership theory for its white male bias and its inherent fallacies (McCall and Lombardo 1978, Shakeshaft 1986).

When theory, and the models and practices that flow from theory, ignore the fact that those structural characteristics filter out women and minorities, then theory is missing a large chunk of the picture. First, research on women and minorities needs to be included in discussions of leadership and organizational socialization. Powerful structural characteristics of organizational life are at work to maintain homogeneity among leaders in organizations. Women expend extra effort getting sponsors and easing others' discomfort over their presence as women in a male-normed career (Marshall 1985a). Edson (1980) destroyed the myth that women do not aspire to leadership positions, and Marshall's grounded theory of *transition* (1979) helps to explain why some women may hesitate and vacillate as they countenance the possibility of entering a male-normed career.

Ortiz (1982) demonstrated that women and minorities are channelled into positions that prevent mobility to the superintendency. In particular, she found that minorities usually enter the career directing special projects and supervising 'their own kind', resulting in few opportunities for interaction or inclusion with majority administrators and few opportunities for line positions (except where minorities constitute the majority). Isolation, tokenism, access to opportunity positions, sponsorship, the burden of being tokens and culture-bearers are all critical concepts that must be added to socialization theory if it is to incorporate the socialization experiences of minorities and women. Socialization theory and practical policy (for example, recruitment and support and selection policy) have not been altered to incorporate these findings.

Previous theory has not adequately recognized the interaction between socio-political values and leadership. Research on education politics calls attention to the pressures of community values on school leaders (Cuban 1985, Iannaccone and Lutz 1970). In their first administrative positions, new administrators learn unstated micro-political rules ('assumptive worlds') that limit their initiative, dictate acceptable values, define the boundaries of work, and teach them how to conform their thinking and behavior to the particular realities of the local site (Marshall and Mitchell 1991). Micro-political analyses of power and rules about power must be included to give full understanding of the socialization of site administrators.

Finally, political lenses must be used to see the dynamics of the organizational, cultural and professional responses to minorities or women who enter administration. We already know that African American teachers and administrators are important role models (Lomotey 1989). We already know of Gilligan's (1982) research proposing that women's moral decision-making focuses on caring and connectedness (while men's focuses on rights and justice). We need to see how politics and power issues affect the careers of women and minorities.

Research design

A qualitative approach was utilized in this study in order to elicit the subjects' ways of conceptualizing their worlds. The study district, Avondale, is in the southern US and has a higher than average number of women and minority site administrators. Within the district, eight 'atypical' assistant principals and principals were selected. These administrators, three white women, three black women, one black man, and one 'risk-taker' white man, were interviewed about their recruitment and observed in their work settings. Document analysis was used to provide the history and policy background affecting the status of women and minority administrators in Avondale.

Findings: The politics of denial

In the 1950s and 60s Avondale experienced forced desegregation, litigation, resistance and violence. Courts monitored Avondale's desegregation but policies focused on the student population. No strong policy statements mandated racial balance in the teaching or administrative staff. No strongly enforced policies emerged asserting the need to promote minorities and women into leadership.

The school board and superintendency retained its tradition of white male leadership throughout the period (the 1950s through the 1970s) when equity mandates were asserted nationally. Thus, Avondale's minority and women administrators' careers evolved in a political context where equity issues were managed publicly and resisted privately.

These Avondale administrators told about learning 'how things are done around here.' They revealed their micro and macro-political understandings when they described the bigger picture about district practices for recruitment and patterns of selection and their learning about how to 'fit in'. They also described career patterns affected by desegregation and by stereotyping and exclusion. Such data demonstrated the need to expand theory to incorporate issues of gender, race and micro-politics.

Incorporating the micropolitical influences

The socio-political environment of the school district does influence the site administrator, but within that sphere of influence lie complex interactions that affect him or her more immediately and daily – those that are site-specific realities.

Every school site is unique; each has special histories, neighborhoods, reputations, community forces and clienteles. Every administrator faces challenges to his or her authority and their areas of responsibility. Administrators learn to establish their territory and protect it; they learn to work within their own boundaries (Marshall 1985b, Marshall and Mitchell 1991). These micro-political lessons are learned in 'troubled' schools, desegregating schools, schools with predominantly blue-collar parents, schools for disabled kids, schools with innovative instructional programs, and schools led by principals who carefully groom assistant principals. Each school has its special micro-politics.

The Avondale administrators gleaned their first clues about the special nature of their schools during the recruitment and interviewing processes. In describing their experiences, they generally explained gender and race issues as micro-political issues.

Race and gender issues in the district and site

Stated and unstated district policies affect career success and 'fit'. Recognizing that each site has specific micro-political nuances helps to bring race and gender issues into focus. Most of the Avondale administrators first denied that people were placed in schools to balance race and gender. Ms. Gaines, a white female assistant principal at a middle school, asserted that 'it's who you know', not race or gender that affects whether you get a job in Avondale. And Ms. Barnette, a black, high school assistant principal, spoke of her school placement as having no discernable rationale – just luck. Mr. Wheeler, however, said he noticed a pattern of selecting 'trouble shooters' for certain schools. Ms. Player, a black assistant principal at a high school, hinted about a pattern in Avondale of matching people to the specific school site:

> I think part of the decision-making process certainly looks at the culture of the schools and the capabilities of the principals and even assistant principals. My experience at central office has taught me that you think of personalities in school and whether or not the personality of the principal is going to work at that particular school.

No one asserted that the matching of 'personalities' included efforts at balancing race and gender on site administrative teams. Ms. Player described a situation where there were two women administrators in one school as occurring 'quite by accident, not by design because this is the first time in a long time that we had two females on the same administrative team. . . . It's very unusual.' So, administrators discerned a pattern of matching and targeting administrators but asserted that it was not race or gender related.

However, there *was* evidence of special placement of women and minorities, and there was abundant evidence of the effects of that placement. It is particularly interesting that Mr. Harding (a black middle school principal) said he had never noticed any ways in which he was treated differently because of his race although every career move he made was to a school with predominantly white professionals and a desegregating population. In one move, he was assigned to a new position as Coordinator of Student Activities in a desegregating high school! Harding said that he had never experienced any obstacles, but subsequently he said he had no one he would call a mentor and that he often felt alone. Some Avondale subjects talked freely about their awareness of being tokens – of being the 'first', isolated, lonely or different as minorities or as women. They did not, however, connect these feelings to district policy. Others denied such feelings and said they had not been treated differently. Ironically, this latter group often went on to describe situations where they were treated a certain way because of their gender or race. In Avondale, then, race and gender *are* factors in recruitment and placement, even though these administrators persistently denied that their race or gender affected their careers.

The influences of gender

All of the women spoke of ways their gender affected their ability to fit comfortably. As the first black woman to be high school principal in Avondale, Ms. Green said: 'One of the things that everybody worries about is, is the lady being too aggressive.' She related vignettes where friends advised her that men have difficulty with women telling them how to do things so she ought to just suggest, rather than order, so it would 'sound better'. She continued: 'You have to be alert to all those nuances where a lady is the principal. Ladies are not supposed to be interested in athletics and I'm an athletic fiend with a son in pro football . . .' Nevertheless, she accepted this advice and described how she slowly gained the respect and friendship of the men 'and especially the coaches'. Ms. Green's explanation of isolation and coping is quite poignant:

> It can be lonely, very lonely. You go to these meetings and when you walk up they've already said something they really didn't want you to hear. They're not talking about you – what they're doing is carrying on men gossip and you're not a part of the men's gossip. I was gracious enough to speak and say 'how do you do' and move on to something else. I always had a book to read or a note pad so I could write on something so it always seemed that I had something else to do. You go through that. That's a compensating way to do it without letting it really get next to you.

She acknowledged that such isolation was difficult, but explained that she had been one of six blacks to integrate her college. She said:

> I'd been through some firsts as a black and I just transferred that information onto being a first female. . . . I know how to sit back and be quiet and I know to speak when I have to. So it's really people skills.

Ms. Player said there was 'no strain whatsoever' . . . and she was 'considered one of the boys'. Nevertheless, she continued, saying:

> They were a little more careful about their language when I was around, like, 'we're not going to say so-and-so when she is around'. But we went out to lunch together. The only thing we didn't do together was meet for weekends to play golf. They did a lot of that. I wasn't invited to those sessions but if we had an in-service at school . . . we'd all go to lunch together. . . . I felt like I was part of the informal network on campus but when we left the campus I felt that they probably participated in some activities where I was not invited.

Finally, Ms. Katz (a white middle school principal) said it was easier for her because another woman principal had preceded her at her school. Although she'd had some difficulty getting certain *fathers* to acknowledge her position, she said, 'I don't dwell on that though'.

Thus, for women, political lessons are: you *must* compensate, you *will be* excluded, and *you must not make a fuss*. Even though they will not really be 'one of the guys', women should not call attention to that fact. Even though they must spend time alleviating other's anxieties about their presence, women learn to do this extra work and stay quiet.

The influence of race

Minority women attributed the exclusion and tokenism more to being females than minorities. The one black male, Mr. Harding, stated that he had not noticed that his race had affected his career (although he had been moved to several different desegregating sites). Ms. Player, in describing her recruitment and selection, said: 'There were some individuals who resented my moving up the ladder so quickly because I was virtually a new teacher having had only five years of teaching'. Her comment is revealing since white males are often promoted to administrative positions even before completing five years of teaching. Yet Ms. Player felt others' resentment toward her 'quick' promotion.

Ms. Barnette, a black high school assistant principal, had to overcome stereotyped expectations to establish territory and authority:

> I found it was very important that I find my turf . . . this school is 86 percent Caucasian. We have some 10–11 percent black and a few Oriental students. . . . When I first came, there would be cases that involved my students, and I'd find other administrators working with them. So I stormed into the executive principal's office and said, 'If there are people I'm not to work with let me know today! If there are areas where you think I'm incompetent, I'd like to know today. And if this is not the case, then I want to work with my students if I'm available. . . . I claim the children that belong to me and if they are mine, they are mine on good days and bad days – black, white or Oriental. . . .' They needed to know that I was their principal, and so we established these lines very early on.

As an administrator, Ms. Barnette had to establish her control over her students. As a black woman, she also had to make it clear that her competencies were not limited to managing black students. She spoke of this as a micro-political issue related to protecting her turf rather than as a race or gender issue.

Resentments toward Ms. Player's advancement, Mr. Harding's career assignments, and Ms. Barnette's turf challenge were not described as race-related. Nevertheless, there is evidence that special race-related issues affected these Avondale administrators as they established their turf and power, even though they deny these effects. Their response is to avoid naming the treatment they received as a race issue. These minority administrators have learned the political lesson: ignore and silently tolerate any race-related events and interactions, and do not label them as race issues (just as the women described earlier learned to tolerate the gender stereotyping and exclusion).

The data from Avondale present several intriguing patterns. First, women learn to be silent about gender-based stereotyping and exclusion as they become socialized. Where minorities experience career assignments and resentments that are race-related, they learn to talk about these as normal aspects of administrator life and *not* as race-related. Finally, all learn to work within special site conditions, and some of the special site conditions are race and gender-based, especially where a school is desegregating.

Summary and implications

In the micro and macro-political context of administrative careers, race and gender conflicts are present but supressed. Race and gender really do affect a person's fit, comfort, power and career progression. These atypicals were taught that they should keep quiet and avoid embarrassing confrontations and situations that emanate from being different. Women learned to downplay isolation and sexism. Minorities learned to obfuscate about special treatment. They know that affirmative action policies are token gestures that do not reach into the depths and subtleties of micro-politics in schools. Adding micro-political lenses reveals political and cultural forces that undermine women and minority administrators.

This research also reveals how, as they learn micro-political lessons, people take on an organization's definitions of their proper sphere and behavior instead of asserting their right to be there. As a result, the potential benefits of diversity and alternative modes for leadership are lost. We know that affirmative action policy has little to no enforcement power. We know that administrators avoid lawsuits because of loyalty norms in their profession and because subtle exclusion does not meet legal standards for racism or sexism (Marshall and Grey 1982). This chapter demonstrates that administrators recognize that affirmative action lacks moral legitimacy, that district policymakers and gatekeepers in the career are not concerned with special issues faced by minorities and women. These minority and women administrators internalize these political lessons. They know better than to assert their rights and demand that district and site policies be examined or to insist that the definitions of their work and working conditions be altered to make then more comfortable and supportive. They must not make trouble. They deny the differences.

This analysis of Avondale administrators demonstrates several themes in micro-politics (Marshall and Scribner 1991). Conflict is privatized and confined and the organization is preserved by avoiding dilemmas. 'One-case-at-a-time microalterations' (Marshall and Scribner 1991: 351) are made and the inherent dilemmas regarding the different treatment of women and minority administrators are avoided.

Note

1. This research was supported by the National Center for Educational Leadership.

References

BELENKY, M., CLINCHY, B., GOLDBERGER, N. and TARULE, J. (1986) *Women's Ways of Knowing: The Development of Self, Voice and Mind* (New York: Basic Books).
BLOOD, R. E. (1966) *The Function of Experience in Professional Preparation: Teacher and the Principalship,* unpublished doctoral dissertation, Claremont Graduate School, Claremont, CA.

BLUMBERG, S. and GREENFIELD, W. (1980) *The Effective Principal: Perspectives on School Leadership* (Boston: Allyn and Bacon).

BRIDGES, E. M. (1965) 'Bureaucratic Role and Socialization: The Influence of Experience on the Elementary Principal', *Educational Administration Quarterly*, 1, pp. 19–28.

BRIM, O. and WHEELER, S. (1966) *Socialization After Childhood: Two Essays* (New York: John Wiley).

CLARK, D. L. and MELOY, J. M. (1988) 'Renouncing Bureaucracy: A Democratic Structure for Leadership in Schools', in T. J. SERGIOVANNI and J. MOORE, (eds) *Schooling for Tomorrow: Directing Reforms to Issues that Count* (Boston: Allyn and Bacon) pp. 272–94.

CUBAN, L. (1985) 'Conflict and Leadership in the Superintendency', *Phi Delta Kappan*, 67 (1) pp. 28–30.

DUNLAP, D. H. (1989) 'Differences Between Men and Women Administrators in Four Settings', a paper presented at the Annual Meeting of the American Educational Research Association, San Francisco, CA.

EDSON, S. K. (1980) *Female Aspirants in Public School Administration. Why Do They Continue to Aspire to Principalships?* unpublished doctoral dissertation, University of Oregon, Eugene, OR.

FERGUSON, K. E. (1984) *The Feminist Case Against Bureaucracy* (Philadelphia: Temple University Press).

GILLIGAN, C. (1982) *In a Different Voice: Psychological Theory and Women's Development* (Cambridge, MA: Harvard University Press).

GREENFIELD, W. (1985) 'Studies of the Assistant Principalship: Toward New Avenues of Inquiry', *Education and Urban Society*, 18 (1) pp. 7–23.

GROSS, N. C. and TRASK, A. E. (1976) *The Sex Factor and the Management of Schools* (New York: John Wiley).

IANNACCONE, L. and LUTZ, F. W. (1970) *Politics, Power and Policy: The Governing of Local School Districts* (Columbus, OH: Charles E. Merrill Publishing Co.).

KANTER, R. M. (1977) *Men and Women of the Corporation* (New York: Basic Books).

KATZ, D. and KAHN, R. L. (1978) *The Social Psychology of Organizations*, 2nd ed. (New York: John Wiley and Sons).

LOMOTEY, K. (1989) *African-American Principals: School Leadership and Success* (Westport, CT: Greenwood).

MCCABE, D. P. (1972) *Bureaucratic Role and Socialization: A Replication of Bridge's Study on the Elementary Principal*, a doctoral dissertation, University of New Mexico, Albuquerque, NM.

MCCALL, M. W. and LOMBARDO, M. M. (eds) (1978) *Leadership: Where Else Can We Go?* (Durham, NC: Duke University Press).

MARSHALL, C. (1979) *Career Socialization of Women in School Administration*, unpublished doctoral dissertation, University of California, Santa Barbara, CA.

MARSHALL, C. (1985a) 'The Stigmatized Woman: The Professional Woman in a Male Sex-Typed Career', *The Journal of Educational Administration*, 23 (2) pp. 132–52.

MARSHALL, C. (1985b) 'Professional Shock: The Enculturation of the Assistant Principal', *Education and Urban Society*, 18 (1) pp. 28–58.

MARSHALL, C. and GREY, R. (1982) 'The Legal Rights of Women in Schools Administration', *Journal of Education Equity and Leadership*, 2 (4) pp. 253–9.

MARSHALL, C. and MITCHELL, B. (1991) 'The Assumptive Worlds of Fledgling Administrators', a paper presented at the Annual Conference of the AERA, Boston, MA.

MARSHALL, C. and SCRIBNER, J. (1991) 'It's All Political: Inquiry into the Micropolitics of Education', in *The Micropolitics of Education*, special issue of *Education and Urban Society*.

MASCARO, F. C. (1973) '*The Early on the Job Socialization of First-Year Elementary School Principals*, unpublished doctoral dissertation, University of California, Riverside, CA.

MERTON, R. K. (1964) *Social Theory and Social Structure* (London: Free Press).

MINTZBERG, H. (1973) *The Nature of Managerial Work* (New York: Harper and Row, Publishers).

ORTIZ, F. I. (1982) *Career Patterns in Education: Women, Men and Minorities in School Administration* (New York: Praeger Publications).

PETERSON, K. D. (1984) 'An Organizational Perspective on Careers', a paper presented at the Annual Meeting of the AERA, New Orleans, LA.

SCHEIN, E. H. (1978) *Career Dynamics: Matching Individual and Organizational Needs* (Reading, MA: Addison-Wesley).

SHAKESHAFT, C. (1986) 'A Female Organizational Culture', *Educational Horizons*, 64 (3) pp. 117–22.

VAN MAANAN, J. and SHEIN, E. H. (1979) 'Toward a Theory of Organizational Socialization', *Research in Organizational Behavior*, 1, pp. 209–64.

WOLCOTT, H. F. (1973) *The Man in the Principal's Office: An Ethnography* (New York: Holt, Rinehart and Winston).

15 The feminization of the principalship in Israel: The trade-off between political power and cooperative leadership

Ellen Goldring and Michael Chen

During the past two decades in Israel, the number of women holding educational leadership positions at the elementary and secondary school levels has steadily increased. Simultaneously, the highly central- ized Israeli educational system has begun a slow process toward system-wide diversity. The resulting structure is a two-tier system in which women principals are highly regarded at the local level yet isolated from major political and policy decisions. Individual school sites as highly feminized work organizations are embedded in power structures that have not altered. Consequently, an increasing gender segregation and devaluing of educational leadership creates a system that often ignores these leaders' highly effective leadership styles.

What happens when women are no longer numerically underrepresented in educational leadership positions? This chapter presents the case of female principals in Israel where women are no longer a minority in the principalship, and reviews the macro-level context that explains the rapid feminization of the principalship. It also presents the results of research that examines the impact of this feminization on schools as workplaces for teachers and principals.[1] The story of Israel illustrates a case in which the numbers of women in the principalship have increased but the political, professional and bureau- cratic power structures continue to be male-dominated. Consequently, meaningful changes are not forthcoming and gender segregation, at different levels of the hierarchy, perseveres.[2]

Women and the principalship

Research on women in educational administration indicates, rather consistently, that female principals differ from their male counterparts, and these differences suggest that women are uniquely suited for educational leadership positions. Studies indicate the typical female principal is better qualified for the job than the typical male principal; woman are better educated, older, and have had more teaching experience (Gross and Trask 1976, Hemphill *et al.* 1962). This body of literature suggests that female principals are more often involved in both participatory and supervisory activities than male principals (Shakeshaft 1987, Fishel and Pottker 1977), are more concerned with instruc- tional processes and learning, and interact more intensively with teachers when com- pared with males (Gilberston 1981, Ortiz and Marshall 1988). Female administrators also are viewed as more effective in representing the school to the wider community and interacting with parents (Sadker *et al.* 1991). Additional marked differences between male and female principals include women's ability to work with others, their sense of caring about students and teachers, and their highly effective communication styles (Shakeshaft 1987, Hemphill *et al.* 1962, Tibbetts 1980).

Table 15.1:   Percent of female principals in elementary and secondary schools in Israel
1972, 1983 and 1989

Year	1972		1983		1989	
School Level	N	%	N	%	N	%
Elementary	1479	20.8	1955	43.4	1883	66.5
Secondary	579	13.8	577	27.5	631	31.1

Source: Adapted from Addi (1992).

Most of this research has been conducted in the US, where women continue to be underrepresented in educational leadership positions (Adkinsen 1981). This chapter addresses the dynamics of gender and educational leadership when numbers are not the issue. The first section presents the political, professional and bureaucratic power structures that have contributed to the influx of women into the principalship in Israel, while the second section presents empirical research results regarding the relationship between gender and leadership in the feminized workplace.

The Context of the Rapid Feminization of the Principalship

One of the unique trends which has dominated the Israeli educational system throughout the 1980s and 90s is the feminization of the principalship. The processes which have led to the feminization of the principalship in Israel are uniquely different from trends in the United States and Europe where males are continuing to dominate administrative ranks throughout the educational hierarchy.

The principalship in Israel can be safely termed a feminine occupation. Between the years 1972 and 1989 the percent of female principals has gone from 21 to 67 percent at the elementary school level and from 14 to 37 percent at the secondary school level, as presented in Table 15.1. Since the total number of elementary and secondary school principals has increased by 27 percent and 9 percent respectively, the increase in the number of female principals can be attributed to feminization, that is, the replacement of male principals, rather than merely an increase in the number of schools or the number of female teachers in the teaching force who can move to administrative positions.

During the 1970s and 80s, in conjunction with the increase in the number of women in the principalship, two other trends were developing. One was the dramatic erosion of the occupational prestige of all educational professions, including the principalship, and the other was the steady increase in the educational attainment levels of school principals (see Table 15.2). In terms of occupational prestige, on a scale out of 100 rankings of occupations in Israel, principals rated in the 90s in 1974 and in the 60s in 1989. This decrease in status for principals is similar to that of teachers. Corresponding to a decrease in occupational prestige, principals have increased their level of education.[3] Hence, it seems that highly educated women are moving into the principalship as the social status of the occupation is decreasing and men with similar levels of educational qualifications are turning to more prestigious and lucrative professions.

The impact of these processes, at the macro level, are obviously very complex. To comprehend them fully it is necessary to describe briefly the structure of the Israeli educational system.[4] The educational system in Israel is both structurally and procedurally

Table 15.2: **Standardized change scores of social indicators of educational occupations in Israel**

Occupation	Occupational Prestige			Education (No. of Years)		
	1974	1989	Change*	1972	1983	Change*
Elementary School Principals	93.1	66.0	−1.52	14.4	15.8	.61
Secondary School Principals	91.1	66.4	−1.44	16.1	16.8	.29
Supervisors	93.1	80.3	−0.75	13.1	15.8	.79
High School Teachers	86.4	63.8	−1.32	15.8	16.3	.21
Elementary School Teachers	78.0	52.9	−1.46	13.8	15.8	.44

Note: *Change is measured in standardized scores.
Source: Adapted from Addi (1992).

centralized. All educational personnel are employees of the Ministry of Education. The Minister of Education is a political appointment, arranged through political negotiations at the time when a newly elected Prime Minister builds a coalition government. Administratively, the Ministry is headed by a director general, appointed by the Minister. There is no lay control of education. The male-dominated Ministry is responsible for the hiring and placement of teachers and principals, who are both members of one very large collective bargaining unit. There is a formal system of supervision carried out by six district superintendents with a cadre of school inspectors. Principals report to their district superintendents. There is a mandatory, uniform elementary school curriculum and most curriculum materials are developed by the Department of Curricula Development, a major department in the Ministry.

It is within this context that the educational system found itself in the beginning of the 1980s. From the point of view of the typical principal in the past, schools were administered as closed systems in a state of relative certainty. Principals received all resources, curriculum and teachers directly from the district offices and consequently, managed the internal functioning of the school in relatively simple external environments which had little impact on their roles. These male principals were integral parts of the central system hierarchy.

Today, the highly centralized system is beginning a slow process to open the system to local initiatives and autonomy along with the rapid feminization of the principalship. The movement toward system-wide diversity comes in response to three trends. First, most aspects of Israeli public services are highly centralized, especially those sectors connected to the public economy. Furthermore, many public services are highly politicized. However, public officials are beginning to acknowledge that Israelis are capable of mature consumer behavior (that is, exit, voice and participation), a relatively new phenomenon in Israeli society. Second, meeting the educational needs of an increasingly pluralistic society is being viewed as a goal to be achieved rather than a problem to be solved. This change in viewpoint is manifested in a change in educational philosophy and emphasis from unity (the single curriculum) to diversity, and from equality (or integration only) to quality (such as special programs for gifted students). Consequently, educational frameworks which promote and sustain unique programs, such as schools of choice (like magnet schools) and community schools are on the uprise (see Shapira 1988). Third, drastic cuts in the national education budget have increased the empowerment of parents and local municipalities, and consequently are reducing the control of the central ministry (Kamanda 1985). In fact, many claim that the catalyst for the move toward decentralization and diversity is rooted in the economic depression and large cuts in the national education budget (during 1981–86 the total number of teaching hours was reduced by 28.5 percent), which have characterized Israel for the last decade (Ministry of Education 1987). Because of decentralization, principals, in essence, were given the burden of deciding how to allocate the new, severely reduced, allotment of financial resources.

Another important impetus for the change of the centralized system is related to educational policymaking mechanisms in Israel. In her article on educational policymaking in Israel, one of the leading policy analysts, Elboim-Dror (1981), proclaimed that the guiding principle of policy formation throughout the educational system is conflict avoidance. Given the heterogeneity of society, which brings to the fore the diversity of ideals and values, there is little consensus around policy issues. Rather than trying to reach consensus through legitimate discussion, fighting and negotiation, the educational system aims to reach consensus by avoiding conflict. The educational system, especially the higher echelons within the Ministry, can no longer avoid conflict at all costs and reach consensus at the national policymaking level. Consequently, decentralization to local levels is a method employed to avoid potential conflicts, especially regarding issues where broad-based consensus cannot be reached: 'Peace through structural separation and autonomy for different ideological orientations has proved to be very effective in reducing conflicts, removing educational policy issues from the top of the national agenda to a peripheral position' (Elboim-Dror 1981: 272).[5]

Thus, the rapid feminization of the principalship is occurring in tandem with the loosening of the central Ministry of Education. In this system, principals are mainly responsible for implementing educational policies which are still formulated at the national level. Although it may seem that these processes would have strengthened the role of the female principal as leaders of comparatively more autonomous institutions, in reality women are being isolated from system-wide influence and social and political networks. Hence, the female principals remain in rather nonauthoritative positions in reference to the larger, male-dominated, educational system, while their male counterparts in the past were highly connected to the very strong and dominant Ministry of Education. Women are underrepresented and often disregarded in the high stakes of the politics of education. In fact many female principals complain about the large amount of responsibility they have as leaders of autonomous organizations in relation to a very small degree of authority to carry out their responsibilities.

The feminization of the principalship is also highly related to political underpinnings which are rooted in the struggle between the central government, that is, the Ministry of Education, and the Teachers' Union, which is one of the largest labor unions in Israel. Surprisingly, principals do not have separate bargaining units, but are represented by the Teachers' Union, which is headed by a male politician connected to the Labor Party. An example of how this political context has influenced the extent to which women enter the principalship is recent contract negotiations. The economic hardship of the 1980s has resulted in drastic budget cuts for education. This has meant difficult bargaining conditions for the union. Rather than receive salary increases, the union, under its male leadership, has fought for 'better' working conditions, conditions that are deemed favorable to the female population, mostly teachers. One clear example is fewer teaching hours. Teachers work on an hourly basis and many teachers work part-time; the average teacher in Israel has 80 percent of a full time position.

The result of this type of bargaining concession by the Ministry, the employers, is that teaching and administrative ranks are being filled with upper socio-economic status females, who view their work as a second income, and who are willing to forego good salary for comfortable conditions in which to raise their children. From the employer's point of view, that of the Ministry of Education, a relatively highly educated, middle-class work force can be had for relatively low salaries. Consequently, the feminization is being supported on both sides, from the educational personnel themselves and from the employers. Male teachers who may have been eligible and interested in administrative positions are leaving the teaching ranks because they can no longer 'afford' to be in the field of education which offers low prestige, and feel misrepresented by their bargaining unit. These trends allow the female principal to support and sustain the traditional role responsibilities of women in Israeli society, that of a second income winner and a homemaker.

The three trends, feminization, decentralization and decreasing occupational prestige are promoting a situation where female principals are focusing on the internal functioning of schools in the feminine workplace. In these feminized organizations the female principals are highly regarded and viewed as successful. They are expected to focus on promoting a harmonious organizational climate with comfortable working conditions in their schools, to compensate both for the low salaries and resource scarcity. They are under extreme pressure to promote educational outcomes that in turn reflect upon the Ministry and its programs, reducing public criticism of schools.

In short, a two tier system has emerged: one at the local school level with its female employees, where the female principals are highly regarded, and one at the Ministry level that is still in charge of the major political and policy decisions. Hence the number of women in the principalship has increased but there are few corresponding changes in the political, professional and bureaucratic power structures. The educational system is still characterized by gender segregation according to occupations. This system has defined the school as a feminized workplace and has changed the nature of teacher/administrator relationships within the school as is discussed in the next section.

The work climate of the feminized school as a workplace

The configuration of interdependencies between educational administration and the major external institutions (the Teachers' Union and the Ministry of Education) that explains the rapid feminization, has affected the nature of the principal/teacher relationship within schools. As has been cited in the literature about the United States (Adkinson 1981), most women principals in Israel emphasize a cooperative, calm, supportive organizational climate as a means of asserting leadership. Consequently, over time, many principals succeed in establishing a participatory, supportive work environment. Teachers are highly rewarded for showing loyalty to the principal. They are rewarded by being assigned to a 'good' class or receiving a convenient work schedule.

Research conducted in a medium sized industrial city in Israel among all secondary school administrators and teachers indicated a number of interesting results (Chen and Addi 1992). First, it seems that male teachers prefer to work in schools with male principals. Most of the male teachers (72 percent) work under male principals, who constitute only a third of all principals, while male teachers constitute only 7 percent of the teaching body under female principals. Thus schools with female principals are practically fully feminized workplaces, while schools with male principals are only partially feminized. In addition, this research indicated that the teachers with female principals reported better cooperation between teachers and management, a stronger sense of collegiality and more job satisfaction than did teachers with male principals.

Other research supports the general assertion that female principals in the feminized workplace use a very cooperative leadership style. In a study of community school principals, where all principals in the sample were women, school effectiveness was related to a leadership style geared toward teacher consideration (Goldring and Pasternack 1992). Effective school principals in this study reported using an interpersonal relations orientation. Teachers in effective schools reported conferring with principals on personal matters more often than their counterparts in ineffective schools. Fuchs and Hertz-Lazarovitz (1991) indicate that male principals who discuss implementing change in schools are concerned with leadership and authority, while female principals emphasize the interpersonal side of implementing change, including feelings about the change, intrinsic motivation and readiness for change on the part of teachers, students and parents.

Additional research (Goldring and Chen 1991) indicates that male principals are more alienated from their work-places than are female principals. It is hypothesized that male principals in female-dominated organizations face a criss-cross social situation because of the incongruence between their perceived upper status as the male incumbent and the low prestige of the female occupations (Berger *et al.* 1966). Furthermore, male principals may face 'status panic'. They invested in a particular status currency (that is, educational training) but it did not yield the benefits, such as a high status occupation.

In summary, the internal climate of the school is emerging to support female principals as leaders of female teachers. These principals are concerned with promoting a positive, supportive school atmosphere, one which leads to results but not at the expense of consideration and good human relations. The supportive work ethos is a reward in itself for principals and teachers.

Conclusions

At the macro level, our analysis suggests that external pressures and gradually diminishing resources have increased the feminization of the principalship, but simultaneously have alienated women from real political power and decision-making authority in the male dominated Ministry of Education. Correspondingly, we suggest that the process of feminization has increased the number of principals who attempt to maintain, develop and foster supportive work organizations since it is primarily from within these organizations that the female principals can reap rewards and establish a basis for power. They do not have very much traditional executive authority due to their weak placement in the formal hierarchy of the Ministry of Education.

Individual school sites, now highly feminized work organizations, are embedded in overall power structures that have not been altered. Consequently, gender segregation is increasing and educational leadership is simultaneously being devalued where lower wages are being paid for more experienced and better qualified incumbents.

In this context of 'ghettoization', men and women educators are in separate worlds. In a workplace where female principals are dependent upon their female teachers for cooperation and loyalty to fulfill their roles successfully, where power is gained from sources internal to the school, and where women view themselves as leaders of other women, a climate of collegiality and management–teacher collaboration can be attributed to the feminized culture. However, this collective culture is most likely the response of a profession declining in prestige than to growing external pressures. The feminization of the principalship is helping women administrators move toward more mutual cooperation and support within schools so they feel satisfaction and gratification in their roles despite low prestige. These effective leadership styles in a supportive school climate often go unnoticed, leaving the women isolated and left out of the arenas external to schools.

Notes

1. In this chapter the terms feminization and feminized refer to the number of women in the occupation and not the feminist culture (see Noddings 1984).
2. The authors acknowledge the helpful comments from Marshall and Zodhiates on an earlier draft of this chapter.
3. The intercorrelations between percent of women in an occupation, occupational prestige, and educational level indicate that the percent of women is significantly correlated to a decrease in occupational status, and an increase of level of education.
4. The chapter refers primarily to the Israeli elementary school system.
5. This section is adopted from Goldring (1992).

References

ADDI, A. (1992) *Changes in the Status of Teachers 1972–1989*, Research Report No. 10, Institute for Social Research, Department of Anthropology and Sociology, Tel Aviv University (Hebrew).

ADKINSON, J. A. (1981) 'Women in school administration: A review of the research', *Review of Educational Research*, 51, pp. 311–413.

BERGER, J., ZELDITCH, M. JR. and ANDERSON, J. (1966) *Sociological Theories in Progress* (New York: Houghton Mifflin).

CHEN, M. and ADDI, A. (1992) 'Gender, Principals and Teachers: Perceptions of Leadership Performance and Job Satisfaction in Secondary Schools', paper presented at the annual meeting of the American Educational Research Association, San Francisco.

CHEN, M. and GOLDRING, E. (1990) 'Tracks of selection and advancement of students of educational administration', in A. BALATZINSKI (ed.) *A Collection of Papers on Educational Issues* (Tel Aviv: Ministry of Education) (Hebrew).

ELBOIM-DROR, R. (1981) 'Conflict and consensus in educational policymaking in Israel', *International Journal of Political Education*, 4.

FISHEL, A. and POTTKER, J. (1977) 'Performance of women principals: A review of behavioral and attitudinal studies', in J. POTTKER and A. FISHEL (eds) *Sex Bias in the Schools* (Cranbury, NJ: Associated University Presses) pp. 289–99.

FRIEDMAN, Y. (1984) *School, Parents and the Community in Israel* (Jerusalem: The Szold Institute).

FUCHS, I. and HERTZ-LAZAROVITZ, R. (1991) 'Principals' thinking about change', *Studies in the Educational Administration and Organization*, 17, pp. 75–104 (Hebrew).

GILBERSTON, M. (1981) 'The influence of gender on the verbal interactions among principals and staff members: An exploratory study', in P. A. SCHMUCK, W. W. CHARTERS, JR and R. O. CARLSON (eds) *Educational Policy and Management: Sex Differentials* (New York: Academic Press) pp. 297–306.

GOLDRING, E. (1992) 'System-wide diversity in Israel: Principals as transformational and environmental leaders', *Journal of Educational Administration*, 30, pp. 49–62.

GOLDRING, E. and CHEN, M. (1991) 'The feminization of the principalship: The effects of gender and social status on sense of accomplishment and alienation', *Curriculum and Teaching Journal*, 6, pp. 23–30.

GOLDRING, E. B. and PASTERNACK, R. (1992) 'Principals who emphasize interpersonal relations: Do they pay the price in school effectiveness?' in J. BASHI and Z. SASS, *School Effectiveness and Improvement* (Jerusalem: The Magnes Press).

GROSS, N. and TRASK, A. E. (1976) *The Sex Factor and the Management of Schools* (New York: John Wiley

& Sons).

HEMPHILL, J. K., GRIFFITHS, D. E. and FREDERIKSEN, N. (1962) *Administrative Performance and Personality* (New York: Teachers College).

KAMANDA, I. (1985) 'The division of power in educational policy', in W. ACKERMAN, A. CAROM and D. ZUCKER (eds) *Education in an Evolving Society* (Jerusalem: Van Leer Foundation) (Hebrew).

MARSHALL, C. (1991) 'Chasm between administrators' and teachers' cultures', in J. BLASE (ed.) *The Politics of Life in School: Power, Conflict, and Cooperation* (Newbury Park, CA: Sage).

MINISTRY OF EDUCATION AND CULTURE (1987) *The Ministry of Education and Culture*, Jerusalem, February (Hebrew).

NODDINGS, N. (1984) *Caring: A Feminine Approach to Ethics and Moral Education* (Berkeley: University of California Press).

ORTIZ, F. L. and MARSHALL, C. (1988) 'Women in educational administration', in N. BOYAN (ed.) *Handbook of Research on Educational Administration* (New York: Longman).

SADKER, M., SADKER, D. and KLEIN, S. (1991) 'The issue of gender in elementary and secondary schools', *Review of Research in Education*, 17,

SHAKESHAFT, C. (1987) *Women in Educational Administration* (Newbury Park, CA: Sage).

SHAPIRA, R. (1988) *Sound Educational Particularism*, Position paper 4–88, Dept. of Sociology of Education and the Community School of Education, Tel-Aviv University (Hebrew).

TIBBETTS, S. (1980) 'The woman principal: Superior to the male?' *Journal of the National Association for Women Deans, Administrators, and Counselors*, 43, pp. 176–9.

What's working for girls?:
The reception of gender equity policy in
two Australian schools[1]

Jill Blackmore, Jane Kenway, Sue Willis and Leonie Rennie

Australia has been relatively unique for its level of national and state-initiated gender reform policies. This chapter offers a critical analysis of both the nature and content of the gender reform policy process, its theoretical underpinnings and limitations in terms of understanding what gender reforms work in schools, how and why. The chapter analyses from a feminist post-structuralist and cultural studies theoretical framework the different responses of teachers and students to what is considered to be sound gender-equity strategies (for example, all-girls maths classes). It explores the ways in which particular equal opportunity messages are produced, circulated and consumed by particular groups of girls and teachers differentially and suggests the need for a more sophisticated understanding of the nature of educational reform and change in specific cultural contexts particularly with respect to gender.

Introduction

This chapter draws from a three-year research project in Australia which seeks to examine the ways in which gender reform initiatives work in schools, why they work, which fail and why. The project involves four major longitudinal case-studies and eight 'spot'[2] studies in Victoria and Western Australia. The focus of this particular chapter is how teachers and girls 'read' and 'respond' to gender reform initiatives in two schools. We first provide an overview of gender reform policy in Australia and the theoretical framework informing the research project. Then, through two case-studies, we consider the ways in which teachers and students have 'read' and 'rewritten' the gender policies available to them in two innovative gender reform schools, and conclude with a discussion about the implications of the studies for policy and practice.

Contextualizing gender reform policy in Australia

Australia is unique for the diversity and extent of its legislative and policy initiatives by the state in gender reform. This was largely due to the rise during the 1970s of 'new social movements' (women's, environmental and various multicultural and multiracial movements) which made political claims on the state for the 'democratising of the distribution of economic, political, cultural and social resources', a demand partially met by federal and state Labor parties by the establishment of EO units and women's policy advisors (Yeatman 1990: xi). While there has been a shift since 1975, when the first major national report on girls and education in Australia, *Girls, Schools and Society*, mapped out the ways girls were disadvantaged in schools, away from a deficit model to one of social justice and the inclusion of structural factors such as curriculum and school organization in the *The National Policy for the Education of Girls in Australian*

Schools (1987), the *Review* of the National Policy in 1992 indicates no significant alteration in the pattern of girls' post-school choices of training/education away from traditional areas, particularly for girls with disabilities, from non-English speaking, Aboriginal or Torres Strait Island backgrounds, or girls who live in poverty. In order to understand why these initiatives have not produced more fundamental and widespread change in girls' occupational choices and post-school options, a re-examination is necessary: first, of the policy process itself, second, of the content and focuses of policy, and third, a consideration of whether the change process is itself different when dealing with gender.[3]

The policy process and gender reform

Gender reform policy has tended not to fall so readily within the dominant paradigm in which schools, teachers and students have generally been ignored in the policymaking process. This paradigm assumes that policy generation and implementation are two distinct phases carried out by two different groups: the policymakers (bureaucrats, researchers, specialist curriculum developers, consultants and teacher union representatives) in the central agency or Ministry of Education; and the practitioners (the administrators, curriculum coordinators and teachers) who work in the school. Any discrepancy between policy and outcomes has been conceptualized as an 'implementation problem' which has been variously interpreted as teacher resistance, inadequate organizational control and/or lack of accountability to the centre. The policy process has therefore been viewed as linear, top-down or as a relatively centralized process negotiated between representatives of specific interest groups and the state (Ball 1992).

In Australia, because gender equity reform has historically relied upon the intervention of the state, EO policy approaches have been framed by the 1980s corporate managerialist approach to policy which emphasizes quantitative outcomes, assumes the neutrality of processes, and demands increased accountability to the centre in a 'state control model' (Ball 1992: 3). EO policy in general, guided largely by liberal feminism, has been criticized for its assumed linearity between policymaking and outcomes, the tendency to ignore the differing cultural contexts, for gauging success for women and girls in male terms, for not fundamentally challenging unequal power/knowledge relationships and the gender biases of organizational structures, for its individualism, and the assumption that policy is 'received' uncritically, passively and in its totality by the 'targeted population' (Tsolidis 1990, Wenner 1990, Wyn 1990, Poiner and Wills 1991, Burton 1991, Kenway 1990: 67). While the *National Policy for Girls* has been the most sensitive of all EO policies to issues of cultural diversity and special needs arising from race, class and ethnicity, what is as yet unclear, though, is the actual rather than assumed capacity of the state to 'reach into schools' and change practice.

Gender reform has also worked through bottom-up developments. In the context of teacher union and parent organization demands during the 1970s for the democratization of decision-making and school-based curriculum development, women teachers, the gender justice workers, individually and collectively initiated school-based activities for gender inclusive curriculum and less organizational discrimination (for example, timetables). School-based gender reform activity has been multifaceted and strategic, relying upon the cross-fertilization of ideas, strategies and policies between EO networks, teachers and parents in ways which have also informed official policymakers. This has also led to an increasing eclecticism in policy as well as the breakdown of the policy generation and implementation divide (Kenway 1990, see MACWAG 1991). So much of the groundwork for EO has already been done in some schools, although there is no widespread groundswell except perhaps in Victoria and South Australia (Taylor 1991), a comparable situation to school-based activities in the United Kingdom where gender reform has largely been brought about by short-term, one-off teacher initiatives, action-research collaboration between academics and teachers, the development of networks and teacher union initiated activities (Weiner 1988) and the United States, given the absence of any coherent state or national policy framework.

While the *The National Policy for the Education of Girls in Australian Schools* (1987) developed a broader definition of post-school options, in the context of a trend towards a more instrumental approach to education with recent moves towards a national curriculum and the development of key learning 'competencies' (Mayer Committee 1992), post-school options have taken on narrower vocational meanings prioritizing maths, science and technology for girls and focusing upon paid work unproblematically, a focus reflected in resourcing, in-service programs and professional activities (for example, unions) (Kenway 1990). 'The implicit message of many such programs is that young men make well-informed choices, young women make ill-informed choices, and that the problem is one of changing choices which individual girls make' (Kenway *et al.* 1991). Particular strategies have developed. Girls-only classes in traditional male-dominated subjects (maths, computers and in some instances, science classes) to provide a separate space to develop their own competencies and self-esteem and girl-friendly pedagogies such as group learning, gender inclusive materials, non-competitive contexts premised on the assumption of girls' underachievement in non-traditional areas (Mahony 1985, Willis 1989, Walkerdine 1989, Kenway and Willis 1990, Wyn 1990, Tsolidis 1990).[4]

Theorizing gender reform policy

At this stage, we are suggesting that who actually 'makes' policy in the case of gender reform is not clear, and that conventional policy paradigms are inadequate. Research on the 'reception' by administrators, teachers, students and parents of gender reform policy is unilluminating. Existing literature embodies a diversity of perceptions about human motivation, behaviour and change ranging from behaviourist to voluntarist positions. In general, this literature tends to view the teacher, parent and student as passive 'recipients' of policy who either implement the policies unproblematically or resist them in their totality. We argue that the dearth of literature and the failure of that which does exist to provide adequate theoretical frameworks is largely due to a lack of empirical investigation of what could be called the 'reception' of *gender* reform initiatives in schools. Hence the focus of this research project on reception, where reception means 'what happens to policy' in schools; that is, how policy is read, interpreted, selected from and acted upon in different contexts by different individuals and groups (Kenway *et al.* 1991). The study of policymaking for *gender* change may, therefore, require us to view the nature of policy, the policy process and change differently. Finally, while the focus of the research project is upon the policy priority of encouraging girls to improve their post-school options, it became clear that this message cannot be disentangled from other reform messages circulating within each school, whether they were about curriculum revision to increase 'access and success' or equal opportunity for women teachers.

Our way of perceiving policy and the policy process in this project draws upon feminist post-structuralism and cultural studies (Kenway 1992). Cultural studies are concerned about social and cultural practices and products and 'the work they do sub-jectively' (Johnson 1983: 2). We argue that 'material, social and cultural conditions – private and public – have an impact on both the production of any cultural text and its reception. That is, the ways in which it is read and used in the social relations of people's daily lives' (Kenway 1992: 4). Furthermore, there are different moments of the cultural process – of production, circulation and consumption – within specific material, social and cultural contexts (Kenway *et al.* 1991). Production refers here to the making of cultural texts. This includes not only the writing, reading and interpretation of policy documents but also the various discourses from which such texts draw (for example, in Australia, the Labor party's and women's movement's commitment to social justice). Texts therefore refer not only to the policy documents themselves, but also to the set of discursive practices and associated documents dealing with issues of equality of opportunity. Writers of policies are therefore both producers and consumers of such texts, as they draw upon several often contradictory discourses.

Policy and curricula, as forms of cultural text, go through this cycle at two levels: the macro-politics of the state and the micro-politics of the school (Johnson 1983). Thus gender reform policies as texts can be seen to have several overlapping and interlocking circuits with specific moments of production, circulation and consumption – at the level of the state, at the level of the teacher and school, and at the level of the student, as each actively produces, then circulates, their own meaning through their particular reading of the text (Kenway *et al.* 1991). So teachers, some of whom have a proclivity to gender reform, will more actively produce new text in a 'writerly' manner, while others will read the gender text uncritically in a 'readerly' fashion (Ball 1992: 11–13). Each group and individual will read the text selectively and not 'receive' it passively or in its totality. In 'consuming' the text, the reader is distanced from the initial process of production. In selecting from and interpreting the text through their own lived experience, how-ever, readers set up or produce their own circuit of production, circulation and con-sumption. This suggests that the authors of any text (such as official policymakers) do not necessarily control the ways in which their products (policy documents) are in-terpreted and translated, that is, 'read' into practice. At the same time, particular readings of the text will be privileged and thereby constrain the possibilities of their reading by teachers. Teachers and students, active in generating and circulating their own meanings of the gender texts available to them, also privilege particular readings, in particular those which have come to be embedded in the popular common sense (which is not necessarily good sense) (Ball 1992). In other instances, particular readings produce counter-hegemonic discourses or interpretations which undermine the original intentions of the policymakers within the school.

Feminist post-structuralism also suggests possible ways of viewing how girls read gender texts. Kenway argues that 'post-structuralism is a term applied to a very loosely connected set of ideas about meaning, the way in which meaning is made, the way it circulates amongst us, the impact it has on human subjects and finally, the connections between meaning and power' (1992: 3). Meaning is not fixed, but shifts within particu-lar cultural contexts. Feminists find such notions valuable in that they emphasize plur-ality and therefore recognize differences among women arising from race, ethnicity and class. Feminist post-structuralists believe that these differences are constantly constituted by discourses. Individuals construct their own gendered identities by drawing from a variety of discourses. A post-structuralist concept of subjectivity, therefore, sees the 'subject' as constituted through a multiplicity of discourses in which the individual is positioned at any point of time; 'one's subjectivity is therefore necessarily contradictory'

(Davies 1990: 3). Fragmentation, discontinuity and contradiction are the focus of such an analysis. Subjects are dynamic and multiple, always positioned in relation to particular discourses and practices and in turn being produced by these as a subject. Feminist post-structuralism raises questions about how policy is interpreted in highly differential ways in specific contexts by those it is expected to assist.

Some methodological issues

For us, as researchers, the problem has been how to get into girls' and teachers' heads. Drawing upon the above ways to theorize policy has been helpful, but also raises different methodological questions. We do not need to rehearse the qualitative/quantitative debate here but, rather, in denying the hegemony of positivism, seek to gain a better understanding of what may be referred to as post-positivist research. Coming from this perspective, Patti Lather suggests that post-positivism focuses upon constructed as opposed to found worlds; it takes what has been called the 'linguistic turn' in social science; it focuses upon consciousness and subjectivity, but . . .

> not false consciousness or distorted perception. . . . [but rather] the organization of material signifying practices that constitute subjectivities and produce the lived relations by which subjects are connected – whether in hegemonic or oppositional ways – to the dominant relations of production and distribution of power . . . in a specific social formation at a given historical moment . . . (Ebert 1988: 23)

It also has led to a focus upon discourse and the 'productivity of language in the construction of the objects of investigation' (Lather 1990: 13). This research, therefore, has focused upon eliciting some understanding of the gender reform texts and other discourses (such as equity) that have informed teachers and students.

The collection of data by the researchers in the two case-studies took place over fifteen months.[5] Data collection took a variety of forms: primary sources were personal and telephone interviews, participant observation; attendance at meetings, planning groups, and focused school activities, informal chats and formal appointments; staff and student evaluations/writings/interviews, etc. Secondary sources included school documents, submissions, reports, surveys of participation rates, school and staff records of activities, lesson plans and so on. Particular all-girls programs were selected for classroom observation. The students were observed on their classroom behaviour, in other meeting situations and interviewed collectively and individually. The collection of data has been primarily through intensive interviewing of the students and their teachers, observation in the classroom, and 'shadowing' of individual girls.

Two approaches to gender reform

The two case-study schools were chosen because of their high level of cultural diversity, their lower middle-class/working-class cultures as inner-city schools, and their reputations for carrying out gender reform programs. Both schools faced closure or amalgamations with nearby schools in 1992 so they could offer the broad comprehensive curriculum demanded under recent changes to post-compulsory schooling in Victoria with the introduction of the Victorian Certificate of Education (VCE) at Years 11 and 12. Both schools have a large proportion of students of non-English speaking background (NESB) with up to twenty different nationalities and cultural groups, the biggest groups being Greek, Italian, Macedonian, Spanish and Arabic and an increasing number of Vietnamese, Cambodian and Malaysian/Chinese students. Both schools have been classified under the national Disadvantaged Schools Program begun in the 1970s, with many families being single parent, welfare recipients especially at Years 7–10. While there is wide diversity in the social class background, both student populations become more middle-class at the senior levels as students from lower socio-economic groups tend to leave school early. Much of the early equal opportunity work in these schools began with two federal programs, School to Work Transition (1979–82) and the Participation and Equity Program (PEP; 1985–9) which focused upon access and success.

Inner City was chosen for this project because of its unique designation as an Affirmative Action[6] School by the state Ministry of Education. This designation, which meant two full-time staff positions for Affirmative Action, was the inducement for the Girls' High School, known for its innovation in gender reform, to amalgamate with the nearby working class 'male dominated' High School in 1988. North Eastern Suburban Secondary College was suggested by the Coordinator of the State Equal Opportunity Resource Centre because of initiatives which had been taken in the interests of girls, some of which could be linked to their post-school options for example, Girls' Council and the Post Primary Professional Development Project run under the Social Justice Initiative to support girls in maths, science and technology.

These two schools provide two models of gender reform and approaches to educational change – the 'add on', ad hoc and relatively marginalized approach to gender reform most common in Victorian schools of North Eastern Suburban; and the 'whole school' or mainstreaming equity approach of Inner City. Both schools had introduced what have become relatively standard strategies for gender reform in many Victorian schools: girls-only maths, science and computer classes; sexual harassment and equal opportunity policies, although again Inner City stands out for the breadth and innovation in gender equity programs which included community oriented activities (self defence, TV and publicity programs in the press; multilingual community nights; girls into science career nights; school–industry links) and work transition for girls; girls-only school camps; special Physical Education Programs; Mathematics Activity Centre; and trialing of pilot 'gender inclusive' curriculum units.

Whereas the discourse of equal opportunity was more widespread and embedded in the common-sense practices of Inner City than at North Eastern, there still is a general assumption at North Eastern among staff that 'everything was OK for the girls because a few initiatives had been taken' (female teacher). Gender issues were increasingly competing in both schools with other reform discourses, such as the curriculum and organizational reform demanded by the new Victorian Certificate of Education and school reorganization due to amalgamations. At the same time administrators and teachers were well aware of 'the political need to acknowledge Ministry Policies for the Education of Women and Girls', particularly since the EO staff position in Victorian schools was legitimated by a special allowance in 1991. Also common to both schools, although to a differing degree, was 'a significant level of resistance to change', especially that associated with gender reform.

In the following two sections we will demonstrate the manner in which various gender reform texts were represented at the level of the school and drawn upon and reinterpreted by both teachers and girls. In turn, teachers and students also drew from institutionally specific discourses arising out of teacher and student subcultures as well as wider, less institutionally specific discourses of feminism, liberal humanism and cultural pluralism.

Teachers' readings and rewritings of gender texts: A whole school approach to integrating gender into the curriculum

At Inner City there was a dominant 'discourse of equal opportunity' which had been produced within the school by the gender workers drawing largely from official policy documents or social justice discourse. A significant shift had occurred since the amalgamation in 1988 as this EO discourse and the democratization of decision-making supplanted the then 'boys club' hegemonic discourse and its less democratic practices with more open debate and gender representative decision-making processes. By the time this research project commenced in 1990, most staff indicated that EO was 'just common sense', although not all agreed with the particular manifestations of the Affirmative Action program in the school. The response generally was: 'Of course we agree that girls should be treated equally and we do'.

At the same time, there existed groupings among the teachers as to how they positioned themselves with respect to EO in general. These could be broadly categorized as follows. First, there were the 'gender workers', that minority of teachers who were most active in the production and circulation of gender texts, a group defined by their membership on the AA team, their activities as EO networkers and proclaimed feminists, as well as their extra-school activities, postgraduate study and interest in the feminist literature. Second, there were the teachers more peripherally involved in the AA program but who were prepared to teach gender inclusive curricula. They read the official text less critically than the gender workers. The third group, 'the silent majority', rarely stated their position publicly with respect to AA. Yet they could, with prompting, recite the popular or common-sense reading of gender texts. This discourse articulated the view that girls were disadvantaged in mixed classes; that boys monopolized space and teacher time; that girls benefit from entering non-traditional subject areas; that girls need to do maths; that girls lacked self-esteem. Finally, there were the active opponents to change in general and gender reform in particular, labelled by their colleagues as the 'troglodytes', who renounced loudly the claims of the disadvantage of women and, less so, girls. They, predominantly men, had little or no inclination to change their teaching practice or curriculum with respect to girls unless coerced. There were those within the school, therefore, who read the policy text in a 'readerly' manner (passively and uncreatively) and those who read creatively and critically and who in turn produced policy text in a 'writerly' manner (Ball 1992).

The latter group included by 1989 the newly appointed principal (male) and Curriculum Coordinator (female). Neither were seen to be associated with either of the antagonistic school cultures forced together in the previous year's amalgamation, but both were committed to AA, with personal histories in curriculum and whole school policy development. Each staff member took a clear stance with respect to the AA program in the school, one informed by the history of the amalgamation and in particular the power shift from male control to the increased representation of the gender workers on school committees. While the initial personal antagonism of the resisters or 'troglodytes' towards those associated with AA, and in particular the new principal, had lessened by 1992, it was not totally obliterated. One member of the AA team recalled being named as a 'rabid lesbian'; another being treated as though she had AIDS; and a male gender worker feeling 'like a missionary amongst my male colleagues'.

Yet each teacher's position drew from a multiplicity of discourses, not only as feminists or 'ockers', but also as professionals, as teachers of a particular subject discipline, as progressive or traditional educators, as teachers in a working-class 'caring' school, as administrators, as heterosexual or homosexual males or females. Subjectivity, therefore, was not acquired in a unified or coherent manner but was 'struggled over and imperfectly held because different discourses offer different subject positions or points of view, many of which are contradictory or incompatible' (Gilbert and Taylor 1991: 135). In turn, each gender worker's consciousness was as Gramsci argues 'strangely composite', always containing contradictions between hegemonic ideology (in this instance the liberal feminist discourse) and critical 'good sense' which arose from their own personal experiences and practice, which was generally a more radical and self critical position in the case of most (Gramsci 1971). So while the gender workers drew significantly from the various gender texts available to them (in particular the *National Policy for the Education of Girls*) and its priority encouraging girls into non-traditional subjects and occupations, they also drew from wider discourses of feminism, progressive education and unionism in highly subjective ways which led to significant internal debates among the AA team. I will focus briefly in this section on the ways in which the gender workers in particular read and rewrote the gender texts available to them as they developed a whole school approach to gender reform.

Given their previous histories in other innovative schools, many of the gender workers were experienced change agents. They were aware that organizational and personal change is more likely to occur when individuals or groups feel as though they influence and own the change (see Fullan 1992, McLaughlin 1987). They determined early in the program that AA needed to be associated with a team and not an individual. They also knew that policies needed to be set in place and that this took time. In the second year of the AA program it was decided by the AA team (of four staff) that strategically it would be better to link curriculum coordination to AA thereby mainstreaming or integrating gender equity throughout the whole school program. This could be done best by utilizing other system level changes such as the major restructuring of post-compulsory school organization, curriculum and assessment with the introduction of the Victorian Certificate of Education at Years 11 and 12 and Curriculum Frameworks for Years 7 to 10. The timeline therefore was first to write school objectives and policy statements for each Learning Area (groups of subjects outlined in Curriculum Frameworks), then to develop and pilot gender inclusive curriculum units, and finally to get all staff to teach these units. Ironically, this model of curriculum integration replicated the top-down linear model of policy of the system, and consequently raised various dilemmas and problems for the gender workers, including the ownership of reform, one exacerbated by the association by many staff of AA with only a small clique of gender workers in the school.

While this whole school policy approach confirmed by 1992 much of the organizational and curriculum change literature which emphasizes critical factors such as the need for adequate resourcing, time, planning, good communication, ownership of change by those affected and some external stimuli, it also suggests that gender reform differs from other forms of reform in a number of significant ways (Blackmore 1992). First, in order to get gender reform accepted and owned among all staff, gender inclusive curriculum and pedagogy has to be legitimized by other discourses, that is, good teaching practice. Thus the whole school-oriented rather than the girl-oriented approach makes equity for girls more palatable as the equity discourse is not accepted on its own merits. Indeed, gender reform was, as suggested above, 'piggybacked' on other reforms which required that gender be addressed. Most staff agreed that the introduction of the Victorian Certificate of Education and Curriculum Frameworks pushed down gender inclusive activities into the classroom.

Second, the whole school policy or 'mainstreaming' approach meant an orientation towards a curriculum approach to change and not a student-centred approach. The curriculum approach favoured producing policies and then implementing them throughout the entire school program, assuming that teachers and students would change accordingly; the student-centred approach argued that you had to begin with what students required at that time – personal development first, curriculum later. Within the AA team, the argument was between the position that students (particularly girls) required a sense of self-esteem before they were receptive to gender inclusive curriculum as 'curriculum went over their heads' unless they were ready, and the view that students would benefit if a gender inclusive curriculum was readily accessible. These approaches became alternatives and not mutually beneficial ways of proceeding because of the need to prioritize and plan. Interestingly, the popular reading that girls lacked self-esteem was accepted uncritically, even by the more radical feminists.

Third, the whole school curriculum policy approach meant that change took longer than was initially anticipated. Consequently, those staff not directly involved with the initial policywriting and consciousness raising activities of the affirmative action team saw the first years as unsuccessful. Again the gender workers themselves debated about the emphasis on too much writing (policy development) and not enough doing (producing classroom materials). They were also aware of the tension between staff members who had AA time allocation and those who didn't. AA team members were not perceived to be 'doing real work' because they were not in a classroom with a piece of chalk in their hand.

Finally, many of the initiatives by the gender workers were subverted or distorted in practice both consciously and unconsciously. For example, most staff agreed that the dominance of the hegemonic masculinity of the 'macho Greek boys' was a problem. Although most female gender workers felt this was the responsibility of male staff members as it diversified their energy, two female AA team members gained funding for an in-service day to allow male staff to address changing the attitudes of the boys and themselves. This caused resentment among even the pro-feminist male staff. According to a pro-feminist male AA team member, when the in-service occurred the male participants not only spent much of the time 'feminist bashing' but ultimately redefined the issue away from looking at the boys and the construction of masculinity to 'what can we do to help the girls'. That is, feminist initiated activity in areas which were threatening to the gender identity of even the more sympathetic males led to collective resistance and subversion (see also Kenway 1990). The collectivity in this specific context constructed feminism as threatening produced an antagonistic rereading of the gender texts.

Most teachers read the gender texts in a non-critical and 'readerly' manner. Indeed there existed a common-sense reading of what constituted gender equity which typified change as meaning the implementation of 'recipe knowledge' or well known strategies (for example, girls-only maths classes, group work in science). This common-sense reading of the official gender text allowed the 'silent majority' in search of quick fix solutions for the 'girl problem' to be readily satisfied with recipe knowledge at the superficial level, thereby not critically re-evaluating fundamental and more subtle aspects of their pedagogy or attitudes such as language practices. Others actively utilized and redefined the central concepts of the official gender texts of equality, individualism and merit to argue against any special treatment of girls. So while most staff accepted gender inclusive curriculum as being good teaching practice, any girls-only activities were still seen to be favouring girls by many students, staff and parents and therefore unfair. Equality was read as meaning equal treatment, not treatment according to the different

needs of girls. Others, drawing upon progressivist discourses of individualized pedagogy, argued that indeed they did provide different treatment to each student, but
according to their individual needs and not because they were male or female. Both
positions tended to shift away from the assumption that girls as a group had been
systematically disadvantaged and therefore may need different or additional programs
and/or resources as a group. This meant the 'silent majority', as did the overt resisters,
rewrote the central messages of AA in highly contradictory ways which were antithetical
to what the original writers of the text intended.

So while the gender workers were able to draw upon official gender texts as powerful legitimators of gender reform activities, they also found it strategically necessary to
draw upon other dominant educational reform discourses (curriculum reform) and
progressivist educational philosophy (equality and individual difference) in creative ways.
At the same time, the gender texts also constrained their activities, first, by the privileging
of particular policy focuses which limited the possibilities of shifting attention to what
they saw as preferred directions. For example, certain policy focuses legitimated certain
forms of gender reform over others (for example, mathematics, science and technology
over personal development.) Second, the absences in policy about issues which were
critical in the school context (such as masculinity) meant these lacked legitimacy. And
finally, the common-sense readings of the discourse of equal opportunity allowed central
concepts to be selectively read in ways which subverted the initial intentions of the
original producers of the text.

The case-study emphasizes the need for strong policy guidelines to initiate or legitimate activities already occurring in the school to provide a framework and justification
to which gender workers could appeal. It also indicates how additional staffing provided
the flexibility and capacity for a school to determine which is the best approach to
gender reform to meet their particular circumstances. It also suggests that centralized
policy guidelines are limited and limiting – limited by the ways in which individuals and
groups rewrite the official gender texts into a situationally specific discourse and limiting in the ways the official gender texts, by privileging particular foci, constrain gender
workers because they ignore the specific contextual, pedagogical and curriculum needs
of the school population. As the next section indicates, the institutionally specific discourse of the teachers in turn overlapped with, defined and was countered by the meanings constructed by students from the gender texts available to them.

Differentiating girls' reading and rewriting gender texts

EO activities at North Eastern Suburban Secondary College prior to 1990 tended to be
add-on or marginal to the mainstream curriculum (improving physical facilities for
girls, purchase of gender inclusive materials; common room for girls; Girls' Council,
self-defence classes, sexual harassment awareness, videos about unequal classroom participation by boys and girls; career advice and individual counselling). With the appointment of the EO coordinator attention shifted to more mainstream matters such as
curriculum and classroom behaviour, participation rates in senior maths and science.
Because of the imbalance of boys and girls in the school, various strategies were attempted, such as all-girls classes. Although some teachers expressed the view that it
may not be worth the trouble and that the boys usually miss out when girls are absent
from classes, gender balance is now an accepted school policy. Yet EO projects were still
largely an issue for action of a small committed group rather than effecting ownership

by the staff. The responsibility for specific projects constantly shifted among individuals calling upon the EO discourses within the system and the school, discourses now legitimated by policy and union prescription. It was therefore maintained that there was 'a level of support for EO within the school'. Despite this, as at Inner City, the equity discourse within the school was subordinate to other more significant reform discourses, like curriculum reform and amalgamation. Furthermore, those women (both teachers and parents) who called upon more radical discourses of feminism which were women or girl-centred continued to be denigrated as being lefty and rampant feminists, and therefore readily dismissed. The EO discourse was superficially accepted, more a matter of lip service as most teachers had not been 'hit over the head with gender inclusive curriculum at all'. Despite this, as at Inner City, most staff members were able to call upon the populist reading of the gender text about girls' disadvantage. These teachers therefore saw single sex classes as recipes for resolving girls' problems, but did not feel that they had to reflect significantly upon or alter their own teaching practice.

Previously funded in 1990 under the Girls in Maths and Science Project, the all-girls maths class was created in 1991 by manipulating the timetable, influencing the choice of subject options and actively counseling girls. The female year level coordinator and the female maths teacher of the girls class, Ms. C. J., persuaded a number of the better achievers among the girls in maths to take on an additional two-period extension class of maths and for most, a two-period science extension class in Year 10. The girls were encouraged, if not 'bullied' in a nice way to take on this class. In turn, they responded positively as they believed the female teachers were motivated out of a concern that girls should 'have more choices in careers . . . because more girls drop out than boys and because . . . more girls don't like maths' (Year 10 coordinator – female). Others were 'rewarded' for taking on the additional maths by being given first preference in a popular outdoor education unit by the year level coordinator.

This group of girls therefore, through self-selection and teacher-selection, appeared to be highly motivated to continue with extension maths. As such, they could be seen to have accepted and internalized the message of the official gender texts.[7] Yet among this particular group of girls there were three dominant but overlapping positionings, which were neither mutually exclusive or independently consistent. All effectively drew elements from the situationally specific, although non-hegemonic, discourse produced and circulating within the school. This discourse focused upon girls remaining in maths and science, girl-friendly environments and the provision of structures and processes which would provide girls with opportunities to voice their opinions and grievances. Three projects were readily identified by the teachers and the girls when asked about the school meeting girls' needs and issues – single-sex maths and science classes, the Girls' Council and the recently launched sexual harassment policy. The gender workers in the school had observed that these three projects had caused debate and even open opposition from among this particular group of Year 10 girls in the all-girls maths class, and through discussion of these projects the different positions of these girls became obvious.

There were three discourses or 'institutionalized language use' upon which these girls drew: feminism, liberalism and cultural pluralism, discourses which were not unitary or coherent, but internally differentiated. At the same time, these girls located themselves within situationally specific and culturally institutionalized ways of talking which led them to categorize themselves and be categorized as 'strong girls', 'feminist' girls and 'non-Australian or nurds'. This self-categorization occurred within the student culture, the classroom and the ritualistic social relationships between boys and girls. As Elizabeth Frazer argues, 'girls' experience of gender, race, class and their personal–social identity can only be expressed and understood through the categories and concepts available to them in discourse' (Frazer 1989: 282). What was clear was that all these girls readily drew upon the gender texts available to them in differential ways according to their positioning within the school culture as well as various discourses of feminism, liberalism and cultural pluralism. The discourse most coherently articulated in this school was the 'strong girl' discourse which was deeply embedded in the culture of a predominantly boys technical school. The least articulated discourse was that of cultural pluralism, although the school prided itself on its multiculturalism due to the presence and diversity of NESB students.

The feminists

The feminists were the girls who actively articulated the discourse of girls' disadvantage and in particular the dominant notions of equal opportunity. In that sense they drew from the wider feminist discourse which was women and girl-centered. They were proud to be seen as feminists, and did not see it as a perjorative label but rather as signifying their maturity and understanding of broader social issues. They also saw the various gender reforms in the school as having made some difference for girls. Donna felt that all the projects were helpful and supportive of girls : 'It is all right as we work much better. I like it better than when the boys are in the class as you get more attention. The girls work together and are quieter. You can ask questions and the boys do not put you down and call you dumb'. There was a general consensus among this group that the boys disrupted classes, called girls names and therefore impacted upon the girls' capacity to learn. They agreed that the recent sexual harassment policy had made some improvement upon the boys' behaviour. As Nicole A stated: 'it is more equal, now girls don't have to take it'. Such policies were, therefore, in the eyes of the 'feminist girls', equalizing the balance. Certainly the 'feminist' girls welcomed the space provided to them by girls-only activities. While their experience confirmed the dominant EO position about the positive benefits to girls of 'boy-free' space and doing maths and science in order to 'get a good job', they still sensed contradictions within the official gender text between its emphasis on individualism and its expectation of equality for girls as a group. This was most evident in Nicole A's comment, where she wished to be fair but was also aware that girls as a group were more disadvantaged:

> I think it's true that there are boys who do want to work in class . . . depends upon the individual . . . we shouldn't be making such a generalization . . . but I think there are more guys who don't care about their education 'cos they think they are going to get into a trade . . . be carpenters, etc. because they will go into the family business . . . girls realize that if we are going to do more than just secretarial work that we need a lot more education . . . I would like something to do with art.

'Strong' girls

Then there were the girls who, although appropriating central terms from the EO discourse about equal opportunity and girls needing to go into science and maths, were careful to disassociate themselves from what they labelled as 'feminism' because it was associated in their minds with 'rabid' feminism, being anti-male and was a common term of abuse used against girls advocating such a position. These girls tended to oppose the differential treatment of girls as being unfair to the boys, arguing that girls as a group were not disadvantaged because they, as individuals, did not feel disadvantaged. Rather than appealing to the notion of group disadvantage, they drew largely from the discourse of liberalism and its notions of individualism, equal access and merit rather than that of social justice or cultural difference. This also tapped into the underlying liberal feminist leanings implicit in the official gender text.

This position is well articulated by Rebecca, who went so far as to make any girls' activities totally irrelevant to herself by denying their existence. When asked about the Girls' Council, she stated: 'I don't agree with it really . . . because if they had a boys council it would be classed as sexist and a big uproar would result . . . they have a girls' council and get away with it. If the girls have a girls' council and the boys don't – I don't think it is right'. When it was suggested that EO policies existed because girls are seen to be disadvantaged, she responded: 'I don't agree . . . I don't feel at all disadvantaged. I really don't agree with that. Equal opportunity is when individuals are treated equally and in this instance they are not being treated equally'. While Rebecca agreed in principle that girls should have equal opportunities, here she asserts what is a popular common-sense reading of the gender reform text: that equal opportunity means the same treatment (See Blackmore 1991b for similar examples). Any different treatment for girls is unfair to the boys. In stating that she did not feel harassed or disadvantaged, she positioned herself as one of the 'strong girls' who were supportive of the boys. She supported her anti-feminist position by arguing that the class did not benefit her. When asked about her presence in the single-sex girls maths class, she again stated she had publicly opposed it in Girls' Council 'as the point of this class was that girls were not supposed to be treated equally in mixed classes . . . now they are not treating the boys equally'. While she agreed that the girls' class was quieter, she suggested that this did not improve her work as they 'gossiped' more anyway. 'I think if you want to work, you do. The type of class does not stop you . . . if the class is noisy you can still work if you really want to'.

Nicole B rejected the all-girls' maths class for different reasons. As a girl who had played junior Australian Rules football until the rules barred her when she turned 14 and who now played competitive sports three nights a week, she took a strong position with respect to her equality with the boys: 'I can do anything a boy can do equally well if not better'. She also drew upon the discourse register within the dominant student culture in which 'strong' girls socially aligned themselves with the boys as their 'mates' and friends. In particular, she was supportive of the male Physical Education teacher who was perceived by the 'feminist' girls as being sexist and chauvinistic because of the way he taught, for example, playing male games only, dividing the class into boys and girls, giving girls different skill-related tasks. She argued in the Girls' Council that this unequal treatment was technically necessary as the girls lacked the same sporting experience as the boys and had to be treated differently when playing football (an argument she rejected as the basis for treating girls differently in maths).

Also drawing from the 'strong girl' discourse register in this group was Tara. While Tara felt that the EO discourse in general had little to do with her personally, she still accepted that science and maths would increase her options, although she was not specifically aware of how. Certainly she was clear that she would not continue with maths into the senior forms, as she was not particularly good at it. Rather, her interest and talent lay with English and art and her preferred occupational area was interior design or decorating as 'she was good with colours'. So she was acquiescent and complied with the dominant claim of the discourse of EO that mathematics would benefit her later although she did not necessarily see it benefiting herself.

So on the one hand, these 'strong girls' recognized that the boys did dominate the public space (playground, SRC meetings and classrooms) and felt that girls needed 'space' within the school for discussion about issues that related to girls. On the other hand, they denied the hegemonic masculinity, with its strong element of anti-intellectualism and its mechanisms of control through harassment, jokes and name calling, as being a constraint on the capacity of girls to speak out. Instead, they attributed this to *other* girls' lack of confidence, as a 'weakness'. Katrina put this position well:

> There are some girls who are not used to the teasing, then [the sexual harassment policy] is OK. But we are used to it [teasing] and know the boys don't mean it. You get used to it as you know they are mucking around. If you don't know they are mucking around it would be hard on some girls. They only do it to the stronger girls. We know what they are really like and others who don't know would get upset.

Katrina was an advocate for the boys in that she felt the video on sexual harassment was unfair as it 'did not put the boys' view'.

Ironically, these girls, although claiming equality (independence, maturity or, in their words, 'toughness') in the sense that they could 'cope' with or 'handle' the boys, were in fact maintaining the dominant hegemonic masculinity of the school which was displayed in various ways such as sexual harassment by protecting the boys. Connell talks about how there is an ordering of various stylized versions of femininity and masculinity (which no particular individual meets). At any one time, a hegemonic masculinity is constructed in relation to other subordinate masculinities and all femininities. Ironically, the strong girls displayed a particular form of 'emphasized' femininity which is complicit in the maintenance of certain hegemonic forms of masculinity (Connell 1987: 183) Other femininities are defined by strategies of resistance or non-compliance (as in the case of the feminist girls in this class). Connell argues that any particular hegemonic masculinity is achieved as a 'state of play' which must be constantly fought for and renegotiated and reformulated in order to maintain its status. That is, hegemonic masculinities utilized effective 'collective strategies', like sexual harassment in relation to women and girls. So in 'coping' with the boys by being strong, these girls were in fact complicit in maintaining this particular form of hegemonic male behaviour in the school. In claiming EO policies were 'unfair', the boys, meanwhile, were utilizing a subtle collective strategy which both appealed to the dominant EO discourse and also to the nurturant and relational aspects of girls' socialization which activates their concern for others (Gilligan *et al.* 1990).

In responding as they did and 'mending the social fabric', the 'strong' girls become complicit in the maintenance of the form of masculinity which is particularly denigratory of themselves as female (See Kenway 1990). In constructing and being constructed in this position of protector and maternal carer for the boys, they blame other girls, who unlike themselves, cannot cope with the boys as they are 'lacking in confidence' and 'weak'. This denigration of other girls as weak or bitchy was an essential aspect of their previous experience and close social bonding with the boys, a relationship which defined them as strong girls, required them to deny that they were affected in any way by the boys' harassment. 'Mucking about' was just part of the hegemonic masculinity of the school culture. Rebecca's response is representative of these girls' position: 'I've always felt comfortable and relaxed with boys and never had any problems being with boys. Girls are too bitchy with each other and critical. Boys accept the way you are'. These girls, because they knew the boys, were, like mothers, prepared to accept the dissonance between the overt public behaviour of the boys which implied dominance, control and high self-esteem and their personal knowledge of the realities of the boys' lives, many of whom lacked academic ability, required nurturance, support and academic help.

At the same time, this meant they were positioned in opposition to those teachers whose anti-sexist practice worked against hegemonic student culture since what teachers saw as sexual harassment was just normal hassling. Trudy spoke of how 'teachers overact to boys hassling girls. We get on better with the boys'. Nicole B and Danielle argued that 'teachers abuse it. The harassment thing is really big now . . . the teachers are being pressured and so are the students. But the students and teachers misuse it and do not get all sides to it'. This distanced the strong girls from those teachers seen to be 'feminist' (although the same teachers did not see themselves as feminist) because anti-feminism was a major element of their individualized reading of the EO discourse and support of the dominant macho boys culture. They saw the sexual harassment policy as providing an opportunity for teacher overreaction, particularly 'feminist' teachers who unsettled teacher–student relationships and for some girls 'who brought it upon themselves' to get at the boys in vindictive ways. Indeed, Nicole B argued that sexual harassment occurred only when the 'victim' was unable to stop the name calling. This meant that the name calling ('dumb bitch', 'slut') was not what constituted harassment in itself. Rather, harassment only occurred when the person being harassed found it necessary to object or was not 'strong enough' to demand that it stop or retaliate. School sexual harassment policies were necessary only to assist weak girls. The strong girls, while taking for granted their equality and individuality in terms of their academic achievement and futures, were simultaneously constructing for themselves a particular type of femininity which did not challenge their relationship with the boys.

'Non-Australian' and 'nurds'

Silva had arrived from Chile seven months previously. She was the only non-Anglo Celtic in the class although there were other minority ethnic groups represented (Croatian, for example). She did not have the same discourse of equal opportunity upon which to draw, but talked about her impression of Australia as offering opportunity and accepting many different ethnic groups. She expressed strong views about fairness and equality and was able to relate these to the EO policies. Silva felt that any harassment she had experienced at the school was largely because of cultural difference, language and appearance, although this was, she conceded also highly gendered:

> Some girls are teased more because of the way they look. They have their problems . . . being fat. It is awful. Girls feel very hurt inside. Is it usually girls who do not fit a model who are picked on . . . even other girls tease girls because they are fat. That's sad. I am glad I'm not fat. If you are friends it doesn't matter what you are. . . . Some of the girls think they are better than other girls and than boys. When you come from another country, when you are black or not white, they tease you. They tease you because of your colour or accent.

Indeed, she pointed out that some of the girls who positioned themselves as 'feminist' were among those who claimed 'superiority'.

Silva shifted the original starting point of my conversation with her away from sexism towards a view of harassment which incorporated racism as well. From her position as a newcomer, an outsider to the student culture and in particular the 'strong girl' culture, she was also positioned as non-Anglo Celtic. Her gender was the least significant factor which constrained her activities or caused her distress. In that sense, the EO discourse and the Sexual Harassment Policy in particular provided her with a starting point or sense that there was some process to which she could appeal. It legitimated her view as to the unfairness and unjustness of such treatment. Culture and race as well as gender actively defined 'the other' in this school. This was evident in the comment by the strong girls about the nature of harassment. Those who were 'picked upon' by both boys and girls, it was agreed, were those who were non-Anglo Celtic, those who did not fit particular hegemonic notions of masculinity and femininity, or who did not fit the anti-intellectual student culture. Or as Danielle put it: 'Some guys will pick on girls . . . not me . . . only those who aren't normal. They are nurds or non-Australian. Boys direct attention at that'. What was also evident, however, was that this form of cultural harassment was practiced among those very girls who utilized the discourse of equal opportunity for their own assertiveness as girls (see also Kenway 1990).

What was significant about all these girls, many of them first-generation Australians from diverse ethnic and racial backgrounds, was their capacity to articulate their current positions and futures in ways which suggested that they did not, as much of the literature assumes, lack self-esteem. Indeed, as Tara, one of the tough girls, stated most succinctly, the girls perceived the boys as lacking self-esteem and ability.

> I think the [all-girls class] is better because the girls are smarter. I think the all-boys class don't do as much work. They muck around more. In our normal class I think we have all the slack boys in our class . . . But they act real smart and fool around. But I know better as I work with them. Because I help them and I know most of them. They are all babies.

Most of the girls saw self-esteem as more of a problem for the boys – hence their false bravado and insistence on being the center of attention. These girls in general had a strong sense of the problems attached to gender stereotyping and did not doubt their own capacity to make decisions about their future when the time came. This is not entirely surprising, given that this was a select group of girls who were obvious achievers in maths and science. But it does require further thought as to the ways in which the concept of self-esteem is universally applied to particular social groups such as girls and women, a tendency exacerbated through policy (Kenway and Willis 1990).

Also implicit is a 'masculine' model of adolescence. Stern (1990) talks about how theories of adolescence describe it

> as a time of separation, individuation and autonomy seeking; theorists of female development have observed that for women, the importance of strong relationships does not abate. In other words, theory tells us that by virtue of being female, adolescent girls especially value their connection; while by virtue of being adolescent, they are attending particularly to their separation. (Stern 1990: 73)

Does connectedness require rejection of separateness or vice versa? In attempting to balance these contradictory imperatives, how are the girls themselves complicit in their own subordination at the personal/private level (verbal harassment) while seemingly portraying independence and autonomy at a more public level (choice of maths and science). The strong girls believed that their maturity allowed them to better understand the motivations underlying the boys' harassment as not being misogynist, but rather an expression of the boys' incapacities to relate and achieve. Perhaps, as Gilligan suggests, girls, in coming from a relational perspective, redefine what is meant by independence and autonomy (and therefore maturity) in terms of changing relationships rather than breaking them – hence their concern with 'mending the social fabric' and the maintenance of congenial social relationships with the boys.

Much of the opposition which arose from the 'strong girls' group to EO was derived from a sense of 'unfairness' when girls received special treatment. It was a selective reading of the EO discourse which equated equality of opportunity to equal treatment. They did not see girls as a group as being 'disadvantaged' in any way as they felt it was within the capacity of each individual girl to act to stop harassment or to achieve despite unfavourable conditions. This draws from the the official gender text which also seeks to abstract the individual from her group or membership and that group's ascribed characteristics (Pateman 1981, Johnson 1988). In so doing, they disassociated themselves from other girls who were, by default, weaker, and therefore in need of intervening policies. Furthermore, such readings can indeed act against the intent of the gender texts from which they draw. Nor do they necessarily translate or transfer into more equitable practices in other areas. Sympathy or even claims for gender equality do not necessarily mean sympathy for claims for race or class equality.

Implications for policy and practice

Where do these analyses take us in terms of how to produce gender reform in schools? We will briefly look at policy, organization and pedagogy. With respect to policy, the study indicates, on the one hand, the power of policy to legitimate the activities of gender workers in schools and to provide a basis for the circulation of a dominant discourse upon which gender workers can draw. On the other hand it indicates the limitations of large-scale policy initiatives which do not cater to the different readings of the text within different contexts. This is in terms of the level of gender awareness and receptivity in the school; the discursive practices which have become embedded in school culture and organization; and the class, racial, sexual and ethnic composition of the school population. It indicates how policy constrains what can be done by the producers of policy text at the school level in that only certain activities are legitimated and the policy text itself is limited by the selective readings of the majority. That is, the popular representations of gender texts become recipe book knowledge for change and do not challenge the underlying relationships and attitudes. The question, therefore, is how to produce policy at the macro-level which provides both a useful legitimating framework informed by research and also takes into account the circuit of production, circulation and consumption which operates at the micro-level of school practice. The study suggests in terms of policy process, that several different policy strategies need to be maintained, such as 'top-down'/'bottom-up', mainstreaming gender reform and specialist programs, (or perhaps it is no longer useful to perceive these even as 'different strategies').

As to the nature of educational and organizational change, it suggests that we have to take into account a number of factors in terms of gender reform. First while it is easy to critique the liberal feminist framework, this particular discourse of feminism has provided necessary and important stepping stones to gender reform in schools, as indicated by the popular currency of its key terms and ideological rationale. It suggests that those concerned with producing educational change within a specific context need to be sensitive to the level of receptivity to particular discourses, working with those of greater legitimacy and currency while seeking to shift the discourse in more radical directions, reconstructing new situationally-specific discourses which gel with the concrete experiences of students and teachers. In this way, it is possible to reformulate and reconceptualize key terms in ways which do not reproduce inequitable discursive practices.

Second, it emphasizes the relational aspects of gender which must be taken into account in gender reform. It is not enough to continue to focus gender equity programs on girls without making masculinity problematic (see Kenway 1991). The two are interrelated. Schools make masculinity, and indeed differentiate between different masculinities and different femininities, both in classrooms and in school organization. These are organized hierarchically, around different forms of knowledge and curriculum and organizational artifacts (Blackmore 1993). As Connell argues, however, compensatory programs (which have been the focus of girls' equity policy) have little relevance to the privileged sex, as masculinity is built around themes of rationality and responsibility, which in turn are redefined and reconstructed in the face of challenge. In terms of political strategy, feminists obviously fear any shift of resourcing away from girls to boys as this merely reinforces the past biases which have only begun to be redressed. The question here, therefore, is how to direct attention to the gender relations and issues of masculinity without shifting attention away from girls?

In terms of school organization, it is important to recognize that policies are being worked upon in specific contexts. In particular, this study indicates how the equity issue is clouded by the lack of resources in a time of economic crisis, which is in turn encouraging an increasingly instrumental and vocational orientation to educational services. Such societal and system level agendas, while espousing gender equity as an objective, can provide an external impetus to gender reform, but can also ultimately continue to divert and even undermine it in more subtle ways. Pedagogically, it raises questions about what constitutes a feminist pedagogy and gender-inclusive curriculum. In these schools, gender reform has addressed the more explicit aspects in terms of content of curriculum – but the hidden curriculum is perhaps more powerful than the explicit one in matters of sexual politics.

Notes

1. This chapter draws from two other papers which elaborate more fully the qualitative data and discussion (Blackmore 1991 a, b). These in turn come out of the collective work of Jane Kenway, Sue Willis and Leonie Rennie in the Australian Research Council's funded research project on *Gender Reform in Schools. EO Policy: Its Reception and Effect* (1990–2). Much of the theoretical framework for this project derives from Kenway (1992).
2. These were short case-studies which focused upon a particular project rather than all activities seeking to produce gender reform in a school.
3. There have been critical appraisals of the successes/failures of Equal Employment Opportunity legislation and policy for women, largely because they also have not produced the expected outcomes; see Burton 1991, Poiner and Wills 1991.
4. The few girls' schools which remain in the state education system rely upon active lobbying by feminist educational groups and community groups based upon the widely held belief that single-sex education is educationally advantageous or culturally preferable for girls (in the Muslim community, for example) when the trend is towards co-education.
5. In 1990, the researcher at one school was Merilyn Evans, who provided much of the background material, although this particular discussion draws from data collected in 1991 by Jill Blackmore.
6. Equal opportunity is the term used in Australia to describe programs designed to compensate various groups such as girls and women, working-class, Aboriginal and disabled people disadvantaged due to their race, ethnicity, sex or disability. Affirmative action, taken up in the mid-1980s, was based solely on merit and not, as in the USA, in establishing quotas.
7. Most of the students in this class came from two-parent, lower and middle-class households, usually with both parents working – a newly arrived Chilean family had both parents unemployed. There was a high level of parental support for these girls' educational and occupational aspirations, encouraging 'choice' but with an emphasis on enjoyable rather than economically rewarding work.

References

ALCOFF, L. (1988) 'Cultural feminism versus post-structuralism: The identity crisis in feminist theory', *Signs* 13 (3) pp. 405–34.

AUSTRALIAN EDUCATION COUNCIL (1992) *Draft of the Review of the National Policy for the Education of Girls in Australian Schools* (Canberra: Australian Government Printing Service).

BALL, S. (1992) 'The policy process and the processes of policy', in R. BOWE and S. BALL, *Reforming Education and Changing Schools* (London: Routledge).

BLACKMORE, J. (1991a) 'The ironies of gender reform in secondary schools: A case study of a whole school policy approach', paper presented to AARE, Gold Coast, 24–28 November.

BLACKMORE, J. (1991b) 'Differentiating Girls and the "Reception" of EO Policy', paper presented to the Australian Sociological Association Conference, December, Perth, Murdoch University.

BLACKMORE, J. (1992) 'Changing schools, changing girls', paper presented to the Australian Association of Research in Education, November, Geelong, Deakin University.

BLACKMORE, J. (1993) 'In the Shadow of Men: The historical construction of educational administration as a "masculinist" enterprise', in J. BLACKMORE, and J. KENWAY (eds) *Gender Matters in Educational Administration and Policy: A Feminist Introduction* (London: Falmer Press).

BURTON, C. (1991) *The Promise and the Price. The Struggle for Equal Opportunity in Women's Employment* (Allen and Unwin, Sydney).

CLARK, M. (1989) 'Anastasia is a Normal Developer Because She is Unique', *Oxford Review of Education* 15 (3) pp. 243–55.

CONNELL, R. W. (1987) *Gender and Power* (Sydney: Allen and Unwin).

CONNELL, R. W. (1989) 'Cool Guys, Swots and Wimps: The interplay of masculinity and education', *Oxford Review of Education*, 15 (3) pp. 291–301.

DAVIES, B. (1989) 'The Discursive Production of the Male/ Female Dualism in School Settings', *Oxford Review of Education*, 15 (3) pp. 229–41.

DAVIES, B. (1990) 'Agency as a form of discursive practice: A classroom scene observed', *British Journal of Sociology of Education*, 11 (3) pp. 341–61.

DUDGEON, P., LAZARE, S. and PICKETT, H. (1990) 'Aboriginal Girls: Self esteem or self determination?', in J. KENWAY and S. WILLIS (eds) *Hearts and Minds: Girls, Schooling and Self Esteem* (Sussex: Falmer Press).

EBERT, T. (1988) 'The romance of patriarchy. Ideology, subjectivity and post modern feminist cultural theory', *Cultural Critique*, 10, pp. 19–57.

ELLIOTT, J. and POWELL, C. (1987) 'Young women and science: Do we need more science?', *British Journal of Sociology of Education*, 8 (3) pp. 277–86.

FRAZER, E. (1989) 'Feminist Talk and Talking about Feminism: Teenage Girls' Discourses of Gender', *Oxford Review of Education* 15 (3) pp. 281–90.

FULLAN, M. (1992) *The New Meaning of Educational Change* (Sussex: Falmer Press).

GILBERT, P. and TAYLOR, S. (1991) *Fashioning the Feminine Girls, Popular Culture and Schooling* (Sydney: Allen and Unwin).

GILLIGAN, C. LYONS, N. and HANMER, T. (1990) (eds) *Making Connections. The Relational Worlds of Adolescent Girls at Emma Willard School* (Cambridge, MA: Harvard University Press).

GRAMSCI, A. (1971) *Translations from Selections of the Prison Notebooks*, Quinti Nuare and Nowell Smith (London: Lawrence Wishart).

HENRY, M. and TAYLOR, S. (1991) 'Gender equity and economic rationalism: An uneasy alliance', unpublished manuscript, Gold Coast, Griffith University.

JOHNSON, L. (1988) 'On becoming an individual: A reassessment of the issue of gender and schooling', *Discourse*, 8 (2) pp. 97–109.

JOHNSON, R. (1983) *What is Cultural Studies Anyway?* Mimeographed paper (Birmingham: Center for Cultural Studies).

JONES, J. (1990) 'Outcomes of Girls' Schooling: Unravelling Some Social Differences, *Australian Journal of Education*, 34 (2) pp. 153–67.

KELLY, A., WHYTE, J. and SMAIL, B. (1984) (1985) *Girls into Science and Technology: Final Report*, Manchester Department of Sociology, University of Manchester.

KENWAY, J. (1990) *Gender and Educational Policy* (Geelong: Deakin University Press).

KENWAY, J. (1991) 'Masculinity – Under siege, on the defensive, and under reconstruction', paper delivered at Bergamo Conference, Dayton, OH.

KENWAY, J. (1992) 'Making hope practical rather than despair convincing: Some thoughts on the value of post-structuralism as a theory of and for feminist change in schools', paper presented to Women's Studies Conference, October, Sydney.

KENWAY, J. (1993) 'Non-Traditional Pathways: Are they the only way to go?', in J. BLACKMORE and J. KENWAY (eds) *Gender Matters in Educational Administration and Policy: A Feminist Introduction* (London: Falmer Press).

KENWAY, J. and WILLIS, S. (eds) (1990) *Hearts and Minds: Self Esteem and the Schooling of Girls* (London: Falmer Press).

KENWAY, J., WILLIS, S., RENNIE, L. and BLACKMORE, J. (1991) 'Studies of Reception of Gender Reform in Schools', *Curriculum Perspectives Newsletter*, June, pp. 3–11.

LATHER, P. (1990) *Feminist Research in Education: Within/Against* (Geelong: Deakin University Press).

MAHONY, P. (1985) *Schools for the Boys? Co-education Reassessed* (London: Hutchinson).

MAYER, E. (1992) *Employment Related Key Competencies*, Mayer Committee, Melbourne.

McLAUGHLIN, M. (1987) 'Learning from experience: Lessons from policy implementation', *Educational Evaluation and Policy Analysis*, 9 (2) pp. 171–8.

MINISTERIAL ADVISORY COMMITTEE ON WOMEN AND GIRLS (MACWAG) (1991) *Working for Gender Justice in Schools* (Melbourne: Ministry for Education and Training).

OZGA, J. (1990) 'Policy research and policy theory: A Comment on Fitz and Halpin', *Journal of Education Policy*, 5 (4) pp. 359–62.

PATEMAN, C. (1981) 'The Concept of Equity', in P. TROY (ed.) *A Just Society? Essays on Equity in Australia* (Sydney: Allen and Unwin).

POINER, G. and WILLS, S. (1991) *The Gifthorse. A Critical Look at Equal Employment Opportunity in Australia* (Allen and Unwin, Sydney).

SCHOOLS COMMISSION (1975) *Girls, Schools and Society*, report by a Study Group to the Schools Commission (Canberra: Australian Government Publishing Service).

SCHOOLS COMMISSION (1984) *Girls and Tomorrow: The Challenge for Schools*, Report of the Commonwealth Schools Commission Working Party on Education for Girls (Canberra: Australian Government Publishing Service).

SCHOOLS COMMISSION (1987) *The National Policy for the Education of Girls in Australian Schools* (Canberra: Australian Government Publishing Service).

STERN, L. (1990) 'Conceptions of Separation and Connection in Female Adolescents', in C. GILLIGAN et al. (eds) *Making Connections. The Relational Worlds of Adolescent Girls at Emma Willard School* (Cambridge, MA: Harvard University Press).

TAYLOR, S. (1991) 'Equity and the Politics of Change: Education Policymaking in Context', paper presented to the Australian Sociological Association Conference, October, Perth.

TSOLIDIS, G. (1990) 'Ethnic Minority Girls and Self Esteem', in J. KENWAY and S. WILLIS (eds) *Hearts and Minds* (London: Falmer Press).

WALKERDINE, V. (1989) 'Femininity as Performance', *Oxford Review of Education*, 15 (3) pp. 267–79.

WEINER, G. (1988) 'Teachers and gender: The unacknowledged makers of education policy', in J. BLACKMORE and J. KENWAY (eds) *Gender Issues in the Theory and Practice of Educational Administration and Policy*, Proceedings of the National Conference, Geelong, Deakin University.

WENNER, J. (1990) 'Culture, Gender and Self-Esteem: Teaching Indo-Chinese Students', in J. KENWAY and S. WILLIS (eds) *Hearts and Minds* (London: Falmer Press).

WHYTE, J., DEEM, R., KANT, L. and CRUICKSHANK, M. (eds) (1985) *Girl Friendly Schooling* (London: Methuen).

WILLIS, S. (1989) *Real Girls Don't Do Maths: Gender and the Construction of Privilege* (Geelong: Deakin University Press).

WYN, J. (1990) 'Working Class Girls and Educational Outcomes: Is Self-Esteem an Issue?', in J. KENWAY and S. WILLIS (eds) *Hearts and Minds* (London: Falmer Press).

YEATMAN, A. (1990) *Bureaucrats, Technocrats, Femocrats*, Allen and Unwin, Sydney.

17 Race, gender and the cultural assumptions of schooling

Fazal Rizvi

The unifying theme of this collection is that educators interested in issues of race and gender reform now work in a new cultural and political context. While at a general level this much is clear enough, what is less clear is exactly how that context should be defined, how it impacts on the politics of educational reform and how it dictates the parameters within which new reforms might be conceptualized. These are issues that are central to any examination of the failure of our schools to provide women and minorities the educational opportunities that might lead to their effective and equitable participation in society. They are also crucial in any assessment of the various reforms that are currently being attempted in schools not only in the United States but also elsewhere. The papers in this collection explore these issues and while they demonstrate a diversity of perspectives, they also indicate a theoretical and political pragmatism which is, in my view, essential for working towards the goals of equality and democracy in education.

What seems clear is that it is not only cultural and political but also theoretical uncertainty that now characterizes the Politics of Education. Thus, this collection is constituted by a range of perspectives, from liberal pluralism to neo-Marxism, from structuralism to post-structuralism. In it major disagreements exist about how best to define and respond to the current political environment. But these diverse viewpoints converge on at least one realization: that through the 1980s, the liberal democratic consensus of the 1960s has been in decline. Not only in the United States but also in other western countries, there is a renewed cynicism about the capacity of schools to work fairly and equitably for women and minorities.

The confidence that educators once had in liberal solutions to educational problems has evaporated under a sustained attack that the Right has been able to mount against the very foundation upon which it was based. In times of economic downturn, it has been relatively easy for conservative movements across the globe to mobilize a popular backlash against equal opportunity and civil rights initiatives. In a cultural era dominated by distrust, disillusionment and despair, the idea of public education has itself lost some credibility. The moral economy of the age has led to a disintegration of community life, and of the political authority of institutions. With this faith in the ability of educational systems to solve social problems lost, we do indeed now confront a new politics of race and gender.

Poverty and education

This politics has as its backdrop the facts of economic dislocation. Over the past two decades, the changes in the structure of the US economy have had major consequences on the cultural lives of people. Within the United States, there is now a new set of social and cultural pressures on women and minorities, clearly affected by a declining inner-city labour market, growing national unemployment, a decline in the number of un-skilled positions, especially for the young, the automation of clerical labour and the shifting of the service sector to the suburbs.

The demographic landscape of the United States has changed dramatically, as Ward's chapter so clearly demonstrates. In it, he argues that recent demographic trends indicate that the United States' population is becoming more diverse, is aging and growing more rapidly in southern and western states. There are now fewer traditional families than there used to be. The number of single-parent and no-parent households are in-creasing at an alarming rate, putting considerable pressure on educational and other social welfare agencies, which are not ideologically fashionable in any case. The legit-imacy of the welfare measures initiated by the state are now openly and widely questioned.

Timar and Shimasaki's contribution demonstrates how issues of demography and politics are inextricably linked. It shows for example, how the current political system in California is 'not adroit at redistributive politics'. Ideological battles, differing effects of local taxation regimes, uneven application of demographic data and bureaucratic struggles over funding formulas all combine to explain growing funding disparities among urban, suburban and rural districts. Timar and Shimasaki suggest that even under the welfarist objectives of redistributive and compensatory politics, a dispropor-tionate amount of educational resources are in fact flowing to the predominantly white, middle-class suburbs, and that the urban areas where most minorities live are now considerably worse off.

The most alarming facet of this profile, however, is the growing disparity in in-come distribution between the suburban and the urban – the rich and the poor. A nation that prides itself in its commitment to the values of liberty and equality now suffers from endemic poverty. Fuelled by an ethic of greed that is institutionalized, the rich have become richer and the poor poorer, but the economic indicators are not sufficient to reveal the full extent and the nature of poverty. For as Edgar (1989: 13) has pointed out, 'the "poor" are not only the unemployed, not only the halt, the sick and the lame, not only the working class. The poor are a moving and multifarious population'. Many families who have jobs are still poor because they have insufficient resources to partici-pate fully in society. They are variously excluded and alienated, unable to take full advantage of the benefits that institutions like schools can give them.

As Ward explains, education is becoming increasingly critical to the financial and career success of students as they pass into adulthood. While this is evidently true, the link between poverty and education is not only instrumental; it is a great deal more complex. Ward's analysis focuses on the individuals, and how poverty is instrumental in making the symbolic capital that schools transmit inaccessible to the children who are poor. Children in poverty are thus less likely to be successful in schools. However, while this analysis of the link between poverty and education is clearly accurate, it appears trapped within a deficit theory that suggests that children who are poor lack some essential condition necessary for educational success.

Ward argues that because of poverty certain children are denied the kinds of edu-cation that are necessary for the needs and attributes of an information-based society and a global economy. This way of looking at issues, however, seems to suggest that inequalities are a problem to do with only a section of the community – those who are poor – and not the whole of the community. Yet as Connell and his colleagues (1991) have pointed out, poverty is not only a problem for individuals. It is also an *educational* issue – about how relations of social distribution are arranged and how curriculum and pedagogy serve the interests of some groups better than others. The problem is about the wider play of class relations. As Connell *et al.* (1991: 24) put it:

> Poor people suffer most from this interplay; their educational problems are indeed the worst. They generally have little power to change educational institutions set up by others, or to make them function in their own interests. For equity reasons, if there are limited dollars or limited political will, it is right to focus action on the education of the poorest groups. But it should never be thought that this will work very well as an isolated enterprise. Many of the educational problems of children in poverty arise from systemic effects which cannot be remedied by action at the school or even the regional level.

Connell and his colleagues suggest that *all* educational policies should be framed in order to take into account the interplay between poverty and education.

One of the main problems with the current views concerning the relationship between poverty and education is they often assume poverty to be a *cause* which has certain educational *effects*. Thus, it is thought, for example, that inadequate income leads to families being unable to afford educational support expenses; or that because of inadequate role models children who are poor focus on the immediate rather than the long-term benefits of education. While there is a great deal of truth in these claims, they do not tell the full story. Indeed, it is this kind of thinking that leads many welfare organizations to believe that education is an issue separate from welfare issues. Similarly, many neo-Marxist educationists believe that schools simply reproduce social class and poverty. There was much talk about 'cycles of poverty'. However, both the popular and neo-Marxist perspectives rest on a set of dualist assumptions that are mistaken. The major assumption is that poverty and education are somehow *external* to each other, related only in a contingent manner.

In my view, this myth needs to be exploded. We need to recognize that the educational system not only reproduces inequality it also *generates* it. A recognition of this kind is helpful in breaking down the assumption that poverty is largely a welfare business, in which schools play only a minor part. Rather, from the point of view of educational theory, it is helpful to think of poverty as a *curriculum* issue. We need to consider how curriculum and pedagogy contribute, over time, not only to the reproduction of poverty but also its production.

Ideology and curriculum

In recent years, it has also become increasingly clear that poverty in the United States is a racialized and gendered phenomenon. It affects in a disproportionate way single women, African Americans, Latinos and other minorities. Curriculum itself is a site where issues of poverty and race and gender articulate with each other. As Cody and her colleagues point out, while desegregation and the civil rights movement of the 1960s and 1970s had finally exploded the myth of a culturally neutral curriculum, the battle over curriculum is far from over.

It is now widely recognized that curriculum contributes to the production of poverty in a number of ways. For example, the ideology of 'credentialism' often works against the interests of women and minorities. Its growth has increasingly become a selection device even where the credentials are not technically relevant to the job, disproportionately affecting those students who cannot stay on in schools and colleges. The levels and kinds of formal education have become definers of social status and boundaries, disproportionately affecting those minority youth whose cultural experiences do not match the symbolic capital in which schools deal.

The emphasis on technical and vocationally 'useful' knowledge that business groups interested in school reform have championed have also disproportionately impacted on women and minorities. As Borman, Castenell and Gallagher argue, business has had a conservative input into the development of educational policy in the United States. It has put its own narrowly defined interests ahead of the pursuit of gender and racial equity.

Business and industry-sponsored attempts to reform schools have been aimed largely at teachers and teaching, state and local school governance and school-to-work transition programs. Business has sought to see schools run in its own corporate managerial image. Not surprisingly therefore business has viewed pedagogy and curriculum with industrial ends in mind, overlooking the cultural contradictions that confront many young people, particularly those living in inner-city areas. There is furthermore a danger that an elaborate and standardized bureaucratic framework of strands and levels, and a managerial scheme for assessing and reporting on them (of a kind that many business groups appear to want), will simply further alienate many young people from the processes of schooling.

It would be a mistake to believe however that the modern discourse of business is so uniform and blunt. It is a contradictory discourse that rearticulates oppositional ideas and popular sentiments so that they are effectively made to serve, seemingly in an indispensable way, the dominant agenda. Its emphasis on diversity, options, opportunities and so on often obscures its desire to develop a social structure that is uniform, standardized and under the control of dominant class interests. It uses many of the terms that were integral to the liberal agenda, but has succeeded in fundamentally rearticulating their meaning and significance. Indeed, the current rhetoric of devolution and the self-managing school is illustrative of the extent to which business and the New Right have captured a liberal democratic vocabulary to serve a set of contradictory political purposes. For example, the idea of self-management has now been converted into a consumerist notion concerning 'the right of individuals to be able to choose in an unconstrained market'.

However, as Glenn's contribution suggests, the ideology of choice is deeply contradictory, and does not 'function by *itself* to produce the benefits frequently claimed'. Thus, Glenn demonstrates how the choice program in Boston has in fact served to reduce the resources available to improve schools that most poor and minority children attend. The theoretical notion of 'choice' itself has not been problematized. The view of choice that business celebrates is derived from the notion of preference in neo-classical economics and a pluralist politics. This view of choice is highly individualistic, however, overlooking its essential *social* character. It obscures the fact that choices are culturally constructed, and that institutions such as schools have a major role in fostering those capacities that enable people to choose intelligently and thereby secure some measure of control over their lives. Also, people's capacity to make certain choices are often dependent upon the material resources they possess, which are frequently defined in class, race and gender terms.

In addition to its rhetoric of choice, much of the rationale of the business agenda is based on another premise which suggests that in order to become more internationally competitive the United States has to develop an educational system that is characterized by quality, depth and flexibility – in effect, to meet the changing needs of capital. Current education and training practices, it is claimed, are too rigid, producing a range of skills which are too narrow to meet the needs of the industry. The new rhetoric suggests that the only way to tackle the problems of the inner city, of employment growth and of social equity is through capital growth and through the skilling of America.

Such an agenda for educational reform represents a resurgence of human capital theory. The theory was developed within the framework of a neo-classical view of the labour market which saw the skills the individual possessed as a kind of human capital which not only benefited the individual but also served to increase a society's economic growth. However, as a number of writers have pointed out, a major problem with such a theory is that its claim that education and training are positively correlated with higher marginal productivity or individual rewards in the form of higher wages has never been established. Maglen (1988) has argued that both macro and micro-level evidence shows no necessary connection between education and worker productivity, and that a narrow instrumentalist education serves rather the interests of social allocation and control of people. In this way, human capital theory is a piece of ideology that has been remarkably resilient.

This conclusion should not be taken to suggest that skills are somehow unimportant or that students should not learn about the world of work. What is being argued instead is that human capital theory serves to narrow the focus of education. As Watkins (1991: 45) has argued Anglo-conformist it obscures the basic questions about the way work is organized and the way young people are socialized into various occupational choices. The human capital theory also individualizes the labour market. So, for example, if a person cannot get a job then it is assumed that this is a reflection of his or her skill levels and ability rather than certain intrinsic weaknesses within the economic structure and the way employment is distributed, and even more significantly, how the availability of work is linked to certain regimes of gender and race. The assumption that the current youth unemployment level is somehow linked to the low skills level of young people, and once this has improved, jobs will simply follow is an ideological hoax which serves only to blame the victims.

Indeed, it is an ideology similar in its structure to the myth of a racially and gender-neutral curriculum. As Cody *et al.* point out, that myth was perpetuated by white, male elites 'to preserve stability and to represent the public interest'. The notion of public interest has never been so simple, especially in light of the realization that the nexus between home and school is extended to institutional ordering of whole school systems on a basis of class, race and gender advantage and disadvantage. The organizational culture of schools in the United States is Anglo, conformist, gendered and middle-class, and this often creates a social distance between teachers and families of the minorities. What is also clear is that the competitive individual selection and assessment practices of schools create difficulties in establishing continuing success orientation for all students.

What these considerations show is that curriculum is a site of contestation, ideological bargaining and political struggle, and that the universalist curriculum has served only to protect dominant interests, and that it is inimical to the notions of social justice and democracy. They also suggest that diversity is a permanent feature in US schools, and that it needs therefore to be dealt with on the basis of sound educational principles.

Diversity and the problems of liberal reform

Currently, the most popular response to diversity in US education is multiculturalism. As Anderson and Herr observe, despite a neo-conservative backlash, the ideas of diversity and multiculturalism are still in vogue. Much has been written about multiculturalism's potential for ameliorating racial inequality. It has been suggested, for example, that diversity need not, and indeed should not, be viewed as a problem; but that the fact that children in our schools come from a variety of family backgrounds and outlooks should be celebrated for the educational potential it clearly has. Multiculturalism is seen to present a new approach to curriculum, pedagogy and evaluation through the promotion of a specific set of cultural attitudes to difference and through the creation of the kind of school environment in which every student can participate.

It is important to note, however, that multiculturalism is not a unitary discourse. McCarthy (1990) has argued that in education at least three discourses of multiculturalism can be identified – those emphasizing the idea of cultural *understanding* and sensitivity to cultural differences; those insisting on a curriculum for cultural *competence* that encourages students to develop competencies to live comfortably in a pluralist society; and those suggesting the possibilities of cultural *emancipation* through education, leading to improved life-chances of minority students.

Each of these discourses focuses on the notion of 'culture', though unlike the educators of the 1960s who had consistently advocated compensatory education as a means of overcoming 'cultural deprivation', the contemporary theorists of multicultural education view culture as something positive. They suggest that cultural differences should be celebrated, and that every effort should be made to ensure that minority students are able to maintain their cultural heritage. Further, they state that such an approach is essential if the problems of racism, understood as a broad notion that describes the practices of racial, ethnic and cultural exclusion, bias and discrimination, are to be adequately tackled.

The basic premise upon which this view is based is that education of minority students can no longer be structured around a notion of linguistic or cultural deficit, and that a program in multicultural education must utilize the social context of children's lives outside the classroom. Unless this is done, students will inevitably be alienated from schools, have low self-esteem and are unlikely to be able to contribute to the mainstream society. The rationale for a multicultural education does not only reside in this defensive logic, however. It was based also on the political imperative that all groups in society should enjoy equal access to power, status and wealth, and that success should not depend on renouncing group values, norms and life-styles. To make schools truly multicultural, it is argued, major changes are required to curriculum, teacher education and development and school organization and administration.

While this liberal rhetoric in US education has indeed been strong, the actual changes it has been able to sponsor in schools are hard to find. As McCarthy (1990) has noted, most programs in multicultural education place an overwhelming emphasis on issues of attitudes, feelings and personal development, at the expense of the requirements of intensive, rigorous or specialized academic teaching. There is a tendency to view culture in very narrow terms, to dwell on the 'traditional', to celebrate festivals and foods, even if these have little significance for minority youth. As Anderson and Herr argue, 'regardless of how well-meaning, educational institutions cannot move from "soft" definitions of multiculturalism to more sophisticated ones without an understanding of the role the educational institution plays in the identity struggles of its students'. They propose a micro-political perspective in order to examine how students' voices are negotiated through the processes of schooling.

The simplistic pluralism implicit in popular views of multiculturalism, Anderson and Herr suggest, serves to silence student voices, making them invisible. It is premised on the ideals of color-blindness, meritocracy and equal opportunity. A micro-political analysis of student lives, however, demonstrates how these ideals are myths which bear little relation to the real dilemmas of minority youth, and are certainly not factors in their life chances. Anderson and Herr also argue that 'these myths are dysfunctional in that they blind members of dominant groups from understanding the very real dilemmas of minority groups'.

In my view this blindness is further accentuated by the commonly held view that assumes that racism is caused by ignorance which is reinforced by prejudices that some individuals hold. Thus, it is argued, racism occurs when minorities are made the scapegoat by people who do not adequately understand the real causes of the material and social problems they confront. The solution to the problem of racism is thus thought to lie in better education. Once people have learnt the real causes of social problems they would be less inclined to 'blame the victims'. Another side of this liberal argument stresses the importance of direct experiential learning about minority cultures as a mechanism for breaking down stereotypes and irrational prejudice and promoting greater tolerance of diversity.

However, a major problem with this argument is that it rests on a number of rationalist assumptions. It is assumed, for example, that racism is primarily a discourse which is falsely premised, and can be ameliorated with a superior logic and better information acquired through education. But, as Cohen (1987: 1) argues:

> popular racism does not work in this way. Its appeal is precisely that it makes 'imaginative sense' of common predicaments; it is a practical, behavioural ideology, rooted in everyday cultural practices, and does not require theoretical legitimation or institutional support to become popular.

It is assumed, moreover, that it is at the cognitive level that a program in multicultural education is best targeted. But racism is not a rational ideology; it is constructed around certain structures of feeling and has a socio-emotional dimension that cannot be adequately confronted either by an academic discussion of racial inequalities or by an experiential encounter with 'other' cultures, such as a visit to a Buddhist temple. As Cohen (1987: 2) contends:

> popular racism cannot be tackled by simply giving students access to alternative sources of experience, or new means of intellectual understanding; rather it is a question of articulating their lived cultures to new practices of representation, which make it possible to sustain an imaginative sense of social identity and difference without recourse to racist constructions.

In treating ethnicity as an educational resource that needs to be celebrated in the multicultural curriculum, for example, teachers have effectively marginalized and subordinated the role ethnicity plays in defining social relationships *within* schools. As Cole (1986) has pointed out, by focusing attention on cultural diversity and ethnic children's self-esteem, multiculturalism does not adequately account for the processes that lead to *culturally biased forms of education*.

Many teachers still regard racism as a problem that is external to the processes of schooling. It is a problem, they assume, that is best tackled by such classroom strategies as providing students better information about ethnic cultures; introducing programs in moral education that emphasize the virtues of tolerance, understanding and diversity; purging school textbooks of their racist biases; presenting positive role models of successful minority individuals; and ensuring that the curriculum is broadened to reflect diversity more accurately. These strategies are certainly valuable and go a considerable way towards challenging the assimilationist assumptions upon which most schooling is still based. They are unlikely to be successful unless they are framed within the political dynamics of interactions that form the borders of what Walker (1988) has referred to as 'intercultural articulation'.

As Kennedy (1991) has demonstrated, 'teachers often assume that knowledge of student diversity is mainly relevant to social issues, and not to issues of academic content and how it is taught and learnt' (p. 15). She has found that most courses and workships about ethnic differences tend to be largely descriptive, providing teachers with generalizations about group characteristics and customs, but such knowledge often reinforces, rather than alters, latent racism. Kennedy maintains moreover that teachers treat issues of difference as a fact to be taken into account rather than a factor constitutive of curricular and pedagogic relations. Her view is on the other hand that teachers cannot assume a position of neutrality in the formation of such relations, as somehow external to the more general processes of racial articulation in society.

What this argument implies is that the relationship between schooling and race needs to be reconsidered in a more dynamic *relational*, rather than instrumentalist, terms. The relations between racism, education and society are complex, and cannot be reduced to some simple essential form. We need therefore to develop a better understanding of the pedagogic processes through which differences are converted into racism. We need to understand how racism works relationally through the structural operations of education, in textbooks, in resource allocation and in practices of assessment which privilege some values and dismiss others. As McDermott and Gospodinoff (1981: 216) explain: 'Our problem is not that people are different, but that differences are made to make more of a difference than they must, that the differences are politicized into borders that define different kinds of people as antagonistic in various realms of everyday life'. And as Cohen (1987: 5) suggests, it should be 'feasible to acknowledge the presence of divisions within and between ethnic communities, whether based on religion, class, gender or generation, without reinforcing them, while also pinpointing the sources of unity or alliance which do or could exist'.

Some of the contradictions that are inherent in the liberal views of multiculturalism apply also to current practices of gender reform in education. Research conducted by Blackmore and her colleagues shows how current policies of equal opportunity for girls in Australia remain trapped within the framework of liberalism. These policies have provided many individuals with particular opportunities, in terms of access and success, but they have not focused on removing structural and procedural impediments that inhibit equity for girls generally, despite some policy efforts to conceptualize girls' disadvantage in terms of structural factors such as curriculum and school organization, the deficit model of gender reform remains dominant in schools. According to Blackmore and her colleagues, this signals the importance of looking more closely at the change process itself.

Blackmore and her colleagues suggest that those working for gender reforms in Australian schools have had to contend with an administrative ideology of corporate management that is 'state-centric'. Corporate management emphasizes quantitative outcomes, assumes neutrality of administrative processes, appeals to notional consultation and demands increased accountability to the center. While acknowledging the importance of the state's role in legitimating reform initiatives, Blackmore and her colleagues argue that a more serious problem with the corporatist approach to gender reform is that it treats 'reception' of policies at the local school level unproblematically. It assumes a degree of passiveness on the part of teachers, parents and students, and ignores the way gender reform efforts articulate with the issues of race and class. Using theoretical resources of post-structuralism, Blackmore and her colleagues seek to show how policy is read, interpreted, selected from and acted upon in different contexts by different individuals.

In many respects, the observations made by Blackmore and her colleagues apply also to the United States. While the United States has lacked centralized policy prescriptions in the area of gender reform, there has been much local activity in schools. As in Australia, however, most initiatives at the school level have been informed by a set of liberal assumptions about 'access and success'. As the work of the Boston Women's Collective and Kathleen Weiler (1988) demonstrates, the initiatives that focus only on greater educational opportunities for girls overlook the issue of how these opportunities are structurally constituted through various gender regimes. It suggests that the definition of equality with which many schools work is a narrow instrumentalist one, confined to issues of occupational advancement and access to participation. It does not address the way the dominant cultural, political and economic order in the United States is patriarchal and the way it legitimizes existing inequalities and perpetuates the myth that liberal reforms promoting the values of tolerance and cooperation are sufficient for the achievement of greater equality of educational opportunity. Weiler (1988) suggests that a more critical examination is needed of the cultural assumptions of schooling upon which alternatives to liberal reforms might be conceptualized.

Alternatives to liberal reforms

The alternative to liberalism that many feminist scholars in education propose is based on the assumptions of critical pedagogy. An educational policy more appropriate for changing gender regimes, they argue, requires a radical appraisal of our society's materialist, racist and sexist culture, which continues to be transmitted by schools. We need to understand how gender is constitutive of this culture, and how gender relations are produced and reproduced in schools.

Critical pedagogy requires the teaching of critical literacy, seeking to develop in students a familiarity with not only the academic skills but also a critical understanding of power and the diverse patterns of cultural reproduction. Girls need to become aware of the worth of their own histories so they can value their own precepts and insights. They need to challenge the history of the dominant culture to validate their own experiences and truths so that they can look at themselves as useful members of a cultural tradition that empowers them to speak with their own voices.

The notion of voice is also central to a more radical discourse of multicultural education, referred to by McCarthy (1990) as 'emancipatory'. As Anderson and Herr's chapter in this collection indicates, this empancipatory discourse is based on the premise that multiculturalism needs to develop a better concept of the cultural mechanisms that affect educational participation. It recognizes that most contemporary textbooks, instructional materials, curriculum, teacher behaviour and school climate continue to be biased in favour of the dominant groups. Thus, critics such as O'Connor (1989) argue that mainstream multiculturalism fails to realize how the 'discourse structures' of schools are constructed to legitimate the existing patterns of power relations. Favoured ways of speaking and acting, as well as favoured conceptions of knowledge and skills, are the cultural capital of such educational discourse structures which govern and control the life chances of many minority students. Thus, for example, the 'success of students who orient themselves to the dominant group's forms of educational discourse are described in personal terms, and viewed as virtually independent of cultural attachments', while students from minority backgrounds who resist the dominant discourse, 'are marked by defensive, closed boundaries, with reference to their cultural background becoming ideologically valuable to certain teachers and students' (O'Connor 1989: 69).

O'Connor (1989: 72) suggests that for multicultural education to be more effective in producing greater educational equity and in tackling the problems of racism, it must permit, 'all cultural voices to search for skills and concepts to reconstruct their cultural principles in their own terms'. For unless learning is made *culturally relevant*, it would simply continue to leave many students confused, disadvantaged and alienated. O'Connor goes on to say:

> To develop an educational response that appreciates the politics of participation, it is necessary to organize educational discourses according to multivoiced and democratic pedagogies. A multivoiced approach to teaching recognizes that teachers must always enter into dialogue with students, all of whom possess various social orientations. To accomplish the task of teaching students how to reconstruct cultural principles and values, teachers must continually search out the relevant connections to these different starting points. Cultural differences add some uncertainty and complexity, but they do not alter the basic process. Teaching must always be engaged in multivoiced dialogues. (p. 70)

The most basic educational task that teachers have, according to O'Connor (1989: 72) is the development of 'democratic practices of representation in the classroom. Reliance on an authoritarian, monophonic classroom will only lead to the development of a fractured society'. Following Freire, O'Connor stresses the importance of dialogic rather than monologic authority of the teacher. Ideally, he argues, the voices of the students should be treated equally with that of the teacher.

O'Connor's view of multiculturalism is based on the insights of critical pedagogy (Giroux 1983). It highlights the importance of democratizing school practices, including its modes of communication and social relations. It suggests that since such educational issues as knowledge, pedagogy and evaluation concern the entire community, all sections of the community should be given an equal voice in the processes of educational decision-making. What goes on in schools should thus be negotiated dialogically rather than imposed by some central authority.

The critical view of multicultural education suggests further that teachers should, above all, attempt to create conditions in their classrooms that help students to understand collaboratively and oppose the construction and maintenance of inequalities that have been created through the assimilatory logic of a meritocratic education that prevails in most schools. As Wood (1984: 235) has argued, 'If students are to develop the civic courage to make it possible for them to act democratically, it is necessary that they understand their own histories'.

Now, while the critical view of multiculturalism certainly represents a significant advance on the mainstream liberal view, in terms of its assumptions concerning the cultural politics of teaching, it is similarly flawed. While it advocates a contrasting view of the teacher's authority, it does not examine the issues of the structural conditions within which this authority resides, is exercised and is accorded legitimacy. Moreover, while it rejects a static reified view of culture, and sees it instead as something dynamic, constantly changing in response to new ideas, beliefs and circumstances, and open to negotiations of various kinds, it does not explain the role of the teacher in the creation of the boundaries of the dialogue within which the critical enterprise is to occur.

Both the mainstream and critical views of multiculturalism thus undertheorize the conditions under which teachers work. If however it is admitted that the goals of race and gender equity are difficult to achieve in mainstream schools then are ethnic and gender-specific schools the only viable alternative? This is an issue central to the chapters by Brown and Alston. Brown argues that the proponents of African American academies have viewed these schools as necessary to respond to the crisis facing black males both within and outside of educational institutions. He examines a number of legal and educational objections to such academies, but suggests that these are not insurmountable.

In contrast, Alston cautions against the enthusiasm for separate schooling experiences for African American males. While acknowledging the validity of many of the claims made by the advocates of segregated schooling, such as those relating to the consequences of educational failure and the complicity of educators in such processes, he nevertheless notes two major concerns. The first relates to the long-term costs of such experiments and the second relates to their consequences for the education of African American girls. Alston contends that the life chances of all African Americans are conditioned on the same material circumstances, and that to assume, even implicitly, that mainstream 'schooling is healthier for girls or that the success of girls is conditioned on the failure of boys is unconscionable'.

The more fundamental point in this debate concerns the negotiating and ordering of gender relations. If all social structures are relationally defined then such ordering in education requires the participation of both sexes in order to combat the historical and cultural pressures that minorities confront. However, the advocates of African American academies seldom discuss the issues of relationality, and what their proposals are for girls.

To suggest that desegregation across race and gender is a goal still worth preserving is not to maintain, however, that there may not be occasions when some separation is not only strategically prudent but also educationally desirable. While there are clearly no fixed rules for making such judgments, what this debate does highlight is the need for the widest possible community participation in educational decision-making. It is only through such participation that minorities can be empowered to express what their interests and needs are. Whatever the particular merits and problems of the Chicago school reform that Hess so strongly defends, his point concerning the importance of giving minorities a voice in their own educational futures seems unexceptionable.

At the same time, however, we have to acknowledge that teachers and administrators are key players in educational reform. Yet, far too little is said, in this collection and elsewhere, about the structural conditions under which they work. Those who propose reforms often assume that by and large teachers are supportive of those reforms, and that they already have the appropriate inclination, background, commitment and ability to work towards the reforming agendas of democracy and equality. Their confidence is often misplaced. In my view, genuine reforms cannot be realized without an adequate theoretical understanding of the various ways in which teachers conceptualize their social world, and the ways these conceptualizations serve to define social relations of pedagogy and curriculum in schools. What is required is a systematic understanding of the nature of teacher subjectivity and how it relates to the structural conditions within which schooling occurs, and within which teachers work.

The cultural assumptions of educational administration

These remarks apply equally to school administrators. Two decades of research have amply demonstrated how hostile the us educational system is to diversity and equity. It seems to rest on the assumptions of uniformity and conformity. The point can be amply illustrated by looking at the failure of the educational system to attract and keep women and minority educational administrators.

The data provided by Bell and Chase confirm once again something that most educators know intuitively: that women and minorities are underrepresented in positions of administrative responsibility in schools. Beyond these quantitative measures, however, it is also clear that those who make it to such positions are not entirely happy with the support they receive. As Marshall argues, many women and minority administrators still feel alienated, subjected to tokenism and isolation. So, why is it that, despite enhanced public awareness about the issues of gender and race and the development of equal opportunity initiatives, women and minorities remain so underrepresented in educational leadership positions; and so dissatisfied, even when they secure such positions?

This question is one of the most complex and perplexing issues confronting contemporary educational administration. In seeking to answer it, Bell and Chase examine four explanations. First, they suggest that gender stratification in schools is maintained by differential access to opportunities for advancement. Second, they contend that gatekeepers in schools are predominantly white men. Third, they point to the persistence of both subtle and blatant forms of sexism and racism. Finally, they argue that recent trends in public policy have had negative effects on equity.

In her chapter, Marshall looks at the way administrators are socialized into the dominant culture of schooling. She suggests that current discussions of organizational socialization do not sufficiently take into account the operations for gender and race in filtering out social differences. Women and minorities are taught to keep quiet, avoid conflict and accept the dominant norms. Assimilation, it seems, continues to be a condition for administrative success. Exactly how this assimilation occurs in schools, however, is an issue that most theories of administration do not address.

The idea of assimilation suggests that in order to maintain its corporate identity and stability, an organization must inevitably strive to ensure that everyone in it is absorbed into its homogeneous culture. Any organizational development is, so it seems, only possible upon the tacit terms of the prevailing ethos. The functionalist emphasis on the need for educational administrators to conform to existing norms means that organizations discourage expressions of social and cultural differences. Any challenges to the existing structural features of schools are regarded as dysfunctional. Those who cannot or do not wish to be assimilated are either excluded or marginalized.

I agree entirely with the explanations Marshall and Bell and Chase provide for the exclusion and marginalization of women and minorities. However, I believe their accounts need to be placed in a broader theoretical context. To do so, we might consider how functionalist theories of educational administration and practice serve in fact to reinforce conservatism, and thus militate against the possibilities of genuine equity reform.

To understand how this happens, we need to explore more fully the cultural politics of schooling – the various ways in which educational administrators conceptualize their social world, including the phenomena of gender and race inequalities; the ways these conceptualizations serve to define social relations in schools; and the ways administrative work is related to the structural conditions within which schooling occurs.

Much of the functionalist research on leadership and organizational socialization rests on the assumption of individualism which implies that social relations are simply the sum of the relations that occur between individuals. This way of looking at such issues as administrative style overlooks the fact that administrative work is also culturally structured. Recent feminist and critical works (see for example, Connell 1987 and McCarthy 1990) have shown how even what is often regarded as personal is in fact connected to the larger social structures of gender, race and class. Just as teaching is a classed, raced and gendered activity, so is administration. Administrative work is socially and culturally formed, and is never neutral in the way functionalist theories assume.

This myth of neutrality lies at the heart of the reluctance that most school administrators display in confronting issues of racism and sexism, except on occasions when their expressions are unambiguously overt. It is not surprising therefore that most educational administrators fail to recognize the role they play in the perpetuation of racism, for example. Indeed, recent research I have conducted (Rizvi and Crowley 1993) clearly demonstrates that most teachers and administrators are uncomfortable about even using the term racism; and when they do use it, they usually refer to incidents on the streets or things said by students or politicians. Preferring to think of themselves as tolerant and liberal and able to inspire these qualities in others, they find it difficult to reconcile the image they have of their role with the idea that institutionalized racism is necessary for the maintenance of existing power relations.

As I have already noted, gender and race are not issues external to the processes of schooling – independent variables, to be taken into account in constructing policies. Rather, they are factors which are *constitutive of* curricular, pedagogic and administrative relations in schools. It is not possible therefore to assume a position of neutrality in the formation of such relations. So long as organizational theory remains wedded to the fiction that school administration is somewhat separate from the more general processes of cultural articulation in society, we will continue to be thwarted in achieving genuine equity reform.

What this argument implies is that the relations between schooling and social difference need to be reconsidered in more dynamic *relational*, rather than instrumental functionalist, terms. The relations between race, gender, education and society are complex, and cannot be reduced to some simple essential form (Miles 1989). Much recent curriculum research has sought to develop a more adequate account of the pedagogic processes through which ethnic differences are converted into racism, and gender differences converted into sexism. Thus, we now know a great deal about how racism and sexism work *relationally* through the structural operations of not only the curriculum but also administration. In my view, we need a similar program of research in educational administration, to understand how such administrative practices as resource allocation, personnel management, teacher supervision and policy formation may also contribute to processes of exclusion and marginalization.

Functionalist views assume educational administration to be neutral with respect to racial and gender voices, concerned only with issues of implementation of organizational goals, but such a view assumes that it is possible for women and minority administrators to suspend any reference to their own social histories. Administrators are assumed to be without class, gender and ethnicity. However, as Martin and Mohanty (1986: 208) have pointed out:

> the claim to a lack of identity or positionality is itself based on privilege, on the refusal to accept responsibility for one's implication in actual historical and social relations, or a denial that personalities exist or that they matter, the denial of one's own personal history and the claim to a total separation from it.

This separation has the consequence of 'disembodying' the administrator, and of creating a dualism between knower and known, administrator and administrated. As Juliet Mitchell (quoted in Weiler 1991: 469) has pointed out, however, it is not possible to live as human subjects without in a sense taking on the history of that subjectivity. Individuals come to administrative work against the background of an already formed subjectivity which is linked to different histories, privilege, power and oppression. Administrators are moreover socially situated actors who are caught up in power relations of gender, ethnicity and class in ways that are not arbitrary but are historically constituted, and may not be entirely understood by them.

It has to be acknowledged that most administrative work takes place in a context of schooling that does not permit radical reform. School administrators, no matter how well-intentioned, work in a context that is inherently conservative. As Carby (1980) points out, a major weakness in the current versions of equity reforms lies in the location of what might otherwise be positive practices in a context of discipline and control. The school is a site for containing the effects of racism and sexism by promoting a fiction of tolerance between social groups in order to produce a society in which a certain truce exists between ethnic groupings and classes – but schools are not generally tolerant of difference and, as Connell (1985: 147) has argued, the formal structure of supervision in schools tends to reinforce educational conservatism.

The various ways in which schools socialize students into the dominant social orders are now widely recognized. Schools legitimate the dominant social ideology by fostering among students a form of compliant thinking which often prevents the formation of their critical understandings of social structures. However, what is seldom realized is that the same processes have implications for the work of administrators as well. Schooling is now widely recognized as involving contradictory processes. On the one hand, it encourages teachers and administrators to promote the values of democracy, creativity, cooperation and diversity. On the other hand, it operates under structural conditions that embody a competing set of values, namely, obedience, compliance, routine, conformity and homogeneity. Whatever the analytical accuracy of the notion of the 'hidden curriculum', it should be noted that it applies just as much to the way teachers and administrators are located within the structure of schooling as it does to the students.

The contradictions that define social relations in schools refer to not only the issues of curriculum and pedagogy but also the administrative principles within the framework of which schools are governed. Bates (1984) has demonstrated how school administration mirrors and reinforces the patterns and dominance and subordination found in the wider society. Schools eschew any examination of cultural concerns and have a tendency to favour the technical. Bureaucratic rationality (see Rizvi 1989) structures much of the discourse of schools, where communication between administrators, teachers, students and parents is often unidirectional and acausal, based upon the cultural assumptions of administration. Given the administrative emphasis on uniformity, differences, whether they be cultural or political, are not easily accommodated, except in certain symbolic ways.

These considerations go some way towards explaining why equity initiatives designed to improve the representation of women and minorities in administrative positions have been unable to make the impact on schools anticipated by their architects. Equity reforms emphasize multivoiced negotiation of cultural differences, and yet, for the purposes of administrative convenience, the functionalist view prescribes uniformity in organizational arrangements. Until we understand how to administer *with* and *for* difference, we will continue, I am to afraid, to be thwarted in our efforts to bring about genuine equality of educational and employment opportunity.

References

BATES, R. J. (1984) *Educational Administration and the Management of Knowledge* (Geelong: Deakin University Press).
CARBY, H. (1980) 'Multiculture', *Screen Education*, 34.

COHEN, P. (1987) *Racism and Popular Culture: A Cultural Studies Approach*, Working Paper No. 9, Centre for Multicultural Education, University of London Institute of Education, London.

COLE, M. (1986) 'Teaching and learning about racism' in S. MODGIL, G. VERMA, K. MALICK and C. MODGIL (eds) *Multicultural Education: The Interminable Debate* (London: Falmer Press).

CONNELL, R. (1985) *Teachers' Work* (Sydney: Allen and Unwin).

CONNELL, R. (1987) *Gender and Power* (Stanford, CA: Stanford University Press).

CONNELL, R., WHITE, V. and JOHNSTON, K. (1991) *Running Twice as Hard* (Geelong: Deakin University Press).

EDGAR, D. (1989) 'The Social Cost of Poverty' in D. EDGAR, D. KEANE and P. McDONALD (eds) *Child Poverty* (Sydney: Allen and Unwin).

GIROUX, H. (1983) *Theory and Resistance in Education: A Pedagogy for the Opposition* (South Hadley, MA: Bergin and Garvey).

KENNEDY, M. M. (1991) 'Some Surprising Findings on How Teachers Learn to Teach', in *Educational Leadership*, November.

McCARTHY, C. (1990) *Race and Curriculum* (London: Falmer Press).

McDERMOTT, R. and GOSPODINOFF, K. (1981) 'Social contexts for ethnic borders and school failure', in H. TRUEBA *et al.* (eds) *Culture and the Bilingual Classroom* (Rowley, MA: Newbury House).

MAGLEN, L. (1988) *Challenging the Human Capital Orthodoxy: The Education–Productivity Link Re-examined* (Melbourne: Economics Department, Monash University).

MARTIN, B. and MOHANTY, C. (1986) 'Feminist Politics: What's Home Got to Do with It?', in T. deLAURETIS (ed.) *Feminist Studies/Critical Studies* (Bloomington: University of Indiana Press).

MILES, R. (1989) *Racism* (London: Routledge and Kegan Paul).

O'CONNOR, T. (1989) 'Cultural voice and strategies for multicultural education', *Journal of Education*, 171, 2.

RIZVI, F. A. (1989) 'Bureaucratic rationality and the promise of democratic schooling', in W. CARR (ed.) *Quality in Schooling* (London: Falmer Press).

RIZVI, F. and CROWLEY, V. (1993) 'Teachers and the Contradictions of Culturalism', in G. VERMA (ed.) *Equity and Teachers Education* (London: Falmer Press) pp. 144–64.

WALKER, J. (1988) *Louts and Legends* (Sydney: Allen and Unwin).

WATKINS, P. E. (1991) *Knowledge and Control in the Flexible Workplace* (Geelong: Deakin University Press).

WEILER, K. (1988) *Women Teaching for Change* (Boston: Bergin and Garvey).

WEILER, K. (1991) 'Freire and a Feminist Pedagogy of Difference', *Harvard Education Review*, 61 (4) pp. 449–74.

WOOD, G. H. (1984) 'Schooling in a democracy: Transformation or reproduction?', *Educational Theory*, 34 (3).

Index